Effective
Group
Discussion

EFFECTIVE
GROUP
DISCUSSION
THEORY AND PRACTICE

Tenth Edition

John K. Brilhart
University of Nebraska, Omaha (Emeritus)

Gloria J. Galanes
Southwest Missouri State University

Katherine Adams
California State University at Fresno

Boston   Burr Ridge, IL   Dubuque, IA   Madison, WI
New York   San Francisco   St. Louis
Bangkok Bogotá Caracas Lisbon London Madrid Mexico City
Milan New Delhi Seoul Singapore Sydney Taipei Toronto

McGraw-Hill Higher Education

*A Division of The **McGraw-Hill** Companies*

EFFECTIVE GROUP DISCUSSION: THEORY AND PRACTICE

Published by McGraw-Hill, an imprint of The McGraw-Hill Companies, Inc., 1221 Avenue of the Americas, New York, NY, 10020. Copyright © 2001, 1998, 1995, 1992, 1989, 1986, 1982, 1978, 1974, 1967, by The McGraw-Hill Companies, Inc. All rights reserved. No part of this publication may be reproduced or distributed in any form or by any means, or stored in a database or retrieval system, without the prior written consent of The McGraw-Hill Companies, Inc., including, but not limited to, in any network or other electronic storage or transmission, or broadcast for distance learning. Some ancillaries, including electronic and print components, may not be available to customers outside the United States.

 This book is printed on acid-free paper.

1 2 3 4 5 6 7 8 9 0 DOC/DOC 0 9 8 7 6 5 4 3 2 1 0

ISBN 0–07–231568–7

Editorial director: *Phillip A. Butcher*
Developmental editor: *Jennie Katsaros*
Marketing manager: *Kelly May*
Project manager: *Christine A. Vaughan*
Production supervisor: *Rose Hepburn*
Coordinator freelance design: *Laurie Entringer*
Supplement coordinator: *Susan Lombardi*
New media: *Kimberly Stark*
Cover design: *Cindy Crampton*
Interior design: *Cindy Crampton*
Cover illustration: *© Bob Commander/ The Stock Illustration Source*
Compositor: *Shepherd, Incorporated*
Typeface: *10/12 Garamond*
Printer: *R. R. Donnelley & Sons Company*

Library of Congress Cataloging-in-Publication Data

Brilhart, John K.
   Effective group discussion : theory and practice / John K. Brilhart.—10th ed.
     p. cm.
   Includes bibliographical references and indexes.
   ISBN 0–07–231568–7 (softcover : alk. paper)
   1. Small groups. 2. Communication in small groups. 3. Group problem solving. 4.
Discussion. I. Title

HM736 .B75 2001
302.3'4–dc21
                                        00–021679

www.mhhe.com

Contents

PREFACE

This is the 10th Edition of *Effective Group Discussion* and we welcome the contributions of Katherine Adams, who joins us as co-author. For all of us, small group work is too important to be left to chance or to "conventional wisdom." Thus, the new edition continues to provide a comprehensive survey and interpretation of the small group research literature accompanied by practical, prescriptive guidance. We believe that small groups provide the initial vehicle by which humans make their contributions to the collective good. Humans have a need to participate, and small groups can serve as vehicles for this participation. People who understand how groups function, and why, can adapt their communicative behavior appropriately to maximize their participation in small groups. Conversely, people who lack this understanding will be frustrated. Even worse, they will be left without the tools of knowledge and skill they need to improve how their small groups function. They don't know why one group produces joy while another produces frustration, and they certainly cannot assess their own contributions to a group's success or failure. That is our mission: to help students become more effective small group members and leaders by providing them with the research-based tools—both theoretical understandings and practical suggestions—for effective participation in groups.

Effective Group Discussion is about secondary groups of all kinds: work groups, committees, task forces, self-directed work teams, and other small groups whose objectives include finding solutions to problems, producing goods, and creating policies. Although the text is written for academically prepared beginning students of small group communication, it is likely to be most useful to upper-division students who appreciate the extensive research base underpinning the narrative. It should also serve well as a reference source for advanced communication students, consultants, or people appointed to leadership positions in groups or organizations—in short, for anyone active in small groups. Instructors in academic fields such as communication, social psychology, business communication, a variety of health-related fields, and education will find it an appropriate and teachable textbook for their small group–oriented courses.

Effective Group Discussion is differentiated from our other small group text, *Communicating in Groups,* by the inclusion of more reports of current research, use of a more extensive vocabulary, and greater emphasis on theoretical principles and models. Visual illustrations are incorporated to illustrate and teach rather than to entertain or capture attention. Upper-division students will find their needs for research summaries and theoretical explanations well met.

THEMES

Systems theory is the theoretical foundation on which *Effective Group Discussion* is based. We believe it provides the most useful, elegant framework for incorporating all the information we know about small groups. We have included all the other major theories that bear on small group discussion, such as structuration, symbolic convergence, and so forth, but systems theory helps us organize what we present in the text. It gives students an accessible handle for assembling the elements.

We think systems theory provides another advantage as well—it reminds our students of the interdependent relationships among all the components of small groups. Our students often come to us wanting *the* answer for why *this* group outperformed expectations or why *that* group bombed. Part of what we try to do is help students understand the complexity of human behaviors and the multiple causes for most outcomes, including in small groups. Systems theory helps us convey that complexity to our students without overwhelming them.

We also believe strongly in the *practicality* of what we present in *Effective Group Discussion.* For this reason in the 10th edition we have incorporated chapter-opening case studies into every chapter, with ongoing discussion of them and questions designed to get the students to think about how the information they have learned in the chapter can be applied to actual situations they might encounter. The information on which the opening case studies are based comes from actual experiences—our own and others'—and illustrates to the student the pragmatic value of understanding how small groups work.

CHAPTER FORMAT, PLAN OF THE TEXT, AND NEW FEATURES

Previous users of *Effective Group Discussion* will recognize that familiar chapter elements have been retained, with two new ones added. As before, each chapter begins with a Central Message, a concise focal point stating the purpose of the chapter. This is followed by the Study Objectives, which delineate the major points to be covered, and the Key Terms, which our students tell us they appreciate. Key Terms are defined in the text and also in the Glossary at the end of the book.

Previous users of *Effective Group Discussion* will be pleased with two new features: the case studies and new "Consider This" boxes. Each chapter begins with an intriguing opening case that illustrates a major point of the chapter. These case studies have been drawn from real-life events and are designed to emphasize the usefulness of the information presented in the chapter. Then, throughout the chapter, "Consider This" boxes ask the students to apply a concept just explicated in the chapter. This feature is designed to help students think about a concept by asking them to apply it. This not only helps students learn the material but also encourages them to understand how the information is useful in everyday small group situations.

The chapter Summaries have been made more concise and put into a numbered format to make them more helpful to the student. Each Summary reflects the chapter's opening Study Objectives with summaries of the chapter's key points. The concise summaries are designed not to repeat information in the chapter but to highlight the main points for purposes of aiding retention and recall. The Exercises remain, providing additional ways for students to apply or experiment with the chapter's concepts. The Bibliographies and Notes at the ends of chapters provide students with extensive leads for additional reading or research.

The chapters are designed generally to move the discussion from systems inputs to throughput processes to outcomes. Part 1 presents an overview of small group theory. Chapter 1 introduces the importance and types of small groups in our lives, and Chapter 2 introduces the organizing framework of systems theory. Part 2, "The Foundations of Communicating in Groups," presents a theoretical description of the communication process, thereby providing a foundation for understanding the centrality of communication in a group's throughput processes. Chapter 3 explains the communication process, Chapter 4 concentrates on verbal and nonverbal signals, and Chapter 5 describes the effects of culture and cultural differences on communication in small groups.

Part 3 focuses on the development of the group as an entity. Chapter 6 discusses the members. Chapters 7 and 8 deal with how members develop from a collection of individuals into a group, with Chapter 7 focusing on structuration and the development of roles and norms, and Chapter 8 on networks, status relationships, cohesiveness, avoiding groupthink, teambuilding, and SYMLOG. Chapter 9 presents theoretical perspectives about leadership, while Chapter 10 offers guidelines for designated small group leaders.

Part 4 links throughput processes with outputs as it presents information about effective problem solving. It begins with an overview of problem solving in Chapter 11, moves to a discussion of decision making in chapter 12, and concludes in Chapter 13 with information about how properly managed conflict can enhance these important small group processes. Part 5 contains techniques and tools for evaluating and improving small groups. Chapter 14 presents specific discussion techniques that maximize small group effectiveness. Techniques and tools for observing, analyzing, and evaluating small group communication are presented in Chapter 15.

As with previous editions, the new 10th Edition was written so the chapters may be used selectively and in an order other than the one presented in the text. After Chapters 1 and 2, the chapters may be presented in any order without loss of comprehension, according to the instructor's preference. Some teachers want to address leadership or problem solving early in the course. Others want their students to know how to observe and evaluate interaction in groups so that the theoretical explanations can be applied to specific real-life examples. Still others may choose to omit some chapters or sections. These and other changes in the order of chapters should not interfere with student understanding of the concepts.

REVISED CONTENT

With every new edition of *Effective Group Discussion,* the problem of what to include becomes more challenging. In making changes, we have relied heavily on the advice of our reviewers, instructors who use the text, and our own experiences in teaching from the text. We have tried diligently to keep the text manageable and affordable for students.

We know also that, in recent years, most students using *Effective Group Discussion* are likely to have completed at least one basic communication course before enrolling in a small group course. As with the previous edition, we continue to take this into account by streamlining our discussion of basic communication processes. The overview we provide will serve as a review for students with previous communication courses, but students without such a background should still receive enough detail to make sense of the communication process in small groups.

Of the helpful changes we have made in this 10th Edition, the addition of the chapter-opening cases is perhaps the most visible and exciting. The cases are based on actual small group experiences, either our own or from the contemporary popular press. We selected stories that students should find interesting and that intrigued us. For example, we've included cases describing the development of cohesiveness in the 1999 World Champion U.S. Women's Soccer Team, the decision-making process used by teams of burglars when they decide what houses to hit, and the conflict-management process used by Common Ground, the organization that promotes small group discussion to foster understanding between pro-choice and pro-life individuals. These stories captivated us; we think they will intrigue students and spark their interest in the chapter material.

We have enhanced our discussion of group culture by presenting information about culture early, in Chapters 1 and 2, before developing it more fully in Chapter 5. We have shortened considerably the church board dialogue in Chapter 2, in response to user comments. Now, we present shorter bits of dialogue designed to illustrate specific concepts. In Chapter 3, we present contemporary examples of how important using good interpersonal communication is in maintaining healthy relationships. We continue to emphasize the importance of intercultural communication concepts to small groups by keeping the intercultural information in Chapter 5 rather than distributing it throughout the text, and we have emphasized ethical communication principles in diversity issues.

We have added information about the Myers-Briggs personality types in Chapter 6. In our experience, students have more trouble managing personality differences than ethnic or gender differences, and we believe this information provides students with tools to begin to appreciate and capitalize on differences rather than dreading them. We have taken the discussion of groupthink out of Chapter 13, the chapter on conflict, and incorporated it into Chapter 8 in the section on cohesiveness, where it seems to fit better conceptually. In Chapter 14, we have added more information about technology, particularly Group Support Systems, which are becoming both more common and more affordable.

Throughout the text, we have updated the research and incorporated the most current information available about the topics covered. We believe you will find especially helpful the new "Consider This" boxes dispersed throughout each chapter that ask students to apply concepts or think about them in more depth. As in previous editions, we have continued to strengthen the communicative focus of the text by emphasizing what members *say* and *do* in small groups and by asking students to consider what effect this communication behavior has on various group processes. We have increased our emphasis on diversity by providing more examples throughout the text to emphasize this highly significant issue.

SUPPLEMENTS

We continue to revamp our *Instructor's Manual* to reflect the new directions we are taking in our own classes. The *Instructor's Manual* is extensive and contains many ideas for activities, assignments, exercises, video resources, and now, Internet resources that help clarify or expand on concepts included in the text. There are also two videotapes created specifically for this and our other text. *Communication in Small Groups: Short Takes* illustrates a variety of small group concepts in short (two- to three-minute) segments. Concepts that are illustrated on the videotape are marked with an icon of a videocassette in the margin of the text; the tape's *User's Guide* is designed to help both instructors and students focus their viewing. *Communicating Effectively in Small Groups,* our original videotape, presents four longer group scenarios and is especially useful as the basis for written case study assignments. The *Instructor's Manual* also suggests other videotapes and films that clarify concepts discussed in the text, along with "writing to learn" and many other kinds of activities.

We gratefully appreciate your use of *Effective Group Discussion.* We welcome your written reactions to its content and composition. You can send such comments to us via McGraw-Hill Company to the Department of Communication and Mass Media, Southwest Missouri State University, Springfield, Missouri, or the Department of Communication, California State University, Fresno, California.

May all your groups be enjoyable and satisfying!

ACKNOWLEDGMENTS

We appreciate the contributions made to this book by numerous persons; we can name only a few. First, we acknowledge our debt to instructors and writers Freed Bales, Ernest Bormann, Elton S. Carter, B. Aubrey Fisher, Larry Frey, Kenneth Hance, Randy Hirokawa, Sidney J. Parnes, J. Donald Phillips, M. Scott Poole, Marvin Shaw, and Victor Wall.

The following reviewers were exceptionally helpful in supplying thoughtful, carefully considered suggestions: Dianne Blomberg—Metro State College; Laurie Arlis—Ithaca College; Ray Collins—San Jose City College; Marifran Mattson—Purdue University; George Nagel—Ferris State University; and John R. Schedel—Medaille College. Their suggestions have helped us improve the book appreciably. Fellow members of many small groups provided numerous examples, many of which we have included in the book. Students in our classes continue to teach us; their insights have been incorporated as well. Finally, our friends and families have supplied support in countless ways. To all these people, and many left unmentioned, our sincere thanks!

INTRODUCTION TO THE STUDY OF SMALL GROUPS

The two chapters in Part 1 provide introductory information to focus your study of small groups. Chapter 1 introduces important terms and concepts used throughout the text, and Chapter 2 presents systems theory as a framework for studying and understanding small groups.

The Small Groups in Everyone's Life

1

Central Message

If you want to succeed in modern organizational and social life, you must understand how to communicate effectively as a member of a group.

Study Objectives

As a result of studying Chapter 1 you should be able to:

1. Explain why you need to understand small group communication and to participate productively in small group discussions.
2. Use correctly the terms presented in this chapter, particularly *group, small group, discussion, small group discussion,* and *ethics.*
3. Describe the two major categories of small groups.
4. Describe the four ethical principles most relevant to small group communication.
5. Consciously and intentionally become a participant-observer during group discussions.

Key Terms

Activity group

Committee
  Ad hoc or
    special
    committee
  Standing
    committee
  Conference
    committee

Discussion (small
  group
  discussion)

Ethics

Group

Grouphate

Interaction

Interdependent
  goal

Learning group
  (study group)

Participant-
  observer

Personal growth
  group

Primary group

Problem-solving
  group

Quality control
  circle

Secondary group

Self-managed
  work group

Small group

Small group
  communication

Social loafers

David Harrison, business owner in Springfield, Missouri (where Gloria, one of your authors, lives), is a successful author of children's books. David has a long-standing interest in encouraging children to write; recently, he has turned his attention to promoting literacy, especially among children. His latest project is the "Sky High on Reading" program, intended to challenge Springfield schoolchildren and youth to read enough books during the 1999–2000 school year to make a stack two miles high. Springfield is a medium-sized city of more than 150,000 people, nearly 30,000 of them of school age. David knew that he couldn't pull off his project alone, so he formed a steering committee to help. The steering committee consisted of teachers and administrators from both the Springfield public school system and private schools in Springfield; librarians from the Springfield public library system; and university teachers who had contact with student teachers and teachers' aides in the schools. The steering committee, once committed to the project, helped organize and promote the program, figured out ways to keep track of the books read by the students, and devised numerous innovative ways to publicize the program throughout the city.

This story illustrates two important points. First, even if you have a brilliant idea, other people can help you improve upon it. Second, if your idea or project is at all complex, you need others to help carry it out. Like David Harrison, you'll probably want to form a small group to help ensure your chances of success.

Small groups—teams, task forces, committees—are the way most work gets done in present-day American society. This is true whether the context is education, business and industry, health care, social services, religion, family life, politics, or government work—small groups are the basic building blocks of our society and are themselves smaller models of social interaction that demonstrate the interactive processes that operate in the society as a whole.[1] We agree with Lawrence Frey, a leading scholar of small group communication, who believes that the small group is *the* most important social formation:

> Every segment of our society—from the largest multinational organization to the political workings of federal, state, city, and local governments to the smallest community action group to friendship groups to the nuclear and extended family—relies on groups to make important decisions, socialize members, satisfy needs, and the like.[2]

We spend a tremendous amount of our time in formal and informal groups. For example, Cole reported in 1989 that executives spent an average of half their time in business meetings,[3] and Lawren noted that there are an estimated 20 million meetings *each day* in the United States.[4] When you add to this the amount of time people spend in groups *not* connected with jobs, you begin to understand how pervasive groups are in modern society. Moreover, the ability to work effectively as part of a team requires skills that must be practiced. In a recent national survey of 750 leading American companies,

71.4 percent of respondents mentioned "ability to work in teams" as an essential skill for MBA graduates—more important by far than knowledge of quantitative and statistical techniques.[5] If you want to get anything *done*—on the job or anywhere else—you must learn how to be a good team member.

To help you with that learning, four important ideas about groups are introduced in this chapter. First, groups exist to meet important human needs, and humans are willing to exchange items of value—time, energy, money—to participate in groups. Schutz explained that groups meet needs for inclusion, affection, and control: a need to belong and be identified with others; a need for love and esteem from others; and a need to achieve and exert power over others and our environment.[6] We humans cannot meet these needs by ourselves—participation with others is mandatory. In addition, these needs are so important that we willingly give of our own resources, especially time and energy, to participate in groups. For example, the Sky High on Reading committee members worked long and hard *as a group*, not only because the issue was so important to them but also because they knew the project would succeed only if they worked collectively rather than individually. But participation in groups always requires trade-offs—you get something, but you give up something, too. In return for being included, getting to use your talents, and accomplishing something important to you, you give up some autonomy and the license to do whatever you want, whenever you want.

A second important point about groups is that because the formation of groups is natural to humans, groups are everywhere. List all the small groups in which you participated during the past week, regardless of how briefly—and don't forget to list your family! Students in college classes average about 8 to 10, and sometimes list as many as 24 groups. For example, one student listed the following: family, *Bible* study, sorority, executive committee of sorority, study group in small group class, project group in marketing class, intramural volleyball team, car pool, work group of clerks in clothing department. Our faculty colleagues often list even more groups than these. In fact, Goldhaber found that the average tenured faculty member served on six committees simultaneously and spent 11 hours per week in meetings![7]

If this seems like a lot of groups, consider this: reliance on groups in our society is increasing and expected to increase further, perhaps dramatically. American managers are recognizing the value of participative decision making, with the small group as one important vehicle for encouraging employee participation and improving corporate decision making. The Ford Taurus and General Motors Saturn success stories are in large part the stories of successful group work. Saturn, for example, was praised by *Consumer Reports* for having a much better than average reliability record in its first year of production,[8] a far cry from the poor records of other General Motors cars throughout the 1980s. Years ago, Ouchi, developer of Theory Z management, warned American managers that their ability to counter Japanese competition depended on how well they learned to work in groups.[9] More recently, Waterman identified teamwork as a key element in companies that have kept their competitive edge.[10] It seems that Americans are getting the message.

Why is group work successful? Groups are usually better problem solvers, in the long run, than solitary individuals because they have access to more information than individuals do, can spot flaws and biases in each other's thinking, and then can think of things an individual may have failed to consider. Moreover, if people participate in planning the work of solving the problem, it is more likely that they will work harder and better at carrying out the solution. Thus, participation in problem solving and decision making helps guarantee continued commitment to decisions and solutions.

The third key point about groups is this: just because we often participate in groups, we cannot assume that our participation is *effective*. Just doing it doesn't mean we do it well! And unless we know something about *why* a group is *unproductive,* we won't know *what* we can do about it and we can't help a group improve. We may laugh at the saying "A camel is a horse designed by a committee," but when our own group's horse looks suspiciously like a camel, we're often helpless to know what to do about it.

Students often groan when we tell them that a major portion of their grade will be based on a group project. Sorensen calls this **grouphate**—the antipathy many people feel toward working in groups.[11] Interestingly, she found that grouphate is partly caused by lack of training in how to communicate effectively as a group member. We hope to reduce any of your grouphate by providing you with information about the process of group communication and with education in effective discussion techniques. Strong communication skills are central to effective discussion and productive teamwork. Donald Petersen, former CEO at Ford Motor Company, learned this during his rise at Ford. At first he envisioned his role as that of a solitary engineer designing cars, but later he discovered that a successful company requires interaction and teamwork: "Communication skills are crucial. And I mean that in both directions—not only the ability to articulate . . . in a good fashion, but to listen."[12]

The fourth and final point is that groups provide the vehicle by which the individual can make a contribution to the organization and the society as a whole. Larkin postulated that humans have a motivation to *give*. The basic ingredient cementing social cohesion is not the satisfaction of needs, but rather the availability for contribution. What best binds individuals to groups may not be so much the pressure to obtain necessities as the opportunities to give of oneself to something beyond merely self-interested acquisition.[13] The dignity of individuals, Larkin states, comes from people's contributions to something greater than themselves. People who give, of their time, money, energy and other resources, live healthier, happier, and more fulfilled lives; they report that their lives are more meaningful than those who do not.[14] For example, in legendary baseball pitcher Nolan Ryan's distinguished 27-year career, he remembers the unity and team spirit of the 1969 pennant-winning New York Mets as a high point.[15] We believe that the success of work-related committees stems largely from this need to contribute collaboratively with others.

The focus of this book is the *communicative* behavior of group members—what people say and do in groups. Although we will draw upon findings from other fields, we will concentrate on the process of communication among members, especially in Western cultures such as the United States, and on how you as a group member can influence this process. In psychology, you may have studied how groups modify the behavior of individuals or provide therapeutic benefits, and, in sociology, how groups help establish and maintain social organization. In communication, you will study what happens as members talk and work together, and what you can do to make your own communication as productive as possible. Moreover, we will use as examples groups from a variety of settings. Although groups in business and industry have captured a great deal of attention, group work is fundamental in *all* arenas of modern life. Thus, our examples come from the educational sphere, political life, sports and entertainment, health care situations, religious settings, social services, and community development organizations as well as the corporate and industrial realms.

Small group discussion, the talk among group members, cannot be reduced to a set of prescriptions; it is far too complex for simplistic rules. Each element of group discussion influences each other element in the group system, which we describe in depth in Chapter 2. Because the only person you can directly control is yourself, this book is designed to promote your awareness of your own behavior in small groups and its implications for other members. We occasionally give guidelines and suggestions for you to consider, but we assume you will remember to take into account your group's entire and unique situation as you follow our guidelines.

In the remainder of this chapter, we present definitions of key terms we will be using throughout the book to reduce the possibility of misunderstanding. We also present information about the types of groups you will encounter in many different kinds of settings, and we conclude with a brief discussion of ethical behavior important to effective group functioning in Western cultures.

IMPORTANT CONCEPTS AND TERMS

Group is the first term we must consider. Although a variety of definitions exists, we believe none surpasses Marvin Shaw's: "persons who are interacting with one another in such a manner that each person influences and is influenced by each other."[16] Shaw's conception of a group emphasizes interaction and mutual influence. **Interaction** implies *communication,* the exchange of signals (words, gestures, and so forth) among people who belong to the group. It also implies that at least some of these signals are perceived and responded to in such a way that each member can potentially affect each other member's behaviors, beliefs, opinions, values, and so on. By this definition, a collection of people in one place would not necessarily constitute a group unless there were reciprocal awareness and influence. Following this logic, group members who are widely scattered geographically, but who interact and mutually influence each other by way of newsletters, telephone conversations, computer networks, closed circuit TV, or radio *do* constitute a group.

The study of groups may include large groupings (e.g., whole societies) or small ones; our focus is on *small* groups. The notion that "each person influences and is influenced by each other" implies that members are *aware* of each other, and from this mutual awareness we derive our definition of *small* as being based on *perceptual awareness*. A **small group,** therefore, is a group small enough that each member is aware of and able to recall each other group member, know who is and is not in the group, and recognize what role each is taking. We admit that this is fuzzy, but attempts to define *small* on the basis of number of members have never worked. At the low end, we can certainly perceive all members in a group of three. We arbitrarily eliminate the dyad, or two-person unit, as a small group because dyads function differently from units of three or more. At the high end, most of us can take in up to 11 members in a unit and, with training, may learn to handle 12 to 14.[17] But at the end of a semester, even a class as large as 25 may seem small to a teacher.

Some authors differentiate teams from small groups. Lumsden and Lumsden see teams as highly functioning groups where members are committed to the goal, leadership is shared, and the team has forged a strong sense of identity.[18] Harris and Sherblom reserve *team* for those groups where leadership is shared, such as the problem-solving or self-managed work groups we discuss later.[19] We do not differentiate between teams and small groups and we sometimes use the terms interchangeably in this text. In everyday life, a group may be called a team (e.g., "the management team" or "the red team"), yet function no better than other groups of its type. Like Larson and LaFasto,[20] we are interested in groups that function well, regardless of what they are called, and our intent in this text is to provide you and your fellow group members with the tools you need to achieve top-notch performance.

One key feature of a group is an **interdependent goal,** meaning that all members succeed or fail together in the accomplishment of the group's purpose. For example, one player on a softball team cannot win while the others on the same team lose. The players' fates are linked—they all succeed or fail *as a group*. Without an interdependent goal, a collection of people is not a group.

Discussion, another term essential to the concept of a group, is the primarily verbal exchange among members through which the work of the group is accomplished. In this book, **small group discussion** refers to *a small group of persons talking with each other (usually face to face) in order to achieve some interdependent goal, such as increased understanding, coordination of*

Breaking a large group into smaller ones gives everyone a chance to contribute and is much more satisfying.

activity, or a solution to a shared problem. We will now "unpack" this definition, which suggests several characteristics of small group discussion:

1. A small enough number of people for each to be aware of and have some reaction to each other (typically 3 to 7, rarely more than 15).
2. A mutually interdependent purpose, making the success of one member contingent on the success of all.
3. Each person having a sense of belonging, of being part of the group.
4. Interaction involving verbal and nonverbal channels, with words conveying the content of the discussion (this definition includes as "verbal" manual languages, such as American Sign Language). Members continuously respond to and adapt their actions to each other. The give and take of impromptu communication, rather than prepared speeches, is the essence.
5. A sense of cooperation among members. Although there may be disagreement and conflict, all members perceive themselves as searching for a group outcome that will be as satisfactory as possible to all, so that no one is frustrated at losing to another group member.

The term **small group communication** refers to the study of interaction among small group members as well as to the body of communication theory yielded by such study. Throughout this book, we will examine in detail this body of theory and principles.

CONSIDER THIS

If you were David Harrison (in our story at the start of this chapter), how big a group would you assemble for the Sky High on Reading project, knowing that you wanted to preserve that "perceptual awareness" that keeps a group small? What groups do you think are essential to have represented on the steering committee (for example, the public schools)? How would you balance the need for broad representation with the need for efficiency?

Communicative behavior of group members is the focus of this book, and its study is a relatively new field. Early researchers, such as Muzafer Sherif, W. F. Whyte, and Robert Bales, were often social psychologists who were particularly interested in how groups influenced individual behavior and how norms developed in groups. Later communication researchers, extending their interest in public speaking, began to examine the communication within groups and to link members' communicative behaviors to group outcomes such as the effectiveness of decisions and the degree of cohesiveness. Now, as the field of communication has matured, researchers have increasingly attended to the process of communication within the group, including how ideas are developed, how the communication creates and maintains group structure, how leadership is enacted by what people say and do, and how groups can best be studied. These trends are expected to continue and are being encouraged as appropriate directions for small group communication scholars.[21]

TYPES OF SMALL GROUPS

There are two major categories of small groups, *primary* and *secondary*. Each focuses on meeting different human needs, but elements of each category are found in most of the groups to which you will belong.

Primary groups focus on the interpersonal relationships among members and exist chiefly to satisfy what are termed *primary needs*—needs for inclusion (affiliation, belonging) and affection (love, esteem). Primary groups are usually long term. Examples include a nuclear family, roommates, several friends who meet daily around a table in the student center, co-workers who regularly share coffee breaks, and other groups principally designed for friendship. Although such groups may make decisions and tackle particular tasks, they exist mainly to provide personal attention and support for the members, who may chat about a variety of topics, let off steam, and generally enjoy each other. The tasks they perform are less important than their primary purpose of providing affection. Their talk may seem disorganized and informal because it is not so much the means to an end as it is the end in itself. More than any other forces in our lives, primary groups socialize and mold us into the people we become; their importance is tremendous. Primary groups are not the main focus of this book; typically, primary groups are studied in sociology, psychology, and interpersonal communication courses. However, the interpersonal relationships at the heart of primary groups are very important to understanding small groups in general.

Secondary groups focus on task accomplishment and are formed for the purpose of doing work, such as completing a project, solving a problem, or making a decision. Secondary groups, such as most work teams and problem-solving groups, meet primarily what are called *secondary needs*— needs for control and achievement. Such groups enable members to exert power over their environment and others. For example, the teams studied by Larson and LaFasto in their efforts to define effective teamwork are clearly secondary in nature because they have "a specific performance objective or recognizable goal to be attained; and coordination of activity among the members of the team is required for attainment of the team goal or objective."[22] All groups initiated to accomplish some task are more secondary than primary, although many task groups also help members achieve primary needs for socialization and affection.

CONSIDER THIS

Is the Sky High on Reading steering committee, described in the opening story, more primary or secondary? Why do you think so? As you may have discerned by this point, there are no *pure* primary or secondary groups. Although groups are classified as primary or secondary according to their major focus, primary groups do engage in work, and secondary groups provide affection and belonging to their members. Thus, most groups blend primary and secondary characteristics and meet many human needs in addition to the ones for which they were initially formed. In fact, Anderson and Martin demonstrated that secondary group members are motivated by a number of factors that are more primary than secondary, including desires for pleasure and to escape. Such factors strongly influence secondary group members' communication behaviors, feelings of loneliness, and satisfaction with the group and are worth examining.[23] Figure 1.1 illustrates this blend of interpersonal (primary) and task (secondary) characteristics for a variety of groups.

In addition to the two major categories just described, there are many other ways to classify groups according to their purposes. Our four classifications exhibit both primary and secondary characteristics in varying degrees, but the fourth is more purely secondary than the first three.

| FIGURE 1.1 | Types of groups and the needs they satisfy. |

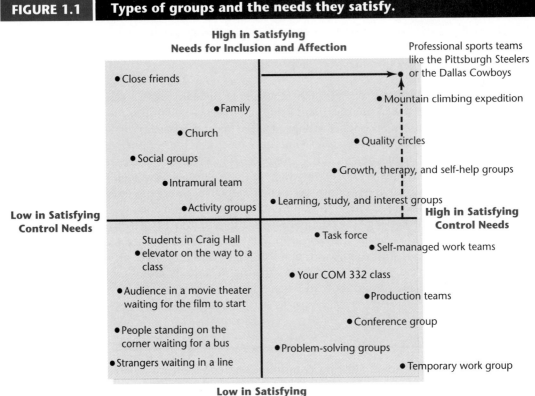

Activity Groups   **Activity groups** enable members to participate in an activity, both for the sake of doing the activity and for the affiliation provided by doing the activity with others. The following are examples: a gourmet club whose members meet regularly to eat together at different restaurants, bridge and poker clubs, road rally clubs, hunting and bird-watching groups, and numerous other interest groups. Members of such groups solve problems and make choices such as when and where to meet, how to pay for their activities, how group membership is determined, and all the other decisions necessary when several people's efforts must be coordinated. Of course, members enjoy the fellowship and camaraderie of others whose interests are similar.

Personal Growth Groups   Therapy and support groups are called collectively **personal growth groups.** They are composed of people who come together to develop personal insights, overcome personality problems, and grow as individuals from the feedback and support of others—to engage in personal learning and growth. Examples include local chapters of 12-step programs such as Alcoholics Anonymous and Al Anon, mutual support groups like gay or women's rights groups, outpatient groups for clients with personal adjustment problems, support groups for parents whose babies died of SIDS, cancer survivors' support groups, and therapy groups for spouse abusers. Members of such groups typically do not choose each other; they join to help themselves with problems that are both highly personal and social. Because no purely *group* goal is sought, goal interdependence is low; rather, members meet their individual needs for personal learning, awareness, and support in the context of the group. Many such groups have a professional facilitator to guide the interaction. Most of these groups have a limited term of existence; in some, membership changes gradually while the group itself continues.

Learning groups, sometimes called *study groups,* are formed so members can understand a subject more thoroughly by pooling their knowledge, perceptions, and beliefs. For example, local public libraries often organize issue-oriented learning discussions so citizens can become better informed regarding important or controversial issues. Members of such groups often learn much more than the specific subject matter they gather to study; participants also learn skills of effective speaking, listening, critical thinking, and effective interpersonal communication.

Learning (Study) Groups

Problem-solving groups formed to address some condition or problem vary widely in their composition and functioning. For example, the teams studied by Larson and LaFasto functioned primarily in one of the following three ways: solving a problem, creating and innovating, or executing a well-defined task.[24] These researchers note that each type of group must have a *results-driven structure,* which means that the group's structure must match the group's purpose to help it achieve its goals. For example, a problem-resolution team, such as the health care task force led by Hillary Rodham Clinton, or our example of the Sky High on Reading group, depends upon trust among team members, effective discussions, and assessment of information for its success. Creative teams, such as advertising agency creative groups or the team that developed the Apple Macintosh, need freedom and autonomy to be able to work without bureaucratic hassles. On the other hand, tactical teams, such as heart transplant and automobile assembly teams, require clearly defined tasks and dependable members.

Problem-Solving Groups

Whatever the main function of a problem-solving group, such groups are so classified because they are created expressly to solve problems. There are many ways of describing subtypes of problem-solving groups. In this book, we deal with three major categories we believe are prevalent in modern organizational and social life: committees, quality control circles, and self-managed work groups. The latter two are relatively new to the American scene but are rapidly gaining in both numbers and acceptance.

Committees are groups that have been assigned a task by a parent organization or person with authority in an organization. Committees may be formed to investigate and report findings, recommend a course of action for the parent group, formulate policies, or plan and carry out some action. All

Committees

©James L. Shaffer

A committee discusses
content of a report.

these tasks require discussion among members. Boards, councils, and staffs
are special kinds of committees. For example, a *board of directors* is often
called an *executive committee* and represents a larger organization. It may
have extensive power to make and execute policy.

Committees are usually classified as either *ad hoc* or *standing*. The **ad
hoc** or **special committee,** established to perform a specific task, normally
ceases to exist when that task has been completed. It is often referred to as a
task force, with members appointed from various departments of an organization or political body. Examples of what special committees might be
asked to do include evaluating credentials of job applicants, drafting bylaws,
hearing grievances, planning social events, conducting investigations, devis-
ing plans to solve work-related problems, advising legislators on what to do
about statewide problems, and evaluating programs and institutions. Once
the task force has reported its action or recommendations, it disbands.

Standing committees are ongoing committees established through the
constitution or bylaws of an organization to deal with recurring types of
problems or to perform specific organizational functions. The most important
standing committee of most organizations is given a name such as *executive
committee, board,* or *steering committee*. Usually this group is charged with
overall management of the organization and can function for the entire organization when general membership meetings are not feasible. Other standing
committees encountered commonly go under names such as *membership
committee, personnel committee, parking and traffic committee, program
committee, bylaws committee,* and so forth. These groups continue indefi-
nitely, even though the membership may change. Frequently, some members

of a standing committee are replaced annually so that the group includes both experienced members and those with a fresh perspective. Standing committees often meet regularly, typically resolving a number of problems at a single meeting.

Conference committees are committees composed of members who represent the interests of two or more other groups. The members serve as representatives of their constituent groups. Most organizations are composed of multiple work groups who must somehow keep each other informed and coordinate their efforts. For example, a community's arts council may consist of representatives from the community theater, art museum, ballet, symphony, and jazz ensemble, who meet to coordinate their scheduling, marketing, and publicity efforts so that individual events do not compete with each other. Conference committees between delegates of the U.S. Senate and House of Representatives routinely meet to resolve differences in legislation passed by each body. Often, conference committees do not have the authority to resolve matters within the conference committee meeting, but must submit their tentative decisions to their respective constituent groups for approval.

A **quality control circle** consists of workers (usually five to seven) in a company who either volunteer or are selected to meet regularly on company time to discuss work-related problems. These groups sometimes go by other names, including *continuous improvement teams, cycle time reduction groups,* or the shortened version, *quality circles.* Regardless of what they are called, their purpose is to improve some aspect of work life—efficiency, quality of finished products, worker safety, and so forth. Quality circles represent attempts to capitalize on the fact that groups usually make better and more readily accepted decisions about complex problems than individuals do, and that individuals actually performing the work are in the best position to recommend ways to improve it. Several conditions are essential for quality control circles to work. The people who lead the groups must be trained as problem-solving discussion leaders who remain open-minded toward all ideas suggested. Members must also be trained in discussion procedures and their responsibility as members. Upper management must be committed to the quality circle concept, must respond to all recommended solutions, and must either act on the recommendations or explain why they are being delayed or rejected. Workers must share in the benefits of any cost-saving ideas, and job security must be guaranteed when efficiency is increased.

Quality Control Circles

Self-managed work groups, also called *autonomous work groups* or *peer-led work teams,* are groups of workers given a defined area of freedom to manage their productive work within certain preset limits established by the organization. For example, an automobile assembly team may be responsible for assembling a car from start to finish. It may be given a deadline by which the car must be fully assembled, but within that limit the team members are free to elect their own leaders, plan their work procedures, and schedule individual assignments for the members. Members of self-managed work groups are often *cross-trained,* meaning that each member can perform several jobs competently. This permits human and other resources to be allocated efficiently and effectively, gives workers the chance to develop a variety of skills, and reduces boredom. As with quality circles, workers in self-managed work groups must be well trained.[25] The organization benefits because the immediate group can allocate resources more expediently than a somewhat distant manager, employees with some say in their work are more committed and productive than workers given less choice, and involvement in decision making meets psychological needs of employees without reducing the technical quality of their work. In the future, more employees will be involved in self-managed work groups and quality control circles, so sensitivity to group phenomena and skills in discussion leadership become increasingly important.

In the same way that no group is purely primary or secondary, most small groups you encounter will combine elements of all four group types just described—activity, personal growth, learning, and problem solving. Several years ago, the Springfield City Council established an *ad hoc* task force to investigate and recommend solutions to the city's solid waste disposal problem. Members had to educate themselves about solid waste, various disposal options, and pros and cons of the options before they could make their recommendations to the city council. They also had to manage their own resources of time and information and be concerned with the comprehensive quality of life in the Springfield area. Thus, this group comprised elements of a learning group, problem-solving group, quality circle, and self-managed work group.

CONSIDER THIS

From the types of groups just described, what kind of group would you call the Sky High on Reading steering committee? Which of the descriptions provided seem to fit that group?

ETHICAL BEHAVIOR OF GROUP MEMBERS

For a group to perform effectively, its leader and members must behave ethically. **Ethics** refer to the "rules or standards for right conduct or practice.[26] Appropriate standards of behavior from the general culture apply also to behavior within groups; however, the unique nature of small groups requires attention, in our Western culture, to special ethical concerns regarding the treatment of speech, of people, and of information.

The first ethical principle for small group communication is that group members should be willing to share their unique perspectives and at the same time refrain from saying or doing things that prevent others from speaking freely. The field of communication has evolved from what was originally the study of speech. Our field has a long and distinguished tradition, dating from Aristotle, that supports the value of free speech.[27] Many groups and teams are formed because several heads perform better than one, but that advantage will not be realized if group members are unwilling or afraid to speak freely in the group. Each member of a group must feel free to share his or her knowledge, beliefs, and opinions within the group, according to the appropriate discussion rules established in the group.

The second ethical principle is that group members must conduct themselves with honesty and integrity. In a small group, an obvious implication of this principle is that group members should not intentionally deceive one another or manufacture information or evidence to persuade other members to their points of view. Integrity also implies that members should support group decisions, but this may present problems for the individual member. We mentioned earlier that participation in a group requires trade-offs. In order to receive the benefits of group participation (such as inclusion, affection, and control), members give up something in return (total autonomy, or the ability to do whatever they want whenever they want). Sometimes you may be asked to do something for a group that violates your own personal values, beliefs, morals, or principles. For example, what if a group on which you serve decides to suppress information that is contrary to a decision the group wishes to make, and pressures you to go along? What will you do? Only *you* can answer that question. One option is to try your best to persuade the group to see things your way; another option is to leave the group. But if you choose to stay with the group, make sure you can support or at least live with the group's actions and decisions. Integrity also implies that you are willing to place the good of the group ahead of your own individual goals. We believe that if groups are to function effectively, members should make public their private agendas so they are not operating from motives unknown to the other members. We have known individuals who are not able to become part of a team because they are unable or unwilling to merge their personal agendas with that of the group. These individuals make poor team members, and the group is better off without them.

Third, members should perform no actions intended to disconfirm, belittle, or ridicule other members, and, before agreeing or disagreeing with another, members should make sure that they have first understood that member. Deetz stresses that ethical interpersonal behavior should strengthen one's personal identity and should have mutual understanding as its goal.[28] Our first goal, as we interact, should be to strive to understand others to their satisfaction. If this happens, we will confirm and support each other's self-concept and identity, even when we disagree strongly.

Finally, it is essential that we mention the ethical treatment of information. The fourth ethical principle for effective group discussion is that members must make a conscientious effort to find and present to the group all information and points of view relevant to the group's work, to set aside personal biases and prejudices when evaluating that information, and to refrain from doing anything that short-circuits this process. Many consequential decisions are made in groups, from how best to get children to read to whether or not it is safe to launch a space shuttle in cold weather. These decisions will be only as good as the information on which they are based and the reasoning that members use to assess the information. It is absolutely crucial that group members consider all relevant information in an open-minded, unbiased way by employing the best critical thinking skills they can; to do otherwise can lead to tragedies such as the fatal decision to launch the *Challenger*. It follows from this that members must credit or document the sources of information they share with the group, and must not falsify data or information. We will return to the subject of ethical behavior at various points throughout the book.

THE PARTICIPANT-OBSERVER PERSPECTIVE

A major purpose of this book is to help you develop a participant-observer perspective. A **participant-observer** is a regular member of the group who engages actively in its discussions, but at the same time observes, evaluates, and adapts to the group's processes and needs. Participant-observers direct part of their attention to participating in the group and part to assessing how the group is functioning; they try always to be aware of what the group needs at the moment. For example, if the group seems confused, a participant-observer will try to clarify; if group members seem tired of the task, a participant-observer may suggest a break. Because such members simultaneously pay dual attention to the group's processes and the content of the discussion, they can supply essential information, ideas, procedural suggestions, and interpersonal communication skills *when needed*. We hope this text gives you the tools you need to participate effectively.

Some members supply valuable information but have little understanding of group processes. As long as the group is operating well, these members contribute needed facts and ideas, but they are of no help in resolving conflicts, reducing misunderstandings, offering procedural suggestions, or helping solve other process problems.

Other people are members in name only; they are **social loafers** who watch and listen but contribute little and seem content to let the rest of the members carry the workload. Even if they detract little from the group's energy and resources, they add almost nothing to the group's inputs. We all have experienced groups with social loafers, such as the committee member who makes no suggestions or the classmate in a discussion group who has not read the assignment to be discussed. Although this behavior may result from a lack of understanding of group processes, it nevertheless is inappropriate and unhelpful.

In contrast to both these types of members, participant-observers who are competent communicators and have extensive knowledge about groups contribute to the quality of both the process and the product of the group. In a recent survey of real-life groups, Broome and Fulbright found, among other things, that members wanted stronger guidance about group methods, procedures, and techniques as well as fellow members skilled in the communication process.[29] To be an all-around valuable member of the group, you need *both* a participant-observer focus *and* information and expertise essential to completing the group's task. This is what *Effective Group Discussion* is designed to teach you.

SUMMARY

1. Small groups play vital and pervasive roles in our lives. They provide a source for our identity, a means for problem solving in a complex society, and a vehicle to satisfy many basic needs. Thus, we willingly give up time, energy, and total autonomy in order to belong to small groups. The use of groups in the workplace and in society will continue to increase, so learning to operate effectively in small groups is an essential skill worth learning.

2. A group is *small* if each member is perceptually aware of the other. *Small group discussion* refers to three or more people interacting in order to achieve an interdependent goal.

3. Primary groups focus on interpersonal relationships and include families and groups of close friends. Secondary groups focus on task acccomplishment. Main types of groups (which may have both primary and secondary characteristics) include activity groups, personal growth groups, learning (study) groups, and problem-solving groups such as committees, quality control circles, and self-managed work groups.

4. Ethical members of groups treat speech, people, and information conscientiously, honestly, carefully, and open-mindedly.

5. Groups are helped by participant-observers who are able to attend to both the content and the process of group discussion.

EXERCISES

1. This icebreaker exercise is designed to help you get acquainted with classmates and reduce the tension and formality that exist among strangers. Each of you should take out a blank sheet of paper. Count the number of people in the room and make a grid on your paper with as many squares as there are people in the room. Your instructor will also make a master grid on the board. Your instructor will then hand out one index card to each of you. On this card, without using your name, write down a personal characteristic about yourself that most people in the class would not know. This could be a hobby, an event in your life, a favorite food, etc. Pass your card in to your instructor. Your instructor will read each card;

as he or she does so, write that characteristic in your grid as the instructor writes it on the master grid on the board.

All of you should stand up, push your desks against the perimeter of the room, and mingle with each other in the middle. Through conversation, try to find out who is linked to each characteristic without directly asking the person a question such as, "Are you the person who owns a rare coin from the Civil War?" When you find someone you think is a match, write that person's name in the appropriate square on your grid. The object is to be the first person to complete one row, column, or diagonal for a "Bingo." The first person to get "Bingo" yells it out loud and activity stops to check the matches. The

student who claimed "Bingo" should read off his or her matches; if one is wrong, all someone has to say is "incorrect" and the game continues. If the matches are correct, a winner is declared and you should all go back to your seats to discuss the activity.

2. For the next week, keep a list of all the small groups in which you actively participate. Classify these groups according to the types presented in this chapter. Next, rate your personal satisfaction with each group, from 1 (very dissatisfied) to 7 (very satisfied). Compare your lists in class. What do you conclude? Do your classmates like and dislike the same things in a group that you do? Using these lists, can you develop a list of general principles for having an effective group?

BIBLIOGRAPHY

Cathcart, Robert S., and Larry A. Samovar, eds. *Small Group Communication: A Reader.* 6th ed. Dubuque, IA: Wm. C. Brown Publishers, 1992, sections 1 and 2.

Larson, Carl E., and Frank M. J. LaFasto. *Teamwork: What Must Go Right/What Can Go Wrong.* Newbury Park, CA: Sage Publications, 1989.

NOTES

1. Kurt W. Back, "The Small Group: Tightrope between Sociology and Personality," *Journal of Applied Behavioral Science* 15 (1979): 283–94.

2. Lawrence W. Frey, "Applied Communication Research on Group Facilitation in Natural Settings," in *Innovations in Group Facilitation: Applications in Natural Settings,* ed. Lawrence R. Frey (Cresskill, NJ: Hampton Press, 1995): 1–26.

3. Diane Cole, "Meetings That Make Sense," *Psychology Today* (May 1989): 14.

4. Bill Lawren, "Competitive Edge," *Psychology Today* (September 1989): 16.

5. Charles C. DuBois, "Portrait of the Ideal MBA," *The Penn Stater* (September/October 1992): 31.

6. William C. Schutz, *FIRO: A Three-Dimensional Theory of Interpersonal Behavior* (New York: Rinehart, 1958).

7. Gerald Goldhaber, "Communication and Student Unrest" (Unpublished report to the president of the University of New Mexico, undated).

8. "Road Test," *Consumer Reports* (April 1992): 266; (July 1992): 427.

9. William Ouchi, *Theory Z: How American Business Can Meet the Japanese Challenge* (Reading, MA: Addison-Wesley, 1981).

10. Robert H. Waterman, Jr., *The Renewal Factor: How the Best Get and Keep the Competitive Edge* (New York: Bantam Books, 1987).

11. Susan Sorensen, "Grouphate" (Paper presented at the International Communication Association, Minneapolis, May, 1981).

12. Quoted in Lisa Stroud, "No CEO Is an Island," *American Way* (November 15, 1988): 97.

13. T. J. Larkin, "Humanistic Principles for Organization Management," *Central States Speech Journal* 37 (1986): 37.

14. Douglas M. Lawson, *Give to Live: How Giving Can Change Your Life* (LaJolla, CA: ALTI Publishing, 1991).

15. Nolan Ryan, personal interview on the *Today Show* (May 25, 1993).

16. Marvin E. Shaw, *Group Dynamics: The Psychology of Small Group Behavior,* 3d ed. (New York: McGraw-Hill, 1980): 8.

17. Robert F. Bales, *Interaction Process Analysis* (Cambridge, MA: Addison-Wesley, 1950): viii, 35–39.

18. Gay Lumsden and Donald Lumsden, *Communicating in Groups and Teams: Sharing Leadership* (Belmont, CA: Wadsworth, 1993): 13–15.

19. Thomas E. Harris and John C. Sherblom, *Small Group and Team Communication* (Boston: Allyn and Bacon, 1999): 123–31.

20. Carl E. Larson and Frank M. J. LaFasto, *TeamWork: What Must Go Right/What Can Go Wrong* (Newbury Park, CA: Sage, 1989): 19.

21. Richard E. Sykes, "Imagining What We Might Study if We Really Studied Small Groups from a Speech Perspective," *Communication Studies* 41 (Fall 1990): 200–211.

22. Larson and LaFasto, *TeamWork,* 19.

23. Carolyn M. Anderson and Matthew M. Martin, "The Effects of Communication Motives, Interaction Involvement, and Loneliness on Satisfaction: A Model of Small Groups," *Small Group Research* 26 (February 1995): 118–37.

24. Larson and LaFasto, *TeamWork,* 66–69.

25. Charles C. Manz and Henry P. Sims, Jr., "The Potential for 'Groupthink' in Autonomous Work Groups," *Human Relations* 35 (1982): 773–84.

26. *The Random House Dictionary of the English Language,* 2d ed. unabridged (New York: Random House, 1987): 665.

27. Ronald C. Arnett, "The Practical Philosophy of Communication Ethics and Free Speech as the Foundation for Speech Communication," *Communication Quarterly* 38 (Summer 1990): 208–17.

28. Stanley Deetz, "Reclaiming the Subject Matter as a Guide to Mutual Understanding: Effectiveness and Ethics in Interpersonal Interaction," *Communication Quarterly* 38 (Summer 1990): 226–43.

29. Benjamin J. Broome and Luann Fulbright, "A Multistage Influence Model of Barriers to Group Problem Solving: A Participant-Generated Agenda for Small Group Research," *Small Group Research* 26 (February 1995): 25–55.

2

The Small Group as a System

Central Message

All components of a small group operate interdependently with one another, and the group itself is interdependent with its environment. To understand a group fully, we must examine the components in relationship to one another, not in isolation.

Study Objectives

As a result of studying Chapter 2 you should be able to:
1. List and explain the major input, throughput, and output variables in a small group system and provide examples of their interdependence.
2. Define the main terms and types of variables pertaining to systems.
3. Describe the characteristics of an effective discussion group.

Key Terms

Boundary spanners
Closed system
Environment
Feedback
Individual-level variables
Input variables
Interdependence
Multiple causation
Nonsummativity
Open system
Output variables
System
System-level variables
Throughput variables
Variables

During one traumatic week, the church board—one minister and three lay people—of a new Unity church faced nearly insurmountable challenges. On Monday the board chair suffered a stroke; on Wednesday the minister died. The remaining members, in shock, recruited three others members to help carry on the work. The board had been working to establish a second Unity church in Springfield, Missouri, following an unpleasant church split two years earlier. The new church had just gotten off the ground when these tragedies occurred, but members, committed to the project, decided to keep the church going. The board elected Bill, a lawyer, as chair. Sally, a widowed secretary whose husband had been a minister, agreed to serve as secretary. The other members included Marina, a college professor; Sunni, director of a university speech and hearing clinic; and Norm, a massage therapist who was also an accomplished musician. No paid employees worked for the church—all the work was accomplished by volunteers, including board members.

Among the challenges board members faced were how to handle Sunday services without a minister, how to pay for the lease they had recently signed on an older building, and how to overcome opposition to the new congregation, both from the denomination's headquarters and the original church's minister. The board quickly decided they needed additional expertise so they soon added two more members: Don, a retired business owner, and Gary, a maintenance worker. The members had diverse experiences and expertise, but they all shared a similar vision for the church and common values to guide them in their work. The board met every week for two years. At the end of that time, members could point to several important accomplishments: Sunday services were held every week and attendance had increased from about 40 members to about 90 members per Sunday; bylaws had been approved by the congregation; the board, originally an informal, self-selected board, was voted in by the congregation; enough money had been set aside to cover a minister's salary for six months; and, most important of all, the formerly renegade congregation had received official approval from the denomination's headquarters and were now "legal."

We have already discussed how pervasive small groups are in our daily lives and why we should study them. In this chapter we will use the church board we just introduced to illustrate the basic principles of general systems theory, a framework for understanding small groups. We periodically present dialogue from the church board to illustrate how various principles of systems theory may appear communicatively. Once you have a communication-based model for understanding systems principles, you can recognize the principles operating in any group.

THE SMALL GROUP AS AN OPEN SYSTEM

You have probably noticed that when a new person joins a group, the group changes in some ways. For example, when a new baby is brought into a family, all family relationships will change, including between the parents, between the other children, and between the parents and the children. In addition, new relationships must be accommodated—between everyone else and the new baby. This illustrates the idea of a **system**—a set of relationships among interdependent, interacting components and forces. General systems theory is built upon an analysis of living entities—including groups and organizations—as they attempt to remain in dynamic balance with the environment by constant adjustments. Systems theory provides a useful framework to help you keep track of all the individual elements and components of a small group as they interact as a complex whole.

Several principles of systems theory are especially relevant to your study of small groups. One of the most important is the principle of **interdependence,** which states that the parts of a system do not operate in isolation but continuously affect each other, as well as the system as a whole. The new baby affects every other family member. Similarly, if the usually cheerful chair of a committee comes to a group meeting in a grouchy mood, the other members will feel uneasy and the group's normally effective decision-making processes may be impaired. In the church board we described, every decision was accomplished through open discussion that emphasized member interdependence. No individual's views (including those of board chair Bill) were treated as more important than another's. Consider the following excerpt from the first board meeting members held after the minister died, at which members were trying to figure out what needed to be done for Sunday services:

Bill: Why don't we make a list of all the things that have to be done on Sunday mornings, and see who wants to do what? Does that sound all right to you?

Group: Yes, that's a good idea. That will help. Sounds fine.

Marina: We have to make sure things are cleaned up for Sunday. Gary, if you come in Saturday morning to clean, I'll help you, then I can get Chandra to decorate the sanctuary on Saturday afternoon.

In this fashion, members listed jobs to be done for the next half-hour while Sally made a list on a flip chart. Often, the member who presented a task simultaneously volunteered to do it. Members jumped in to claim the "unclaimed" tasks or to recruit someone from the congregation to do them. Even though each member ended up with several unglamorous tasks, she or he recognized that the success of the entire enterprise—having a good Sunday service—depended on everyone doing the jobs effectively. They acknowledged their interdependence with each other, as well as their interdependence with the congregation.

A column by George Will in *Newsweek* dramatically illustrates the principle of interdependence and also reminds us that, because we are all interdependent, actions we take sometimes have unanticipated consequences.[1] When the Lincoln Memorial was illuminated at night, the lights attracted insects, which attracted the spiders that fed on them, which then attracted the birds that fed on the spiders. To keep the monument beautiful for visitors, workers scrubbed the bird droppings and the spider webs that had accumulated, but the act of scrubbing the marble made it susceptible to the exhaust fumes from the traffic in Washington, D.C. Lighting the monument, intended to have a positive effect, also set in motion a chain of events that is contributing to the monument's deterioration. We cannot know in advance all the effects our actions will cause.

Another key principle is the system property of **nonsummativity** (nonadditivity), which states that the whole system is not the sum of its parts. It may be either greater or less than the sum of its parts, with either positive synergy or negative synergy operating. Imagine a collection of individuals when they first begin to interact and coordinate their efforts to form a competitive basketball team. The team involves much more than the simple addition of the abilities of each player. The group will take on a life of its own and become an identifiable entity. Sports fans know they will lose money on a basketball or football game if they add up the statistics for each player, arrive at team totals, and bet on the team with the higher total. On any given day, a so-called poor team can play beyond its apparent potential (positive synergy), or a terrific team can have an off day (negative synergy). Why? Because each team or group is a living system in which everything is interdependent, and no one can predict precisely how the new system will function during any particular time.

In other arenas of endeavor, groups frequently design technologies beyond the collective capacities of the individual members. For example, most recent Nobel prizes in science have been given for breakthroughs that required teams of scientists. On the other hand, groups of intelligent, knowledgeable, and committed members sometimes make bad decisions, such as the groups of scientists and managers who decided to launch the space shuttle *Challenger* on its ill-fated trip.

No one can predict whether a group will experience positive or negative synergy. In our classes, we have often had groups composed of bright students whose final products disappointed us. However, Salazar has posited that the amount of ambiguity a group faces plays a major role in process losses and gains.[2] Ambiguity determines the types of obstacles a group will encounter. Whether the obstacles are dealt with in a facilitative or disruptive way determines whether a process loss (negative synergy) or gain (positive synergy) will occur. In any case, the communication behavior of the members is the principal determining factor for process gains or losses.

CONSIDER THIS

The church board introduced at the beginning of the chapter clearly demonstrates positive synergy—seven ordinary people who, together, accomplished an extraordinary result. What do you think are the factors that helped produce this positive synergy? What effect do you think members' commitment to the task had on the group? How might one member's commitment affect another member's? What does this say about member interdependence?

The systems perspective helps keep us from oversimplifying our understanding of how a group functions and perhaps missing something important. For example, systems theory emphasizes **multiple causation,** the fact that whatever happens in a system is not the result of a single, simple cause, but is produced by complex interrelationships among multiple forces. For example, several factors contributed to the church board's successful efforts, including the board's shared leadership, Bill's democratic coordination, the commitment and expertise of the members, the fact that creation of a new congregation filled a need in the community, and probably some fortuitous factors, such as the availability of an affordable location.

The **variables** of a system are its characteristics or dimensions. They may be classified as either *individual-level* or *system-level* features of a group.[3] **Individual-level variables** are properties of the individual members, such as their traits, skills, abilities, expertise, values, and attitudes. **System-level variables** are characteristics of the group as a whole, including preexisting societal and cultural norms, the degree of cohesiveness, and procedures the group uses. The individual-level and system-level variables are interdependent within themselves and with each other. For example, a new member may be well informed about a topic the group is discussing (an individual-level variable), but if the group has established a norm that new members should be seen and not heard until they have "paid their dues" (a system-level variable), the group will not benefit from that member's information. In the church board, Sally, whose husband had been a minister, had expertise in the creation of church bylaws—an individual-level variable. But her expertise would not have been made available to the group in open discussion if the board had not developed a democratic structure in which everyone, not just lawyer Bill, got a chance to contribute their expertise—a system-level variable. Thus, individual characteristics and group (system) characteristics mutually influence each other, as well as the group's final outputs.

System variables have been classified into three broad categories: *input, throughput,* and *output.* In a small group, **input variables** are components from which a small group is formed and that it uses to do its work, including the members; the reasons for the group's formation; resources such as information, expertise, money, and tools; and environmental conditions and forces that influence the group. In the church committee, members with their diverse areas of expertise were inputs. For instance, both Sunni and Sally had examples of bylaws from other churches, and Bill knew what to do to incorporate and receive tax-exempt status. All this information, possessed by individuals but shared with the group, served as resource input variables that ultimately affected both the group's deliberations and its success. Consider this exchange, after the minister died:

Sunni: I'm in shock from the past week, but I don't want to give up.

Norm: Me, neither. We're just on the verge of creating something that people have been wanting for two years, and I want to see us keep going.

Marina: Me, too. It's really important for me to have a church where I feel comfortable, so I'm willing to give whatever time is necessary to pull this off!

Communicatively, members demonstrate the high level of commitment they bring to this daunting task and their willingness to see it through—important input variables.

   Throughput variables of a group involve how the group transforms inputs into final products and are characteristics of how the system functions, what it actually does. Examples include roles, rules, and norms; procedures the group follows; the group's leadership; communication among members; and all the other things that are part of the process in which the group engages as it works toward completing its task. In our church board, observe how certain rules and procedures evolved. First, the members complimented each other and affirmed their commitment to the group's task. This led to a pattern of expressing cohesiveness and mutual respect, which later made it easier for members to contribute freely and frankly. Bill operated as a democratic chair who supported the group's norms of equality and shared leadership. This made other members feel comfortable to jump in with suggestions or comments. Look at the following exchange:

Bill: Well, here's draft one of the bylaws! They aren't carved in stone. I suggest that everybody take them home, read them carefully, and come prepared with changes next week. Then we can make the changes and have them copied and distributed for the congregation to look at. Sound OK?

Norm: Hang on a second, Bill. We said we were going to give these to Reverend Lacy [minister of another congregation who agreed to give the denomination's perspective] for feedback. That will take longer than one week.

Bill: You're right, I forgot. Let's schedule our discussion of the bylaws after Norm gets Reverend Lacy's perspective.

In this exchange, chair Bill's original suggestion is challenged, politely, by Norm. Bill acknowledges that he made a mistake and backtracks. This illustrates a throughput process that is democratic, where members can contribute without fear of repercussion and the leader has no more power to control events than the others do.

   Output variables of a group are the results or products of the group's throughput processes, including the tangible work accomplished (such as written reports, items built, and policies developed), changes in the members (such as increases in commitment and increased self-confidence), the group's effect on its environment, and changes in the group's procedures. The church board's most obvious output to its environment was the formation of a church now serving many people in southwest Missouri. Within the group, though, strong bonds of affection, cohesiveness, and pride at a job well done were intangible outputs that developed. In one meeting, after the group had been together for over a year, members articulated their feelings:

Don: As much as we complain about how much work we have to do, look at our finances! We have nearly half a year's salary in the minister's fund.

Bill: I know. At times when I'm swamped and feel like giving up, I think about what we've created and I'm energized again.

Marina: When I get discouraged about all that we *haven't* done and all the things that have fallen through the cracks, I think about how enthusiastic the congregation is, and how wonderful you all are, and I'm overcome with gratitude!

Gary: Speaking of gratitude, I haven't told you all how hesitant I was to be part of this group at first. You all have a lot more education than I do, and I didn't feel like I could express myself as well. But this has been one of the best experiences of my life, and I'm grateful for your encouragement and support.

Clearly, this is a cohesive, supportive group. Gary could admit something like this only if he trusted the others.

CONSIDER THIS

The church board was a secondary group with a well-defined task to perform, but its strong primary characteristics made it unique. How did members communicate their commitment to each other and their caring? How were Schutz's (see Chapter 1, page 5) human needs of affection, inclusion, and control met in this group? Can *any* group become this cohesive and productive? Why or why not?

Feedback is a response to a system's output. It can come in the form of information or tangible resources and helps the system determine whether or not it needs to make adjustments to reach its goals. For instance, a car company that sells many cars (outputs) receives money for those cars (response to the outputs). This positive consumer response to the cars also provides the company with the information that it will likely reach its profit goals. One goal of the church board was having its bylaws approved by its denomination's Ministerial Association. To achieve this goal, the board sought feedback:

Sally: I used to know people at the association, but everyone I knew has moved on. The association's approval is critical—if they don't like our bylaws, we won't get official approval as a church.

Sunni: Is there any way we can get a preliminary reaction, before we send our final draft?

Norm: Yes—remember Reverend Lacy, from Columbia? She said she'd help us however she could, and she's on a couple of committees at the association. She could look at the bylaws and tell us how the association is likely to react.

Reverend Lacy did have several suggestions for modifying the bylaws. Her reaction (feedback) to the draft of the bylaws (the output) produced several changes in the bylaws that strengthened them and enhanced their chances of being approved.

As you can see, input, throughput, and output variables are not separable; everything influences and is influenced by everything else. For example, attitudes affect interaction, which in turn affects the outcome.

Just as input, throughput, and output variables are interdependent, so is a group highly interdependent with its **environment,** the setting in which the group exists. Most groups are part of a larger organizational structure and must interact with individuals and other groups within that structure. But even nonorganizational groups are also part of an environment. For instance, the environment of a family may be the neighborhood or the general society in which it lives. It is critical to remember that groups are affected by their environments. The church board described here was highly influenced by its environment, the congregation. As effective as this group's throughput processes were, how successful do you think it would have been without the financial, moral, and informational support of its congregation? Not very successful!

Many small group researchers have criticized small group research for ignoring the effect of the group's environment on the group.[4] Some group researchers have implied that the quality of a group's output is entirely or largely within a group's control. So long as the group has skilled and knowledgeable members (inputs) and effective leadership with helpful norms such as a conscientious attitude and good listening behaviors (throughputs), then the group will produce high-quality outputs. This oversimplifies the case because most groups are not self-contained entities but in fact are highly dependent on their environments. For instance, Broome and Fulbright asked real-life group members what factors hurt their efforts.[5] They found that organizational factors beyond a group's control often had strong negative effects on a group's performance.

Recognizing the important role of the environment on the group system is an important first step in understanding group processes; however, it is only a first step. Putnam and Stohl remind us that, while the group's environment influences its internal communicative dynamics, that very environment is shaped by the group.[6] The boundaries between groups and their environments are fluid and permeable. Members of a group are simultaneously members of other groups; they bring the influence of those other groups into the first group. For instance Sunni, an original member of the church board, was also director of a university speech and hearing clinic. Members also carry into the group their outside role interests or agendas, which can subtly or overtly affect group interaction. Sally brought to the church board a sample of bylaws from the church where her husband had ministered. Fluctuation in group membership also affects the permeability of the group's boundaries, as was shown by the different perspectives Gary and Don brought to the group. Lastly, fluidity and permeability of group boundaries vary depending on the commitment members demonstrate to the various groups to which they belong. How well one group's identity is constructed in light of multiple memberships influences the group's dynamics and the strength of that group's self-identity. A major strength of the church group was the sense of belonging that members created and acted on.

Several realities of our social world help account for the reciprocal relationship between a group and its environment. First, members of groups, because they belong to other groups, create situations in which they often communicate between groups. Bill, the lawyer on the church board, talked to his office partners about the board and vice versa. These interactions simultaneously influenced both groups—the church board and his office partners. Second, groups often have to coordinate their actions with other groups within the same parent organization. The church group had to coordinate with other church committees, such as the finance committee and the worship committee. Third, there is frequent internal and external communication about how group goals should be interpreted, the extent of the group's authority, and support (or lack of it) for the group's actions. At one point in a board meeting, Norm relayed Reverend Lacy's feedback about the proposed bylaws, which resulted in some changes to the bylaws. Fourth, members all bring their own ways of speaking, their own sense of "group." The church board established a democratic discussion format early in its history with comments such as this one of Bill's: "Why doesn't everybody think of the important things that must be accomplished over the next, say, six months, and next week let's make a tentative schedule and organize how we're going to get everything done. Does that sound all right to you?"

Putnam and Stohl's *bona fide group perspective,* by focusing on group boundaries and interdependence with the environment, help us to see that a "group" is not easily identified and that its relationship with its environment is both reciprocal and complex.

One recent study by Hirokawa and Keyton of actual organizational groups supports the overall utility of the systems framework, including a focus on the group's context, for examining small groups.[7] These researchers asked several continuing groups what factors helped and hindered their group's progress. The factors fell into three categories: individual (e.g., member motivation and interest), group (e.g., group leadership), and organizational (e.g., assistance from the organization, including continuing informational support as needed). These findings emphasize the complexity of the group process and suggest that outcomes depend on input factors relating to members, on throughput processes such as leadership, and on environmental factors often beyond the group's control.

CONSIDER THIS

From what you know about the Unity church board, what were the individual, group, and organizational factors that contributed to this group's success?

The model in Figure 2.1 illustrates several of the many variables included in each of the main system categories. The hopper at the top of the figure represents inputs flowing into the machinery of the system, where they are processed and changed during the throughput process. The exit channel at the bottom represents the system's outputs. The tube on the right side represents the feedback channel that provides responses to the system's outputs. Surrounding the entire system is its environment, or setting, which also provides resources that affect the system. This particular model represents an **open system,** meaning that the group interacts freely with its environment. The perforations in the system's boundaries illustrate this characteristic that lets resources flow freely between the environment and the group. For example, a classroom group that receives relevant information from the instructor, from other classmates, from friends outside class, and from media or news sources is an open system. The church board had a high degree of interchange between itself and the congregation that was a main part of its environment, which made it an extremely open system. For example, board meetings were open and anyone from the congregation could attend them. In addition, the board frequently held "town meetings," at which congregation members were invited to share their opinions about the running of the church. In contrast, a **closed system** has relatively little interchange between the group and its environment. Its boundaries are more solid. A cloistered monastery, where monks interact with each other but have little contact with outsiders, illustrates a closed system. However, there is no completely closed human system.

In our previous discussion, we have stated that a group's environment is important to a group's success. This implies that how well a group manages its relationship with that environment is equally important. Ancona and Caldwell note that this aspect of group processes has been largely ignored by group researchers.[8] They suggest that groups need members who serve as boundary spanners by constantly monitoring the group's environment to bring in and take out information relevant to the group's success. The first of the three major functions that boundary spanners serve is initiating transactions to import or export needed resources, such as information or support. For instance, in our example of an effective group, Norm contacted Reverend Lacy for advice about organizing the new congregation and help in gaining approval from the Association. Another boundary-spanning function consists of responding to initiatives of outsiders. Someone may ask a group member what the group discussed at a particular meeting; that member must then decide whether and what information to relate. The final function involves changes in the membership of the group—new people may be brought into the group either temporarily or permanently. For example, in an unorthodox move, members decided to invite Gary's wife, Christy, to attend church board meetings in his place as a nonvoting member during a two-month stretch when he was unable to attend meetings. This enabled Gary to keep up with the board information and maintain, through Christy, relationships that he had formed. The management of the group's relationship with the

Model of a group as an open system.   **FIGURE 2.1**

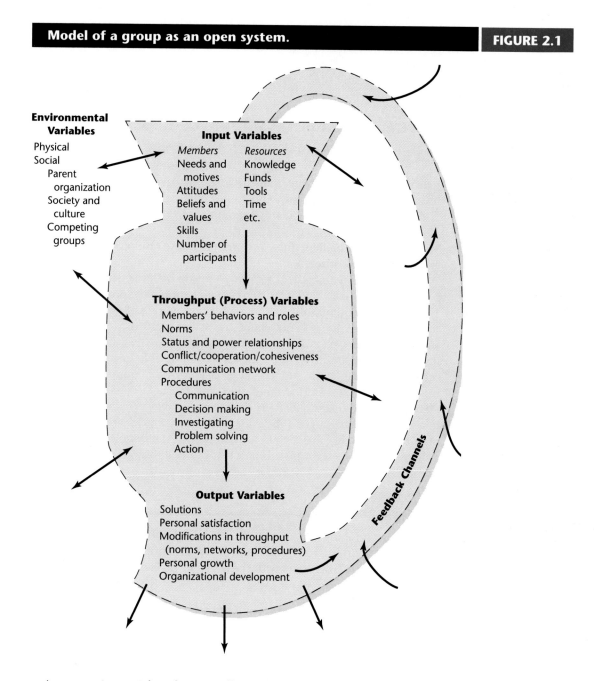

Environmental Variables

Physical
Social
   Parent
     organization
   Society and
     culture
   Competing
     groups

Input Variables

Members
Needs and
  motives
Attitudes
Beliefs and
  values
Skills
Number of
  participants

Resources
Knowledge
Funds
Tools
Time
etc.

Throughput (Process) Variables

Members' behaviors and roles
Norms
Status and power relationships
Conflict/cooperation/cohesiveness
Communication network
Procedures
    Communication
    Decision making
    Investigating
    Problem solving
    Action

Output Variables

Solutions
Personal satisfaction
Modifications in throughput
  (norms, networks, procedures)
Personal growth
Organizational development

Feedback Channels

environment is crucial and can spell success or failure for the group. If the church board had decided to be secretive and not share openly with the congregation what was discussed and decided at board meetings, the congregation would have been unlikely to support the church with time, energy, and resources.

The church board operated effectively. Seeing how the members interacted with each other and with their environment should help you identify standards against which you can evaluate the major input, throughput, and output variables of any small group to which you belong, too.

CHARACTERISTICS OF EFFECTIVE PROBLEM-SOLVING GROUPS

A secondary group's effectiveness can be determined only by comparing its accomplishments (outputs) with its stated goals and assessing its impact on its environment. The following standards, summarized in Figure 2.2, represent the ideal input, throughput, output, and environmental variables toward which discussion groups should strive, even though most will fall short.

Input Variables   1. **Members share basic values and beliefs about the purpose of the group and each other.**
For instance, if one member of a project group believes deeply that the project is worthwhile and intends to commit substantial time to it but another member thinks the assignment is busywork and decides to "blow it off," the group is not likely to reach consensus or interact smoothly. Ideally, members' attitudes toward each other, the group, and the group's task are positive. Members should be able to count on each other to complete tasks, support the decisions of the group, and act in a trustworthy way toward the other members. In our story about the effective church board, members demonstrated their commitment to the group and to doing a good job with such statements as "It's really important to me to have a church where I feel comfortable" and "I'm willing to give whatever time is necessary to pull this off!"

CONSIDER THIS

From what you know about the church board, what values do you believe were important to the members? What kind of group culture, or personality, would members with these values be likely to create?

2. **The number of members is small enough for all to be active participants and to be perceptually aware of each other as individuals, yet large enough to supply the variety of knowledge and competencies needed to achieve high-quality outputs.**
A divergence of backgrounds and perspectives is needed, but similarity in goals and values will make it possible for all members to support group decisions. Ideal groups achieve a balance between diversity and similarity; this balance is more important than size. For example, five people with different perspectives but similar values might agree on a

Characteristics of an effective discussion group.

FIGURE 2.2

Input Variables

1. Members share values and beliefs toward the purpose of the group and each other.
2. The number of members is small enough for all to be active participants who are aware of each other, yet large enough to supply knowledge and competencies.
3. The group's purpose is understood and accepted by all members.
4. Resources needed to achieve group goals are available.
5. The group's relationships to other groups and organizations are clear.
6. The group has sufficient time to do its work.
7. The group has a meeting place that provides for members' needs and is free of distractions.

Throughput Variables

1. Members can predict each other's behaviors.
2. Roles are stable, mutually understood, and accepted.
3. Members have relatively equal status, so they can exert influence based on knowledge, ideas, and skills.
4. Norms and the values underlying them are understood and adhered to, or discussed openly and changed if counterproductive.
5. Communication flows in an all-channel network.
6. Members are skilled and considerate when expressing themselves.
7. All members understand and share procedures that are efficient and lead to goal achievement.

Output Variables

1. Members perceive that the group purpose has been achieved.
2. Members feel satisfaction with their roles, the group process, and their relationships with other members.
3. Cohesiveness is high.
4. There is consensus on the role and leadership structure.
5. The parent organization (if one exists) is strengthened by the group's work.

Environmental Factors

1. The environment (usually an organization) should publicly recognize the accomplishments of the group and reward the group as a group.
2. The environment should supply whatever informational resources a group needs.
3. The environment should supply whatever resources and expertise are needed by the group.
4. The environment should provide a supportive atmosphere for the group.

goal, yet supply different sets of information about the problem and possible solutions. Thus, they will perform more effectively than 10 people whose perspectives are exactly the same or three people who can't agree on either basic values or goals.

3. The group's purpose is understood and accepted by all members. All members perceive the goal alike and give it priority over personal goals or needs incompatible with group objectives. Members whose personal values or goals are at odds with a group goal interfere with efficiency. For example, if the purpose of a religious study group is to share and understand a variety of beliefs, but one or two members attempt to convert others, the group will have problems.

4. **The group's relationships to other groups and organizations in its environment are clear, and members know what resources are available from these groups and organizations.**

   Group members perform the appropriate boundary-spanning activities and know how they relate to the organization that created the group, to competing groups, and to the environment. The area of freedom and limitations on the group are understood both by the group and by affected people in the environment. The group knows how to adapt to changing environmental circumstances.

5. **The group has sufficient time in which to do its work.**

   If research is needed to understand the problem, group members should have enough time to do it thoroughly. Groups need time to work through all the phases of the problem-solving process or to digest and process information and ideas. In short, members must have and commit enough time to do their work as a group thoroughly and well. For example, they should not try to find a solution to a city's congested traffic in a 40-minute meeting. Recall that the church board met *every week* for two years before it considered its main goals met.

6. **The group has a place to meet that provides for members' needs and allows discussions without distractions.**

   A committee that has no adequate room in which to meet regularly will expend much energy just finding and changing meeting places and trying to get members to those places. A quality circle cannot discuss problems well in a noisy assembly room, nor can a personnel committee evaluate job candidates in a room where privacy is compromised by strangers wandering in and out.

Throughput Variables

1. **Members are dependable and reliable.**

   A member who undertakes an assignment can be counted on to carry it out, whether that involves gathering information, typing and distributing a report, or scheduling a Sunday speaker for the service. Members can be counted on to attend scheduled meetings, notify the group if this is not possible, and perhaps send a knowledgeable substitute in their place if appropriate.

2. **Roles of members are relatively stable, mutually understood, and accepted by all members.**

   There is both sufficient role definition to permit members to predict each other's behavior (for example, on the church board Marina was consistently task oriented and organized and Bill was consistently democratic), as well as sufficient flexibility to permit anyone to make needed contributions to either the task or interpersonal relationships (for instance, other members besides Marina were task oriented and organized, and Marina also contributed to the positive feelings: "I'm overcome with gratitude!"). There is an equitable division of labor. The leadership position has been settled satisfactorily, but leadership functions are shared by all members.

3. **Members have relatively equal status, so all can exert influence based on their own knowledge, skill, and ideas rather than status differences internal or external to the group.**

On the church board, Bill's external status as a lawyer was relatively high, but that didn't stop Norm, the massage therapist, from saying, "Hang on a second, Bill . . . That will take longer than one week," when he reminded Bill of the need for Reverend Lacy's perspective. That was possible because inside the group, the status of members was relatively equal. Equal status promotes teamwork. Members spend their energies achieving the goals of the group, not competing against each other for power and position. When all members feel equal, they freely contribute ideas, opinions, and suggestions; they don't hold back. This gives the group more information to work with.

4. **Norms (rules) and the values underlying them are understood and adhered to, or are discussed openly and changed when found to be unproductive.**

A consistently productive problem-solving group has a culture of beliefs, values, and standards that encourages thorough searching for and testing of facts and ideas. For example, diversity of opinion was important to the church board; at one point, Bill suggested putting one or two people on the bylaws committee who felt strongest about limiting the power of the minister; Marina said, "Bill, that's a good idea! We need to make sure their point of view is included." When a member expressed a concern, that member would often conclude by asking, "Does anyone else feel bothered by this or is it just me?" This allowed the others to express their views, to address the problem, and to participate in finding a solution.

5. **The flow of communication reveals an all-channel network.**

A high proportion of remarks is directed to the group as a whole, not to individual members. There are no sidebar conversations during the group meeting, yet members are free to approach any and all other members when a meeting is not in progress. Members build on each other's ideas.

6. **Members are skilled in expressing themselves interpersonally and are considerate of other members.**

In the church board, Gary felt insecure about his ability to express ideas, but he was willing to share his opinions, did so clearly, and was encouraged by the other members. Group members should express their ideas with sensitivity so as not to evoke defensiveness in the others. Bill, although he was the designated leader of the group, often followed suggestions he made with, "Sound OK?" or "Is that all right with all of you?" or something similar that affirmed his respect for the others' opinions.

7. **All members understand and share procedures that are efficient, prevent overlooking important issues and facts, and lead to goal achievement.**

   In a problem-solving group, all members understand and follow a procedure that is based on systematic methods of problem solving, and they share in exercising control over this procedure. The group decides what changes should be made in its procedures. In addition, it is helpful for group members to share specific discussion techniques appropriate to the purpose of the group, and to participate in establishing the agenda. For example, at one point, the church board tried biweekly meetings for a while, but Norm concluded they weren't working for him. He brought it up to the group, gave the members reasons why they might reconsider ("Things really pile up in two weeks, and sometimes there's a big delay in our response . . . "), and asked the others what they thought. The whole group then had a chance to evaluate and modify their procedures.

Output Variables

1. **Members of the group perceive that its purpose has been achieved.**

   Decisions and solutions to problems are supported by members as the best ones possible. The church board members talked about several accomplishments they had achieved, including receiving bylaws approval from their congregation and their association, and saving enough money for half a year's salary for a minister. Solutions decided upon by a group should be accepted by most or all of the people affected.

2. **Members experience personal satisfaction with their respective roles in the group, the discussion and group-work process, and their relationships with the other members.**

   For example, Bill says, "I think about what we've created and I'm energized again," and Gary says, "I'm grateful for your encouragement and support." The fact that at one point the board decided to meet *more* frequently, not less, indicates a high degree of satisfaction with the activity.

3. **Cohesiveness is high.**

   Members have a strong sense of identification with the group and give it high priority among competing demands for their time and attention. Cohesiveness among board members was evident ("This has been one of the best experiences of my life . . . "). A high degree of trust exists among members, as when Gary revealed his original insecurity about being a member of the board.

4. **There is consensus on the leadership and role structure of the group.**

   If asked independently, each member would name the same person(s) as designated leader of the group and as choice for leader in the future. For example, Bill emerged as the group's designated leader because he organized well, was democratic, and put in considerable work. He was drafted to coordinate the steering committee, and was later elected board chair. The rest of the members' roles developed as a result of their interests and expertise in relation to the needs of the group. Thus, members shared in leading the group.

5. **The group creates a culture that reflects its unique qualities and values.**

   Each group creates a culture or personality that is different from every other group. In effective groups, that culture is a positive one that supports the values of the members and reflects to the members what is most important in that group. For example, in the church board, members sometimes stopped a discussion for a brief prayer, particularly if a disagreement was under way. The prayer reminded members that disagreeing with ideas was acceptable but being disagreeable to other people was not. These brief prayer breaks were an important part of the group's culture. Clearly, in a different kind of group, prayer breaks would not have been appropriate or welcomed.

6. **The parent organization (if one exists) is strengthened as a result of the small group's work.**

   The organization is better off as a result of the group's work. In the church board's case, this requirement clearly was met. The board helped create a viable church that grew, received its denomination's approval, and eventually hired its first minister.

1. **The environment (usually an organization) should publicly recognize the accomplishments of the group and reward the group as a group.**

   Praise and recognition for one's efforts are highly motivating. In contrast, ignoring someone's efforts is demoralizing. Group members will be motivated to work efficiently and productively when they know there will be praise and other rewards for their efforts. The church board was publicly recognized and thanked by the congregation at several points during the process of creating the new congregation.

2. **The environment should supply whatever informational resources a group needs.**

   Nothing is more frustrating to group members than to be given a charge but not the information or data needed to complete the charge. In addition, as members begin their work, they often find that they need information they had not anticipated. It is especially important that the parent organization continue to give the group access to whatever information members find they need to complete their task in a timely manner.

3. **The environment should supply whatever resources and expertise are needed by the group.**

   Sometimes organizations provide initial training and orientation for group members, especially for brand new groups, but often forget that groups may need continuing training and access to specialized procedures and expertise. For instance, a problem-solving group may benefit from bringing in a consultant to help them develop their

Environmental Factors

creativity as a group. Ideally, the group's environment is supportive of such group needs and continues to supply resources, training, expertise, coaching, or whatever else a group needs to be productive.

4. The environment should provide a supportive atmosphere for the group.

Groups are sometimes demoralized when their efforts are consistently second-guessed or interfered with by the parent organization. In addition, organizations sometimes tend to load a group, particularly one that has been successful in the past, with too many priorities to handle well. Instead, the ideal environment for a group is a nurturing and supportive one that gives the group room to negotiate without stifling or overburdening it.

Few groups you experience may measure up to these standards as well as the church board did. However, you now have a model of an effective small group as a basis for comparison and should be able to spot at least some of the sources of difficulty in any group that is not producing satisfactory outputs.

SUMMARY

1. Systems theory provides a framework for understanding something complex, such as small groups. The small group was described as an open system with input, throughput (process), and output variables, and having the properties of interdependence among components, nonsummativity, and interdependence with its environment.

2. Input variables include such items as members' skills, knowledge, and other resources. The group, as a system, processes these resources through communication among members, thereby transforming them into outputs including tangible products, such as reports or recommendations, and intangible products, such as cohesiveness or changes in members' perceptions.

3. Ideal input, throughput, output variables, and environmental factors were described, with examples provided from the church board introduced at the beginning of the chapter.

EXERCISES

1. Compare the church board discussed in the chapter to the Mafia. Compare each group in terms of the concepts listed below.
   a. Open versus closed systems.
   b. Interdependence of the parts of the system.
   c. Nonsummativity.
   d. Boundary-spanning activity.
   e. Characteristics of the group's culture.

2. In this chapter, several input, throughput, and output variables of small secondary groups were identified. What others do you think should be included? Why? Your answer should include a modification of Figure 2.1.

3. Think of the best and the worst small secondary groups in which you have participated. Why were they the best and worst? What characteristics of the inputs and the throughputs seem to have made the most difference? As a class, generate your own criteria for effective inputs and throughputs.

BIBLIOGRAPHY

Katz, Daniel, and Robert L. Kahn. *The Social Psychology of Organizations*. 2d ed. New York: John Wiley, 1978. See chapter 2.

Von Bertalanffy, Ludwig. *General System Theory*. New York: George Braziller, 1969.

Wood, Julia T., Gerald M. Phillips, and Douglas J. Pedersen. "Understanding the Group as a System." In *Small Group Communication: A Reader*. 6th ed. Robert S. Cathcart and Larry A. Samovar, eds. Dubuque, IA: Wm. C. Brown Publishers, 1992, 5–17.

NOTES

1. George F. Will, "A New Level of Worrying," *Newsweek* (July 22, 1996): 72.

2. Abran J. Salazar, "Understanding the Synergistic Effects of Communication in Small Groups: Making the Most Out of Group Member Abilities," *Small Group Research* 26 (May 1995): 169–99.

3. Randy Y. Hirokawa and Dierdre D. Johnston, "Toward a General Theory of Group Decision-making: Development of an Integrated Model," *Small Group Behavior* 20 (November 1989): 500–23.

4. Benjamin J. Broome and Luann Fulbright, "A Multistage Influence Model of Barriers to Group Problem Solving: A Participant-Generated Agenda for Small Group Research," *Small Group Research* 26 (February 1995): 25–55; Cynthia Stohl and Michael E. Holmes, "A Functional Perspective for Bona Fide Groups," *Communication Yearbook* 16, (1993): 601–14; Jeremy Rose, "Communication Challenges and Role Functions of Performing Groups," *Small Group Research* 25 (August 1994): 411–32.

5. Broome and Fulbright, "A Multistage Influence Model."

6. Linda L. Putnam and Cynthia Stohl, "Bona Fide Groups: An Alternative Perspective for Communication and Small Group Decision Making," in *Communication and Group Decision Making*, 2d ed., eds. Randy Y. Hirokawa and M. Scott Poole (Thousand Oaks, CA: Sage, 1996): 147–78.

7. Randy Y. Hirokawa and Joann Keyton, "Perceived Facilitators and Inhibitors of Effectiveness in Organizational Work Teams," *Management Communication Quarterly* 8 (May 1995): 424–46.

8. Deborah G. Ancona and David F. Caldwell, "Beyond Task and Maintenance: Defining External Functions in Groups," *Group & Organization Studies* 13 (December 1988): 468–94.

THE FOUNDATIONS OF COMMUNICATING IN GROUPS

©Bob Daemmrich/The Image Works

The three chapters in Part 2 provide theoretical information about communication particularly relevant to communicating in small groups. These chapters are intended to serve as a foundation on which to build your understanding of throughput processes in a small group. This foundation includes information about the communication process itself, how nonverbal and verbal behaviors function together, and how individuals from different cultures communicate differently in small group settings. Specific guidance is provided to help improve your personal competencies as a group member, especially in speaking, listening, and interpreting during group meetings.

Human Communication Processes in Small Groups

3

Central Message

Communication is a complex, symbolic process that group members must both understand and observe so they can coordinate their efforts to achieve the group goal.

Study Objectives

As a result of studying Chapter 3 you should be able to:
1. Explain communication as a symbolic, personal, transactional process that is not always intentional.
2. Differentiate among the content, relationship, and affective levels of interpersonal communication.
3. Explain the fallacy in each of five communication myths.
4. Describe how signals are encoded, transmitted, received, interpreted, and responded to in a communication transaction.
5. Give an example of a complete communication transaction and explain why such transactions are important.
6. Identify and describe the four general listening preferences.
7. Identify and describe each of seven pitfalls to effective listening.
8. Demonstrate both active and focused listening.

Key Terms

Action-oriented listener
Active listening
Communication
Content-oriented listener
Defensive listening
Feedback
Focused listening
Listening
Message
Noise
Paraphrase
People-oriented listener
Pseudolistening
Sidetracking
Signs
Signals
Symbols
Time-oriented listener

Po and some of his college friends started a small software company in the Silicon Valley. Po, Tony, May, Tamika, and Kevin took computer classes together and over time discovered they had one thing in common—the desire to get rich quick in the computer business and retire early. Po had been working on a software program to benefit utility companies in their billing. He shared his ideas with his friends, who decided to join Po in creating a software company. With the program in its final stages it was time for them to decide how to market their product. They conducted a series of meetings to develop a marketing plan. Their first task would be to assess their finances, and Kevin, their accountant, was assigned to give a report to the group. But lately, Kevin tended not be on time to their meetings. During one meeting Tamika remarked, "Man, what time is it already? Kevin—he's ten minutes late! If he had gotten here on time, we'd have been done by now. I'm tired of this." Po, in frustration, declared, "I'm tired of waiting on the jerk, too, okay?" And May replied, "I don't have time for this." Po, growing impatient, switched directions with, "Let's just go ahead and get started and try to get the ball rolling. Tony, did you find out who our major competition is?" The meeting proceeded without Kevin.

In Chapter 1 we made a case for recognizing small groups as our most important social formation and thus central to our lives, with communication central to the life of a small group. As this story shows, what and how we communicate with each other as group members creates the nature of the small group we participate in. *Communication* is like the nerve network of a small group; it is the verbal and nonverbal process by which individuals forge themselves into a group, maintain the group, and coordinate their efforts: "Communication is the lifeblood that flows through the veins of groups. Communication is not just a tool that group members use; groups are best regarded as a phenomenon that emerges from communication."[1] No communication, no group. This chapter provides a foundation for understanding the term *communication,* which is *the* fundamental throughput process of all groups.

If you have previously studied communication, the next two chapters may be a review for you. Nevertheless, because communication scholars sometimes use key terms in different ways, we recommend that you at least survey these chapters to understand how we use key terms.

WHAT IS COMMUNICATION?

Many definitions of the term *communication* exist. We define **communication** as the process by which people create and send signals that are received, interpreted, and responded to by other people. The purpose of this process, for the small group, is to develop meaning that is shared sufficiently for the members to accomplish the group task. Meaning is never completely shared between two people, let alone among the four or five who typically constitute a small group. However, for group members to achieve their interdependent goal, at least *some* shared meaning must occur.

In this section, we first present several principles that govern the communication process before we elaborate on that process in greater detail and discuss several myths about communication. Different authors subscribe to different communication principles, but the following are the ones that are generally accepted by scholars and to us seem particularly important for understanding communication in small groups. We consider several of these principles in greater detail in Chapter 4.

Principles of Communication

1. **Human communication is symbolic.**

   This, perhaps, is the most important principle of communication. *Meaning* is not transferred from one person to another; rather, people send messages to each other that must be interpreted. In the movie *Brainstorm,* the main character invented a headphone device that could transfer experiences directly from the brain of one person to another without first having to *encode* the experiences into words. Of course, we can't do this—yet! We must use verbal and nonverbal signals to send our thoughts to another person. In this encoding process, we convert our thoughts, feelings, beliefs, and experiences into the words, sounds, and gestures that we hope others will interpret as we mean them. The receiver then uses the reverse process of *decoding,* attending to what was sent and interpreting it, to try to determine what was meant.

   The **signals** that humans exchange may be either *signs* or *symbols.* **Signs,** nonverbal elements such as tone of voice, face and body characteristics, have an inherent, natural connection with what they represent. For example, if you scowl because you hear something you dislike, there is a natural connection between your feeling of dislike and your scowl. Similarly, your blush of embarrassment is a sign directly connected with your feeling of embarrassment. In contrast, **symbols** are arbitrary signals created by people to represent experiences, objects, or concepts. For example, there is no automatic reason why we call something we write with a *pen.* We could just as easily have agreed to call it a *dog, tree, or la plume.* Similarly, the *okay* gesture, the circle we make with thumb and forefinger, is an arbitrary symbol; it means something different in other cultures, such as in South America, where it means something obscene. This reliance on symbols is an important characteristic of human communication and is a major reason why meaning can never be shared exactly.

2. **Communication is personal.**

   Meaning itself is not conveyed. A person sends signals that evoke meaning in a receiver; the signals will have different associations for the receiver than they do for the sender. Because much human communication is symbolic, the same word can have different meanings to different people. Thus, as it is sometimes stated, "meanings are in people, not in words." This principle is even more important when we consider that many of the concepts we necessarily use in everyday conversation are abstract: *fairness, excellence, effective.* For instance, excellence to you may mean striving for an A grade on a project, with no typographical errors and all information thorough and complete; for a fellow group member, excellence may mean getting the project completed on time, even if there are mistakes and missing information. Both of you are using the same word, but you aren't meaning the same thing at all! Your backgrounds, experiences, the culture from which you came—all of these things affect the meanings you give to the words you and others use. We discuss in detail the effects of culture on the communication process in Chapter 5.

CONSIDER THIS

In our story, Po, Tamika, May, and Tony believe that Kevin has a problem being "on time." Note Tamika's exclamation, "he's ten minutes late!" But what does it mean to be late? "Being on time" and "late" are interpretations of behavioral events (e.g., we agreed to meet at 2 PM and it is 2:30 and Kevin has not shown up). In this case, the group members are sharing with each other their own experiences of time. Can you think of examples which show how time is experienced differently in different cultures, perhaps one in which 30 minutes past a set time for a meeting would not be considered "late"?

3. **Communication is a transactional process.**
   This principle follows from the previous two. *Transactional* implies that participants in a communication encounter must cooperate and work together to achieve mutual meaning and understanding. From the previous example, if we know that the verbal symbol (i.e., word) *excellent* has different connotations to different people, and we want to make sure we understand each other about our project, then we must work together, communicatively, to determine what we jointly mean by *excellent*. In addition, *transactional* implies that the sender-receiver roles occur simultaneously, not alternately. While I am describing what an excellent project means to me, I simultaneously see your frown, and guess that you don't agree with my description. Thus, communication is *both* a sender *and* receiver phenomenon simultaneously for each person involved in the process. Finally, the concept of *process* implies that communication is an ongoing event with no clear beginning or end. If we argue about how excellent our project will be, then the next time we meet we will carry the memory of that argument with us. Thus, communication is ever-changing, not static, but constantly in flux.

4. **Communication is not always intentional.**
   This principle is sometimes stated as "You cannot NOT communicate," and not all communication scholars agree with this position.[2] For

example, Infante et al. believe that for an event to "count" as communication, the sender must have intended to communicate with the receiver.[3] "You cannot NOT communicate" was never meant to imply that all behavior is communication, only that all communication in a social setting (e.g., a group) is behavior and behavior has no opposite (i.e., you cannot *not* behave). For instance, when two or more humans are in each other's perceptual awareness, they cannot stop sending nonverbal signals to each other, which the receivers pick up, interpret, and respond to. Kevin's absence from his group communicates various things to his group. Thus, in a social setting, one probably cannot avoid communicating.[4] The way signals are interpreted may not be the way they were intended. Kevin may not at all intend to communicate to his colleagues that he does not care enough for the business to be on time. Moreover, people do not always *know* what they intend, and may have multiple intentions for their words or actions.[5] Nevertheless, in a social setting like a group, you do not have the option of not communicating, because even silence will be interpreted by your fellow group members.

5. **Communication involves content, relationship, and affective levels.**

A **message,** the set of signals from one person to others, contains all three levels. The *content* or denotative level of the message is the subject or topic of the message. The *relationship* level of the message refers to what the message reveals about how the speaker views his or her relationship to the other participants, and the *affective* level of the message reveals how the speaker feels about what he or she is saying. These latter two levels provide the connotative, or implied, level of the message.

At the content level, Tamika's first remark presents a fact—that Kevin has not arrived at the designated time—and an opinion—that the group could have finished its meeting if members had been able to start on time. However, the level of communication most striking here, and in Po's and May's subsequent remarks, is the affective level. Clearly, these colleagues feel angry and frustrated that Kevin has failed them again. Po's calling Kevin "a jerk" indicates that Kevin's behavior pattern is straining the good will of the others. Now notice Po's final remark: "Let's just go ahead and get started . . . Tony, did you . . . ?" This comment clearly illustrates the relationship level of communication, which concerns how the speaker views his or her relationship to the other members. Po takes charge here by suggesting the group begin without Kevin, then asks Tony for a report. At the content level, Po seems to be making a procedural suggestion ("Let's get started") and asking Tony for information. At the relationship level, however, Po is saying, "I have enough authority in this group to suggest how to proceed, and I'm taking charge now." The rest of the members accept Po's definition, and the meeting gets under way. Why? Po is the designated leader of the group, and he is behaving appropriately for his position. The actions of the others support this behavior and thus Po's authority is sustained. In this instance, Po does not overstep his relational bounds.

The relationship level, which is often conveyed nonverbally through tone of voice and movement, can show that the speaker considers him- or herself to be dominant, subservient, or equal to the other members. Attitudes of arrogance, dominance, submissiveness, distrust, superiority, neutrality, or concern are not often stated; rather, listeners interpret them from nonverbal cues or how a message is expressed. In our experience, this level causes many of the misunderstandings we observe in small groups. To illustrate, what if May had turned to Tamika and said, in a commanding tone of voice, "Tamika, you take notes for the meeting." Tamika would probably have wanted to say, "Who died and made you queen?" Group members often react strongly to a peer who seems to command and direct because the manner suggests superiority to the other members.

So far, we have discussed small groups that meet in real time and face to face. But, since the advent of computers and more recently the explosion of Internet capabilities, groups no longer need to meet face to face in real time. Group members can overcome the limitations of space and time with computers. *Computer-mediated communication,* or CMC, is the phrase used to refer to the use of computers to interact with others. Although this may appear to be a different kind of communication, the communicative processes involved are still symbolic, personal, transactional, not always intentional, and involve content, relationship, and affective dimensions. We will elaborate on CMC in later chapters.

Myths About Communication

Misunderstandings about communication are perpetuated by a number of communication myths. Here are five of the most pervasive ones:

1. **I understand communication. I've been communicating all my life!**
   What if your 90-year-old Aunt Tilly said, "I know how to drive—I've been driving all my life!" Just because we do something often doesn't mean we do it well. Most people do not think reflectively about their communication behavior so they can improve it.

2. **All human problems are communication problems.**
   This statement trivializes the very real value differences that divide humans. Environmentalists who want to save the Bering Sea ecosystem, one of the world's richest and commercially valuable marine environments, may understand perfectly well the concern of fishermen who fear for their jobs and livelihoods—but they disagree over values and appropriate courses of action. Communicating more and better may do nothing to resolve their disagreements.

3. **If communicators use good communication techniques, they will automatically have good communication.**

It is true that becoming a good communicator requires practicing techniques of effective encoding and decoding. However, communication involves much more than that. The most important "skill" for improving communication involves having an attitude of wanting to be a good communicator. You can make mistakes with the techniques you use, but if people sense your basic good intentions they will often forgive your communicative lapses and you can be quite effective in coordinating meanings with them. Only if you *want* to be a good communicator can the skills and suggestions in most communication books help you.

What promotes good communication? Almost always, good communication is enhanced by group members' understanding of the communication process, their attitudes toward both the process and other people, and their abilities to listen well.

4. **I didn't misunderstand him; he misunderstood me.**

Both sender and receiver must cooperate to create clear, mutually understood messages; remember, communication is not linear but transactional. If a message is misunderstood, the effective communicator will accept a share of the responsibility (not blame!) and work to improve future transactions.

CONSIDER THIS

Kevin finally arrives an hour after the scheduled time for the meeting. Tamika confronts him and asks him why he does not care enough to get to their meetings on time. Kevin tells her that he swore he heard Po tell him the meeting was scheduled for 3 PM not 2 PM. If communication is seen as linear then who is to blame for Kevin's "lateness"? On the other hand, from a transactional perspective, how do they all share in this circumstance? What might they say to each other if they looked at their circumstance transactionally—that is, if they took the point of view that they all created the situation?

5. **Good communication achieves perfect understanding among participants.**

Perfect understanding is impossible. Moreover, some messages are intended to mislead rather than enlighten. Have you ever answered vaguely to the question, "How do you like my new hair style?" In this case, the lack of clear, unambiguous communication purposefully avoids hurting someone's feelings. In addition, because communication is both symbolic and personal, the best we can do is come close enough to understanding that we can complete the work of the group.

A Description of a Communication Transaction

Now that we have looked at main principles and widespread myths about communication in general, let's go back to our definition of communication (*the process by which people create and send signals that are received, interpreted, and responded to by other people*) and use it to analyze a communication transaction, which is modeled in Figure 3.1. **Noise,** or interference with the participants' ability to achieve mutual understanding, can happen at any point in the communication process. Noise is always present to some extent; that doesn't mean that communication has broken down, but that the limitations of human communicating always make perfect understanding an impossibility.

To start the process, something occurs to a group member that he or she wants to share. That member then encodes the thought, feeling, or idea by putting it into words and gestures. This process, of course, happens without a lot of conscious thought. You typically don't stop to think how to arrange your face into a scowl when you are expressing your displeasure—you just *do* it. However, you probably have had the experience of intending to say something, but the words came out wrong, or the thought was not expressed as precisely as you would have liked. This glitch in encoding is a type of noise.

In small group communication, we usually assume the communicators are face to face. After the speaker has encoded the thought and sent it (i.e., spoken the words with accompanying nonverbal signals), another person must then receive the communication. This may sound simple, but the receiving process, which we call *listening,* is tricky, an additional source of noise. First, the receiver must *hear* what the speaker has said. Listeners often mishear or hear only part of what a speaker said. One of us attended a group meeting where a member said, "I don't have time to do that," but another member failed to hear the *don't,* and assumed the first member would handle a particular task. Fortunately, the problem was quickly straightened out by a third member, who suspected the misunderstanding and clarified it.

Once the receiver has physically heard the message sent, he or she must then *interpret* the message, another stage where noise interference often occurs. Major misunderstandings can occur during this step because of the symbolic and personal nature of communication. We may use the same words or gestures but mean very different things by them. For example, Raul comes to the first meeting of his group early. He greets everyone in a friendly way when they arrive, sits at the head of the rectangular table, and makes numerous suggestions. One member thinks, "Wow, I like his self-confidence. He'll really be an asset to the group." Another member thinks, "What an arrogant jerk. What makes him think he's in charge?" Same actions, different interpretations on the part of the receivers. Later, as the members get to know each other better, they may modify their interpretations. The second member may conclude, "Well, he comes on a little strong to begin with, but actually he's really friendly and hard working." A vital determinant of how we interpret

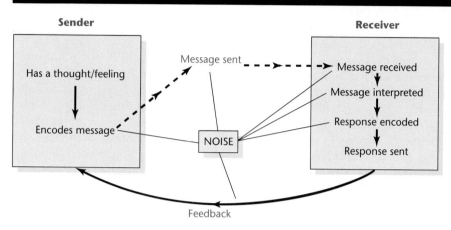

An interpersonal communication transaction.   **FIGURE 3.1**

messages comes from the culture in which we were raised. Our culture gives us the rules for what is appropriate communication behavior. Differing cultural rules can interfere with understanding in a small group. The effects of culture are covered in detail in Chapter 5.

The final step in the communication transaction is **feedback.** As with feedback to a system, feedback in the context of a communication transaction is the listener's response to a message (i.e., output) from the sender, and it provides a number of important functions in the communication process. First, it helps reduce the harmful consequences of noise that interfere with mutual understanding. For instance, a member who isn't sure she heard a speaker correctly can say, "I didn't catch that, could you run it by again?" Or, a member who heard the speaker but isn't sure how to interpret the statement can say, "Does that mean that you can help me with that assignment, or not?"

In addition, giving feedback to other members implies, "I am listening to you and you are a valued member of this group." Chopra observed, for instance, that when group members did not give each other supportive feedback, retaliation, withdrawal, and defensive behaviors increased.[6]

In the groups to which you belong, notice whether there is a difference in how much members typically respond to each other. Are you, like most of us, more comfortable in groups in which members react openly and clearly (even to disagree), or in ones in which reaction is minimal? Do you agree with Jablin, who found that subordinates would rather have a boss disagree openly than ignore them, which is perceived as highly insulting?[7] We suggest you monitor your own feedback and change it if you routinely fail to respond to speakers.

LISTENING AND RESPONDING DURING DISCUSSIONS

The level of understanding among group members depends more on how they listen and respond than on how they speak. Earlier, we explained that communication involves encoding, sending, hearing, interpreting, and responding to messages. **Listening** comprises the steps of hearing and interpreting. *Hearing* is a physiological process that involves the reception of sound waves by the ear. It is only the first element of listening, which also includes the *interpretation* of those sound waves (and other signals). A person with acute hearing may be a poor listener who does not interpret others' statements accurately or respond appropriately. In contrast, someone with considerable hearing loss may be a good listener who is motivated to understand others the way they want to be understood.

CONSIDER THIS

In 1996 someone estimated that every morning in the United States 15 million meetings take place. Consider that in a six-person group, every time 5 minutes of information is repeated because of poor listening, a total of 30 minutes is wasted.[8] Taken together that is a lot of wasted time! Are you a good listener? Why? When you are not as effective a listener as you would like to be, what has happened? Interested in improving your listening? Read on.

Roach and Wyatt suggest four important things good listeners remember.[9] First, good listeners pay attention to the context of what is said. Have you ever been quoted "out of context"? If so, you know that context can change the entire meaning of what is said. Suppose Tiffany says she's not sure the president of your organization will read your group's entire report right away because the president is in the middle of performance reviews with all the committee heads. Saying "Tiffany said the president won't bother to read our report" seriously distorts what Tiffany said and ignores the context of the president's being too busy *at the moment* to give the report full attention.

Second, good listeners pay attention to the feelings of the speaker. Remember the affective component of a message? When Malcom says, "Yes, that idea is fine," in a resigned, flat tone of voice, he's probably expressing a negative feeling about the idea, without actually saying so. A good listener will verify that interpretation: "Malcom, you said you like it but you don't sound too enthused. Would you share your concerns with us?"

Third, when the organizational pattern a speaker uses is confusing, good listeners help speakers make themselves clear by asking questions to clarify. For example, Shanda is a statistics whiz who completed all the computer analyses for your group's project. She knows her stats so well that she skips steps in explaining them to the rest of you, who are lost. You can help her communicate more clearly by asking her questions that encourage her to fill in the gaps.

Finally, it is important to interpret silence carefully. Silence may mean that people don't understand what was said, that they don't agree, that they are apathetic, or that they are hoarding information as a power play. Group leaders often mistake silence for agreement when it is something else. Again, a well-timed question will help interpret silence correctly.

Poor listening is easier to detect in a dyad than in a small group where one person can "hide" for long periods of time.[10] Compare a nine-person group to a dyad. In a nine-person group, if all members are participating equally, then each member listens about 90 percent of the time! Thus, the social pressure on members to listen is not as intense in a group as it is in a dyad and bad listening is easier to hide. Because people can fake listening, only when someone speaks do other participants have a basis for judging that person's listening behavior. Making irrelevant comments and asking questions about something that has already been explained are evidence of poor listening.

Most of us think we are good listeners, but evidence suggests otherwise. At times, group members are not even aware of the current topic of discussion. Berg found, for instance, that topics were switched about one time per minute in discussions he observed. Members were hardly listening or responding to what previous speakers had said.[11] This finding was confirmed by other investigators in a variety of cultures and situations.[12] Nichols and Stevens reported that students listening to lectures on which they knew they would be tested retained only about half of the new information presented.[13] We have found that when members of small groups (whether college students or corporate personnel in training groups) are required to paraphrase what a previous discussant said to that person's satisfaction, they can do so only about half the time. This is true even when participants know that they will be assessed for accuracy in listening. How much, then, must group members misunderstand when they are *not* on guard?

The cost of poor listening is high. Jobs are completed incorrectly, shipments go awry, and people are hurt or killed because they or someone else didn't listen well. A good listener is, unfortunately, a rare commodity of great value to a group. Bechler and Johnson found that individuals who are perceived by their fellow group members as being skilled listeners (e.g., stayed focused on the discussion, maintained eye contact with the speaker, and so forth) are also perceived as being leaders.[14] In fact, we think good listening is one of the most important skills a leader can exhibit.

By now we hope you have gotten the idea that good listening in a group is an invaluable skill and poor listening can produce terrible group outcomes. We have mentioned why some of us are not very good listeners and suggested four things to remember if you want to improve your listening. In addition, you should understand that all of us bring to our group experiences different listening preferences which, if not recognized, can produce

**Listening
Preferences**

problems for the group. Have you ever thought that perhaps your strengths and weaknesses as a listener are tied to your learned listening preference?

Kittie Watson, a specialist in listening and small group communication, has identified four general listening preferences: people-, action-, content-, and time-oriented listeners.[15] No one preference is better than another because each has its advantages and disadvantages. The trick to managing different listening preferences is to be able to identify the listening preferences of all members, including yourself, in group interaction and shifting your preference to fit the needs of the group.

People-oriented listeners are concerned about how their listening behavior affects relationships. Appearing attentive and nonjudgmental, these listeners are the ones people go to when they want someone to listen to them. Behaviors indicative of this preference are the use of "we" more than "I," use of emotional appeals in discussion and debates, and willingness to show vulnerability. These members may be heard telling a personal story to calm down members who may be upset or angry. People-oriented listeners may also become distracted by others' problems, may avoid conflicts to maintain a sense of harmony, and may engage in too many side conversations during meetings.

Action-oriented listeners in your groups are focused on the job at hand. They help the group stay on task by remembering details and providing feedback about the goal. They enjoy listening to well-organized material. On the other hand, these members can appear overly critical, may interrupt too much if they believe the group is getting off track, and may lose interest if the discussion appears to be going nowhere.

Content-oriented listeners are the group members who really enjoy analyzing the things they hear and are drawn to highly credible sources. You may observe these members using graphs, quoting sources, bringing research to the group, and dissecting the information and arguments of others. These listeners can also be seen as overly critical and maybe even intimidating to other members. Their analytical skills, while valuable, may also slow the group down and can even serve to devalue information they do not see as important, such as anecdotes.

Time-oriented listeners can be identified by their attempts to schedule group meeting and activity times, their sensitivity to nonverbal cues that may indicate impatience, and their focus on moving the group along in a timely manner. The creative and spontaneous discussions so necessary to problem solving can pose difficulties for these listeners. They also discourage additional discussion as the group nears the end of its scheduled meeting time.

CONSIDER THIS

Look back at the story about Po and the others at the beginning of the chapter. Given the information you have, which listening preferences are manifested in the dialogue? How do the preferences help the discussion? How might they hinder the discussion?

No one preference is the best. They are learned, so you are not locked into one of them. Each group member preference is influenced by many factors, including the nature of the relationships between group members and time constraints. Observe the members in your group for behavioral patterns that identify their preferences. Be willing to shift your preference to suit the immediate needs of the group and be willing to encourage the productive use of all the preferences. Let's turn now to a discussion of some of the more common behaviors that stand in the way of our becoming better listeners and of optimizing our listening preferences.

Our listening is impaired when we are tired, preoccupied, or overloaded with information and noise. But even when we are not bothered by such interference or concerns, we still may listen poorly as a result of bad habits we are not aware of. We either do not pay attention carefully to the speaker, or we pay too close attention—to the wrong things! The following are behaviors that interfere with good listening:

Pitfalls to Listening Effectively

1. **Pseudolistening.**
   Pseudolistening refers to faking the real thing. Pseudolisteners nod, smile, murmur polite responses, look the speaker in the eye, and may even give verbal support like "right" or "good idea." But behind the mask, the pseudolistener has "zoned off" on a daydream, a personal problem, sizing up the speaker, or mentally preparing a response. When such behavior is challenged, most pseudolisteners blame the speaker ("That stuff he was saying was boring") when they really hadn't given the speaker a chance.

2. **Sidetracking.**
   Related to pseudolistening is **sidetracking,** when you allow something another member said to send you off into your own private reverie. As a consequence, sometimes you may sidetrack the conversation in a completely inappropriate direction, thereby wasting the group's time.

3. **Focusing on irrelevancies and distractions.**
   Sometimes distractions such as background noises, room furnishings, and the air temperature make it difficult for us to concentrate on the speaker. At other times, undue attention to speaker characteristics such as dialect, appearance, or personal mannerisms causes us to miss important points. As one woman from Georgia said to her group: "Damn it, listen to what I have to say, not to how I speak. It makes me really mad when someone says, 'Oh, how you talk is so cute, I just can't pay attention to what you are saying.' "

4. **Silent arguing.**
   Many people listen selectively for information that confirms views they already hold. When they hear information that contradicts their chosen positions, silent arguers carry on an internal argument that opposes what they think the speaker has said.

You cannot mentally rehearse a reply at the same time you are striving to understand another. If you listen primarily to find flaws and argue them in your mind, you are unlikely to understand the speaker, the context of the remarks, and the meaning the speaker intends. We are not saying, "Don't argue." We are suggesting that you make sure you understand others first, well enough to be able to paraphrase their remarks *to their satisfaction,* before you disagree.

5. **Premature replying.**

   Similar to silent arguing, premature replying need not involve disagreement. Most commonly, a person prepares mentally to make a remark before fully understanding the speaker's comment or question. Also, group members who know each other well think they know what others are going to say before they say it—but they aren't always right! Jumping to a conclusion before the other has finished speaking results in a disjointed discussion in which the subject keeps switching.

6. **Listening defensively.**

   When we feel psychologically threatened, we don't listen well. Feeling vulnerable, we generally quit listening in order to invent ways to defend ourselves and attack the perceived threat. This is called **defensive listening.** For example, later in the meeting of our software colleagues, May verbally attacks Kevin several times. Kevin defends himself by attacking May back: "What's your problem? You've been riding my case all day!" Unfortunately, this won't help solve the group's problem. When we feel attacked is often the very time when we most need to understand the perceptions and values of the other person. Still later, after Tamika politely but directly confronts Kevin's behavior, his honest, nondefensive response to her indicates that he is not feeling attacked.

   You may have noticed that evaluation or judgment is part of most of these nonlistening behaviors. The sequence is entirely reversed from what it should be. Only *after* we understand each other's ideas are we able to judge appropriately. We need to be empathic listeners who try to understand what the other means *from his or her point of view,* with the motivation to receive information being greater than the motive to evaluate and criticize.[16]

We assume now that you want to improve your listening behavior in groups. With your attitude in the right frame of mind and armed with an understanding of listening preferences and pitfalls, we present some tested techniques to help you take responsibility for your listening habits.

Effective Listening in the Small Group

Small group members must work at understanding each other while they keep the group discussion structured and organized. Two listening techniques are especially helpful for accomplishing this: active and focused listening.

Effective listening is an *active* process requiring as much effort as speaking. Engaged listeners trying hard to understand and recall show signs of physical activity, including an accelerated heartbeat and postural shifts. In contrast, heart rates of poor listeners frequently slow to the level of sleep! Listening takes an act of will, a decision to listen. No matter how great the speaker is, it is the listener who chooses how to listen, to whom, and when. Thus, Watson reminds us, it is the listener who holds the power in small group interaction and, therefore, it is to our advantage to understand and use effective listening techniques.[17]

A good test of how well you have been listening is a technique called **active listening.** This technique virtually forces the listener to understand a speaker before replying or adding to a discussion. The main rule is that you must state in your own words, or **paraphrase,** what you understand the previous speaker meant, then ask for a confirmation or correction of your paraphrase. Active listeners paraphrase, not repeat word for word. After all, a parrot can repeat, but that doesn't mean that the parrot has understood! A paraphrase in the listener's own words forces the listener to process the information cognitively, allowing the original speaker to determine whether the message was understood as intended or not. The original speaker can then reply to the paraphrase (i.e., give feedback) by accepting or revising it or asking the listener to try again. Only when the original speaker is fully satisfied that the listener has understood what was intended does an active listener proceed with agreement, disagreement, elaboration, change of topic, or whatever. The following dialogue illustrates the technique:

Active Listening

Ed: Requiring landowners to farm in such a way that topsoil is not lost is absolutely necessary if we really want to protect the Earth for our children. (opinion)

Gail: If I understand you, you think we should require that farming practices prevent possible erosion of the topsoil because erosion destroys the Earth for living things? (paraphrase of Ed's opinion)

Ed: Right, Gail. (confirmation and acceptance of the paraphrase)

Another example:

Consuelo: If every college graduate were required to demonstrate some competence in using a computer, that might help right at graduation. But computers are changing so rapidly that grads would be no better off in a few years than if they had no such training, unless they kept up to date or had to use a computer all along. (opinion)

Taylor: Do I understand you right? Are you saying that a computer science course should *not* be required to get a degree? (attempted paraphrase of Consuelo's opinion)

Consuelo: No, just that it should be more than just how to use a computer. You ought to understand computers, and what they do and don't do. (rejects the paraphrase and attempts to clarify)

Taylor: So you think there should be a requirement for a graduate to be able to explain what computers can and can't do, as well as be comfortable with a computer. (second attempt at paraphrasing Consuelo's opinion)

Consuelo: Yes, more than a course as such. (confirms Taylor's paraphrase)

Taylor: I agree with that idea, and think we should also have a requirement for ability to investigate, organize, and write a term paper. (His paraphrase confirmed, Taylor is now free to add his opinion, on a new topic, to the discussion.)

Every idea proposed in a discussion should be evaluated, but only when you are sure you understand it to the satisfaction of the speaker. Active listeners confirm their understanding *before* they express their positive or negative evaluation. Only at that point is critical listening in order, evaluation by the listener as to whether the statement is relevant, defensible, likely to be effective, was carefully thought through, and so forth.

Sometimes active listeners cannot hear adequately or are not confident of their understandings. If so, they will say so quickly, asking the speaker to repeat or clarify. Only then will they disagree, add more information, or express whatever is their honest reaction.

Active listening slows the pace of interaction. If you are not used to listening actively, you may at first find yourself with nothing to say for a moment after the other finishes speaking. Keep practicing; soon you will find yourself making spontaneous responses instead of preplanned or irrelevant remarks. Above all, don't pseudolisten, which often damages trust and cooperation.

Focused Listening

Group members often have problems recalling what was discussed. During the excitement of exploring a new idea, it is easy to forget vital information, even though that is the responsibility of each member. **Focused listening** helps members recall important information, ideas, and issues discussed during a meeting.

Human memory is limited. We have a terrible time memorizing unrelated lists of items, but we can more easily recall information grouped into sets of related items. Try to remember the following list of numbers: 4178365218. Now try again: (417) 836-5218. Grouping a string of digits into area code, exchange, and number helps you remember it better. This is the key to focused listening.

Effective group members maintain their perspective on the discussion as a whole by focusing their listening on the *main points* of the discussion. They organize the details—specific facts and opinions—by issue. Ironically, focusing on the main points and issues helps them remember details better.

If you want to be a productive group member, keep a notepad to record important information, listen for and record the main issues by using key words rather than complete sentences, and keep track of essential facts by issue. This type of focused listening helps you keep on track so you can reorient the group when someone switches topics before closure has been reached. Focused listeners can serve as process observers who readily keep track of the discussion. They often provide an internal summary, or brief review, of what has transpired up to that point in the discussion, thus keeping the discussion orderly and easy for other members to follow.

SUMMARY

1. Human communication is a complex transactional process that involves the generation, transmission, receipt, and interpretation of verbal and nonverbal signals. Effective small group communication is about sharing enough meaning that group members can coordinate their efforts to complete the task of the group.

2. Human communication is necessarily an inexact process because it is a complex symbolic, personal, transactional, and often an unintentional process. Messages include content, relationship, and affective levels. Several myths help perpetuate misunderstandings about its process

3. During a communication transaction, a sender encodes a message by putting it into words and nonverbal signals; a receiver then decodes the message by hearing it, interpreting it, and responding to it.

Noise, or interference with understanding meaning, can occur at any time. Thus, understanding is facilitated through feedback.

4. Listening is a complex process that involves both hearing and, more important, accurate interpretation.

5. People have four general listening preferences: action-oriented, content-oriented, people-oriented, and time-oriented.

6. Several specific pitfalls to listening include focusing on irrelevancies, pseudolistening, sidetracking, silent arguing, premature replying, and defensive listening.

7. Mutual understanding is helped by active listening, when a listener paraphrases what the speaker has just said and asks for confirmation. Focused listening helps group members recall details by focusing on the main points or issues.

EXERCISES

1. Discuss the following in small groups, then share your ideas with the class as a whole: "How and where in the small group system can noise interfere with the process of communication?"

2. Select a topic (preferably a controversial one) and then discuss it in small groups while you practice active listening. A discussant may not have the floor or add anything new to the conversation until he or she has paraphrased what the previous speaker meant (both ideas and feelings) to the speaker's complete satisfaction. If the paraphrase is not accepted, the discussant tries again until the speaker accepts the paraphrase. One member of the group should not participate but should keep count of how many times paraphrases are accepted or rejected. Be sure to count every

attempt to rephrase. Afterward, discuss the implications of active listening, how to improve communication, and how you felt during this discussion.

3. Prepare a chart for recording observations of listening behaviors and responses of members of a discussion group. This chart should have three columns headed as follows: *active listening, premature replying,* and *sidetracking.* With several classmates, observe either a live or recorded discussion. As you observe, note each instance of these behaviors.

   Now compare your observations with those of your fellow observers. What do you conclude about the listening-responding behavior of discussants? What was the effect of the members' listening behaviors on the group outcomes?

BIBLIOGRAPHY

Mader, Thomas F., and Diane C. Mader.
*Understanding One Another: Communicating
Interpersonally.* Dubuque, IA: Wm. C. Brown
Publishers, 1990.

Roach, Carol A., and Nancy J. Wyatt. "Successful
Listening." In *Small Group Communication: A*

Reader. 6th ed. Robert S. Cathcart and Larry A.
Samovar, eds. Dubuque, IA: Wm. C. Brown
Publishers, 1992, 301–25.

Stewart, John. *Bridges Not Walls.* New York:
McGraw-Hill, 1990.

NOTES

1. Lawrence R. Frey, "The Call of the Field:
Studying Small Groups in the Postmodern
Era," in *Group Communication in
Context: Studies in Natural Groups,* ed.
Lawrence R. Frey (Hillsdale, NJ: Erlbaum,
1994): ix–xiv.

2. See especially Michael T. Motley, "On Whether
One Can (Not) Not Communicate: An
Examination via Traditional Communication
Postulates," *Western Journal of Speech
Communication* 54 (1990): 1–20.

3. Dominic A. Infante, Andrew S. Rancer, and
Deanna F. Womack, *Building
Communication Theory* (Prospect Heights,
IL: Waveland Press, 1990): 8–10.

4. Janet B. Bavelas, "Behaving and
Communicating: A Reply to Motley,"
*Western Journal of Speech
Communication* 54 (1990): 593–602.

5. Glen H. Stamp and Mark L. Knapp, "The
Construct of Intent in Interpersonal
Communication," *Quarterly Journal of
Speech* 76 (1990): 282–99.

6. Amarjit Chopra, "Motivation in Task-Oriented
Groups," *Journal of Nursing
Administration* (1973): 55–60.

7. Fred Jablin, "Message-Response and 'Openness'
in Superior-Subordinate Communication,"
Communication Yearbook ii, ed. Brent
Ruben (New Brunswick, NJ: Transaction-
International Communication Association,
1978): 293–309.

8. Kittie W. Watson, "Listener Preferences: The
Paradox of Small-Group Interactions," in

*Small Group Communication: Theory and
Practice,* 7th ed., eds. Robert S. Cathcart,
Larry A. Samovar, and Linda Henman
(Madison, WI: Brown & Benchmark,
1996): 268–82.

9. Carol A. Roach and Nancy J. Wyatt,
"Successful Listening," in *Small Group
Communication: A Reader,* 6th ed., eds.
Robert S. Cathcart and Larry A. Samovar
(Dubuque, IA: Wm. C. Brown, 1992):
301–25.

10. Watson, "Listener Preferences," 270.

11. David M. Berg, "A Descriptive Analysis of the
Distribution and Duration of Themes
Discussed by Task-Oriented Small
Groups," *Speech Monographs* 34 (1967):
172–75.

12. Ernest G. Bormann and Nancy C. Bormann,
Effective Small Group Communication, 4th
ed. (Minneapolis: Burgess, 1988): 120.

13. Ralph G. Nichols and Leonard Stevens,
"Listening to People," *Harvard Business
Review* 35 (1957): 85–92.

14. Curt Bechler and Scott D. Johnson,
"Leadership and Listening: A Study of
Member Perceptions," *Small Group
Research* 26 (February 1995): 77–85.

15. Watson, "Listening Preferences," 271–75.

16. Charles M. Kelley, "Empathic Listening," in
Small Group Communication: A Reader,
4th ed., eds. Robert S. Cathcart and Larry
A. Samovar (Dubuque, IA: Wm. C. Brown,
1984): 296–303.

17. Watson, "Listening Preference," 269.

Verbal and Nonverbal Signals in Small Group Communication

4

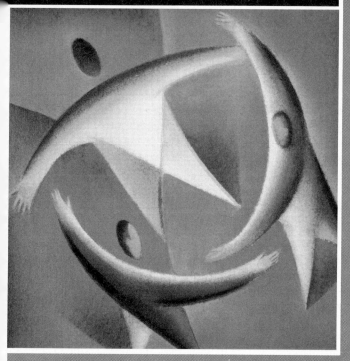

Central Message

Members who want to be effective send and interpret verbal signals in harmony with nonverbal signals and realize that all their actions are potential messages to other members.

Study Objectives

As a result of studying Chapter 4 you should be able to:
1. Describe the nature and function of each of the three major components of language.
2. Describe the nature of bypassing, abstract language, and emotive words, including their disruptive effects on discussions and how to prevent or correct such disruptions.
3. Express your ideas during a discussion so that your statements are organized, clear, and relevant to the preceding remarks.
4. Explain three major principles of nonverbal communication.
5. Explain six major communicative functions performed by nonverbal signals.
6. Name and give examples of eight types of nonverbal signals, and explain how each contributes to communication among small group members.

Key Terms

Ambiguity
Bypass
Concrete
Control touches
Emotive words
Hidden antagonizers
High-level abstractions

Kinesics
Nonverbal signals
Paralanguage
Proxemics
Referent
Regulators

For some months, a small neighborhood in Fresno, California, had been the site of vandalism resulting in damaged property. Neighbors were upset about what had happened to their quiet neighborhood. Taking the lead, one neighbor, a retired school teacher, contacted her next-door neighbor, a small farmer from Laos. Together neighbors decided to ask three other families to join their efforts to stop these crimes. A meeting was called one weekend evening in the hope that they could all draw up a plan of action. One neighbor entered the room carrying a stack of articles on how homeowners could best arm themselves. He took the chair at the head of the table and boldly asked when they were going to get this meeting going. Another neighbor shyly asked if everyone was present, only to be interrupted by the take-charge neighbor who proclaimed, "We have to stop those Hispanic gang bangers with the only thing they understand—force at the end of a gun barrel." The retired school teacher, thinking, "This guy is going to be trouble," asked him to please refrain from labeling all criminals as "Hispanic gang bangers" and noted that arming themselves was one option they would consider, but first they needed to hear from the rest of the group. At this point, the neighbor slouched down in his chair, threw his papers on the floor, and, pushing back his chair, isolated himself from the rest of the group. The small farmer then clarified that this meeting was not about reaching a decision but to hear the concerns of the neighbors and ask questions of a police officer they had invited to the meeting.

Group communication begins before any member says a word. We begin to form opinions about each other on the basis of what we see and hear. One member slinks into the room without looking at anyone and takes a seat in a corner: "Better not count on much from that one," you think. The next person, dressed in a dark business suit, strides confidently to the head of the table and deposits a briefcase: "Arrogant, will try to boss us around," you think. Members' clothing, looks, manners, where they sit, how much space they claim—all these and other nonverbal signals affect how relationships among members develop. Given the verbal and nonverbal behaviors of the boisterous neighbor in our story, what first impressions might you have drawn?

In a small group, the primary medium for exchange of information and ideas is the words members use. Although discussion is the heart of group interaction, verbal and nonverbal signals operate together to create meaning; they are indivisible. "It is impossible to study either verbal or nonverbal communication as isolated structures. Rather, these systems should be regarded as a unified communication construct."[1] We artificially separate verbal from nonverbal signals only in order to help you assess the contribution each makes to *meaning* during discussions. At different times and for various reasons we may attend more to the words or more to the nonverbal signals, but almost no group communicating is entirely verbal or nonverbal.

In this chapter, we first present an overview of the nature of language, some things that often go wrong when we speak to each other, and how informed word choices and arrangements can facilitate group process. The latter part of the chapter summarizes research and theory about the characteristics of nonverbal communication.

THE NATURE OF LANGUAGE

Any language—Spanish, Vietnamese, English—consists of a language code (words) and rules about how to use them. In addition, each community of users of a language (i.e., subculture) develops its own unique subcode. Cultures, subcultures, corporations, families, clubs, and other groups often have their own special codes that identify someone as belonging to that group or culture. For example, theater students call the *waiting room* the *green room.* Your author Gloria's stepdaughter Molly and her friends call boys they don't like *corndogs.*

Language and culture are intimately tied to each other in an ever spiraling, reflexive relationship. On one hand, language use helps to fashion the complex, multiple cultural realities you navigate daily; on the other hand, those cultural realities help give meaning to what you say and how you say it. We are all deeply immersed in language and as such there is not anything we perceive that is not somehow affected by our language.[2] A tenet of the commonly known Sapir-Whorf hypothesis is "The background linguistic system (in other words, the grammar) of each language is not merely a reproducing instrument for voicing ideas but rather is itself the shaper of ideas, the program and guide for the individual's mental activity, for his [or her] analysis of impressions."[3]

CONSIDER THIS

You are an avid snow skier and have learned all sorts of terms to describe the varying snow conditions you might encounter. What might a list of such terms look like? Given all these terms, can you see how you are able to distinguish or perceive different kinds of snow compared to a group member who has never seen snow?

In addition, how you behave verbally and nonverbally helps identify you as a member of any number of cultural groups, probably before you even say a word. In turn, your behavior is given meaning by placing it in any number of cultural contexts. In this chapter, we will examine general characteristics of verbal and nonverbal signals in small group communication before we move on to describe more specifically how culture affects small group communication in Chapter 5.

The appropriate way to use language depends on the situation and we all have learned to adapt our codes for a variety of situations. For instance, we use a different code when we meet someone in a church or synagogue from the one we use during a tailgate party at a football stadium. Physicians use a different code to explain a medical procedure to a patient from the one they use to discuss the procedure among themselves. We must use the code shared by group members if we want to be understood and accepted.

Of all the characteristics of language, the most important to keep in mind is that all *language is symbolic.* As we said in Chapter 3, words have no inherent

Symbolically, he is a chien, hund, cane, perro, and dog; or Wolf to his best human pal.

© Jean-Claude Lejeune

meanings. As symbols, *words have no meaning or reality apart from the persons using them and responding to them.* The object or experience to which a symbol refers is called the **referent.** For instance, the referent Americans call a *dog* is symbolized in other languages by the words *chien, hund, cane, perro,* and *hunt.* Same referent, different symbols. The main point is this: human communication is symbolic, and only if speakers and listeners have approximately the same referent for a word will they have perceptual similarity. *This cannot be taken for granted!* For instance, our neighborhood group at the beginning of the chapter had to decide collectively what *they* meant by "taking action" to restore their neighborhood, not just what one member may have meant.

Speakers in a discussion must use the same or similar codes in order to be understood. Even if discussants speak the same language, they may use the same word to refer to different things. Consider a word less concrete than *dog,* such as *food.* As illustrated in Figure 4.1, when Joe says "Let's go get some food," his referent is a cupcake and soft drink from the nearest vending machine. Mary envisions alfalfa sprouts on whole wheat bread, and Herbie pictures a five-course meal at a fine restaurant. Obviously, Joe's words have different meanings to these three people. If this were a group recommending a break for lunch, clarification would be necessary!

Clearly, we communicate effectively with symbols only when we have similar referents for them. Imagine that the designated leader of your group asks you to keep a "detailed" list of what the group discussed. The leader means "word for word account of the entire discussion," and you assume that "a broad description of major decisions" will suffice. Your group will

One statement, different referents. **FIGURE 4.1**

have problems, even though neither of you was wrong. Each of you used the same symbol ("detailed") to refer to something different, which emphasizes the personal nature of communication—meanings are in people, not in words. To complicate matters, language is not static but dynamic and changes constantly as our world changes.

CONSIDER THIS

Our language has changed to reflect and give meaning to the influence of computer technology on our world. A bit of computer humor recently passed along on the Internet pokes fun at this change. Remember when a "window" was something you hated to clean and a "ram" was the cousin of a goat? "Meg" was the name of your girlfriend and "gig" was a job for the night. "Memory" was something that you lost with age, a "CD" was a bank account, "log on" was adding fuel to the fire, "hard drive" was a long trip, "mouse pad" was where a mouse lived, and "backup" happened in your commode. Now they all mean different things and that really "mega bytes"!

Problems Resulting from Language Choices

You have seen how easy it is even for people who speak the same language to misunderstand each other, and you already know that an important ethical principle for group members is to make a sincere effort to comprehend one another. Fortunately, understanding that symbols (including all words) have no absolute or certain referents can help you prevent a variety of misunderstandings and problems common in discussions. Three of the most troublesome problems include bypassing, lack of clarity, and using emotive words.

Bypassing

Two discussants **bypass** each other when they have different referents for the same word or phrase but think they have the same meanings, or when they think they disagree but really do not, because they use different words to indicate the same referent. For example, one of us observed a group arguing about whether *feminism* was good or bad. One young woman, believing feminism meant that men and women should have the same rights, particularly in the workplace, could not understand how another group member could be opposed to it. On the other hand, the man who disagreed with her believed *feminism* meant that women should be preferred over men and should receive higher salaries than men because of past discrimination and underpayment. This group wrangled for fifteen minutes before someone, listening carefully, said, "I think you two actually agree," and asked each to explain what *feminism* meant. When they realized they had been using the word to refer to different phenomena, they were then free to discover that they actually *agreed* with each other that men and women performing the same work should receive the same pay.

Bypassing is particularly problematic when discussants become self-righteous, with each believing the other is wrong or stupid. In the earlier example of the word *detailed,* if both you and the designated leader act as if the other's use of the word was wrong, then feelings will be hurt, as will the group's productivity. Our boisterous neighbor in our opening story insisted that "taking action" meant nothing less than using force to fight force. Instead, remember that it is normal for people to use words differently and that effective communication occurs only if discussants use the same code and definitions; they must be in agreement on the referents for their words at any given time. Whenever a symbol is used that could be misunderstood, ask for clarification: "What do you mean by *detailed?* How much detail do you want me to go into?" Taking a bit of extra time initially saves time in the long run.

Lack of Clarity

Two factors contribute to lack of clarity in discussions: abstractness and ambiguity. In discussions of ideas, many statements are necessarily **high-level abstractions,** lacking specific referents. Think of such terms as *justice, fairness, democratic, high quality, civil rights,* and so on. As we move away from terms referring to specific and unique items, the degree of abstractness increases, as does the potential for misunderstanding. Consider the following set of terms, each of which is more vague than the ones before:

The 2000–2001 Curriculum Committee of the Department
 of Communication

Departmental committee

Committee

Problem-solving group

Small group

Group

Living system

When the first term is used among members of the Department of Communication, the picture in the listeners' minds is almost certain to be similar to the picture in the speaker's mind. However, when we talk of a *committee,* any one of many committees could come to mind. Only terms that name unique objects are likely to be completely clear. For example, one member of a group discussing classroom procedures and policies said, "Lecturing is a poor method of teaching." Another responded, "Oh, no it isn't." An argument ensued until a third member asked for **concrete** examples (lower-level abstractions). The speakers were then able to agree on specific instances of effective and ineffective lecturing, and particular contexts in which lecturing was both a good and a poor choice of teaching strategy. The vagueness thus reduced, the group agreed on a less abstract statement: "Lecturing, if well organized, filled with concrete examples, and done by a skilled speaker, can be an effective means of presenting factual information and theoretical concepts. It is usually less effective than discussion for changing attitudes or developing critical thinking skills."

Leathers found that highly abstract statements consistently disrupted subsequent discussion, with the degree of disruption increasing as the statements became more abstract. His groups contained "plant" discussants who were trained to make abstract statements like "Don't you think this is a matter of historical dialecticism?" After such a statement, most of the other discussants became confused and tense; some withdrew from further participation.[4]

Lack of clarity is also produced by **ambiguity,** or communication that could reasonably be interpreted in more than one way. Several factors can cause ambiguity. Sometimes words can be interpreted in more than one way. For example, one of our colleagues once wrote in a letter of recommendation: "You will indeed be fortunate if you can get him to work for you." The writer meant that the person being "recommended" was a lazy employee and "you'll be lucky if you can get him to do any work." However, the recipient of the letter likely took it to mean that the future employer of this job candidate would be fortunate indeed to have such a promising employee.

A mixed message, one in which the words seem to imply one meaning but the actions indicate something different, can produce ambiguity, too. For example, the group leader might say, "Take as long as you like to consider this item," while at the same time looking at the clock and stuffing things into a briefcase. Such ambiguous messages are difficult to interpret and disrupt effective communication in the group.

Lack of clarity sometimes results when opinions are uttered in sentence fragments or in an evasive manner. Spontaneous participants quite commonly utter sentence fragments; they mention a subject, but never finish making a point about it, at least not in words. Sometimes, a nonverbal signal—a shrug, a facial expression, a gesture—completes the sentence, but anyone not watching will miss the point, and those watching may misunderstand. A fragment like the following can confuse listeners:

> Maybe we should divide . . . there seem to be a lot of issues . . . a lot of confusing bits and pieces . . . will make a lousy solution.

This statement could have easily been uttered directly and clearly, leaving little doubt in listeners' minds about what was intended:

> Maybe we should divide our investigation of how student-athletes are treated academically by dividing the issue into component topics, such as recruitment, advising during orientation, advising after enrollment, and monitoring compliance with NCAA rules. Otherwise, we may get all these topics mixed up, overlook some problems, and produce an incomplete or shoddy report.

People use vague language for several reasons. Occasionally, a group member will try to enhance personal status by using technical jargon the others don't use. Sometimes, this is done to conceal ignorance of the issue. At other times, the speaker may be trying to cover up or evade answering the question directly, such as a politician saying: "Revenue enhancement is very important, and we will have to explore every available avenue for overcoming the economic paralysis caused by the deficit. No one likes new taxes, and I can promise you we'll investigate all options." (We think that means taxes are going up!) When you encounter this, don't be snowed by a show of technical expertise or jargon. Ask the speaker to explain in terms you know.

Members can and should try to prevent the confusion that results from abstractness and ambiguity by asking for clarification. Remember that group members who are ethical strive for mutual understanding; this means they try to be clear and to help others make themselves clear. So, as a speaker, you help produce clarity by using language appropriate to the particular group situation, by providing specific examples to illustrate the abstract terms you use, and by making your actions and words congruent. For example, the statement "I think we can produce an excellent report, one that addresses all three major aspects of the topic, uses references no older than two years, and is grammatically perfect" tells your listeners what you mean by the abstract term "excellent." Encourage others to give you feedback, and welcome questions from other members as opportunities to improve mutual understanding.

As a listener, when you aren't sure what a speaker means, ask for clarification or for a specific illustration: "Jamal, you said we could take as long as we liked, but you seem rushed. Would you rather we table this discussion to a later meeting?" or "What do you mean by a 'detailed' report, Maria?" Paraphrase and ask the speaker to confirm or correct your understanding. Work transactionally *with* the speaker to create a baseline of common meaning.

Emotive words are words that evoke strong feelings in others; these connotative words recall highly pleasant or unpleasant images and experiences. Some emotive words are the fighting, snarl, or trigger words that produce strong reactions—unthinking, instantaneous responses by a person reacting to the word as if it were the actual thing. For instance, the man mentioned earlier with the strong negative feelings about the word *feminist* had an image of feminists as man-hating, bra-burning, controlling females with no sense of humor. Powerful physiological reactions to words with highly negative connotations are normal, but they involve nonthinking responses. Recall that group members are ethically obliged to strengthen, not weaken, one another's identity and self-concept; therefore, intentionally using emotive words to hurt someone or to see if you can get a rise out of someone is not only inappropriate, it is unethical.

Emotive Words

When a discussant, or something he or she values, is called one of these negative terms, the response is usually defensive or hostile. Constructive, open-minded discussion ends. But this doesn't need to happen. You can state your opinion, even if it is controversial and others are likely to disagree, in a way that does not deliberately push somebody's "hot button." Most negative emotive words have neutral alternatives you can use instead. For example:

Negative Connotation	Neutral or Positive Connotation
Egghead	Intellectual
Broad	Woman
Manipulative	Persuasive
Jock	Athlete

Why should we pay attention to such language? Groups can get sidetracked from their goals by hurt feelings and lost harmony. Remember, you want your ideas and opinions to get a fair shake in your group's discussions, but someone you have offended with an emotive word will be unable to consider fairly and objectively the merits of what you propose. So, using such language hurts the group's ultimate outcome.

Discussants must be sensitive to current usage and to the feelings of other group members; in other words, remember the *observer* part of being a good participant-observer. Sometimes the use of trigger words is not intentional.

We might use a word and only afterward find out a group member was offended. These unintentional trigger words are referred to as **hidden antagonizers.** For example, a Caucasian group member with no prejudicial intention may say *colored* and a black member may respond defensively. Our black students have told us they now prefer the term *African American* to *black,* which was the preferred term for many years. One discussant might say, "Nebraska has socialistic electric power distribution," meaning that such facilities are owned by the public and managed by a voter-elected board. Although *socialistic* is used appropriately to define a company owned by a social body (the citizens of Nebraska), some Nebraskans wouldn't take kindly to that adjective. *Publicly owned* would have been a better choice; it is equally descriptive, but doesn't carry the negative connotations of *socialistic.*

The use of sexist terms is a major problem for many groups. Terms that once were used interchangeably to refer to all people, as well as males specifically, are now rejected as biased against women. For instance, the word *man* has been used in the past when the person referred to could be either male or female (patrolman, chairman, businessman, postman). Language is dynamic; it changes to fit changing circumstances. What was once acceptable is now inappropriate. Any word that implies a sex criterion for filling a role or performing a task may disrupt many discussions. Ivy and Backlund, experts in gender and communication, propose, "If people would spend more time figuring out how a listener will best hear, accept, understand, and retain a message and less time figuring out how they want to say something to please themselves, then their communication with others would vastly improve."[5] We believe this is a worthwhile golden rule for managing all forms of potentially hurtful word choice.

The worst form of stigmatizing is name-calling. Adrenaline rises as we prepare to fight physiologically and psychologically when called by such names as *pig, chauvinist, feminazi, whitey,* or *nigger.* Name-calling is unethical. It deflects attention from the issues before a group, destroys trust, elicits defensive reactions, and does nothing to promote effective group discussion.

What can you do to prevent or reduce the negative effects of stigmatizing? First, recognize that people have feelings about everything and these feelings are not to be rejected. When people or their beliefs are challenged, their concepts of self are also challenged and must be defended. Monitor your own behavior; be aware that your feelings and evaluations are just that—YOUR feelings and opinions, *not truths.* Take responsibility for your own opinions and express these opinions provisionally: "It seems to me that . . . ," or "I don't like . . . ," for example, makes it clear you know you are expressing your opinion only.

Finally, when you hear someone else express a trigger term, you can reduce the potential harm by restating the emotive statement in neutral form and inviting contrasting feelings or points of view. For example, a statement like "Doctors are money-grubbing pigs at the American feed trough and we can't get health care reform because of their greed!" might be rephrased as follows: "Jamisha believes that health care reform will be difficult because physicians have strong concerns about losing their current incomes. What do the rest of you think?" Replacing the emotive terms with neutral ones and soliciting a variety of opinions and feelings allow the group to examine the idea objectively, in a mood of skeptical inquiry, so the conclusion will be based on more complete information.

CONSIDER THIS

Review the story that began the chapter. During the meeting one member asked the loud neighbor not to use the phrase "Hispanic gang bangers." How might the neighbor who used the phrase and called for the neighbors to arm themselves have stated his ideas in a less threatening manner, yet still showed how serious he was about his idea?

As we noted, stigmatizing and name-calling are unethical behaviors because they attempt to undermine other members' self-concepts. They sidetrack the group into arguments that deflect it from its goal and cause the group to reject what may be valuable information because it was poorly stated. As a speaker, you should be sensitive to other group members so as not to stigmatize them, their values, or their beliefs. As a listener, rephrase stigmatizing statements so that they are neutral. That way, if members disagree, it will be on the merits of the idea, not because of the trigger words. If a member persists in stigmatizing others, make it clear—politely, but directly and firmly—that such behavior is not acceptable.

The ability to speak in a fluent and polished style is not essential to being a valuable group member but, as we have already discussed, clarity is. Organizing your remarks makes it easier for others to interpret them as you intend. The following are guidelines for organizing remarks:

Improving Communication by Organizing Remarks

1. **Relate your statements to preceding remarks.**
   It should be clear to your fellow group members how your remark contributes to the discussion. Your statement should not appear to come out of the blue, but should connect to the topic under discussion and, most of the time, to the immediately previous remark. Furthermore, you should state your idea, support it with evidence, and make the connection to the topic clear. For example, in a group investigating the loss of widely used library reference materials, Nguyen has just said, "A major problem for the library is replacing magazines with articles that have been cut out." You say, "Yes, that is a major reason why reference materials aren't available, and I *also* found out that every encyclopedia had articles removed. The librarian told me it costs $2,000 per year to replace them." Your remark will make sense to other group members

because it relates directly to Nguyen's statement, it is relevant at this particular time in the discussion, and the point is clear.

2. **Speak concisely.**

When other members' eyes glaze over, shut up; you've talked too long. State your ideas simply, briefly, and clearly—once! We all know participants who restate every point several times or use 200 words for what could be said in 20. This causes listeners to tune out and hogs "air time."

3. **State one point at a time.**

This is not an absolute rule, but usually you should not contribute more than one idea in a single speech because a group can discuss effectively only one idea at a time. For instance, if you say, "Many people are injured when bumpers fail. Furthermore, I think cars should be required to have antilock brakes, and there's also a problem of the steering wheel that locks when the ignition shuts off," one person might reply about the bumpers, another about the brakes, and a third about the steering. A confused discussion will result. An exception to this guideline might be if you are submitting a multipoint report to the group, in which case it will be helpful if you distribute a handout that lists or outlines the main points.

In this section we have described the nature of spoken language and several of the pitfalls to avoid during small group discussion. We now turn to an equally important component of messages, nonverbal signals.

NONVERBAL SIGNALS IN SMALL GROUP COMMUNICATION

Nonverbal signals include all signals *except* the actual words themselves. They are vital to small group communication. For instance, Birdwhistell, an early pioneer in the study of body-movement signals, believed that only about 35 percent of meaning is communicated verbally when people are face to face; the other 65 percent is evoked by nonverbal signals.[6]

Nonverbal signals supplement our words and tell listeners how to interpret our words. However, nonverbal codes are culture bound. Most of what follows is about mainstream American culture and is *not necessarily valid* for people from other countries or from certain subcultures of the United States. We address the effects of culture in Chapter 5; here, we first consider general principles about nonverbal communication, then the specific functions performed by nonverbal signals.

Principles of Nonverbal Communication

There are three major principles necessary for understanding nonverbal communication. These principles concern the flow of nonverbal signals, their lack of specificity, and what happens when nonverbal and verbal signals contradict one another.

1. **You cannot stop sending nonverbal signals to other members of a small group.**

   This is often stated as "you cannot *not* communicate" and means that, in the presence of another person, you cannot help sending signals that others can potentially receive and interpret (although the interpretation may be completely incorrect). One of us taught a small group seminar in which one member, afraid that others would get to know her too well,

   "Are you *sure?*" Nonverbal signals supplement the verbal ones.

   decided she would not communicate. She refused to look at the other members, made few verbal contributions, and even turned her chair slightly aside so others could not see her face. Of course she communicated—that she did not care about other members and was "too good" for the rest of the group. Although this was not the message she intended, this was the meaning attributed to her by the others. You may not participate verbally, but you cannot be physically present without affecting the mood, climate, cohesiveness, and interpersonal relationships of the group. The question is not "Will I communicate?" but "*What* will I communicate?"

2. **Nonverbal signals are highly ambiguous.**

   Consider what a smile can mean: feelings of friendship, agreement with a proposal, amusement, acknowledgment of another, gloating over someone's misfortune, feelings of superiority, or simple liking. Looking at your watch might be interpreted as boredom, but it could also mean the person has to take medication on a fixed schedule or has another meeting in a few minutes. To prevent misunderstandings, verbal clarification is needed.

CONSIDER THIS

In our neighborhood story, one of the members asked "shyly" if everyone was present. What are the nonverbal behaviors which are often taken to mean *shy*? Can you think of any other ways those very same behaviors may be interpreted?

3. **When nonverbal and verbal signals seem to contradict each other, people will usually trust the nonverbal signals.**

   A fellow group member, fists clenched and brows drawn tight, shouts, "NO, I'M NOT MAD!" Do you believe him? Marriage counselors are taught to look for these discrepancies, such as the wife who says, "I love my husband," while she shakes her head to indicate "no." There is good reason why we tend to believe nonverbal elements when there is an inconsistency: nonverbal signals are less subject to a person's conscious control. Few of us are able consciously to control sweating, blushing, blood pressure, tension levels of internal organs, and so forth. Most of the time in group meetings we are not fully aware of what our feet, hands, faces, and bodies are doing. Some of us have been taught to control our speech rate, vocal tone, or pitch, and most of us exercise considerable control over the words we utter. Thus, nonverbal communication is relatively spontaneous and easier to trust than the more easily manipulated stream of words. This is especially the case when the nonverbal and verbal signals conflict and less so when they are more congruent; then we pay more attention to the verbal signals.

Just as nonverbal signals can be inconsistent with verbal ones, nonverbal signals are sometimes inconsistent with each other. For example, consider the group member who leans forward, nods at what you say, and seems to be paying rapt attention, but stifles a yawn while sneaking a peek at the clock. What are you to make of that? The pattern of overall nonverbal behavior is more important than any individual signal.

Sometimes, inconsistent nonverbal signals result from the sender's internal confusion or uncertainty. For example, a group member may both like and dislike different elements of someone's proposal; this genuine confusion may appear as mixed signals in the form of a positive head nod with a frowning face.

To avoid sending mixed messages, be honest and clear. If you as a speaker are confused, help other members interpret your remarks by honestly revealing your confusion. If you are confused or puzzled by the mixed messages of another, say so, and help the other person clarify his or her intent.

Functions of Nonverbal Communication

Awareness of the functions of nonverbal communication will enable you to respond appropriately to others and make your own signals more clear to them. Nonverbal signals serve six major functions during group interaction:

1. **Supplementing the verbal.**
   Nonverbal signals may repeat and reinforce the verbal message. For example, a person points to item three on a chart and simultaneously says, "Now look at the third item on our list of ideas." Sometimes, nonverbal signals elaborate what is said. For instance, a discussant may say, "It will be about *this* high when it is finished," and holds his hand three feet from the ground.

2. **Substituting for words.**
   Many gestures are substitutes for spoken words. Thumb and forefinger forming an O with the other three fingers held out stands for *okay* in the United States, as does the thumbs-up signal. If a committee chair asks, "Are we ready to vote?" and members shake their heads from side to side, the group will not vote.

©Nita Winter/The Image Works

Nonverbal signals supplement the words.

3. Contradicting verbal messages.

As we discussed earlier, sometimes nonverbal signals contradict what a person says. For instance, a member might say, "Yes, I'll go along with that," but in such a way that you expect him or her to give no real support to the idea. In such a case, point out the contradiction and ask for clarification: "You said you'd go along with the proposal, but something about the way you said it sounded as if you really don't like it very much. What do you feel?"

4. Expressing emotions.

As the previous example illustrates, our feelings are communicated more often by nonverbal signals than by what we say. Say, "I agree with you," in a variety of ways, and notice how each seems to indicate a very different feeling. A smile or nod can signal, "I like your proposal." Negative feelings are communicated nonverbally as well. For instance, some vocal aspects of anxiety are immediately detectable.[7] Particular voice characteristics are associated with both passive and active feelings.[8] Vocal qualities, posture, and facial expressions can all communicate feelings.

5. Regulating interaction.

Certain nonverbal messages, called **regulators,** direct the flow of interaction among group members. For example, turn-taking is communicated nonverbally by such things as leaning forward, taking an audible breath, or relaxing. Turn-taking happens almost automatically, without much conscious thought, but discussion leaders also consciously employ head nods, eye contact, and hand movements to indicate who should speak next. Favorable nods indicate "keep talking," but lack of response or looking away may signal "shut up." Students raise their hands in classes to show they want to be recognized. Many of these regulatory cues are visual. A group that one of us observed had a blind member who could not see visual regulatory cues. He frequently talked out of turn or cut the other members' speaking turns short. The others were upset at what they perceived to be arrogant and self-centered behavior, but a discussion about regulatory cues helped the group discover the extent to which we depend on visual regulatory cues to regulate interaction. The discussion increased members' sensitivity to the communicative problems some blind people experience.

6. **Indicating status relationships.**
Sitting at the end of the table indicates leadership or a desire for high influence in the group. A member who stakes out more than an average amount of territory at a table (briefcase, books, coffee cup, etc.) shows dominance or superiority, as does suddenly getting very close to another, a penetrating stare, loud voice, or a patronizing pat or other touch.[9] High-status members tend to have more relaxed postures than lower-status members. On the other hand, uncrossing arms and legs, unbuttoning a coat, and a general relaxation of the body often signals openness and a feeling of equality.[10] Emergence as a perceived leader has been related to shoulder, head, and arm gestures.[11] Body orientation, the angle at which a participant's shoulders and legs are turned in relation to the group as a whole or another person, indicate how much one feels a part of the group and often that one is more committed to a subgroup than to the group as a whole.[12]

CONSIDER THIS

Identify as many functions as you can of the nonverbal behavior displayed by the boisterous neighbor in our opening story.

Effective group members understand the principles and functions of nonverbal communication we have just discussed and use their understanding to be sensitive to nonverbal behavior. For example, one of us observed a normally quiet group member fold his arms in a closed gesture in response to a statement made by the group's chair. The chair, recognizing that this gesture could be interpreted in a number of different ways, asked the member to share his opinions directly with the group. It turned out that the member strongly disagreed with the emerging group consensus for several excellent reasons the others had not considered. The chair's alertness and sensitivity helped make this member's information available to the entire group.

Interpreting nonverbal signals appropriately requires that we look at the *pattern* of signals rather than at just a single cue. At the same time, we need to be aware of the various types of nonverbal signals so as to avoid overlooking any. Those listed below are especially relevant to communication among group members.

Types of Nonverbal Signals

Members of a new group react to each other's appearances long before they begin to judge each other's expertise and competencies. The judgments may or may not be correct, but they are formed initially from nonverbal signals that cannot be concealed, such as race, sex, physique, and mode of dress. We attribute factors such as intelligence and likability to people on the basis of what we initially observe of them. Of course, we may change our judgments later, but they are formed initially from a variety of nonverbal signals.

Physical Appearance

Cultural factors influence our responses to physical appearance. Americans apparently have a clear picture of what a leader should look like. We tend to be prejudiced against endomorphs (heavy bodies), whom we often perceive as lazy, sloppy, stupid, and undependable, but also as jolly and easy to get along with. Ectomorphs (tall and skinny) are perceived as frail, studious, and intelligent. Mesomorphs (muscular types) are more likely than others to be perceived as leaders. Height is particularly important. The taller a person is, the more likely she or he is to be looked up to, literally, as a leader; short people have to try harder to be seen as potential group leaders.[13] We often are not aware we have these prejudices, so it is especially important that we teach ourselves to react to what a person does rather than to physical appearance.

There have been many studies of how we use **proxemics,** or personal space and territory, to communicate. We signal our need to be included by how we orient our bodies to the group. The neighbor who wants to arm the neighborhood pushes his chair away from the group when he is challenged by another member of the group. A person who sits close to other members, directly in the circle in a flexible seating space, close to a circular table, or at a central point at a square or rectangular table signals a need to belong or a sense of belonging; a member who sits outside the circumference, pushed back from a table, or at a corner may be signaling a desire to withdraw. Sitting within range of touch indicates that we feel intimately or personally involved, whereas sitting from just outside touch distance to several feet away signals a more formal, businesslike relationship.[14] Patterson found that group members making collective (group) decisions sit closer together and in more of a circle than when making individual judgments.[15] Stacks and Burgoon discovered that closer distances (18 inches) make group members more persuasive and credible than distances of 36 or 54 inches.[16]

Space and Seating

What is a comfortable distance varies from one individual or one culture to another. Females tend to sit closer than males and tolerate crowding better. People of the same age and the same social status sit closer together than people of different ages and statuses. The better acquainted people are, the closer they tend to sit. Thus, members of a long-standing group characterized by high interpersonal trust would be comfortable sitting close together in a small room, but people just beginning to form into a group would need more space. Even so, humans are highly adaptable, so when a room or other constraint violates our preferred distances, we adjust, at least for a short time.

A member's status affects how others react to violations of space norms. Burgoon et al. found, for instance, that if low-status group members violated the group's norm regarding space, other members saw them as less persuasive, sociable, and attractive. In contrast, high-status members enhanced their status by moving closer than the group norm specified, and even more if they moved farther away.[17] Thus, it is generally advisable for you to follow group space norms rather than violate them, but if you are a high-status group member, you may have some leeway.

Leadership emergence in a group is related to space. Dominant people and designated leaders usually choose central positions in the group, such as at the head of a rectangular table or across from as many others as possible. Other members frequently avoid sitting next to a designated leader, so the circle ends up looking like the diagram in Figure 4.2.[18] This reinforces the leader's position, allows the leader a comprehensive view of the group, and facilitates the leader's coordination and control.

People sitting across from each other speak more often to each other than people sitting side by side.[19] However, when a group has a dominating leader, "sidebar" conversations tend to break out between people sitting next to each other. Thus, we can conclude that conversation normally flows across the circle, and leaders should sit where they can maintain eye contact with as many group members as possible.

Seating and spatial features of the group's environment, such as fixed-space permanent features like walls and doors, and movable features like furniture, influence the group's interactions.[20] In a large room, group members may choose to sit closer together than normal. If a group is meeting in a space normally used for another activity, the normal use of that space may change the group's interaction; for example, meeting in a member's living room may encourage informality. Meeting around a formal conference table encourages somewhat formal interaction, whereas meeting in a lounge with comfortable sofas does not. Sometimes, simply rearranging a group's meeting-place can turn a chaotic group into a productive one. One of us advised a student committee whose meetings were characterized by general disorganization, repetition, and sidebar conversations. The room used by the group was normally set up for large assemblies, with a head table on a raised platform at the front, which the members used for their discussions. The president sat at the center of the long table, with the rest of the members sitting on either side of her along one side of the table. Only the members directly next to the president could both see and hear her without great difficulty. The

Typical spacing between designated leader and other members of a small task group. | **FIGURE 4.2**

group was advised to stop using the table and instead to rearrange the chairs in a circle. After just one meeting, members reported substantial improvement.

Eye Signals

Eye movements can signal disgust, dislike, superiority, or inferiority, as well as liking; the rules for eye contact are highly culturally dependent. For most middle-class white Americans, establishing eye contact is the first step to conversing. Americans use eye contact when they seek feedback, when they want to be spoken to, and when they want to participate more actively.[21] For many middle-class Americans, lack of eye contact is perceived as dishonesty, rudeness, apathy, or nervousness.[22] Burgoon reported that students given free choice of seating arrangements in small classes chose to sit in a circular or U-shaped pattern for their meetings so they could maintain eye contact with as many other members as possible.[23] Although a stare may indicate competitiveness, in a cooperative group it shows friendship and cohesiveness.[24] Eye contact is important, but must be interpreted carefully in context with other verbal and nonverbal signals.

Facial Expressions

Facial expressions indicate feelings and moods. Without a word being spoken, you can perceive anger, support, disagreement, and other sentiments. Eckman, Ellsworth, and Friesen found that at least six types of emotion could be detected accurately from facial expressions.[25] People with poker faces, who change facial expression very little, tend to be trusted less than people whose expressive faces signal their feelings more openly. But even poker-faced people leak their feelings by physiological changes they can't readily control, such as sweating or blushing.[26] If group members show few facial expressions, watch for other revealing physiological signs.

Movements

The study of how we communicate by movement is called **kinesics.** We reveal our feelings with bodily movements and gestures. We show tension by shifting around in a chair, drumming fingers, swinging a foot, or twitching an eye. Such behavior may signal frustration, impatience with the group's progress, or annoyance. Alert group members will attempt to track down the source of tension by pointing out the kinesic signs and asking what may be producing them.

According to Scheflen, body orientation indicates how open to and accepting of others a group member feels.[27] Members turn directly to those they like and away from those they do not like. Leaning toward others indicates a sense of belonging, whereas leaning away signals a sense of rejection. Members who sit at angles tangential to the rest of the group may not feel included or want to belong.

When members are tuned in to each other, they tend to imitate each other's posture and movements. This behavior is called *body synchrony*. Scheflen observed many instances of parallel arm positions, self-touching behavior, and leg positions indicating congruity.[28] Several studies found that group members are more likely to imitate the movements and gestures of members with high status and power than those with low status.[29] We can infer who has power and status in a group by observing which members are mimicked by others.

In discussion groups, body movements often regulate the flow of discussion. For example, speakers often signal that they are finished speaking by relaxing and stopping hand gestures.[30] Scheflen reported that a speaker who is concluding a point makes a noticeable postural shift.[31] A listener can bid for the floor by leaning forward, waving a hand, and simultaneously opening the mouth.

Vocal Cues   Vocal cues, or **paralanguage,** are any characteristics of voice and utterance other than the words themselves. Included are variables such as pitch, rate, fluency, pronunciation variations, force, tonal quality, and pauses. Extensive research since the 1930s indicates that listeners attribute certain characteristics to speakers based on these vocal cues,[32] including such things as attitudes, interests, personality traits, adjustment, ethnic group, education, and anxiety level and other emotional states.[33] Tone of voice is an excellent indicator of a person's self-concept and mood. For instance, frightened people tend to speak in tense, metallic tones; anxious people have nonfluencies such as interjections, repetitions, hesitations, sentence correction, and even stuttering in their speech.

How we react to statements such as "I agree" or "Okay" depends much more on the pitch patterns and tone of voice than on the words themselves. For example, sarcasm and irony are indicated primarily by a tone of voice that suggests the words should be taken *opposite* to what they seem to mean. Children generally do not understand sarcasm, and even one-third of high school seniors take sarcastic statements literally.[34] Sarcasm in a group is easily misunderstood.

In both movement and voice, animation tends to increase status within the group. People who speak quietly in a low key have little persuasive impact. They seem to lack much personal involvement with what they say. However, members whose vocal qualities change too extensively may be seen as irrational, not to be trusted as leaders or credible sources. Taylor found, however, that excessive vocal stress was judged more credible than a monotonous vocal pattern.[35] You are advised to vary your vocal tone and use vocal cues to emphasize the verbal content of your remarks.

Few of us think of time as a nonverbal dimension of communication. Perceptions of time are highly culturally dependent. We will discuss this cultural dimension in detail in Chapter 5; here, we introduce you to the concept of time as a component of nonverbal communication. Americans think of time as a commodity to be spent or saved. People in Western cultures tend to regulate their activities by the clock, but people in many other cultures act according to inner biological needs or natural events.

Time Cues

In the fast-paced culture of the American business world, being considerate of group members' time is important; Americans usually will allow only about a five-minute leeway before they expect an apology.[36] People who come late to meetings (except because of absolutely unavoidable circumstances) are judged to be inconsiderate, undisciplined, and selfish. Likewise, it is considered improper to leave a meeting before the announced ending time, unless some prior arrangement or explanation has been made. Forcing others to keep to your time schedule is the prerogative of high-status individuals.[37] It implies that your time is more important than that of the other members, and marks you as inconsiderate and arrogant.

Time also is a commodity in the group's interaction (i.e., "air time"). People can abuse this resource by talking too much or too little. Harper, Weins, and Matarazzo found that persons who talked somewhat more than average were viewed favorably on leadership characteristics. Those who talked an average amount were the most liked. Extremely talkative members were regarded as rude and selfish, members the group could do without.[38] Derber refers to excessive talking as *conversational narcissism.*[39]

Touch is an important nonverbal dimension in interpersonal communication. It is vital to group maintenance in most primary groups and athletic teams, but may be nonexistent in many American work groups and committees. The kind of touching people expect and enjoy depends on their acculturation and the type of relationship they share with others. For instance, touch between strangers, other than a handshake, tends to threaten most Americans.

Touch

Touch between individuals may occur to show play, positive feelings, or control, to get a job done, as part of a greeting or farewell, and of course we touch each other accidentally. Jones and Yarbrough found that *control touches* occur most often followed by positive affect touches.[40] **Control touches** are efforts to gain attention or request compliance and are most often accompanied by some sort of verbalization such as "Move over." Positive affect touches are most often signs of affection and associated with our primary groups but can occur in business settings. They found that some work teams may engage in spontaneous and brief touches to show support.

Touch among group members can strengthen unity and teamwork. Families join hands to say grace before a meal; football players pile on hands in a huddle; actors hug each other after a successful performance. The type of touch, as well as the setting, determines the reaction. Pats are usually perceived as signs of affection and inclusion. Strokes are generally perceived as sensual, inappropriate in a small group meeting. A firm grip on an arm or about the shoulders is usually a control gesture, interpreted as a one-up maneuver; among a group of equals, this may be resented. A gentle touch may be a means of getting someone to hold back and not overstate an issue. Many a group member has been restrained from saying something hostile by a gentle touch on the arm during a heated argument.

As with other nonverbal cues, people vary widely in the extent to which they accept and give touches. Andersen and Leibowitz found that people range from those who enjoy touch to those who react negatively to being touched.[41] It is crucial that you touch others in a group only when you sense they accept both you and the touch. Although touching can strengthen team bonds, you must respect the rights of those who prefer not to be touched, and never touch unless it is comfortable for you. A forced touch is detectable and seems phony or manipulative.

On the other hand, it is appropriate to give a gentle pat as a sign of solidarity to those who like being touched, even in work-related committee and task force meetings. You should go easy on touching in secondary groups, but you need less diligence in primary groups, many of which have norms of showing warmth and affection physically.

SUMMARY

1. Effective discussion requires appropriate use of language. If coordination is to be achieved, people must work to ensure that the same words refer to the same referents.

2. Troublesome language problems and misunderstandings include bypassing, lack of clarity, and emotive words that stigmatize others, all of which should be recognized and avoided.

3. Because you cannot stop sending nonverbal signals, you cannot *not* communicate in the presence of other group members.

By their nature, nonverbal signals are ambiguous. When verbal and nonverbal signals contradict each other, most perceivers trust their interpretations of the nonverbal rather than the verbal signals.

4. Language and nonverbal signals function jointly. Nonverbal signals communicate emotion, establish relationships among members, supplement and clarify verbal expressions, substitute for words, and regulate the flow of talk.

5. Interpretation of nonverbal signals is highly culturally dependent. Major cate-

gories of nonverbal signals particularly relevant to small groups include appearance; spatial relations, seating arrangements, and distances; eye contact; facial expressions; body movements and gestures; vocal cues; time; and touch.

EXERCISES

1. Listen to a recorded discussion or to a discussion among several classmates. Each time someone utters a cliché you recognize, write it down. Record your impression of any effect the cliché had on subsequent discussion. What did you discover? Share your findings with fellow observers.

2. Describe an instance of misunderstanding resulting from each of the following types of verbalization. You may do this from memory, direct observation, or recorded discussion. Describe specifically what was said and what happened in response.
   a. High-level abstraction or ambiguity
   b. Sexist language
   c. Ethnic or racial epithet

3. In a practice group discussion session, all members should refrain from giving any bodily or vocal responses to the comments of others (i.e., no head nods, leaning forward, hand gestures, "uh huh" comments, facial expressions, etc.) for about 10 minutes. Each person should make at least one major comment. Then, for the next 10 minutes, everyone should react nonverbally (physically and vocally) as fully and completely as possible. Finally, talk about what you felt during each nonverbal response pattern and what this shows about group communication.

4. Watch a videotape of a small group meeting, but turn off the sound so the words cannot be heard. What do you think the members are talking about? What does each member's individual behavior seem to indicate? Watch the group again, this time with the sound, and see how accurate you were. Discuss what specific nonverbal behaviors contributed to your judgments.

5. Secure a play script. Choose a scene at random, and practice changing the meaning of the scene by varying the vocal qualities: pitch, rate, expression, tonal quality, and so forth. Next, practice reading the scene several times, this time keeping the vocal qualities constant but changing the gestures, distances between characters, facial expressions, and so forth. What did you discover?

BIBLIOGRAPHY

Andersen, Peter A. "Nonverbal Communication in the Small Group." In *Small Group Communication: A Reader*. 6th ed. Robert S. Cathcart and Larry A. Samovar, eds. Dubuque, IA: Wm. C. Brown Publishers, 1992, 272–86.

Andersen, Peter A. *Beside Language: Nonverbal Communication in Interpersonal Interaction*. Palo Alto, CA: Mayfield, 1995.

Burgoon, Judee K. "Spatial Relationships in Small Groups." In *Small Group Communication: A Reader*. 7th ed. Robert S. Cathcart, Larry A. Samovar, and Linda D. Henman, eds. Dubuque, IA: Brown & Benchmark Publishers, 1996, 241–53.

Burgoon, Judee K., David Buller, and W. Gill Woodall. *Nonverbal Communication: The Unspoken Dialogue*. New York: Harper & Row, 1989.

Condon, John C. *Semantics and Communication*. 3d ed. New York: Macmillan Company, 1985.

Leathers, Dale G. *Successful Nonverbal Communication: Principles and Applications*. 2d ed. New York: Macmillan Company, 1992.

NOTES

1. D. J. Higginbotham and D. E. Yoder, "Communication within Natural Conversational Interaction: Implications for Severe Communicatively Impaired Persons," *Topics in Language Disorders* 2 (1982): 4.

2. See John Stewart and Carol Logan, *Together: Communicating Interpersonally,* 5th ed. (New York: McGraw-Hill, 1998): 80–86.

3. John B. Carrol, ed., *Language; Thought and Reality: Selected Writings of Benjamin Lee Whorf* (New York: Wiley, 1956): 212–13.

4. Dale G. Leathers, "Process Disruption and Measurement in Small Group Communication," *Quarterly Journal of Speech* 55 (1969): 288–98.

5. Diana K. Ivy and Phil Backlund, *Exploring Genderspeak: Personal Effectiveness in Gender Communication* (New York: McGraw-Hill, 1994): 17.

6. Ray L. Birdwhistell, lecture at Nebraska Psychiatric Institute, Omaha, NE, May 11, 1972.

7. J. Starkweather, "Vocal Communication of Personality and Human Feeling," *Journal of Communication* 11 (1961): 63–72.

8. Joel R. Davitz and Lois J. Davitz, "Nonverbal Vocal Communication of Feeling," *Journal of Communication* 11 (1961): 81–86.

9. Erving Goffman, *Relations in Public* (New York: Harper & Row, 1971): 32–48.

10. Gerald E. Nierenberg and H. H. Calero, *How to Read a Person like a Book* (New York: Pocket Books, 1973): 46.

11. Edward A. Mabry, "Developmental Aspects of Nonverbal Behavior in Small Group Settings," *Small Group Behavior* 20 (1989): 192–203.

12. Stewart L. Tubbs, *A Systems Approach to Small Group Interaction* (Reading, MA: Addison-Wesley, 1978): 185.

13. J. B. Cortes and F. M. Gatti, "Physique and Propensity," in *With Words Unspoken,* eds. L. B. Rosenfeld and J. M. Civikly (New York: Holt, Rinehart and Winston, 1976): 50–56.

14. Edward T. Hall, *The Silent Language* (Garden City, NY: Doubleday, 1959).

15. M. L. Patterson, "The Role of Space in Social Interaction," in *Nonverbal Behavior and Communication,* eds. A. W. Siegman and S. Feldstein (Hillsdale, NJ: Lawrence Erlbaum Associates, 1978): 277.

16. D. W. Stacks and J. K. Burgoon, "The Persuasive Effects of Violating Spacial Distance Expectations in Small Groups." Paper presented at the Southern Speech Communication Association Convention, Biloxi, MI (April 1979).

17. J. K. Burgoon, D. W. Stacks, and S. A. Burch, "The Role of Interpersonal Rewards and Violations of Distancing Expectations in Achieving Influence in Small Groups," *Communication* 11 (1982): 114–28.

18. R. F. Bales and A. P. Hare, "Seating Patterns and Small Group Interaction," *Sociometry* 26 (1963): 480–86; G. Hearn, "Leadership and the Spacial Factor in Small Groups," *Journal of Abnormal and Social Psychology* 54 (1957): 269–72.

19. B. Steinzor, "The Spatial Factor in Face to Face Discussion Groups," *Journal of Abnormal and Social Psychology* 45 (1950): 552–55.

20. Judee K. Burgoon, "Spatial Relationships in Small Groups," in *Small Group Communication: A Reader,* 6th ed., eds. Robert S. Cathcart and Larry A. Samovar (Dubuque, IA: Wm. C. Brown, 1992): 289–90.

21. J. McCroskey, C. Larson, and M. Knapp, *An Introduction to Interpersonal Communication* (Englewood Cliffs, NJ: Prentice-Hall, 1971): 110–14.

22. Peter A. Andersen, "Nonverbal Communication in the Small Group," in *Small Group Communication: A Reader,* 6th ed., eds. Robert S. Cathcart and Larry A. Samovar (Dubuque, IA: Wm. C. Brown, 1992): 274.

23. J. Burgoon, "Spacial Relationships in Small Groups," 295.

24. R. V. Exline, "Exploration in the Process of Person Perception: Visual Interaction in Relation to Competition, Sex and the Need for Affiliation," *Journal of Personality* 31 (1963): 1–20.

25. P. Eckman, P. Ellsworth, and W. V. Friesen, *Emotion in the Human Face: Guidelines for Research and an Integration of Findings* (New York: Pergamon Press, 1971).

26. R. W. Buck, R. E. Miller, and W. F. Caul, "Sex, Personality, and Physiological Variables in the Communication of Affect via Facial Expression," *Journal of Personality and Social Psychology* 30 (1974): 587–96.

27. A. E. Scheflen, "Quasi-Courtship Behavior in Psychotherapy," *Psychiatry* 28 (1965): 245–56.

28. A. E. Scheflen, *Body Language and the Social Order: Communication as Behavioral Control* (Englewood Cliffs, NJ: Prentice-Hall, 1972): 54–73.

29. J. K. Burgoon and T. Saine, *The Unknown Dialogue: An Introduction to Nonverbal Communication* (Boston: Houghton Mifflin, 1978).

30. S. Duncan, Jr., "Some Signals and Rules for Taking Speaking Turns in Conversations," *Journal of Personality and Social Psychology* 23 (1972): 283–92.

31. Scheflen, *Body Language and the Social Order*.

32. N. D. Addington, "The Relationship of Selected Vocal Characteristics to Personality and Perception," *Speech Monographs* 35 (1968): 492; Ernest Kramer, "Judgment of Personal Characteristics and Emotions from Nonverbal Properties of Speech," *Psychological Bulletin* 60 (1963): 408–20.

33. Davitz and Davitz, "Nonverbal Vocal Communication of Feeling."

34. P. A. Andersen, J. F. Andersen, N. J. Wendt, and M. A. Murphy, "The Development of Nonverbal Communication Behavior in School Children Grades K–12" (Paper presented at the International Communication Association Annual Convention, Minneapolis, May, 1981).

35. K. D. Taylor, "Ratings of Source Credibility in Relation to Level of Vocal Variety, Sex of the Source and Sex of the Receiver" (M.A. thesis, University of Nebraska at Omaha, 1984).

36. Hall, *The Silent Language.*

37. Martin Remland, "Developing Leadership Skills in Nonverbal Communication: A Situational Perspective," *Journal of Business Communication* 3 (1981): 17–29.

38. R. G. Harper, A. N. Weins, and J. D. Matarazzo, *Nonverbal Communication: The State of the Art* (New York: John Wiley and Sons, 1978).

39. C. Derber, *The Pursuit of Attention* (New York: Oxford University Press, 1979).

40. Stanley E. Jones and A. Elaine Yarbrough, "A Naturalistic Study of the Meanings of Touch," *Communication Monographs* 52 (1985): 19–56.

41. P. A. Andersen and K. Leibowitz, "The Development and Nature of the Construct 'Touch Avoidance,' " *Environmental Psychology and Nonverbal Behavior* 3 (1978): 89–106.

The Effects of Culture on Small Group Communication

5

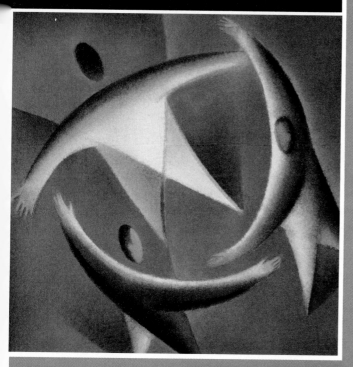

Central Message

The United States is a pluralistic culture comprising many different subcultures. This, and the fact that American business is becoming increasingly transnational, means that members of small groups must recognize, accept, adjust to, and welcome cultural differences in communication.

Study Objectives

As a result of studying Chapter 5 you should be able to:
1. Define *culture* and explain why knowledge of cultural differences in communication is important for effective group discussion.
2. Describe five major dimensions on which cultures differ.
3. Describe specific ways in which cultures differ in language use and nonverbal behavior.
4. Explain why gender and race differences may be viewed as cultural differences, and describe differences that have been observed between male and female behavior in Western culture, and between African American and European American behavior.
5. Describe the ethical principles group members should use to address and embrace cultural differences.

Key Terms

Activity
  orientation
Backchannel
Collectivist
  cultures
Cultural identity
Culture
Dialect
Ethnocentric
Gender
High-context
  communication
Individualistic
  cultures

Intercultural
  communication
Intracultural
  communication
Low-context
  communication
Power distance
Sex
Subculture
Uncertainty
  avoidance
Worldview

Martha, who grew up and attended college in New York City, had always wanted to work in California. During spring semester of her senior year, with her degree in computer science almost in hand, Martha landed a job interview with a software development firm in Silicon Valley. The firm's software development team, a self-managed work group, was responsible for its own interviewing and hiring. Members wanted to have a strong sense of any person they were considering for a position—would that person be a good "fit" with the rest of the team?—and they had a good track record. Martha would spend an entire day with the team, attending their meetings, shadowing various members, eating lunch with them, and so forth. The team wanted to see how she handled herself in the kinds of work situations that were everyday occurrences for them.

Martha prepared carefully for her interview. She read up on the company, knew the kinds of software it was known for, updated her portfolio of projects she had worked on in college, and selected her clothes for the interview very carefully—new navy blue suit, matching pumps, white shell, discreet jewelry. She was ready!

Martha's first inkling that something might go wrong occurred when team representative Jorge met her at her hotel. Jorge was wearing jeans, a San Francisco 49ers' cap, and a T-shirt with a fish tie handpainted on the front. When they got to the company's building, she noticed that all the workers were similarly dressed—casually, with a certain irreverent style. Team members asked her to talk a bit about her background before they started their meeting, and she relaxed a bit. After all, she had prepared for how to sell herself. About five minutes into her presentation, Jorge interrupted to suggest that he take her on a tour of the building before the next meeting. They left, and the other team members began to talk. "Thinks a lot of herself, doesn't she," said Akimi. "She talks so fast I couldn't follow half of what she said," complained Scott. "She's wired pretty tight," agreed Montana. The group concluded that Martha would probably not be a good fit with the culture of this particular team, in part because she didn't seem like a team player. Within a half-hour of first meeting her, they decided not to extend her a job offer.

This story underscores three important points we make in this chapter. The first is that cultural diversity presents a tremendous challenge to small groups because it forces members to pay more careful attention to their communicative behavior and to give up preconceived stereotypes if the group is to succeed. The second point is that cultural differences can exist even among individuals from the same country, who speak the same language and have similar educations, as Martha's failed job interview demonstrated. Finally, cultural differences represent a potentially valuable resource and should be embraced, not eliminated.

In this century, Americans of Asian, Hispanic, African, Middle-Eastern, and eastern European ancestry will outnumber Caucasians of western European ancestry. Called the "browning of America" by *Time* magazine,[1] this phenomenon will have a profound effect on *all* forms of communication.

©Gary A. Conner/PhotoEdit

Effective groups, more and more, require sensitivity to cultural differences.

Transactions between people of different ethnic and racial groups require patience and attention to the communication process. You don't have to visit another country or travel extensively for this phenomenon to affect you. The change, already well under way, will come to you; you will soon participate in groups with people whose backgrounds are markedly different from your own, if you haven't already.

You may have heard discussions recently about the value of diversity in the workplace. Recent studies suggest that cultural diversity can be a real plus. Diversity can enhance a group's performance, assuming that the group's communication process allows members to integrate their diverse perspectives.[2] McLeod and her associates explicitly studied the effects of ethnic diversity on a brainstorming task.[3] They compared ethnically homogeneous (all–Anglo American) groups with ethnically diverse (Anglo, Asian, African, and Hispanic American) groups and found that the diverse groups came up with more creative solutions. However, they also found that the diverse groups had more negative feelings about their groups than the homogeneous groups. To us, these findings highlight the importance of studying the effects of culture; diversity can be an important source of energy and creativity in all areas of American work, but we must somehow learn to appreciate our differences so we can work together productively.

The culture in which a person is raised profoundly affects every aspect of that person's communication behavior, starting with the interpretation process we discussed in Chapter 3. Communication among people of diverse backgrounds (and hence with diverse communication patterns) is challenging. Unfortunately, most people are **ethnocentric:** they believe in the superiority of their personal native culture and interpret the behavior of all people by the norms of that culture. But successful communication among culturally diverse individuals requires them to give up their ethnocentricity.[4] The software development team members who interviewed Martha couldn't get past her New York style, with its fast-paced talk and aggressive verbal pattern. In relaxed California, that style says "Stuck on herself," but in New York, people are taught to promote their accomplishments and talents when given an opportunity. The team concluded, ethnocentrically, that Martha was not a team player because she promoted her accomplishments and spoke fast without pausing for others to jump in. They interpreted her actions through their own cultural filter.

The software development team isn't unusual. Many of us stereotype the behavior of cultural groups different from our own, then negatively evaluate that behavior. Speicher's analysis of a conflict between an African American male and a white female concluded that the participants' failures to recognize cultural differences contributed to the conflict and to the negative evaluation of the other person.[5] Leonard and Locke examined stereotypes held by African Americans about whites, and vice versa.[6] Each group evaluated the other negatively on the basis of the group's stereotypical communication behavior. African Americans had worse impressions of the whites than the other way around, but neither group's evaluations suggested a supportive climate for communication. Perhaps enhanced cultural understanding can begin to undo such negative assessments.

In this chapter we try to sensitize you to ways in which other cultures and subcultures differ from the "dominant culture" of the United States, thereby improving your sensitivity and your communication in groups. Instead of presenting a laundry list of cultures and the characteristics associated with each (a lengthy catalog!), we focus primarily on several broad dimensions on which cultures differ. We offer three important caveats. First, from the vast and growing field of intercultural communication, we present only information we believe to be most relevant to small group communication. Second, in many instances we are overgeneralizing. For example, when we say that "white, middle-class Americans prefer direct eye contact," we know there is a lot of variation in the preferences of white, middle-class Americans. We urge you to remember that sometimes there will be as much within-group as between-group variation, especially for pluralistic cultures such as the United States. Third, there has been relatively little research on intercultural communication *within small groups*. While much is known about how Mexicans and Arabs behave within their own cultures, almost nothing is known about how Mexicans and Arabs behave when they work *together* in the same small group. In many instances, we are making logical, best guesses about what happens when individuals of different cultures must interact within the same setting. We rely heavily on findings from studies of interpersonal intercultural communication, applying them to small group settings. We turn now to a definition of terms important to your understanding of the effects of culture on small group communication.

We have already used several terms in common usage, but now we define them according to our usage in this book. These terms are *culture, cultural identity, subculture, intracultural,* and *intercultural communication.*

WHAT IS CULTURE?

Culture refers to the pattern of values, beliefs, symbols (including language), norms, and behaviors shared by an identifiable group of individuals. During enculturation, or becoming part of a culture, you are taught how to perceive the world, to think, to communicate, and to behave. The teaching is done both formally and informally as you learn the lifestyle of the family and community. Small groups, starting with the family, are vital to this process and are the primary way individuals become enculturated. This process happens so gradually and automatically that, unless something happens to make us question our behavior, we rarely are aware of how culture affects us; our own culture's effect on on us is invisible, unless we make a point of looking for it. **Cultural identity** refers to the degree to which a person learns, accepts, and identifies with the symbols, meanings, and standards of behavior common to a particular group.[7] Individuals are *taught* such things as language, how and when to speak, how to perceive the world, what is and is not appropriate behavior, and so forth. Each of us belongs to a culture, but, for the most part, we do not examine the cultural values and norms we accept. Martha's interview team misinterpreted her behavior, but members seemed to be oblivious to how their cultural identities affected their own communication behavior and their interpretation of Martha's behavior.

Our definition of *culture* is intentionally broad. *Culture* as we define it refers to *any* group of people with a shared identity. For example, a *cultural grouping* can refer to ethnicity (black, white, Hispanic, Greek), a professional grouping (college students, communication professors, nurses, accountants), an interest grouping (hunters, duplicate bridge players), or even gender. In short, any symbol system that is "bounded and salient" to individuals may be termed a culture.[8] Sometimes a grouping that sees itself as distinct, but is part of a larger culture, is termed a **subculture.** For example, your coauthors consider themselves to be part of the subculture *professional educators.* We share certain values and beliefs with other professional educators that are very important to us: a belief in the value of education, similar ideas about what does and does not constitute a good education, a desire to place education high on a list of funding priorities, and so forth. When we interact with professional educators (at our university, at professional conferences, during chance encounters on airplanes, etc.), we take these beliefs for granted—we accept them as "givens." Other examples of subcultural groupings include rural and urban; white collar and blue collar; eastern, southern, western, and midwestern United States; Roman Catholic and Jewish; and many more. "Sub" in subculture does not mean "less important" or "less valuable." It simply means that the subculture in question is smaller in numbers—although perhaps highly influential—than the larger culture of which it is a part.

Each of us belongs to several different subcultures simultaneously. For example, Gloria is white, middle-class, AND Greek American; Jack is white, middle-class, AND a shepherd; Kathy is white, middle-class, AND a military brat. Whether a particular subcultural identification is important in a given circumstance depends on the specific features of that circumstance. For example, Gloria's identification as a Greek American is more salient when she attends festivals where there is Greek food and dancing than when she attends professional conferences. Kathy thinks of herself as a military brat when she talks about how much she has moved or when she attends high school reunions with those who went to Wagner High School on Clark Air Force Base in the Philippines.

We pointed out in Chapter 4 that it is important to understand your culture because it affects *everything* you do, particularly your communication behavior.[9] The behaviors and attitudes we adopt from our culture are learned, not innate, but they are lasting. Cultures do change, but slowly. During **intracultural communication** (among individuals from the same culture or subculture), much of the communication behavior can be taken for granted. But during **intercultural communication** (among individuals from different cultures or subcultures), participants must be alert to the added potential for misunderstanding.

It is important to note here that intercultural communication is not limited to encounters between people from different countries. An Anglo American manager talking to an Arabic counterpart is certainly an instance of intercultural communication, but so is a native of Cupertino, California, talking to someone from New York City. In fact, a conversation between people from different countries can be more *intra-* than *inter*cultural (e.g., as between an Anglo American and an Anglo Canadian).

In a sense, *every* act of communication has intercultural elements because each individual is a *unique* blend of learned behaviors.[10] Intercultural communication is a continuum with *intercultural* communication at one end and *intracultural* at the other.[11] As is shown in Figure 5.1, all encounters are more or less intercultural, but none are purely one or the other. Thus, communication among members of an Inuit family living in a remote area of Alaska will be almost purely *intra*cultural, whereas a conference of Japanese and American legislators who do not speak each other's languages would be extremely *inter*cultural. The more intercultural communication becomes, the greater the potential for communication malfunctions.

Now that we have introduced you to these important terms, we turn to a discussion of five broad characteristics that differ from culture to culture and that significantly influence group members' communication behaviors.

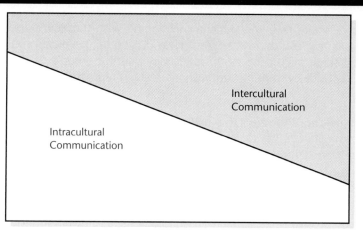

Degrees of intercultural communication. FIGURE 5.1

CULTURAL CHARACTERISTICS THAT AFFECT COMMUNICATION

A number of researchers have investigated particular characteristics that differ across cultures.[12] We focus on five that are especially relevant for communication in small groups. These are *worldview; individualism versus collectivism; power distance; uncertainty avoidance;* and *high- versus low-context communication.*

Worldview encompasses how we perceive the nature of the world around us, our relationship to it, and the purpose of life. Every culture has a worldview that serves to explain why things are the way they are and where humans fit into the grand scheme of life; this cultural characteristic is highly resistant to change. For example, people from cultures that believe fate controls all human events are more likely to "go with the flow" because they believe their destinies are predetermined. They are not likely suddenly to become "movers and shakers" of events. In contrast, people from cultures that believe people control events will respond quite differently. Asian and many Native American cultures are much more likely to conceive of life as a river that flows, making it more appropriate for individuals to flow with the river than to try to navigate against it. North Americans and some western Europeans have the opposite conception. They say things like, "If at first you don't succeed, try, try again," indicating a worldview that hard work, with or against the river, is valued. In terms of communication behavior in small groups, developing *patience* and allowing discussion to proceed at its own pace without forcing it to a conclusion may be more natural in a go-with-the-flow culture, but difficult for many Americans who want to get to the point in a hurry so they can get things done. Worldview affects one's activity orientation, values, customs, and beliefs.

Worldview

CONSIDER THIS

There is value to being patient and "going with the flow," *and* there is value to "making things happen." How do you think a group could potentially benefit from each worldview? How might a group's decisions be affected positively from having both worldviews represented in the group?

Activity Orientation

Activity orientation refers to whether a culture emphasizes *being* or *doing*.[13] Some cultures (e.g., the Hopi) emphasize spontaneity, being "in the moment," and being in harmony with nature. In contrast, the majority culture of the United States represents a *doing* orientation, where activities that produce tangible accomplishments are highly valued. For instance, Americans usually ask, "What do you do for a living?" when they first meet someone. We tend to define people more by what they *do* or what they have achieved than by what they *are*. When members from both *doing* and *being* cultures meet in a group, communication may be difficult and consensus decisions may be impossible.

Values

Worldview also affects values. The following story, highlighting differences between American and Arab values, exemplifies the types of value differences that can create communication challenges in a small group. Imagine that a man is in a small boat with his mother, wife, and child when it capsizes. Only he can swim, and he can save only one of the other three people. Whom should he save? Rubenstein found that *all* the Arabs he asked would save the mother because a man can always get another wife and child, but he has only one mother. Of 100 American college freshmen, 60 said they would save the wife and 40 the child. They laughed at the idea of saving the mother.[14] Such fundamental differences in values may be impossible to resolve.

Customs and Beliefs

The customs, habits, and beliefs of a culture are also affected by that culture's worldview and values. Thus, in a culture where one's purpose in life is associated with bringing honor and good fortune to one's family, communication is likely to center on one's family. A Nigerian student told us how unfriendly he thought Americans were when he first came to the United States. His friends on campus said "Hello" to him and kept walking. In Nigeria, the friends would have stopped, inquired about his mother, father, brothers and sisters, aunts and uncles, and so forth. They would have had a long conversation about their respective families. Imagine that Nigerian student in a group of focused, "get down to business" American students!

Individualism versus Collectivism

Some cultures place higher value on individual goals, but others value group goals more. Gudykunst and Ting-Toomey note that in **individualistic cultures** the development of the individual is foremost, even when this is at the expense of the group, whereas in **collectivist cultures** the needs of the group are more important, with individuals expected to conform to the group.[15] As is suggested by the terms, conformity is valued in collectivist cultures, but diversity and dissent are more esteemed in individualistic cultures. People in the United States admire the person who "marches to a different drummer." The identity of *I* takes precedence over *we,* so we give high priority to *self*-development, *self*-actualization, and individual initiative and achievement. We go so far as to encourage group members to leave a group if they feel their individual values, beliefs, and preferences are being compromised. In contrast to this are most Asian and Native American cultures. For example, a Chinese proverb states, "The nail that sticks up is pounded down." This means that if a member is standing out from the group, the group has the right—even the obligation—to force the individual to conform. In collectivist cultures, the goals, wishes, and opinions of the in-group (the dominant group) always prevail; such cultures value cooperation within the group and slow consensus building rather than direct confrontation in which individual opinions are debated.

This distinction between collectivist and individualistic cultures is important in mixed-culture small groups, primarily because of the effect on communication behaviors. For example, members of individualistic cultures, who see themselves as relatively more independent than interdependent, value verbal clarity more than members of collectivist cultures.[16] You may have noted that much of the advice we give in this text about speaking clearly, concisely, and to the point reflects our own enculturation into the mainstream, individualistic culture of the United States.

CONSIDER THIS

Brislin et al. provide an example of the collectivist versus individualistic cross-cultural theme.[17] Native Hawaiian children come from a collective culture. A Caucasian teacher from the individualistic mainland found that her attempts to motivate the children by having them compete against each other for prizes were not working. How do you analyze this situation? What could you do to remedy it?

Power Distance

Cultures differ with respect to their preferred **power distance,** which is the degree to which power or status differences are minimized or maximized.[18] In low power-distance cultures, such as Austria, Israel, and New Zealand, people believe that power should be distributed equally. For example, in the United States, a relatively low power-distance culture, we prize equality under the law; our Declaration of Independence asserts that "all men are created equal." We regard it as unfair for some to receive privileges accorded to them only by accident of birth instead of being earned by hard work or merit. In contrast to this are high power-distance cultures, such as the Philippines, Mexico, Iraq, and India, where there is a rigid, hierarchical status system and large power distances are preferred. In high power-distance cultures, people believe that each person has his or her rightful place, that leaders or others with power should have special privileges, and that the authority of those with power should not be questioned.

Hofstede noted that larger cultures usually develop higher power distances. Larger groups need more formalized leadership and communication structures to maintain themselves than smaller groups do. Power tends to be concentrated in the hands of a few people, with others accepting the fairly rigid hierarchy as normal and desirable.

Lustig and Cassotta have summarized research that examines how power distance might affect small group communication.[19] They found that power distance is related to leadership styles and preferences, conformity, and discussion procedures. High power-distance cultures value authoritarian, directive leadership, whereas low power-distance cultures value participative, democratic leadership. We Americans tend to assume, ethnocentrically, that everyone wants a chance to participate in decisions that affect them. That reflects our deeply held cultural values stemming from our relatively low power-distance culture. However, an American group leader trying to use a participative leadership style in a group of Mexicans or Filipinos is likely to be seen as inept or incompetent. Power distance is also related to the discussion procedures members prefer. Participation in group discussions and decisions is preferred by persons who believe their individual opinions should be valued regardless of status (i.e., low power-distance cultures), but decision making by the leader, with minimal participation from the group, is the norm in high power-distance cultures. People from high power-distance cultures believe it is appropriate for low-status group members to conform to the desires of high-status members; however, in low power-distance cultures, members will be less likely to conform.

Uncertainty Avoidance

Uncertainty avoidance refers to how well people in a particular culture tolerate ambiguity and uncertainty.[20] Does unpredictability make us anxious or eager? Low uncertainty avoidance cultures have a high tolerance for ambiguity, are more willing to take risks, have less rigid rules, and accept a certain amount of deviance and dissent. Great Britain, Sweden, and Hong Kong are such countries. At the other end of the continuum are countries such as Greece, Japan, and Belgium, where people prefer to avoid ambiguous situations. These cultures use rules to help establish security and clear-cut norms of behavior; all members of the culture are expected to behave in accordance with the standards of behavior, and dissent is not appreciated. People from such cultures often have a strong internalized work ethic. The United States is a fairly low uncertainty avoidance culture.

When low and high uncertainty avoidance individuals come together, they may threaten or frighten each other.[21] Low uncertainty avoidance people, such as most Americans, are perceived as too unconventional by their high uncertainty avoidance counterparts. On the other hand, high uncertainty avoidance people are seen as too structured or uncompromising by the low uncertainty avoiders.

Uncertainty avoidance affects preferences for leadership styles, conformity, and discussion processes.[22] Cultures high in uncertainty avoidance rely on clear rules, consistently enforced, with the leader expected to structure the work of the group and behave autocratically. Low uncertainty avoidance cultures prefer democratic leadership approaches. High uncertainty avoidance cultures value predictability and security; nonconformist behavior threatens this predictability. Conformity to the leader and group opinion is the norm for high avoidance cultures, whereas dissent and disagreement are tolerated, even encouraged, in low avoidance cultures. The need for structure and clear procedures is characteristic of high avoidance cultures. Lustig and Cassotta postulate that this should produce groups that are more task-oriented in high uncertainty avoidance cultures and more relationship-oriented in low uncertainty avoidance cultures.

Low- versus High-Context Communication

The final cultural characteristic we will consider is what Hall termed low- versus high-context communication.[23] A culture with **low-context communication** is one where the primary meaning of a message is carried by the verbal, or explicit, part of the message, whereas in **high-context communication** the primary meaning is conveyed by certain features of the situation. In other words, in a high-context culture, what is *not* said may be more important in determining meaning than what *is* said. In low-context cultures, such as those of Germany, Switzerland, the Scandinavian countries, and the United States, direct, clear, and unambiguous statements are valued. The suggestions we provided in Chapter 4 for conducting organized and effective group discussions are appropriate for low-context cultures such as ours. We expect people to state precisely what they mean so there can be little room for doubt, no matter what the situation (i.e., context) happens to be. The same verbal message given in different contexts means about the same thing. For example, "No, I don't agree with that idea" means much the same thing whether you are in a meeting of co-workers, at the family dinner table, or meeting with your church board. In contrast, high-context cultures such as China, Japan, and South Korea prefer ambiguity, with several shades of meaning possible, because this helps preserve harmony and allows people to save face. In China, instead of "No, I don't agree with that idea," you are more likely to hear, "Perhaps we could explore that option." You would have to be well versed in Chinese communication patterns to know whether that statement means "No, we don't like it" or "We like it very much, but we must build consensus slowly" or "We don't know whether we like it or not until we explore it more fully." Moreover, you would also have to be astute at reading clues in the situation—for instance, is this in reaction to the boss's suggestion, or to a younger co-worker's? Complicated, isn't it? To us, with our low-context bias, it seems as though the Chinese are beating around the bush.[24]

Low-context cultures also tend to be individualistic, and high-context cultures tend to be collectivist.[25] Collectivist cultures operate by consensus of the group; individuals try not to risk offending another member of the group as this might upset a delicate balance of agreement and harmony. Apparently, ambiguity allows individuals to express opinions tentatively rather than directly without the risk of affronting others and upsetting the balance. Because low-context cultures such as the United States display cultural diversity where little can be taken for granted, verbal skills are probably more necessary, and thus more valued.[26] In a high-context culture such as Japan, the high degree of cultural homogeneity means that more can be taken for granted (and thus remain unspoken) during the communication process. In fact, most Japanese value silence more than we do and are suspicious of displays of verbal skills.[27]

You can imagine how difficult group communication can be when members from a high-context culture try to interact with members from a low-context culture. Your author, Gloria, once observed a student group that included Qing-yu, who was from Taiwan. The American students were used to lively debate and accustomed to speaking out in favor of or in opposition to one another's ideas, but in Qing-yu's culture, disagreement is indicated very subtly. Qing-yu's quiet, subdued behavior in the group irritated the American students, who kept trying to get her to behave more like them. The harder the Americans tried to force her to take a stand, get to the point, and be direct, the more she retreated into her familiar orientation of ambiguity and indirectness. The misunderstanding was severe.

COMMUNICATION DIFFERENCES CAUSED BY CULTURE

The five characteristics we have just discussed determine what is considered appropriate verbal and nonverbal communicative behavior in a particular culture. We now present information about how communication behaviors differ from culture to culture.

Language   Differences in language and language use are probably the most obvious sources of misunderstanding. Our most important symbol system is our language, including both vocabulary and rules of usage. As we explained in Chapter 4, it is not just the fact that we use different symbol codes that makes communication difficult. Some researchers also believe that language in fact *determines* how we experience our world; although such deterministic views have been softened, it is clear that our language code helps shape what we perceive in several fundamental ways.[28] For example, several languages, including German and Spanish, have more than one form of the pronoun *you*. A formal or polite version is used to address people the speaker doesn't know very well; another informal or familiar form is used to address family members and friends. What does this say about the relative formality, display of respect, and egalitarianism in such cultures? Some Native American languages, such as that of the Hopi, have no past, present, or future verb tenses. These cultures are spontaneous and experience *time* as what happens in the present moment. Thus, language barriers are not limited to different word usages; they are also caused by *perceptual* differences that can be equally troublesome.

Not only are symbol systems and usages different, but preferred organizational patterns differ as well.[29] Consider what many of you have been taught by your English teachers, who suggest starting an essay with a main thesis, developing the thesis and supporting it with evidence, and presenting a clear conclusion that summarizes the main points. That linear presentation is the preferred organizational pattern for U.S. English. However, other cultures prefer different patterns. Many Eastern cultures, for instance, prefer a narrative approach to the topic and use a more inductive than deductive pattern. Sometimes students who complain about experiencing difficulty in courses taught by non-native teaching assistants or professors are reacting more negatively to organizational patterns than to the mispronunciation of some words.

Inability to use the same language code (i.e., to speak the same language) presents significant obstacles to understanding. Consider how stressful it must be for the many international students in colleges and universities throughout the United States who must expend considerable energy listening and trying to decipher the content of messages; little energy is available for the nuances and subtleties of the interaction. Even something as simple as the word *yes* can cause problems. Koreans sometimes use *yes* when an American might say *no*. "Didn't you go to school yesterday?" elicits the following Korean response: "Yes, I didn't."[30] Although *yes* sometimes means agreement, it can also acknowledge that the Korean listener has heard a question, or that the Korean fully understands what the speaker is saying and is encouraging him or her to continue. Koreans use *yes* to maintain harmony and the appearance of harmony by avoiding appearing negative.

Communication difficulties can occur even between native speakers of the same language. For example, one of our colleagues, a native-born Canadian, circulated a memo asking us to provide our yearly activity reports in "point form." Faculty members were confused until someone noted that *point form* to a Canadian means *outline form* to someone from the United States. Misunderstandings between native language speakers can be humorous and are usually cleared up quickly, but misunderstandings between non-native speakers can sometimes be deadly. Many air traffic controllers around the world issue their instructions in English. When a controller in Madagascar said, "Clipper 1736 report clear of runway" the American pilot interpreted that as clearance to take off. The controller had meant, "Report that you have cleared the runway." The result of this linguistic mistake was a crash where 600 people died.[31]

One final example illustrates pitfalls that can occur with the verbal aspects of intercultural communication. In graduate school, Gloria worked on a committee to analyze data by computer. Two Arab students were members of this committee. Responsible for writing the instructions for the computer analysis, Gloria named the file "BEGIN" to indicate "here's where to start." The Arab students, believing she had named the file *BEGIN* after Menachem Begin, prime minister of Israel, felt they had been deliberately insulted and protested vehemently to the course professor. They were focusing on cues most salient to them. It took a long time to unravel the source of the friction, but even though the mistake was innocent, trust among the group members was permanently impaired.

As important as language is to intercultural communication, nonverbal signals are often more important, as well as more difficult to interpret. In the next section, we highlight several of the best-documented cultural differences in nonverbal signal use.

Nonverbal Signals   As we explained in the previous chapter, nonverbal signals include every perceivable signal except the words themselves. There is considerable cross-cultural variation in the types of nonverbal behavior exhibited by people from different cultures.

Paralanguage   Intertwined with language is paralinguistic behavior, or the *way* a person speaks—speed, pitch, force, pronunciation, and so forth. Often what people react negatively to in another's speech is not the content of what is said so much as the manner in which it is spoken. Pierce relates the story of a woman from New York City who offended many guests by her bossiness at a party.[32] She appeared to be ordering everyone around, but Pierce observed that her words seemed perfectly polite and appropriate for the situation. It was her *intonation pattern* that was offensive. Her particular pattern, appropriate and customary for New York City dwellers, was perceived as domineering by persons from other areas.

Cultural differences have been observed in the use of the **backchannel,** which refers to vocalizations such as *mm-hmmm, uh-huh,* and *yeah-yeah-yeah* that are uttered while another is speaking to indicate interest and active listening. White Americans do not give such backchannel responses as frequently as African Americans, Hispanics, and people of southern European origins.[33] This can lead to friction if members who use the backchannel frequently think those who do not are not really attuned and listening well, while the less active backchannel responders perceive their fellow members as being rude for interrupting so often.

Dialect may also cause misunderstandings. **Dialect** entails regional and social variations in pronunciation, vocabulary, and grammar of a language. Because dialect influences perceptions of a speaker's intelligence and competence, it can seriously affect employability and performance,[34] as well as credibility. Most countries including the United States, Canada, Great Britain, and Japan, have regional and social class language deviations to the "standard" dialect. We tend to stereotype individuals with nonstandard dialects. People who use *dees* and *dose* instead of *these* and *those* are identified as lower-status speakers and accorded lower credibility ratings. Speakers of the general American dialect are rated higher than Appalachians and Bostonians on socio-intellectual status, dynamism, and being pleasant to listen to. Those who speak a French-Canadian dialect are rated as poor and ignorant in comparison with those who speak an English-Canadian dialect. Teachers tend to rate students who use dialects other than general American as less confident and more ignorant.

It is important to be aware of judgment errors that result from such perceptions. However, as intercultural communication becomes more widespread, cultures become increasingly similar.[35] Surprisingly, William Labov, a renowned professor of sociolinguistics, has not found this to be the case with respect to dialect.[36] He predicted that, due to the homogenization of the American marketplace, he would find a standardization of dialect in the United States. In a three-year attempt to create a "phonological atlas" of the United States, he found that our dialects are stronger and more distinct than ever before. Even areas of the country, such as the West Coast, that have not had strong accents show regional dialects. For instance, "bed" in California is pronounced "bad"; in the Great Lakes region, it is pronounced "bud" and in the south, "bayed." Communities show their distinctiveness by how they speak; individuals show their uniqueness by consciously varying their accents.

Kinesic behavior varies considerably from culture to culture.[37] Even facial expressions such as smiling cannot be assumed to mean the same in all cultures. For example, a smile in Japan may be a spontaneous expression of pleasure, but it may also represent the desire not to cause pain for someone else.[38] A smiling Japanese may say to you, "I just came from my mother's funeral." According to Japanese rules of etiquette, it is extremely bad form to inflict unpleasantness on someone else; thus, no matter how bad someone feels inside, a cheerful face must be presented to the world.

Kinesics

Americans prefer direct eye contact with their conversational partners, but in some cultures (e.g., most Native American cultures) this is perceived as rude, while in still others (e.g., Arabic cultures) intense staring is the norm.[39] Hispanic children are taught to lower their gaze to indicate respect, but this can backfire in cases where Hispanic children interact with members of the dominant American culture.[40] For example, white American teachers and police officers sometimes misinterpret a lowered gaze as sullenness. Many African Americans, too, tend to avoid eye contact, especially with someone of higher status.[41]

The handshake, a standard American greeting, is by no means universal. The willingness to touch hands suggests a belief in the equality of people.[42] This typically Western notion contrasts with the Hindu belief in a hierarchical society. Hindus greet each other by bringing their own palms together at the chest. Muslims, who according to the *Koran* are all brothers, hug each other shoulder to shoulder. The Japanese bow in greeting, but prefer to avoid physical contact. You can see how a culture's power distance (such as a belief in equality versus a belief in hierarchy) influences such things as the appropriate nonverbal form for a greeting, and also how easy it is for misunderstandings to occur in small groups with members of different cultures.

Space   The use of space differs widely among cultures. In the high-contact cultures of South America, southern and eastern Europe, and Arab countries, people prefer to stand close, whereas in low-contact cultures such as northern Europe, North America, and Japan, people prefer more space.[43] In fact, members of Arabic cultures feel reassured when they stand close enough to be able to smell their conversational partners. Westerners, however, are usually uncomfortable with such close contact and tend to back away, causing Arabs to mistrust their intentions.

In small groups, individuals usually try to place themselves at a comfortable conversational distance according to the norms of their own cultures. Naturally, this can cause problems if the participants are members of cultures with divergent norms about appropriate distance; they may interpret unexpected behavior of others as rudeness or aggressiveness. We know a New England native who becomes extremely uncomfortable in crowded spaces and perceives as pushy those who try to close the space. On the other hand, one of us once had a friend from Alabama who kept moving closer to her co-workers in Ohio, who kept backing away. Finally, they began to joke about her "invasion of their personal space," and both she and her co-workers learned something about their own subcultural rules.

Seating preferences have been found to vary across cultures. Summarizing research in this area, Ramsey explains that Americans show liking with close interpersonal seating, a forward lean, direct orientation toward the other, and eye contact. Leaders seem to gravitate to head positions, with high-status individuals sitting nearby. Similar behaviors occur in Japan, where the leader sits at one end of a rectangular table, and, the lower the rank, the farther away the seat. In some cultures, teachers and others need to be careful in assigning seats for fear of inadvertently violating cultural taboos about who may sit next to whom. In a few cultures, people sit opposite each other when they have differences to settle, but sit side-by-side in rows when eating or enjoying one another's company.[44] Most of what we know about seating patterns comes from research on Westerners; it may not hold true for people of other cultures.

Time   In the previous chapter we explained that concepts of time are not consistent from one culture to another. Hall describes the Spanish culture of New Mexico as *polychronic,* while the Anglo culture is *monochronic.*[45] The Spanish do several things at a time, while the Anglos tend to do one thing at a time. The Spanish are casual about clocks and schedules; they are frequently late for appointments and meetings. Anglos are offended by such behavior. The collectivist cultures of Latin America, the Middle East, Japan, and France are polychronic, whereas the individualistic cultures of northern Europe, North

America, and Germany are monochronic.[46] In individualistic cultures, time is treated as a tangible *thing* that can be spent, killed, and wasted; time is perceived as more relational in collectivist cultures, which integrate task and social needs and hold more fluid attitudes about time. People from individualistic cultures believe time can be controlled, but those from collectivist cultures tend to see time and space as renewing themselves without the imposition of people. These differences in time and space patterns can cause irritation and resentment during intercultural encounters.

Often the unconscious nonverbal signals we have discussed determine how much we like or trust someone. We all have a tendency to like people we perceive as similar to us, but we are unaware that our feelings are often based on *nonverbal* similarity.[47] It is important for us to recognize this normal tendency and consciously suspend judgments of others in intercultural settings where the same nonverbal behaviors have different meanings.

GENDER AND RACE AS CULTURE

Earlier we described *culture* as something that is learned, a set of expectations and behaviors that we absorb. *Gender* and *race* behavior, too, can be viewed as largely culturally transmitted. With little conscious effort we learn to become *a female* or *a male,* or *an African American* or *a European American,* in the same way we learn to become a salesclerk or a Protestant.[48]

Gender

We refer to learned characteristics and psychological attributes of masculinity and femininity as **gender,** and to the inherent biological characteristics with which we are born as **sex.** Researchers do not know precisely which differences have biological origins (i.e., sex differences) and which have cultural origins (i.e., gender differences); however, research suggests that many differences are learned, not inborn. Moreover, research findings are often inconsistent. Female and male gender roles have been changing rapidly in the past 30 years, so differences observed many years ago do not necessarily hold true today. In addition, current research findings will almost certainly be out of date years from now because our roles as men and women continue to change.

We caution you that while there appear to be differences in the way men and women communicate, there are far more similarities between the genders than differences. Whether men and women represent two distinct communicative cultures is a highly contentious issue. Burleson argues that to study gender as a culture inaccurately characterizes men and women as more different than similar, promotes harmful stereotypes, and misrepresents differences that actually do exist in the communication between men and women.[49] Thus, to conceptualize communication between men and women as "intercultural communication" is not the same as identifying the cultural variables in male-female communication; in fact, it may obscure them.[50] We

cannot resolve the issue here but we want to introduce it to you so you remember that we are still have a lot to learn about sex and gender in small
group communication.

An extensive review of findings about gender differences has been provided by Stewart et al.[51] In spoken communication gender differences have
been observed in verbosity, interrupting, and initiating behaviors. Men talk
more and interrupt more, but that may be changing, as recent research with
college students did not find these differences. Women initiate more topics
but, in part because men provide more minimal responses ("uh huh," or
"yeah") without elaboration, more topics introduced by women are dropped
in conversation than those introduced by men. Women often ask questions
to maintain conversations; however, men usually ask questions to acquire information. Women speak more deferentially and tentatively. In the past,
women were reported to ask more *tag* questions ("It's a good idea, *isn't it?*"),
but recent research does not confirm those early findings.

Most researchers propose cultural rather than biological or psychological
explanations for the differences that have been observed. For instance, Maltz
and Borker concluded that men and women seem to have different rules
about what constitutes friendly conversation, about how to conduct such
conversation, and what certain behaviors mean.[52] For women, backchannel
responses seem to mean, "I'm paying attention to you, keep talking," but for
men they seem to mean, "I agree with you" or "I follow you so far." A male
speaker receiving "mm-hmms" from a woman is likely to believe she agrees
with him, but a woman speaker receiving only occasional "mm-hmms" from
a man is likely to believe he is not listening. Men often complain that women
say they agree with them but it's impossible to tell what women *really* think;
women often complain that men don't listen. Both complaints may stem
from misunderstandings caused by two conflicting sets of cultural rules for
conducting conversation.

The view that male-female differences in communication are primarily
culture based is further supported by a review of recent gender comparison
studies.[53] Mulac et al. characterize men's talk as direct, succinct, personal
(heavy use of "I"), and instrumental (task-oriented). Women's talk is characterized as indirect, elaborate, contextual, and affective. Note that these differences are tendencies, not inviolable rules. The differences between men's
and women's communication are attributed to to cultural learning rather than
biology.

McCroskey et al. report that women display more facial and other signs
of emotion than men.[54] In situations where males tend to sit or stand upright
with their legs apart and hands on hips, women often clasp their hands together and fold their arms across their bodies. Women sit and stand closer to
others, especially other females, than men do. Men sit closer to women than
to other men, but require more personal space than females. Stewart et al.
suggest that men's normal behavior signifies power and status, whereas
women's conveys subordination.[55] Women display more signs of interper-

sonal liking (immediacy), men more signs of power (potency). Both sexes display responsiveness, although the nature of the responsiveness differs.

In the small group field, gender differences have been investigated more than other intercultural phenomena. In an early summary of such research, Baird reported that women were more expressive (paying attention to the relationships among group members, expressing concern for others, displaying emotions) and men were more instrumental (oriented to the task, factual, analytical).[56] More recent research indicates that male-female behaviors have changed, but some differences still appear. For example, Smith-Lovin and Brody found that men interrupt women more often than other men, but women interrupt men and women equally.[57] Men give more supportive interruption attempts ("I agree. We should . . .") in all-male groups, and the more women in the group, the less likely the men are to interrupt supportively. Men are less likely to yield to negative interruption attempts, women much more likely to yield to them. They concluded that men seem to consider sex to be a status variable, whereas women do not, but the findings are more complex than previously thought. Women do not simply give in to higher-status individuals; instead, an interplay of sex, status, group composition, and gender salience affects the specific interaction.

There are questions as to whether the differences exist. Verdi and Wheelan suggest that differences are exaggerated.[58] They found that all-male and all-female groups behaved the same, but mixed-sex groups behaved differently; group size seemed to be a more important factor than sex. Although early findings showed that men talked more than women, recent studies have produced mixed results. Mabry even found that women dominated group interaction and seemed to prefer interaction with other women more than with men, and that men showed subtle forms of resistance to a dominant presence of women.[59]

Some researchers have found that male leaders of small groups are more effective, but recent findings show that both men and women can behave in similar ways in groups, and neither sex is more effective than the other. Jurma and Wright observed that the leader's sex made no differences in members' perceptions of leaders who lost reward power during group discussions.[60] They concluded that men and women are equally capable of leading task-oriented groups. This conclusion is supported by Andrews, who noted that it is more important to consider the unique character of a group and the skills of the person serving as leader than sex.[61] She suggested that a complex interplay of factors (including how much power the leader has) influences effectiveness. Power was also a factor in Duerst-Lahti's study of successful, high-status business women and men.[62] Contrary to the findings of others, women were not frozen out of conversations. The women talked more often but for shorter periods, gave more indications of verbal support, and freely challenged the men. They had power in the group, and their ideas and proposals were included in the final product. They seemed to have mastered the use of power just as effectively as the men.

Several studies suggest that, despite *actual* behavior, men and women are *perceived* differently. For instance, Carli found that men and women behaved similarly, but that women spoke more tentatively in mixed-sex dyads. However, they were more influential with men, but less so with other women, when they spoke tentatively.[63] Burrell et al. compared trained and untrained mediators of both sexes.[64] No male-female differences were observed in the behavior of trained mediators, but untrained female mediators were more controlling. However, the men, whether trained or not, were *perceived* as more controlling.

Shimanoff and Jenkins lament that an individual's gender alone can change how a person or message is heard and evaluated.[65] They stress that group members need to remember that they constitute a system; members' focus should not be on one person fulfilling the role of leader but on leadership as the responsibility of all group members. Thus, it behooves group members to acknowledge and challenge sex role stereotypes which, if left unchecked, can deprive the group of valuable human resources. After all, group members have been found to be more satisfied and productive when the most qualified members lead, and research has shown repeatedly that such individuals are just as likely to be female as male.

Biological sex often serves as a status characteristic that may affect women's credibility in groups. Propp found that in mixed-sex groups, information provided by women is evaluated more stringently.[66] Information introduced by males was twice as likely to be used by the group in its decision-making process. This was especially true when that information was new and not known generally by the rest of the members. Propp suggests that biological sex is used as a status cue, and this puts women's expertise at a disadvantage during decision making. In another study by Taps and Martin, how female behaviors were evaluated depended on whether the group was sex balanced or lopsided.[67] In all-female groups, women who gave internal accounts for their opinions (e.g., "Based on my previous experience, I think . . .") were more influential and more well-liked. However, the reverse was true for male groups with only one woman. In that case, women who gave external accounts (e.g., "Based on research done by Dr. Smith, I think . . .") were more influential. In sex-balanced groups, the types of accounts didn't seem to matter. These findings have strong implications for how groups are constituted, especially in the workplace.

Other studies indicate that perceptions depend on factors other than gender. Canary and Spitzberg examined how men and women handled conflict episodes.[68] They concluded that the *approach* (i.e., using win-win strategies), not the sex, determined effectiveness, with each sex perceived as being equally effective.

About the only things we can conclude from this brief review are that gender expectations and behaviors are in a state of rapid flux, and that differences are largely a result of culture rather than sex. Remember, whatever is learned can be changed.

If multicultural societies like the United States are to succeed, it is absolutely imperative that we learn to interact with people who are different from us. As we noted earlier, intercultural groups of diverse Americans will become the norm in the coming century. In this section we discuss several of the communication differences between black and white Americans. We do not intend to imply that relationships between Hispanics and whites, or Asians and blacks, are not equally important. In fact, in the near future, Hispanics will be the largest minority group in the United States, with profound implications for communication. However, we elected to discuss black-white communication because misunderstandings here appear to be among the most serious and volatile at this time. African Americans and Caucasian Americans perceive each other as threatening and have generally negative evaluations of each other,[69] so it seems especially important to help each group understand the other. We remind you again that even though we discuss African American communication patterns as though African Americans were a uniform group, this is not the case. We agree with Orbe, who notes that the considerable diversity *within* the African American community has been largely ignored by researchers.[70]

Race

Foeman and Pressley have summarized research that describes "typical" (although we caution you again that there is no such thing as "typical") black communication, particularly in organizational settings.[71] Black culture in the United States is an oral culture, so verbal inventiveness and virtuosity of expression are highly valued. What many whites perceive as boastfulness Foeman and Pressley call assertiveness, which takes both verbal and nonverbal forms (trying to top someone else's boast, strutting across the street). Black managers are perceived as forthright or overly reactive. In a conflict, for instance, a black is more likely to confront an individual directly, whereas a white manager is more likely to approach the problem indirectly. Consequently, some blacks perceive whites as underreactive, but some whites see blacks as overreactive. Degree of responsiveness (expressiveness) differs; blacks are more likely to respond both verbally and physically (e.g., gesturing often with their hands), whereas whites tend to focus on verbal responses. Blacks make less direct eye contact, but they compensate by standing closer to their conversational partner than most whites. These differences in cultural communication patterns can create serious misunderstandings. For instance, a white expecting more eye contact may be likely to repeat or rephrase statements in order to get the expected signs of understanding (such as eye contact), while the black feels the white is being condescending.

The black culture is more collective than the more dominant white culture of the United States. According to Foeman and Pressley, this may lead to such strong black identification with blacks *as a group* that a black person may be unwilling or unable to work with people of different ethnic groups. However, the communal structure of the black culture helps offset the discrimination and prejudice blacks still receive in this culture.

Blacks and whites express themselves verbally in different ways. Blacks are more playful than most whites in their use of language and relish playing verbal games. Foeman and Pressley explain that blacks *signify* (or hint) at questions rather than asking them directly because they perceive disclosure of personal information to be voluntary; thus, questions are implied so that the person being asked will not feel vulnerable or obliged to answer. In addition, blacks use the backchannel (or *call-response*) to indicate interest and involvement in the discussion. For example, in black churches the services resemble a dialogue, with congregation members freely calling *Amen, Go ahead, Preach* to the minister; such responses would be less frequent in most white churches. Differences in black-white uses of the backchannel, as we discussed earlier, can create misunderstandings and cause hurt feelings.

One of us recently noted an illustration of verbal differences between blacks and whites. The week after John Kennedy, Jr., was killed in an airplane crash, Rev. Jesse Jackson was being interviewed by Cokie Roberts in a television tribute to Kennedy. In response to a question about Kennedy's work with the disadvantaged, Rev. Jackson began to speak movingly and at length about the young man. He was using the cadences and extended style of many black preachers and it was clear that he was just getting started when Cokie interrupted him to say, "So in other words, there was substance to [Kennedy]." In one short sentence, Cokie, who seemed a little frustrated at how long it was taking Rev. Jackson to answer her question, summarized concisely what he had been saying and went on to the next question. The "typical" white, to-the-point style bumped up against the "typical" flowery, elaborated style of black preachers in an interesting way.

In the United States, it is often difficult for someone from one subculture to participate fully in a group dominated by members of a different subculture. Many African Americans, including some of the most successful, say they must behave cautiously and carefully in groups of white Americans; they can never fully relax.[72] In many ways they have developed bicultural competencies—one set of behaviors for African American groups, another for primarily white groups. This balancing act can be exhausting, but many African Americans believe that if they do not conform to the communication rules of the dominant, European American culture, they will pay a high price.

This discussion of race and gender has only scratched the surface, and is not intended to be exhaustive. It is intended to encourage you to think about your own behavior with an eye toward sensitizing you to ethnocentric behavior that may cause problems in a group. Two recent studies by Kirchmeyer indicate that minority members of groups are often the lowest contributors.[73] Two plausible explanations for this are that minorities may lack a sense of belonging to the group and that, while they may be skilled in communication within their own culture, they may lack the skills to communicate effectively in groups composed primarily of whites. Kirchmeyer found that the *gender* characteristics of low masculinity, high femininity, and minority status affected contribution levels, and she cautions that multicultural groups may not be encompassing the multiple perspectives of all their members in the final products. This represents a significant loss to all of us. Whether we are black, white, female, male, urban, rural, or whatever, we must begin to recognize that differences are just that—differences! They do not imply that someone from another culture is wrong, stupid, or uneducated. Ethical group members learn as much as they can about other cultures to help prevent serious misunderstandings and to ensure that all views are represented.

CONSIDER THIS

Assume you are the only woman in a group of men, the only man in a group of women, the only black in a group of whites, and the only white in a group of blacks. How do you think you would feel in each of these circumstances? What thoughts would run through your head? How, if at all, do you think your behavior would change?

BEHAVING ETHICALLY IN INTERCULTURAL INTERACTIONS

By now, you know that what is considered rhetorically sensitive and appropriate communication depends on the culture.[74] If communication rules differ in each individual culture, are there any universal or overarching principles that preserve the integrity of individual cultures, yet let members of those cultures work together? Kale suggests two broad principles that should govern intercultural interactions: we should protect the worth and dignity of all human beings, and we should act in such a way as to promote peace among all people.[75] The following ethical guidelines follow from these broad principles:

1. **Communicate in a way that extends empathy and respect to all members of the group.**
   Similar to the ethical principle described in Chapter 1, this principle requires that you work to understand others as they want to be understood. This is more challenging between group members of different cultures because there are fewer "givens," but there are things you can do. First, remember that all discussions are to some extent intercultural; be aware of and sensitive to cultural differences and view them as potential strengths for a group, not liabilities. Resist making judgments about the intelligence or motives of others. Encourage all members to get to know each other beyond the task demands of the group. Finally, initiate discussion of the differences. You will help group members move toward greater understanding and empathy if you explicitly acknowledge differences and willingly discuss them, not in a judgmental way but as an opportunity to learn more about your fellow group members and yourself.

FIGURE 5.2	Guidelines for ethical intercultural communication.

In intercultural small group communication,

Remember that every discussion is intercultural to some extent. Because each of us has a unique background, we do not use verbal and nonverbal signals to mean exactly the same things.

Recognize and accept differences; view them as strengths of the group, not liabilities. Instead of judging others wrong for behaving in ways different from yours, recognize that each of us is the product of our culture. Resolve to learn from each other, not to try change each other.

Resist making attributions of stupidity or ill intent; ask yourself whether the other member's behavior could have cultural origin. When another member's behavior seems rude, inconsiderate, our unusual, ask yourself whether you could be observing a cultural difference in what is considered appropriate behavior before you decide the other member is worthless to the group.

Be willing to discuss intercultural differences openly and initiate discussion of differences you observe. Instead of being uncomfortable or pretending that differences do not exist, be willing to ask for and share information about cultural norms and rules. When you observe differences, you can enrich everyone's understanding by pointing them out and initiating a discussion about how cultures vary.

Be willing to adapt to differences. Instead of insisting that others follow the prescriptions of your culture, be willing to adapt your behavior to different cultural practices when appropriate. Try to incorporate the key values and needs of each culture into the group's procedures and outputs.

2. **Work to incorporate the key cultural values of all members into the group's procedures and outputs.**

   Of course this is easier said than done, but failure to do this denigrates the cultural values of those members who are ignored. This also means that all members must adjust their normal ways of interacting to accommodate differences. Bantz's work with an intercultural research team provides several specific suggestions for managing cultural diversity.[76] In that team, explicitly establishing common goals and deadlines addressed the needs of members high in uncertainty avoidance, and differences in power distance norms were handled by segregating tasks and varying the leadership styles accordingly. Differing needs for cohesion were addressed by alternating task and social aspects of the work. Notice that these ways of handling the diversity recognized the legitimacy of the differing cultural norms, showed the members' ability to adapt, and demonstrated respect for all concerned—all ethical goals.

   Specific suggestions to help you put these ethical principles into effect in your small groups are summarized in Figure 5.2.

SUMMARY

1. All interactions are to some extent intercultural, but some much more than others. Being able to work effectively in intercultural small groups will be increasingly necessary in the next decades. Everyone must abandon ethnocentricity and learn to appreciate, rather than denigrate, diversity.

2. Cultures vary along several key dimensions, including worldview, or beliefs about the nature and purpose of life, which help determine our values, activity orientation, customs, and beliefs; the degree of individualism; the degree of power distance; the extent to which people avoid uncertainty; and the extent to which people rely more on the words or the context to determine the meaning of something.

3. Language differences between cultures are dangerous enough, but more subtle differences in nonverbal behaviors, such as paralanguage, body movements, use of space, and conceptions of time, can also cause major misunderstandings.

4. Gender and race differences can be viewed as cultural differences. However, both gender and race roles are undergoing rapid change, and there are often more similarities than differences.

5. Two ethical principles should guide intercultural interactions in groups: the worth and dignity of humans should be protected, and peace among all people should be promoted.

EXERCISES

1. List all the cultures and subcultures with which you feel a strong identification. Form groups of five or six; share and discuss your lists. What do you think are the most salient characteristics of the cultures or subcultures on your list? How do the members of each one expect you to behave? Do the features of any of the cultures contradict each other? If so, how? How do you handle it when you experience conflict between the expectations of two subcultures to which you belong?

2. One important subcultural grouping is your family. Form groups of five or six and have each person discuss what the communication norms are in his/her family. (You may want to narrow this to focus on only one kind of situation, such as having dinner with your family.) Are there norms that might surprise family members? Are there norms your family follows that differ from the norms of your classmates' families? Are there norms governing what you should *not* talk about?

3. As a class, look at movies that depict intercultural encounters of various kinds, including male-female encounters. For example, *Witness, Moscow on the Hudson, The Four Seasons, When Harry Met Sally, The Joy Luck Club, Gandhi,* and *A Stranger Among Us* depict international or intercultural encounters. As a class, address the following questions:
   How did the two cultures in the movie differ? (Be sure to discuss the characteristics of worldview, collectivism versus individualism, low versus high power distance, low versus high uncertainty avoidance, and low versus high context.)
   What communication problems did the differences create?
   Were the communication difficulties resolved? If so, how?
   How were the people from the two cultures changed by the encounters?
   How realistic were the portrayals of the two cultures?

4. Ask several international students to visit your class and describe communication customs and behaviors in their home countries. Ask them what they found most different or hardest to adjust to in conversations in the United States. How do they think their communicative behaviors have changed as a result of encounters with Americans?

5. Ask native-born American students who have either traveled extensively or lived for long periods of time in other places to talk about their experiences adjusting to other cultures. What did they find most different or hardest to adjust to about the communication behavior of the people in the other cultures? How has their behavior changed as a result of their travels?

6. Use one or more of the intercultural "critical incidents" described in *Intercultural Interactions: A Practical Guide* (listed in the Bibliography below) to create a role-play or skit for the class. Discuss what each individual in the role-play or skit might do to repair the interpersonal damage that may have occurred and to prevent such "mistakes" in the future.

7. Go to a public place (e.g., airport, restaurant, or museum) and observe the differences between how men and women behave. Take note of such things as how they sit and stand, how they seem to use personal space, their facial expressions and gestures, and so forth. What generalizations are you comfortable making from your observations? Share your findings with the class.

BIBLIOGRAPHY

Brislin, Richard W., Kenneth Cushner, Craig Cherrie, and Mahealani Yong. *Intercultural Interactions: A Practical Guide*. Beverly Hills, CA: Sage Publications, 1986. Provides 100 realistic intercultural case studies and asks the reader to speculate upon the sources of misunderstanding.

Kim, Young Yun, and William B. Gudykunst, eds. *Theories in Intercultural Communication, International and Intercultural Communication Annual*. Vol. 12. Newbury Park, CA: Sage Publications, 1988.

Lustig, Myron W., and Laura L. Cassotta, "Comparing Group Communication across Cultures: Leadership, Conformity, and Discussion Processes." In *Small Group Communication: A Reader*. 6th ed. Robert S. Cathcart and Larry A. Samovar, eds. Dubuque, IA: Wm. C. Brown Publishers, 1992, 393–404.

Porter, Richard E., and Larry A. Samovar. "Communication in the Multicultural Group." In *Small Group Communication: A Reader*. 6th ed. Robert S. Cathcart and Larry A. Samovar, eds. Dubuque, IA: Wm. C. Brown Publishers, 1992, 382–92.

Stewart, Lea P., Alan D. Stewart, Sheryl A. Friedley, and Pamela J. Cooper. *Communication between the Sexes: Sex Differences and Sex-Role Stereotypes*. 2d ed. Scottsdale, AZ: Gorsuch Scarisbrick, Publishers, 1990, especially chapters 2, 3, and 4.

NOTES

1. William A. Henry, "Beyond the Melting Pot," *Time* (April 9, 1990): 29–35.

2. Martha L. Maznevski, "Understanding Our Differences: Performance in Decision-Making Groups with Diverse Members," *Human Relations* 47 (May 1994): 531–52.

3. Poppy Lauretta McLeod, Sharon Alisa Lobel, and Taylor H. Cox, Jr., "Ethnic Diversity and Creativity in Small Groups," *Small Groups Research* 27 (May 1996): 248–64.

4. Young Yun Kim and Brent D. Ruben, "Intercultural Transformation: A Systems

Theory," in *Theories in Intercultural Communication: International and Intercultural Communication Annual,* Vol. 12, eds. Young Yun Kim and William B. Gudykunst (Newbury Park, CA: Sage, 1988): 299–321.

5. Barbara L. Speicher, "Interethnic Conflict: Attribution and Cultural Ignorance," *Howard Journal of Communication* 5 (Spring 1995): 195–213.

6. Rebecca Leonard and Don C. Locke, "Communication Stereotypes: Is Interracial Communication Possible?" *Journal of Black Studies* 23 (March 1993): 332–43.

7. Mary Jane Collier and Milt Thomas, "Cultural Identity: An Interpretive Perspective," in *Theories in Intercultural Communication: International and Intercultural Communication Annual,* Vol. 12, eds. Young Yun Kim and William B. Gudykunst (Newbury Park, CA: Sage, 1988): 113.

8. Ibid., 103.

9. Donald W. Klopf, *Intercultural Encounters: The Fundamentals of Intercultural Communication* (Englewood, CO: Morton, 1987): 27–30.

10. Larry E. Sarbaugh, "A Taxonomic Approach to Intercultural Communication," in *Theories in Intercultural Communication: International and Intercultural Communication Annual,* Vol. 12, eds. Young Yun Kim and William B. Gudykunst (Newbury Park, CA: Sage, 1988): 22–38.

11. Young Yun Kim, "On Theorizing Intercultural Communication," in *Theories in Intercultural Communication: International and Intercultural Communication Annual,* Vol. 12, eds. Young Yun Kim and William B. Gudykunst (Newbury Park, CA: Sage, 1988): 12–13.

12. Edward T. Hall, *Beyond Culture* (New York: Anchor Press, 1977); Geert Hofstede, *Culture's Consequences: International Differences in Work-Related Values* (Beverly Hills, CA: Sage, 1980);

F. Kluckhohn and F. Strodtbeck, *Variations in Value Orientations* (New York: Row, Peterson, 1961); Charles H. Kraft, "Worldview in Intercultural Communication," in *Intercultural and International Communication,* ed. Fred L. Casmir (Washington, D.C.: University Press of America, 1978): 407–28; Larry E. Sarbaugh, "A Taxonomic Approach to Intercultural Communication."

13. Kluckhohn and Strodtbeck, *Variations in Value Orientations.*

14. Moshe F. Rubenstein, *Patterns of Problem Solving* (Englewood Cliffs, NJ: Prentice-Hall, 1975): 1–2.

15. William B. Gudykunst and Stella Ting-Toomey, *Culture and Interpersonal Communication* (Newbury Park, CA: Sage, 1988): 40–43.

16. Min-Sun Kim and William F. Sharkey, "Independent and Interdependent Construals of Self: Explaining Cultural Patterns of Interpersonal Communication in Multi-Cultural Organizational Settings," *Communication Quarterly* 43 (Winter 1995): 20–38.

17. Richard W. Brislin, Kenneth Cushner, Craig Cherrie, and Mahealani Yong, *Intercultural Interactions: A Practical Guide* (Beverly Hills, CA: Sage, 1986): 207–8, 219.

18. Hofstede, *Culture's Consequences.*

19. Myron W. Lustig and Laura L. Cassotta, "Comparing Group Communication across Cultures: Leadership, Conformity, and Discussion Procedures," in *Small Group Communication: A Reader,* 6th ed., eds. Robert S. Cathcart and Larry A. Samovar (Dubuque, IA: Wm. C. Brown, 1992): 393–404.

20. Hofstede, *Culture's Consequences.*

21. Myron W. Lustig and Jolene Koester, *Interpersonal Competence: Interpersonal Communication across Cultures* (New York: HarperCollins, 1993).

22. Lustig and Cassotta, "Comparing Group Communication across Cultures."

23. Hall, *Beyond Culture.*

24. Linda Wai Ling Young, "Inscrutability Revisited," in *Language and Social Identity,* ed. John J. Gumperz (Cambridge: Cambridge University Press, 1982): 79.

25. Gudykunst and Ting-Toomey, *Culture and Interpersonal Communication,* 45.

26. Roichi Okabe, "Cultural Assumptions of East and West," in *Intercultural Communication Theory: International & Intercultural Communication Annual,* Vol 7, ed. William B. Gudykunst (Beverly Hills, CA: Sage, 1983): 21–44.

27. Donald W. Klopf, "Japanese Communication Practices: Recent Comparative Research," *Communication Quarterly* 39 (Spring 1991): 130–43.

28. Lustig and Koester, *Intercultural Competence.*

29. Ibid.

30. Myung-seok Park and Moon-soo Kim, "Communication Practices in Korea," *Communication Quarterly* 40 (Fall 1992): 398–404.

31. "Englishes Are the International Language," *Michigan Today* (June 1995): 17.

32. Joe E. Pierce, "Life Histories of Individuals and Their Impact on International Communication," in *Intercultural and International Communication,* ed. Fred L. Casmir (Washington, D.C.: University Press of America, 1978): 525.

33. Peter A. Anderson, "Nonverbal Communication in the Small Group," in *Small Group Communication: A Reader,* 6th ed., eds. Robert S. Cathcart and Larry A. Samovar (Dubuque, IA: Wm. C. Brown, 1992): 278.

34. Klopf, *Intercultural Encounters,* 178.

35. Stewart L. Tubbs and Sylvia Moss, *Human Communication,* 5th ed. (New York: Random House, 1997): 414.

36. William Labov, "Acute Inflection: Speech Patterns Buck National Homogeneity," *Civilization* (June/July 1999): 30.

37. Klopf, *Intercultural Encounters,* 177.

38. Branch Lotspiech, personal conversation, June, 1990.

39. Klopf, *Intercultural Encounters,* 177.

40. Tubbs and Moss, *Human Communication,* 414.

41. Dorothy L. Pennington, "Black-White Communication: An Assessment of Research," in *Handbook of Intercultural Communication,* eds. Molefi K. Asante, Eileen Newmark, and Cecil A. Blake (Beverly Hills, CA: Sage, 1979): 387.

42. Klopf, *Intercultural Encounters,* 178.

43. Gudykunst and Ting-Toomey, *Culture and Interpersonal Communication,* 124–28.

44. Sheila J. Ramsey, "Nonverbal Behavior: An Intercultural Perspective," in *Handbook of Intercultural Communication,* eds. Molefi K. Asante, Eileen Newmark, and Cecil A. Blake (Beverly Hills, CA: Sage, 1979): 129–31.

45. Edward T. Hall, "The Hidden Dimensions of Time and Space in Today's World," in *Cross-Cultural Perspectives in Nonverbal Communication,* ed. Fernando Poyatos (Toronto: C. J. Hogrefe, 1988): 145–52.

46. Edward T. Hall, *The Dance of Life,* summarized in Gudykunst and Ting-Toomey, *Culture and Interpersonal Communication,* 128–30.

47. Walburga von Raffler-Engle, "The Impact of Covert Factors in Cross-Cultural Communication," in *Cross-Cultural Perspectives in Nonverbal Communication,* ed. Fernando Poyatos (Toronto: C. J. Hogrefe, 1988): 96.

48. Brent D. Ruben, *Communication and Human Behavior,* 2d ed. (New York: Macmillan, 1988): 402.

49. Brant R. Burleson, "Proponents of 'Alien Cultures View' Need to Come Down to Earth," *Chicago Tribune* (November 23, 1997).

50. Aki Uchida, "Bring the 'Culture' Back In: A Culture-Building Approach to Gender and Communication," *Women & Language* XX (Fall 1997): 15–24.

51. Lea P. Stewart, Alan D. Stewart, Sheryl A. Friedley, and Pamela J. Cooper, *Communication between the Sexes: Sex Differences and Sex-Role Stereotypes,* 2d ed. (Scottsdale, AZ: Gorsuch Scarisbrick, 1990): 43–114.

52. Daniel N. Maltz and Ruth A. Borker, "A Cultural Approach to Male-Female Miscommunication," in *Language and Social Identity,* ed. John J. Gumperz (Cambridge: Cambridge University Press, 1982): 195–216.

53. Anthony Mulac, Pamela Gibbons, and Stuart Fujiyama, "Male/Female Language Differences Viewed from an Inter-Cultural Perspective: Gender as Culture," paper presented at the *Speech Communication Association Annual Convention* (November 1990), Chicago.

54. James C. McCroskey, Virginia P. Richmond, and Robert A. Stewart, *One on One: The Foundations of Interpersonal Communication* (Englewood Cliffs, NJ: Prentice-Hall, 1986): 244–47.

55. Stewart, Stewart, Friedley, and Cooper, *Communication between the Sexes,* 92–106.

56. John E. Baird, "Sex Differences in Group Communication: A Review of Relevant Research," *Quarterly Journal of Speech* 62 (1976): 179–92.

57. Lynn Smith-Lovin and Charles Brody, "Interruptions in Group Discussions: The Effects of Gender and Group Composition," *American Sociological Review* 54 (June 1989): 424–35.

58. Anthony F. Verdi and Susan A. Wheelan, "Developmental Patterns in Same-Sex and Mixed-Sex Groups," *Small Group Research* 23 (August 1992): 356–78.

59. Edward A. Mabry, "Some Theoretical Implications of Female and Male Interaction in Unstructured Small Groups," *Small Group Behavior* 20 (1989): 536–50.

60. William E. Jurma and Beverly C. Wright, "Follower Reactions to Male and Female Leaders Who Maintain or Lose Reward Power," *Small Group Research* 21 (1990): 97–112.

61. Patricia H. Andrews, "Sex and Gender Differences in Group Communication: Impact on the Facilitation Process," *Small Group Research* 23 (February 1992): 74–92.

62. Georgia Duerst-Lahti, "But Women Play the Game Too: Communication Control and Influence in Administrative Decision Making," *Administration and Society* 22 (August 1990): 182–205.

63. Linda L. Carli, "Gender, Language, and Influence," *Journal of Personality and Social Psychology* 59 (1990): 941–51.

64. Nancy A. Burrell, William A. Donahue, and Mike Allen, "Gender-based Perceptual Biases in Mediating," *Communication Research* 15 (1988): 447–69.

65. Susan B. Shimanoff and Mercilee M. Jenkins, "Leadership and Gender: Challenging Assumptions and Recognizing Resources," in *Small Group Communication: Theory and Practice,* 7th ed., eds. Robert S. Cathcart, Larry A. Samovar, and Linda D. Henman (Madison, WI: Brown & Benchmark, 1996): 327–44.

66. Kathleen M. Propp, "An Experimental Examination of Biological Sex as a Status Cue in Decision-Making Groups and Its Influence on Information Use," *Small Group Research* 26 (November 1995): 451–74.

67. Judith Taps and Patricia Yancey Martin, "Gender Composition, Attributional Accounts, and Women's Influence and Likability in Task Groups," *Small Group Research* 21 (November 1990): 471–91.

68. Daniel J. Canary and Brian H. Spitzberg, "Appropriateness and Effectiveness Perceptions of Conflict Strategies," *Human Communication Research* 14 (1987): 93–118.

69. Leonard and Locke, "Communication Stereotypes."

70. Mark P. Orbe, "Remember, It's Always Whites' Ball: Descriptions of African American Male Communication," *Communication Quarterly* 42 (Summer 1994): 287–300.

71. Anita K. Foeman and Gary Pressley, "Ethnic Culture and Corporate Culture: Using Black Styles in Organizations," *Communication Quarterly* 35 (Fall 1987): 293–307.

72. Orbe, "Remember, It's Always Whites' Ball"

73.   C. Kirchmeyer and A. Cohen, "Multicultural Groups: Their Performance and Reactions with Constructive Conflict," *Group & Organization Management* 17 (1992): 153–70; C. Kirchmeyer, "Multicultural Task Groups: An Account of the Low Contribution Level of Minorities," *Small Group Research* 24 (February 1993): 127–48.

74.   Stella Ting-Toomey, "Rhetorical Sensitivity Style in Three Cultures: France, Japan, and the United States," *Central States Speech Journal* 39 (Spring 1991): 28–36; Mary Jane Collier, "A Comparison of Conversations among and between Domestic Culture Groups: How Intra- and Intercultural Competencies Vary," *Communication Quarterly* 36 (Spring 1988): 122–44.

75.   David W. Kale, "Ethics in Intercultural Communication," in *Intercultural Communication: A Reader,* 6th ed., eds. Larry A. Samovar and Richard E. Porter (Belmont, CA: Wadsworth, 1991).

76.   Charles R. Bantz, "Cultural Diversity and Group Cross-Cultural Team Research," *Journal of Applied Communication Research* 21 (February 1993): 1–20.

PART 3

DEVELOPING THE SMALL GROUP

©Larry Dale Cordon/Image Bank

For a collection of individuals with diverse backgrounds and personalities to coalesce into a small group, members must develop such group variables as roles, norms, communication patterns, a status hierarchy, effective procedures, cohesiveness, and a stable leadership structure. This section examines key characteristics of the individuals who compose a group and explains how members develop these important throughput processes. In addition to theoretical perspectives, practical information to help you function as a group leader is also provided.

The Members

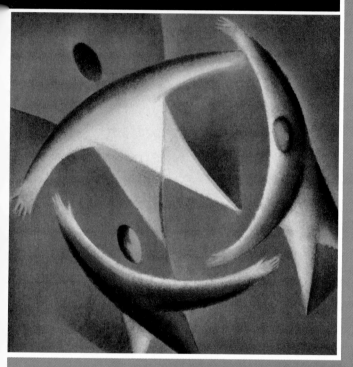

6

Central Message

The number of members and their personal characteristics are input variables that seriously affect group communication and productivity.

Study Objectives

As a result of studying Chapter 6 you should be able to:
1. Know how many members should compose a specific small group.
2. Describe traits such as preference for procedural order, cognitive complexity, and self-monitoring and explain what each has to do with problem-solving discussions.
3. Describe each dimension of the Myers-Briggs Type Indicator® and explain the positive contribution each type can make to group discussion.
4. Describe behaviors that indicate an attitude of responsibility for the success of a small group, and the ethical standards supportive of such an attitude.
5. Explain how a high level of communication apprehension can affect group outcomes.
6. Describe attitudes such as authoritarianism, egalitarianism, and open-mindedness; behaviors associated with each; and their effects on a group.

Key Terms

Aggressiveness
Assertiveness
Attitude
Authoritarianism
Cognitive complexity
Communication apprehension
Dogmatism
Egalitarianism
Extraversion-introversion dimension
Least-sized groups
Myers-Briggs Type Indicator®

Passiveness
Perceiving-judging dimension
Preference for procedural order
Prejudice
Rhetorical sensitivity
Self-monitoring
Sensing-intuiting dimension
Thinking-feeling dimension
Trait

Advertising agencies typically accomplish much of their work in teams. A client—a car manufacturer, a restaurant, a line of cosmetics—is assigned a team of individuals. One particular agency we know about had an exceptionally productive and successful team of five people. Ben, the team's leader, was the head of the retailing division and handled the meetings. Candi, the account executive, served as liaison between the agency and the client. The others described her as "buttoned down." Marija was the media buyer, Vinnie was the art director, and Toni was the copywriter. The team members took it as a matter of personal pride that they were often given the most demanding clients and toughest assignments. The team also represented a variety of perspectives and work styles. Such a combination often derails a team if members don't know how to work with others whose styles, perspectives, and approaches are different. But members of this team worked well together. Ben and especially Candi were highly task focused and able to keep everyone on track. Both took seriously their responsibilities for keeping the project within budget. But they both truly appreciated Vinnie and Toni who, although sometimes taking the group's discussion on a tangent, often came up with just the right theme, just the right visual image, or just the right slogan for a particular ad campaign. Marija, the number cruncher, had an excellent command of figures about how much exposure per dollar various media would provide. Toni, though usually fulfilling a creative role, consistently helped the team focus on the project by asking lots of questions about the client, the target market, the product, and the main images the client wanted to project. In other circumstances, it would be easy to imagine this group self-destructing over differences in work styles, but these open-minded, committed, and competent members had learned both to appreciate and work with their differences, and they were highly successful.

Both the individual characteristics of members and their mix affect how a small group functions and how productive it is. Larson and LaFasto, in a study of outstanding teams of all sorts, found that two types of member competencies were crucial: technical competencies essential for the task, and personal competencies necessary for working well with other members.[1] Members of the advertising team mentioned in our story had both competencies. Productive group members are, or become, skilled and knowledgeable regarding the group's task, really want the group to succeed, and are communicatively competent collaborators. The right people can make group work rewarding, even joyous. Whether we like it or not, group members evaluate each other on such things as their perceived interaction skills and, more often than not, dislike is often based on *lack* of interaction skills. In Chapter 5 we discussed cultural influences that affect member behaviors. Here, we describe how the number of members and their individual characteristics can help produce a winning team.

GROUP SIZE

Theoretically, each member brings some different knowledge, perspectives, and skills relevant to the group's purpose. For complex, nonroutine problems, groups of individuals with diverse skills, information, and perspectives are more effective than homogeneous groups.[2] But that does not mean the more, the better. At some point the increasing cost and difficulty of coordinating the work of more people outweighs the gain. Thelen's principle of **least-sized groups** says we should strive for a group as small as possible, but that has all the expertise and diverse points of view necessary to complete the task well.[3]

As group size increases, the complexity of interpersonal relationships increases geometrically. In a three-person group, only three two-person relationships can exist, but in a group of 10 members there can be 45. As numbers increase, so does the discrepancy in the amount of talking done by different members, with a tendency for one person to do relatively more talking.[4] Leadership tends to become more centralized and formal, with increasing demands on designated leaders to regulate and keep order. Increased size produces lower member satisfaction and cohesiveness, higher competitiveness, increased aggressiveness, increased withdrawal, and fragmentation of work,[5] although some of the negative effects of group size can be offset by a teambuilding program,[6] which we discuss in Chapter 8. On the other hand, groups of fewer than four members can produce tension and may feel constraining.[7]

Other factors being equal, five to seven members is an optimal size for participant satisfaction and cohesiveness. This size is small enough to permit informality, allow everyone a chance to speak up, keep down social loafing (nonparticipation), and facilitate consensus decisions, yet provide the diverse information and points of view needed for quality decisions. In practice, many groups are larger for reasons that have little to do with efficiency or effectiveness.

CONSIDER THIS

The Sky High on Reading Steering Committee we introduced you to in Chapter 1 actually had 19 members. Can you think of reasons why the organizer felt so many people were needed? Do you think these reasons are legitimate? Why or why not? What can you do if you find yourself in a group that is larger than ideal?

©Tom McCarthy/ Unicorn Stock Photos

Groups as large as this is are harder to coordinate, have less equal participation rates, and are less satisfying than smaller groups.

PERSONAL BEHAVIOR: CHARACTERISTICS, ATTITUDES, AND COMPETENCIES

A small group's most important resource is its members. A group cannot be productive if members are lazy, uncooperative, or incompetent. Your personal traits, personality characteristics, attitudes, and competencies certainly affect every group to which you belong. We encourage you to use this chapter as a tool for self-evaluation and personal goal setting.

A **trait** is a consistent pattern of behavior or other observable characteristic. Traits are influenced by both genetics and environment, and our behavior is also determined by our attitudes. An **attitude** is a cluster of values and beliefs held by a person toward an object, person or type of persons, or concept. We infer attitudes from what people say and do. Recent research has confirmed that some personal traits and attitudes produce behaviors that are better for groups than others.[8] For instance, an extremely individualistic attitude makes it hard for someone to operate well as a member of a team.

Personal Traits

A number of personal traits have been shown to influence behavior in groups, including psychological sex type[9] and verbal argumentativeness.[10] We will now discuss three general traits that have a significant bearing on the type of group member someone can be. These traits are thinking patterns (cognitive complexity), self-monitoring, and preference for procedural order.

Cognitive Complexity

How members act in discussions of complex problems, especially when there are wide differences among members' perspectives and preexisting beliefs, is seriously affected by a trait psychologists call *cognitive complexity.* Related to but different from general intelligence, **cognitive complexity** refers to an individual's ability to interpret multiple signals simultaneously: how differentiated, abstract, and organized is someone's ability to process information. In common terms, this is a measure of complex-to-simplistic thinking—do you think in only either/or terms, or can you perceive shades of gray? People high in cognitive complexity employ more differentiated arguments in speaking, are better able to integrate their goals with those of listeners in these arguments, and can better accept and build on others' feelings and beliefs during discussions than people lower in cognitive complexity.[11] Cognitively complex discussants ask more questions and provide more objective information during discussions of class policies than do their less developed classmates; complex people do not assume to know the other's viewpoint. Less developed discussants use their own frames of reference as if these are also the viewpoints of others. During group decision making, high complexity persons can arrive at consensus much better than less complex persons, who speak as if they already know the experience and viewpoints of fellow group members.[12] We suggest you seek out and listen closely to feedback about your own speaking. If you seem to be low in cognitive complexity, you can begin to assume less, ask more questions, check out what you think others want, feel and think, and perhaps learn to evaluate reasoning to become a more analytical, critical thinker.

A second cognitive variable important to how we interact with others in problem solving is called *self-monitoring*. **Self-monitoring** refers to the degree to which a person monitors and controls self-presentation in social situations: "*High self-monitors* attend closely to cues from other participants regarding situationally appropriate behavior and use these cues to guide their social actions. *Low self-monitors* . . . rely on their own attitudes in determining what social behavior to exhibit. . . . "[13] High self-monitors, then, are keenly aware of whether others' responses to their behavior suggest approval or disapproval of that behavior. They can adjust their behavior to achieve desired responses better than low self-monitors by displaying behaviors and role functions appropriate to the group. Modifying behavior instead of following initial inclinations ". . . is the primary mechanism by which high self-monitors emerge as leaders."[14] In other words, sensitivity to cues from others is not sufficient; flexibility and skill in *adjusting one's behavior* as a small group member is also necessary. We discuss how self-monitoring is related to leadership emergence in Chapter 9.

Self-Monitoring

Overlapping the trait of self-monitoring is the characteristic called **rhetorical sensitivity.** Rhetorically sensitive persons monitor what they say, adapting their statements to how they think other members of the group may react.[15] You might have doubts about the ethical standards of self-monitors who are rhetorically sensitive, but we do not. The rhetorically sensitive person is not a *reflector* who says what she thinks others want her to say, or a *noble self* who says whatever comes to mind. Rather, before speaking out, rhetorically sensitive people search consciously for the most effective way to express their point in order to help ensure that other members give their points the fairest possible hearing. They are careful not to insult or inflame other members.

Preference for Procedural Order

A third cognitive trait desirable in members of problem-solving groups is the ability to think critically and systematically. Gouran reported a tendency for most discussion participants to accept inferences without challenging them, even when patently flawed reasoning was involved.[16] For thorough evaluation of proposed solutions, individuals skilled in all aspects of critical thinking along with group procedures that encourage thorough critical evaluation of all solutions are needed. Critical thinking and systematic thinking may be linked in a personality trait referred to as **preference for procedural order** (PPO), which is characterized by a need or desire to follow a clear, linear structure during problem solving. Putnam described the rationale for such a personality measure, development of a questionnaire for measuring it, and its importance to how groups function as problem solvers.[17] Later research by Hirokawa and associates suggests that high PPO persons do much better in choosing among alternatives when a highly structured problem-solving procedure (such as is presented in Chapter 11) is followed by the group. High PPO persons do not seem to think as well as possible during loosely structured discussions. However, groups of low PPO persons who are comfortable with less structured discussion did equally well whether following a procedure of high or low structure. No mixed-PPO groups were considered, but this research suggests that systematic procedures would improve (or at least not reduce) the output quality of most decision-making groups.[18]

Most groups are likely to be composed of members with varying preferences for order and structure. Half of the students Pavitt surveyed preferred a loose "reach testing" decision-making process and the other half preferred a more linear structure, perhaps combined with reach testing.[19] Groups whose members' preferences are similar will have an easier time conducting a discussion.

Personality Characteristics

In our experience, personality differences and differences in how members approach work create the most frustration in groups. The differences themselves are not the problem, but the fact that group members do not know how to work with (much less appreciate) people who are very different from themselves. Of the hundreds of personality characteristics we could have selected to discuss here, we have chosen to talk about the Myers-Briggs Type Indicator® because it is one of the most widely known and researched classification systems. In addition, we think you will have a relatively easy time recognizing yourself within this classification system.

The **Myers-Briggs Type Indicator®**(MBTI) is a personality measure, based on the work of psychologist Carl Jung, that categorizes individuals along four dimensions based on how they relate to the world around them.[20] A mother and daughter psychologist team, Isabel Briggs Myers and Katherine Briggs, extended Jung's work and developed the personality measure currently in widespread use. The MBTI dimensions each assess a particular aspect of how we interact with the world. Each dimension represents a continuum, with a descriptor anchoring each end of the continuum (e.g., extravert and introvert). We each have a preference, sometimes strong but sometimes mild, for one end or the other of the continuum. The MBTI measures our preferences along each of the four dimensions and describes our personality types on the basis of what combination of dimensions we exhibit. No one is a "pure" type—each of us displays some characteristics of all the dimensions. However, the anchor points for each dimension display markedly different communication and behavior preferences from each other.

The **extraversion-introversion dimension** assesses whether you focus on the outer world or your own inner world. Extraverts focus outwardly. They are sociable, like people, often talk to figure out what they think, and generally enjoy working with others in a group. Not so introverts, who much prefer to work alone. Introverts think things through and don't share ideas unless they've figured out first what their positions are. Extraverts don't mind being interrupted, but introverts hate it. Extraverts happily collaborate with others to make decisions, whereas introverts are comfortable making decisions independently. It may seem that extraverts are ideally suited for group work and introverts are not, but introverts can be very thoughtful and careful in evaluating information and can contribute a great deal to group interaction. These two types operate so differently within a group that they may easily misunderstand one another or fail to appreciate each other's contributions to the group. The MBTI code letter for extraversion is E and the letter for introversion is I.

The **sensing-intuiting dimension** assesses the type of information group members prefer to use. Its code letters are S (sensing) and N (intuiting). Sensing individuals prefer and trust facts and figures. They operate in the here and now and are very much rooted in what they can actually apprehend through their physical senses. Intuiting individuals, in contrast, prefer to dream about possibilities and to make connections between seemingly unconnected ideas and thoughts. They easily make intuitive leaps, which sensing individuals mistrust because they prefer concrete information. Intuitives see the big picture whereas sensing individuals tune in to the details, which bore the intuitives. Imagination, invention, and creativity are important to intuitives. In a group, these are the idea people who comfortably leap from idea to idea, but may be short on follow-through. Sensing individuals, however, are careful, able to provide specific facts and illustrations to support the big ideas, and can provide the grounding that intuitives sometimes lack. Both types provide skills groups need.

The **thinking-feeling dimension,** coded T and F, refers to how individuals prefer to make decisions, through careful analysis of objective evidence (thinkers) or empathy and subjective connection with others (feelers). Thinkers are comfortable with a systematic, critical thinking process. They like to analyze data and arrive at verifiable conclusions. They are task oriented and like holding everyone to a single standard. In contrast, feelers tune in readily to the interpersonal relationships among group members and prefer to adjust the standards to meet individual circumstances. Feelers worry about group harmony and will make sure a group takes individual feelings into account in making a decision. Thinkers may forget to take others' feelings into account, but will evaluate evidence critically and come to a logical conclusion. Clearly, thinkers and feelers operate by different internal logic systems in making decisions, yet each system is an important one for a group to consider.

The last dimension, the **perceiving-judging dimension,** concerns how people organize the world around them. Perceivers, coded P, are spontaneous and flexible and react well to change. They like to gather as much information as they can prior to making a decision. At their worst, they are easily distracted and will postpone making a decision until they've collected every piece of information possible—usually an impossible accomplishment. Judgers, coded J, are decisive and sure in making decisions. They make a plan and can stick to it. However, they don't like to change plans once they are made and can become stubborn and rigid. Perceivers constantly second-guess decisions they have made, worrying that they may have forgotten something important. Judgers are never truly comfortable until the group's work is completed and are excellent at keeping the group focused on the task; however, perceivers can roll with the punches if the group's plan falls through. Perceivers are more excited by starting new projects, whereas judgers are more excited by completing them. You can probably see how perceivers and judgers frustrate each other, yet how each one's strengths balance the weaknesses of the other.

These dimensions combine to form 16 different personality types. For instance, someone assessed as ESTJ is extroverted, relies on facts and figures, likes to think things through objectively, and is decisive. A person with an INFP configuration is likely to be shy and quiet, dreamy, empathetic with the other group members, and spontaneous. The most important point to remember about the Myers-Briggs Type Indicator® classifications is that each dimension provides a potential benefit to the group—but only if members recognize the potential strengths in having diverse personalities in the group. If members do not recognize this, they may let frustrations, natural when different personality types try to work together, escalate into unproductive conflict. The chart in Table 6.1 summarizes the MBTI dimensions.

CONSIDER THIS

Which people on the advertising team introduced earlier would be likely to have the most difficult time working together? Why do you think some people are able to work with others whose personalities and styles are very different, and others are not? What do you think your MBTI profile is? What types of individuals do you have the most difficulty working with?

Extraversion-Introversion (where is your focus?)

Extraversion (E)	Introversion (I)
Focus on external world	Focus on inner world
Sociable	Shy, reserved
Use talk to clarify their own thinking	Think things through before sharing verbally
Enjoy working in a group	Enjoy working alone
Don't mind being interrupted	Hate being interrupted
Comfortable making decisions collaboratively	Comfortable making decisions independently

Sensing-Intuiting (what type of information you prefer to use)

Sensing (S)	Intuiting (N)
Trust facts and figures, what can be perceived through the senses	Trust imagination and intuition, what can be imagined
Prefer concrete information and ideas	Prefer to dream about possibilities
Detail oriented	"Big picture" oriented
Stay in "here and now"	Future oriented
Can find specific facts/evidence to illustrate an idea	Dream about possibilities and make intuitive leaps among seemingly unconnected ideas
Grounded	Inventive

Thinking-Feeling (how you make decisions)

Thinking (T)	Feeling (F)
Carefully analyze objective information to make decisions	Use empathy and subjective feelings to make decisions
Systematic, critical thinker; like to analyze data to arrive at conclusion	Tune in to feelings of others and take them into account
Task-oriented	Relationship-oriented
Hold all to a single standard	Adjust standards to meet individual circumstances
Use evidence to come to logical conclusion, regardless of individual feelings	Take others' feelings into account in group decision

Perceiving-Judging (how you organize your world)

Perceiving (P)	Judging (J)
Gather as much information as possible before deciding	Decisive; can make quick decisions
Spontaneous and flexible; react well to change	Stick to a plan once made; dislike change
Excited by starting new projects	Excited by finishing projects
Second-guess decisions they've made	Certain; don't second guess themselves.
Make sure group considers all relevant information	Keep group focused on task

Communicative Attitudes

Attitudes about personal responsibility, other people, and ways of expressing thoughts are vital to how much a member contributes to group goal achievement. Pay particular attention to your attitudes about your group and your fellow group members, and give yourself an attitude adjustment if you need to!

A Sense of Responsibility for the Group's Success

Perhaps the most important attitude of ideal small group members is summarized by the phrase *a sense of responsibility for the success of the group.* Constructive members feel a personal responsibility to do whatever they can to help the group achieve its goals. They are *dependable.* Responsible members put accomplishment of group goals ahead of selfish wants. They are guided by a number of ethical standards, such as:

1. No member has a right to act in a way that would be disastrous if done by all members.
2. No one has a right to expect more effort from other members than he or she makes for the group.
3. Every member should be faithful in carrying out assignments for the group, and if prevented from doing so, should immediately notify the group and explain what went wrong.
4. A member should share any relevant information and ideas for the group to use in solving problems.

The kinds of pronouns used by such members to refer to the group reveal a sense of commitment: *we, us,* and *our* rather than *you* and *your.* These members volunteer to do a fair share of the work, and can be counted on to get it done. Failure to do a fair share of the group's work is the biggest source of friction among members of student project groups in our classes. In sum, the valuable group member is fully responsible and trustworthy. If you will not act that way, other members are better off without you; maybe they can replace you with a useful member.

Egalitarianism-Authoritarianism

Egalitarianism and *authoritarianism* are contrasting ways of seeing human relationships. **Egalitarianism** is the belief in the equal importance of all persons; this is a tenet of the U.S. Declaration of Independence. Egalitarian people encourage full participation by all group members; they tend to be free of bigotry and stereotypes. They abhor bossiness and dictatorial behavior in self and others. In contrast, members high in **authoritarianism** prefer a controlling leader and will dominate a group when placed in a position of leadership. High authoritarians accept uncritically information and ideas expressed by or attributed to authorities (i.e., experts). They ask opinions of others less often, act less friendly, and make more directive comments ("Do this!") than egalitarians.[22]

In our culture, we value egalitarian behavior and expect our group leaders to involve us in decision making. In other cultures, as we suggested in the previous chapter, members do not assume that everyone has an equal right to participate; they expect the leader to assume strict, authoritarian control. However, for most of the groups in which you will find yourself in the United States, you are safest to adopt an egalitarian attitude.

To be a productive member, your *willingness to communicate* must be greater than your need to protect yourself from disagreement or embarrassment. People who have relevant information or see flaws in proposals but do not speak up actually harm the group by taking up a member slot that a more outspoken person with needed resources might have occupied. They could be called *excess baggage* of the group. These people manifest the trait of **communication apprehension** (CA, sometimes called *shyness* or *reticence*), which manifests itself with varying degrees of self-concern, self-doubt, fear, anxiety about speaking, and defensiveness toward others. In this book we are concerned only about communication apprehension experienced by participants in a group's discussion, not in public speaking, family relations, etc. Communication apprehension has far greater negative repercussions in group settings than in those other settings.[23] For example, McCroskey and Richmond say that high CA group members speak much less than members low in CA, choose seats where leaders can overlook them, make more irrelevant comments, are less likely to become a group's leader, and are likely to express strong agreement, even when inwardly they disagree. High CAs are perceived as making little contribution to the group. Others see them as less desirable members than low CAs. High CAs even have a lower opinion of *themselves* than other members have of them.[24]

If you are relatively high in CA as a group member, what can you do? Your college or university may have a center where you can learn such helpful techniques as *systematic desensitization* or *cognitive restructuring*. Although fearful of group settings, if high CAs are willing to engage in small group activities, this exposure can help lessen their anxieties.[25] McCroskey and Richmond add that an in-depth understanding of the communication process and of specific skills can help. To that end, we next consider the attitudes and skills of communicating assertively as opposed to communicating either aggressively or passively.

Assertiveness refers to communicative behavior reflecting respect both for oneself and for other group members. Assertive people communicate openly to other members as equals. Assertiveness lies on a continuum, illustrated in Figure 6.1, between **passiveness** (nonassertiveness) and **aggressiveness** in communicating. Aggressive people are highly dominant and often authoritarian; they try to force ideas and practices on others. They call names, demand, insult, threaten, command, shout, pound the table, and frequently drown out others who are speaking. Rather than challenging information or reasoning as such, they attack other people. Emotional bullies, their motto might be, "Do it my way or fight!" Aggressive behavior may stem from psychopathology, from cultural practices, inability to handle frustration, or just a lack of verbal skills for dealing constructively with conflict.[26] No matter what the cause, this behavior is destructive to productive discussion, cohesiveness, and teamwork. We think that both aggressive and passive behavior violate the ethical principles described in Chapter 1 and earlier in this chapter.

Willingness to Communicate

FIGURE 6.1   **Assertiveness lies between aggresiveness and nonassertiveness.**

Aggressive   Assertive   Nonassertive (passive)

Passive discussants, like high CAs, go along with a majority rather than argue, even when they disagree. In going along despite doubts, they are unethical, untrue to themselves, and therefore untrue to the group. Passive members tend to make little eye contact, speak so softly they are hard to hear, and won't resist aggressors. The stereotyped "yessers" shown in Figure 6.2 epitomize passive behavior. Their motto might be, "We'll do it your way; nothing is worth fighting over." The most harmful type of passive member engages in *passive-aggressive* behavior, which is highly destructive to teamwork. Passive-aggressives attempt to get their way subtly; they sabotage rather than confront in the way an assertive person does. Instead of saying, "I don't like that policy" or "I disagree," they may be late with an assigned report, "forget" to carry out an assignment, fail to attend a meeting, or neglect to do their share of the group work.

In contrast to both aggressors and passives, assertive members disagree openly and explain why. They explain what they think as clearly as possible and state what they want. Even more important, they try hard to understand the information, ideas, perspectives, and wants of other members, and to co-orient so a mutually satisfactory decision may be found.

Attitude toward New Information and Ideas   The preceding description of cognitive traits and attitudes toward other persons and communicating has implied the ideal attitude of productive team members toward new information and ideas—*open-minded,* or curious and low in prejudices. Open-minded members are low in the trait called **dogmatism.** The more dogmatic people are, the less willing they are to try to understand new ideas, to listen to or accept evidence that contradicts their present beliefs, and to base conclusions on the total pool of information available to the group.[27] Arguments based on evidence and sound reasoning can change the positions of open-minded persons, but will not influence dogmatic persons, whose decisions are based more on prior beliefs, internal needs, and emotions than a desire to know the truth and be logically consistent.

Dogmatic people see things in either-or, black-or-white terms. One of us, while discussing the relative merits of collective bargaining with several highly educated individuals, was dismayed to hear such dogmatic utterances as, "I'm just against unions in principle. They're wrong. I wouldn't even consider joining one." Others said, "Unionism is good. Management just doesn't care about us who do the real work." Neither statement demonstrates open-minded use of evidence or reasoning, and neither makes allowance for exceptions. People who talk like this, without qualification, question, or evidence, can block group consensus.

Passive "yessers" do not express genuine agreement. **FIGURE 6.2**

"Aye." "Aye." "Aye."   "All those in   "Aye." "Aye." "Aye."
                          favor say 'Aye.'"

CONSIDER THIS

The advertising team described at the beginning of this chapter succeeded in part because members were willing to hear each other out. What effect do you think a dogmatic team member would have had? What are the biggest problems a dogmatic member creates for a group? How could the members have handled a dogmatic member?

A special kind of closed-mindedness is called **prejudice,** which indicates a judgment or opinion formed without full and sufficient inquiry into the matter. Actually, we can never know everything about anything, so we need to be open to new ideas and evidence. As Allport said, "Attitudes become prejudices only if they are not reversible when exposed to new knowledge."[28] Your mind is closed to the degree that you consistently reject ideas you disbelieve, cannot distinguish nuances among beliefs and practices different from your own, and see no similarities between your own beliefs and disbeliefs.[29]

Ideally, group members would all be open-minded and free of prejudices. We are sure you do not want to behave dogmatically and so create roadblocks to group co-orientation and unity. A little self-monitoring can help a lot. *Ask* for points of view that differ from yours, and be sure you listen actively to them. If you observe dogmatism to be a problem in a continuing group, tackle the problem head-on by describing it. Keep reminding the group that mutual respect is essential for group cooperation.

SUMMARY

1. Groups need diversity of information, perspectives, and skills, but too many members complicate the discussion process. Groups should be *least-sized:* as small as possible with the requisite diversity and variety needed to do the job.

2. Ideally, group members facing a typical discussion task should be high in cognitive complexity so they can deal with complex multifaceted problems. Groups, particularly those with members high in preference for procedural order, generally perform better when they follow some systematic process for solving problems.

3. Members should be open-minded and free of dogmatism or prejudice, and be high self-monitors, and thus rhetorically sensitive, which means that they think carefully before speaking.

4. The Myers-Briggs Type Indicator® helps members understand basic personality differences rooted in how people perceive the world; ideally, members appreciate the diverse strengths these differences bring to the group.

5. Members should have a sense of responsibility for the success of the group, exhibited by their dependability, commitment to group goals, and follow-through in completing their fair share of the group's work.

6. Members who are high in communication apprehension, are passive, passive-aggressive, or aggressive, create problems for a group. Ideal members are assertive.

7. Group members should strive to develop egalitarian rather than authoritarian attitudes, which inhibit optimum group functioning.

8. Successful group members are willing to communicate within the group openly, without prejudice or dogmatism about their own opinions, which is the point of small group discussion.

EXERCISES

1. Discuss the following question with your classmates, first in small groups, then as an entire class: How much can we trust each other to be truthful and to carry a fair share of work in the small groups we form in this class?

2. For one week keep a journal in which you write daily reports of examples of self-monitoring and rhetorical sensitivity. These may be your own efforts or those of others. At the end of the week, share your examples with your classmates.

3. Are you low or high in preference for procedural order? Have all the lows meet in one corner of the room and all the highs in the other. Each group should make two lists:
   a. In what ways is a member like me (high or low PPO) an asset to a group?
   b. In what ways is a member like me (high or low PPO) a detriment to a group?
   After the class reconvenes, the highs should read their list to the class as a whole. The lows should feel free to contribute assets or detriments the highs forgot. Next, the lows should share their list, with the highs contributing. What did you learn from this exercise?

4. Look again at the descriptions of the Myers-Briggs Type Indicator® dimensions and

determine your own classifications. In a small group of fellow students, share with each other what you believe your classifications are and make two lists:

a. For the pole position of each dimension (e.g., extraversion as one pole, introversion as the other pole), what are the advantages of having a member like that in the group?

b. For the pole position of each dimension (e.g., extraversion as one pole, introversion as the other pole), what are the disadvantages of having a member like that in the group?

5. In a small group of fellow students discuss each of the following questions. One person should report your conclusions to the class.

a. What kinds of behaviors suggest that a discussant was open-minded? Dogmatic?

b. What effects have dogmatic persons had in groups to which you have belonged?

c. How do you feel when a fellow group member speaks dogmatically? When a member speaks with an open-minded, attitude?

6. After a topical discussion of some issue on which class members are widely divided in opinions (such as abortion, gun control, smokers' rights, or responsible sex), have every participant rate each of the others on the degree to which his or her behavior manifested open-mindedness versus dogmatism.

7. List two or three prejudices you once held, but have now abandoned. Then describe how you changed them. With fellow classmates discuss what you can learn from this review of your collective pasts.

BIBLIOGRAPHY

Kroeger, Otto, and Janet A. Thuesen. *Type Talk: The 16 Personality Types That Determine How We Live, Love, and Work.* New York: Dell Publishing, 1988.

Larson, Carl E., and Frank M. J. LaFasto. *Teamwork: What Must Go Right/What Can Go Wrong.* Newbury Park, CA: Sage Publications, 1989, 59–72.

McCroskey, James C., and Virginia P. Richmond. "Communication Apprehension and Small Group Communication." In *Small Group Communication: A Reader.* 5th ed. Robert S. Cathcart and Larry A. Samovar, eds. Dubuque, IA: Wm. C. Brown Publishers, 1988, 405–19.

Rokeach, Milton. *The Open and Closed Mind.* New York: Basic Books, 1960.

Shaw, Marvin E. *Group Dynamics: The Psychology of Small Group Behavior.* 3d ed. New York: McGraw-Hill, 1981, chapter 6.

NOTES

1. Carl E. Larson and Frank M. J. LaFasto, *Teamwork: What Must Go Right/What Can Go Wrong* (Newbury Park, CA: Sage, 1989): 59–72.

2. Susan E. Jackson, "Team Composition in Organizational Settings: Issues in Managing a Diverse Work Force," in *Group Process and Productivity,* eds. Stephen Worchel, Wendy Wood, and Jeffry A. Simpson (Newbury Park, CA: Sage, 1992): 138–73.

3. Herbert A. Thelen, *Dynamics of Groups at Work* (Chicago: University of Chicago Press, 1954): 187.

4. Robert F. Bales et al., "Channels of Communication in Small Groups," *American Sociological Review* 16 (1952): 461–68.

5. J. A. Schellenberg, "Group Size as a Factor in Success of Academic Discussion Groups," *Journal of Educational Psychology* 33 (1959): 73–79; E. B. Smith, "Some Psychological Aspects of Committee Work, " *Journal of Abnormal and Social Psychology* 11 (1927): 73–79; Richard B. Powers and William Boyle, "Common Dilemma Choices in Small vs. Large Groups" (Paper presented at American Psychological Association, Anaheim, CA, August 1983).

6. Albert V. Carron and Kevin S. Spink, "The Group Size–Cohesion Relationship in Minimal Groups," *Small Group Research* 26 (February 1995): 86–105.

7. Phillip E. Slater, "Contrasting Correlates of Group Size," *Sociometry* 21 (1958): 129–39.

8. Brian H. Spitzberg, "Interpersonal Competence in Groups," in *Small Group Communication: A Reader,* 6th ed., eds. Robert S. Cathcart and Larry A. Samovar (Dubuque, IA: Wm. C. Brown, 1992): 431.

9. James Joseph A. Diliberto, "A Communication Study of Possible Relationships between Psychological Sex Type and Decision-Making Effectiveness," *Small Group Research* 23 (August 1992): 379–407.

10. Dean Kazoleas and Bonnie Kay, "Are Argumentatives Really More Argumentative? The Behavior of Argumentatives in Group Deliberations over Controversial Issues" (Paper presented at the Speech Communication Association Conference, New Orleans, LA, November 1994).

11. Susan L. Kline, Cathy L. Hennen-Floyd, and Kathleen M. Farrell, "Cognitive Complexity and Verbal Response Mode Use in Discussion," *Communication Quarterly* 38 (1990): 350.

12. Ibid., 357–58.

13. Robert J. Ellis and Steven F. Cronshaw, "Self-Monitoring and Leader Emergence: A Test of Moderator Effects," *Small Group Research* 23 (1992): 114–15; see also Robert J. Ellis, Raymond S. Adamson, Gene Deszca, and Thomas F. Cawsey, "Self-Monitoring and Leadership Emergence," *Small Group Behavior* 19 (1988): 312–24.

14. Ellis and Cronshaw, "Self-Monitoring and Leader Emergence," 123.

15. Roderick P. Hart, Robert E. Carlson, and William F. Eadie, "Attitudes toward Communication and the Assessment of Rhetorical Sensitivity," *Communication Monographs* 47 (1980): 2–22.

16. Dennis S. Gouran, "Inferential Errors, Interaction, and Group Decision-Making," in *Communication and Group Decision-Making,* eds. Randy Y. Hirokawa and Marshall Scott Poole (Beverly Hills, CA: Sage, 1986): 93–111.

17. Linda L. Putnam, "Preference for Procedural Order in Task-Oriented Small Groups," *Communication Monographs* 46 (1979): 193–218.

18. Randy Y. Hirokawa, Richard Ice, and Jeanmarie Cook, "Preference for Procedural Order, Discussion Structure, and Group Decision Performance," *Communication Quarterly* 36 (1988): 217–26.

19. Charles Pavitt, "Describing Know-How about Group Discussion Procedure: Must the Representation be Recursive?" *Communication Studies* 43 (Fall 1992): 150–70.

20. Synthesized from the following sources: Isabel Briggs Myers, *Introduction to Type: A Description of the Myers-Briggs Type Indicator* (Palo Alto, CA: Consulting Psychologists Press, 1987); Otto Kroeger and Janet Thuesen, *Type Talk: The 16 Personality Types That Determine How We Live, Love, and Work* (New York: Dell, 1988); Otto Kroeger with Janet A. Thuesen, *Type Talk at Work: How the 16 Personality Types Determine Your Success on the Job* (New York: Dell, 1992); and Paul D. Tieger and Barbara Barron-Tieger, *Nurture and Nature: Understand Your Child's Personality Type—And Become a Better Parent* (Boston: Little, Brown, 1977): 5–62.

21. Ibid.

22. William A. Haythorn, Arthur Couch, D. Haefner, P. Langham, and L. F. Carter, "The Behavior of Authoritarian and Equalitative Personalities in Groups," *Human Relations* 3 (1956): 54–74; Stanley Milgram, "Some Conditions of Obedience and Disobedience to Authority," *Human Relations* 9 (1965): 57–76.

23. James C. McCroskey and Virginia P. Richmond, "Communication Apprehension and Small Group Communication," in *Small Group Communication: A Reader,* 5th ed., eds. Robert S. Cathcart and Larry A. Samovar (Dubuque, IA: Wm. C. Brown, 1988): 405–19.

24. K. W. Hawkins and R. A. Stewart, "Effects of Communication Apprehension on Perceptions of Leadership and Intragroup Attraction in Small Task-Oriented Groups," *Southern Communication Journal* 57 (1991): 1–10.

25. Rebecca B. Rubin and F. F. Jordan, "Effects of Instruction on Communication Apprehension and Communication Competence," *Communication Education* 46 (1997): 104–14.

26. Dominic A. Infante and Charles J. Wigley III, "Verbal Aggressiveness: An Interpersonal Model and Measure," *Communication Monographs* 53 (1986): 61–67.

27. Milton Rokeach, *The Open and Closed Mind* (New York: Basic Books, 1960).

28. Gordon Allport, *The Nature of Prejudice* (Garden City, NY: Doubleday, 1958): 9.

29. Dale G. Leathers, "Belief-Disbelief Systems: The Communicative Vacuum of the Radical Right," in *Explorations in Rhetorical Criticism,* eds. C. J. Stewart, D. J. Ochs, and G. P. Mohrman (University Park, PA: The Pennsylvania State University Press, 1973): 127–31.

From Individuals to Group: Norms and Roles

7

Central Message

When individuals collaborating on an interdependent goal begin to interact, their communication shapes them into a group with its own unique culture. The norms and roles that are developed are the building blocks of that culture.

Study Objectives

As a result of studying Chapter 7 you should be able to:

1. Describe the structuration process whereby member communication creates and maintains the group.
2. Explain the sources, characteristics, and remedies for both primary and secondary interpersonal tensions among group members.
3. Describe the two major phases through which most small groups pass and the kinds of group behavior prevalent during each.
4. Explain how group rules and norms develop; be able to recognize, state, and describe their effect on the group.
5. Explain the relationship between member behaviors, the functions of those behaviors, and the development of roles in a group.
6. Describe task, maintenance, and self-centered behavioral functions.

Key Terms

Behavior
Behavioral
 function
Group culture
Maintenance
 functions
Norm
Phases
 Formation
 phase

Production
 phase
Primary tension
Role
Rules
Secondary tension
Self-centered
 functions
Structuration
Task functions

Six medical school faculty members, three psychiatrists with M.D.s, a psychologist, and two social workers, were selected by their deans to develop an instructional program to teach new methods for identifying psychological disorders.[1] All six members were outstanding teachers and competent in their respective areas. They were given the freedom to develop any program they wished as long as it could be funded by outside grants.

During their first meeting, the members decided to base all group decisions on sound reasoning. Julian was selected leader, perhaps because of his "take charge" nature. The members insisted that he was expected to encourage input by all members and equalize member influence. Julian made strong efforts to meet their expectations because he strongly believed that their best decisions would be those based on input from all members. He even went so far as to consult books on small group communication for ideas on how best to equalize participation and influence.

The group ran into problems, however, over time. First, group members, strongly entrenched in the medical culture, allowed the M.D.s higher clout. As a result, those without medical degrees found their comments lacked influence. They talked less and less, did not push for their ideas, and after meetings would complain to each other. Second, the group was under pressure to continue to seek funding or their project would end. This pressure led to Julian's increased influence because his contacts enabled him to secure funds for two years.

Soon the group formed into a small clique with Julian as its authoritarian leader. His take-charge manner resulted in his talking more than any other member. When he rephrased other's remarks, he did so in a way that mirrored his own ideas. Those without M.D.s came to rely on his interpretations and lost influence in the group. Tension rose, conflicts were not dealt with in a constructive manner, and meetings were tense. Despite all their best intentions, Julian found himself the leader of an autocratic clique. How did their initial democratic spirit get away from them? We will look for answers in this chapter and the one that follows.

We have described verbal and nonverbal communication in a small group as the most important throughput variable by which a group's work is accomplished. In this chapter, we begin our focus on how communication helps a group develop from a collection of individuals into a team; later chapters will extend this discussion. The system perspective serves as our framework. Small group systems are created through the communication behavior of members, producing outcomes like cohesiveness, a status hierarchy, and decisions. Likewise, small groups can change themselves by revising their interaction and, as we saw with our medical group, can go astray from their original intentions. Note that these group characteristics can be discussed as *both* throughput and output variables because the development of group processes (throughput) is also one of the accomplishments (outputs) of small group interaction. The "pecking order" of the medical group emerged out of their interaction (as output) and simultaneously served to guide and give sense to their discussion (as throughput). Rather than focus on individual characteristics per se, as in Chapter 6, we look at the impact of member behavior on system-level variables as a whole.

DEVELOPMENT OF GROUP CULTURE

We discussed *culture* in Chapter 5 as a group of individuals which can be identified by its shared patterns of values, beliefs, symbols, language, rules, and so forth. We discussed different ethnicities, international groupings, and race and gender as culture. In this chapter we see that small groups develop unique cultures, just as do societies and other large groupings. So when we talk about culture and small groups, we mean three things: members bring their own cultural experiences into the group as input variables, each group has its own unique small group culture (output), and the members' communicative processes create and maintain the group's culture (throughput and output).

Group culture is the pattern of values, beliefs, norms, and behaviors that are shared by group members and that shape a group's individual "personality" (sometimes called *syntality*). Many factors weave together to create a group's culture, including the content and pattern of interactions, the roles members enact and their interrelationships, and the norms and rules guiding the group's interactions. Each group has a unique mix of members, purposes, rules, and behaviors that cannot be duplicated exactly in other groups. For instance, some groups behave informally, with lots of joking and low power distance. Other groups display hostility, aggressive verbal behavior, and divisive conflict. Still others adhere to strict, formal interaction rules with polite, controlled communication. How do these differences come about? We examine some of the processes most important to the development of a group's culture in this and the next chapter. We remind you that a group's culture is never static; rather, it continually evolves, adapting to the changing circumstances of the group. In a sense, a group's culture is always developing, but never completed.

COMMUNICATION AND THE STRUCTURING OF SMALL GROUPS

We have consistently noted the role communication plays in the creation and maintenance of a small group. This is explained by the theory of **structuration,** which refers to how individuals form a small group by exchanging verbal and nonverbal signals that ultimately establish the norms and rules shaping members' behaviors. The theory of structuration, developed by Poole, Siebold, and McPhee, embraces three important assumptions.[2] First, the behavior of group members is constrained by such things as the general rules of the society in which they live, the structures of the particular group in which they find themselves, and the behavior of the other members. For example, the rules of corporate America frown on executives settling their differences with a fist fight. Members of a group that has developed a formal, polite atmosphere would be embarrassed by a member who slaps another on the back and says, "Hey, babe, how's your sex life?" The other members would disapprove of the offending member's behavior, and if the behavior continued, might try to remove that person from the group. The medical group in our opening story was constrained by the presence of the M.D.s and the need to secure external funding.

The second important assumption is that people have free will—they can choose to follow the rules of the group or not. Although there may be unpleasant consequences for a member who doesn't follow a group's rules, there is no *law,* like the law of gravity, that forces conformity. In our medical group, despite all attempts by Julian and members' original wishes, a majority of them did not follow the "spirit" of democracy.

The third important assumption of structuration is that group creation is a process; the group not only creates itself initially but continuously *re-creates* itself, changing in incremental ways, always in a state of *becoming,* with communication as the instrument for this creation and constant re-creation. This incrementalism is often the reason groups like our medical group can find themselves "off track" long after the initial changes started happening; the patterns sneak up on you and become entrenched.

The theory of structuration is quite complex. However, the main point is this: the *communication among members* is what creates group rules in the first place, and once rules and structures are in place, communication is what keeps them there, or changes them, as the case may be. Suppose a company appoints a group of several managers to develop long-range strategy. Two members, Mauricio and Cary, have worked together before and naturally call each other by first names. Mauricio introduces Cary to Carol, an acquaintance of hers, by his first name, and pretty soon the rest of the group members are calling each other by first name instead of Mr., Ms., or Dr. As they wait for the meeting to begin, members talk about mutual interests such as sports and jazz music, and several find common outside interests with other members. Norms of informality and friendliness have begun to develop among these members, and these norms will begin to affect other aspects of the communication among members, such as how they deal with disagreement. For instance, assume that at a later group meeting, Cary says, in a formal and accusing tone of voice, "I respectfully disagree with the proposal offered by my esteemed colleague Ms. Hernandez," and continues to make a formal speech relating his objections. The rest of the members will probably say something like: "When did we get so formal, Cary? What's the big deal here? Why are you sounding like a prosecutor?" What they are saying, in another way, is: "We've developed norms of informality and friendliness, which you are violating. Your behavior seems inappropriate to us." Of course, Cary has free choice about his behavior. He can choose to continue in his formal, prosecutorial way, but if he does, that may either change the informality and friendliness norms to ones more formal and adversarial, or it may cause the other members to ignore Cary and ostracize him from the group.

CONSIDER THIS

You are no doubt currently a member of at least one group. Think about one way your group does something. For instance, how do you work, play, greet each other, etc.? Now consider how your group created that practice and currently maintains it.

A variety of internal and external factors influences the types of structures groups create, including member characteristics and preferences, the nature of the group's task, and such structural dynamics as the interplay between important (but perhaps conflicting) values. The members of the medical group valued democratic principles, but the pressure to get the job done and the deference given to a medical degree led members to encourage controlling leadership.[3] This contradiction caused tension within the group and an eventual split. Sunwolf and Seibold found several conflicting values in their study of jury decision making resulting from numerous contradictions between internal and external factors.[4] For instance, although the jury was told to use judicial resources should any confusion occur, the jury developed the norm that no jury member could send a note outside the group asking for help before first securing permission from the group. In addition, several members of the jury struggled with reporting inappropriate behavior to the court. The expectations that the law should be followed clashed with the social rule of not telling on your friends. Sunwolf and Siebold concluded: "One of the inherent contradictions of group life in jury deliberations occurs in situations in which the attempt to obey the directive to maintain their group's existence simultaneously requires them to collaborate in a reluctant cover-up of member misconduct."[5] These examples also illustrate the point we made in Chapter 2 regarding the fluid nature of boundaries between groups and their multiple environments. Often these boundaries are constructed in group interaction and simultaneously serve to connect the group to *and* separate it from its environment.

We agree with Poole that structuration offers advantages over other social scientific theories. Structuration captures the complexity of human behavior by recognizing that, although human beings are free agents, certain limitations and constraints keep their behaviors in small group systems within certain boundaries while recognizing that change is possible. It also explains why unintended consequences can occur in group interaction. We especially like the communicative focus of structuration theory, for it reminds us to look at the *communicative behavior* of members to learn about a group. We now turn to a discussion of how this communication behavior affects tension in the group and serves to develop the group's norms and roles.

TENSION AMONG MEMBERS

Somehow, what starts as a collection of individuals with an interdependent purpose must become a group that functions as a unit to complete that purpose. One of the first issues a group must address is how it will manage the interpersonal tensions that are a normal part of its development. Just as individuals experience varying levels of tension, so do entire groups. In fact, a certain amount of tension is desirable. Can you imagine taking an exam when you felt so relaxed you could barely motivate yourself to read the questions? An optimum amount of tension can help us perform at peak capacity, but too much or too little impairs our ability to function well. The same is true of groups, which must learn to manage tensions productively for the ultimate good of the group.

Primary Tension

Bormann first dichotomized group tension into two categories, primary and secondary. **Primary tension** results from primary sources, or the interpersonal relationships among members, whereas secondary tension is directly task related. Bormann describes primary tension as being ". . . the social unease and stiffness that accompanies getting acquainted."[6] He describes the symptoms of primary tension as extreme politeness, apparent boredom, yawning and sighing, a lot of long pauses, and tentative statements uttered in soft tones. At this point, members are asking themselves, "Will they like me? Will this be a group I enjoy working with?" The politeness and apparent boredom are only a facade covering the tensions we all feel when we are with people we don't know well. However, if this primary tension is not overcome, group members will get stuck in a mode of overpoliteness, formality, and hesitancy to disagree, which will hurt their ability to think critically.

A second form of primary tension, also resulting from relationships among members, can arise abruptly when there is self-centered competition for power and status within the group. Although the issue may appear to be a matter of who will perform certain jobs for the group, the real issue is the desire and struggle for personal power, which underlies much human behavior. Thus, what appears to be secondary tension is really primary tension disguised as disagreement over ideas.

CONSIDER THIS

How did all the group members, including Julian and the non-M.D.s, contribute to the emergence of their "pecking order" which turned out to be a source of this form of primary tension?

Several things can be done to reduce a group's primary tension. For example, taking time to get acquainted is worthwhile. Members can talk about themselves, their backgrounds, interests, and hobbies, experiences relevant to the group's purpose, feelings about being in the group, and so on. In fact, this movement toward intimacy via self-disclosure is a characteristic of cohesive groups.[7] It may pay to have a social hour or party, with no formal agenda. Joking, laughing together, and finding common interests can help diminish primary tensions. Even members of a group that will meet only once can profitably spend a few minutes introducing themselves so they can orient themselves to each other as parts of a group. Indeed, members who have worked together in many meetings often spend the first few moments of their meeting chitchatting and confirming their relationships before getting down to work.

Primary tensions over power are more difficult to resolve. Rules and procedures for making decisions and assigning work can help prevent or alleviate these tensions. Other times, direct confrontation may be needed. We develop these ideas in several subsequent chapters.

Secondary tension is work-related tension resulting from the differences of opinion among members as they seek to accomplish their task. It is inevitable because members perceive problems differently, disagree about goals and means for achieving them, and criteria by which to evaluate ideas. Secondary tensions are a direct result of the need to make decisions *as a group*. Sometimes these tensions become uncomfortably high.

Secondary Tension

Secondary tension looks and sounds different from primary tension. Voices become loud and strained. There may be long pauses followed by two or more members trying to talk at once. Members twist and fidget in their seats, bang fists on the table, wave their arms, interrupt each other, and may even get up and pace around the room. They may try to shout each other down, call each other names, or aggressively question each other's intelligence or motives. While a couple of members verbally attack each other, the rest of the group may sit stiffly and awkwardly, not knowing what to do.

Although it may seem easier to ignore secondary tensions because dealing with them can be uncomfortable or even painful, groups that deal with these tensions directly will experience several advantages. First, attempts to duck the tension-producing issue don't work. As Bormann says, "The problem . . . if ignored or dodged will continue to . . . impede their progress. Facing up to secondary tensions realistically is the best way to release them."[8] If secondary tension is not managed, it will continue to disrupt the group. Second, groups that find integrative ways to manage their secondary tension experience greater cohesiveness as a result of having worked through the tension. The members know they can disagree with each other yet still experience a sense of trust and commitment. Finally, the group may find that the tensions have caused the members to look more carefully at task-related issues, which usually produces a better final product.

What can group members do to manage secondary tension? Bales found that three categories of behaviors reduced tension among members: agreeing, showing solidarity, and tension release.[9] Showing agreement is socially rewarding to the person agreed with, as if to say to that person, "I value you and your opinion." The more often people are agreed with openly, the more they relax and communicate positively with each other, and the less defensive they become.

A member can show solidarity by indicating commitment to the group. Using *we* to refer to the group, speaking well of other members, offering to help, expressing confidence in the group, and talking about the importance of the group and its task are all ways to show solidarity and encourage members to move away from self-centeredness and antagonism.

Humor, too, can help release secondary tension, so long as the humor does not ridicule another member or is used to ignore the disagreement. Enjoying a joke together makes it easier to listen better and find agreement. In *Pattern for Industrial Peace,* Whyte described how a union staff representative did this repeatedly by using fishing photos whenever discussion among representatives of the steel company and union got overheated with secondary tension.[10]

PHASES IN THE DEVELOPMENT OF SMALL GROUPS

Just as the occurrence of primary and secondary tension is predictable and normal in groups, other developments are relatively predictable, too. The more you know about these typical group processes, the more you will be able to identify what is usual, what is helpful, and what should be changed for the group to function more effectively. A number of researchers have studied how groups develop and change over time; they have found that groups progress through identifiable **phases.** This is an evolutionary process that happens gradually, without clear demarcations to separate the phases.[11] Each phase can be identified by the types of interactions and behaviors the members exhibit.

Bales was one of the first researchers to investigate a group's progression through predictable phases.[12] He identified two concerns with which a group must deal. First, the group must develop the kinds of interpersonal relationships that provide stability and harmony, allowing the group to function cooperatively. These are the *socioemotional concerns.* Second, the *task concerns* involve the group's attention to its job, to completion of whatever is its task. Groups tend to cycle between these two concerns, focusing first on one, then the other. Early in the group's **formation phase,** the socioemotional dimension predominates as members attempt to work out the kinds of relationships they will have with each other. Note the connection here to primary tension. Initial reduction of primary tension, by working through interpersonal concerns, allows a group eventually to become maximally efficient in completing its task. Groups that resolve their early socioemotional issues become increasingly able to take relationships among group members for granted, and thus can shift their attention and energy to the task. As socioemotional remarks and behaviors in a group decrease, task-related remarks and behaviors increase and eventually surpass them. In the **production phase** of a group's life cycle, when the group has reached socioemotional maturity, task behaviors will predominate. The group will achieve its peak in task efficiency. This progression can be seen over the life of an effective group, as well as over the course of a single group meeting.

Balancing task and socioemotional concerns. **FIGURE 7.1**

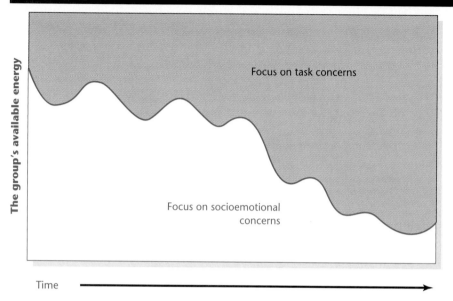

The group's available energy

Focus on task concerns

Focus on socioemotional concerns

Time

It is important to recognize that groups must handle process (formation) and production (task) concerns *simultaneously*. At the very first meeting, a group must begin the process of forming into a functioning unit by establishing the interpersonal relationships, leadership structures, and status hierarchies that enable it to work efficiently—the formation function. The group *also* must deal with its task: what its charge is, how the task should be approached, who is to do what, and so forth. Thus, the group must contend with both kinds of functions throughout its life span. Although the interpersonal concerns predominate at first, task concerns are still present. If everything proceeds smoothly for the group, gradually more and more of its time can be spent directly on task concerns and less on interpersonal concerns as it moves to its production stage. However, at no point can group members disregard socioemotional concerns. Thus, we envision a group following essentially two broad developmental stages, a formation phase where process norms unfold and a production phase where group members focus on the task, as depicted in Figure 7.1. These phases are not distinct. Instead, a group's attention shifts gradually, but never completely, from process to production concerns.

DEVELOPMENT OF GROUP NORMS

When individuals begin to interact as members of a group, the full range of human behaviors is potentially available to them. Perhaps they will listen politely to each other, or maybe they will interrupt and insult one another. Somehow, the members must develop a set of rules and operating procedures to coordinate their individual behaviors into a system. Some **rules** are formalized guidelines for behavior that may be written down. For example, *Robert's Rules of Order, Newly Revised* is used by many organizations as a guide for governing face-to-face interaction.[13] Robert includes an entire section of rules that apply to any committee of an organization using his parliamentary manual.

However, most of the normal operating procedures for a group are developed gradually, with tacit rather than explicit consent of the group members. For instance, if Sam comes late to a meeting and other members make a point of chastising him, Sam will likely arrive on time for subsequent meetings and the group has "decided" on a rule that members should arrive on time. Such an informal rule, or **norm,** is seldom written down; instead, it is ". . . an idea in the minds of the members of a group, an idea that can be put in the form of a statement specifying what the members . . . should do, ought to do, are expected to do, under given circumstances."[14] This section focuses on these informal rules, or norms.

Norms reflect cultural beliefs about what is appropriate or inappropriate behavior, as we discussed in Chapter 5. Although the norms of an individual group may be specific to that group, chances are they will mirror general cultural norms. For instance, if physical violence is prohibited by the general culture, with disagreements handled through discussion, then a group established in the context of this larger culture will also be likely to use discussion instead of physical violence to settle disputes. As Shimanoff stated,

> When group members come together for the first time, they bring with them past experiences and expectations regarding cultural and social rules and rules for specific groups they assume may be similar to this new group. It is out of these experiences and expectations as well as its unique interaction . . . that a particular group formulates its rules.[15]

Norms are not imposed by an authority outside the group but are imposed by members on themselves and each other. They are enforced by various types of peer pressure, ranging from slight frowns to ostracism. It is important for group members, particularly new members, to be aware of these norms because to violate them may mean punishment, loss of influence, and perhaps exclusion from the group.

Norms guide and regulate the behavior of group members. They govern how and to whom members speak, how they dress, what they talk about and when, what language may be used, and so on. The whole process of communication among group members is rule-governed.[16] Rarely do norms specify absolutes; rather, they indicate ranges of acceptable and unacceptable behavior. For instance, a particular group may endorse a prompt starting time for its meetings. However, being four minutes late may be tolerated without comment, but coming 15 minutes late would not.

CONSIDER THIS

Review the story of our medical group. Besides the norm related to rational decision making, what other norms developed in this group?

During the formation stage of a new small group, norms are developed rapidly via the structuration process described earlier, often without members realizing what is occurring. The group's first meeting is particularly critical in establishing that group's norms. At that time, behaviors typical of primary tension in the formation phase—speaking quietly, suppressing disagreement, making tentative and ambiguous statements—can become norms if not challenged. Although members may openly discuss and state rules at their first meeting, norms usually evolve over time and seem to exist below the level of conscious awareness of most members. Often, a norm is brought to a group's awareness only after a member violates it, a new member questions it, or an observer points it out.

General norms direct the behavior of the group as a whole, whereas *role-specific norms* concern individual members with particular roles, such as the designated leader. The medical group developed a general norm related to rational decision making. Role-specific norms for Julian included his rephrasing and redefining of the others' ideas. He also developed the norm of talking more than the others. Notice that these norms are stated as rules, even though they are not imposed on the group by an external authority or parent organization. Examples of each type of norm follow:

General Norms (applicable to every member)	**Role-specific Norms** (applicable to specific members)
Members should sit in the same position at each meeting.	The leader should prepare and distribute an agenda in advance of each meeting.
Members should address each other by first names.	The leader should summarize from time to time, but other members may do so if a summary is needed.
Other members should not disagree with the chair's ideas.	The secretary should distribute minutes of the previous meeting at least three days before the next meeting.
No one may smoke during meetings.	Gulshan may play critical tester of all ideas by asking for evidence.
Members may leave the meeting to get something to drink, but should return to their seats promptly.	Terrell should tell a joke when the climate gets tense during an argument.
Members should arrive on time for meetings.	Julian should restate other members' remarks in his own words.

If norms generally exist below the level of conscious awareness, how can group members discover what their norms are? Norms can be inferred and confirmed by observation. New members, especially, should be sensitive to the group's norms so they do not inadvertently violate important ones. There are two types of behavior to watch for especially:

1. **Behaviors that occur repeatedly and with regularity, by one or all members.**

   Repetitions of a behavior are evidence that a norm exists regulating it. Thus, group members should look for answers to questions such as: "Who talks to whom?" "How do members speak?" "What kind of language do they use?" "What do they talk about and for how long?" "Where do they sit?" "When do they move about and for what reasons?" and "How is the group brought to order?"

2. **Punishment of a member for infraction of a rule.**

   The strongest evidence of a norm is a negative reaction or punishment directed at a member who violates it. Weaker support for the existence of a norm is provided when the violators correct themselves and the other members visibly approve the correction. Observers looking for norms should pay attention to behaviors that elicit negative reactions, ranging from a bit of head shaking, to surreptitious and disapproving glances passing between members, to forceful negative comments or even threats. Notice behaviors to which members react with gestures of rejection, such as frowns, head shaking, and tongue clucking. What acts do members studiously ignore, as if out of embarrassment? Listen for negative comments: "It's about time you got here," "Let's stick to issues and not go blaming each other," and "Maybe you'll have your report ready for our next meeting." Note, particularly, those actions that elicit negative responses from more than one person, a sure bet that a norm important to the group has been infringed.

Changing a Norm

Norms have a tremendous impact on the processes and outcomes of the group. Group members should not only be aware of them but act to change them if they appear to be detrimental. For instance, a norm implying that low-status members may not disagree with high-status members interferes with the critical evaluation of ideas as we saw in our medical group. Or, groups that permit members to criticize ideas as soon as they have been proposed may find that members are reluctant to make innovative suggestions, so that creativity is stifled. In such cases, individuals should not "sit back and take it" but work to change the rules. Small persistent changes can be effective because they are not as noticeable to those who may resist the change.[17] A social worker in our medical group was successful in temporarily moving the group into a more democratic climate. She decided to refuse Julian's attempts to rephrase her comments, which in turn helped him be more aware of his pattern of changing other's ideas to reflect his own. The group managed this new pattern for awhile but when a crisis arose, members, including Julian, fell back into old ways. Had the social worker persisted in her attempts, she might have been successful in changing the autocratic norm. As long as the resources and rules upholding the norm persist, then that norm of discussion will continue.

Using a full frontal assault, particularly one that may be perceived as a personal attack, will not be successful either and will make the person demanding the change seem like a deviant. Instead, following a few simple guidelines can help you change norms without unnecessary trauma. First, the member desiring the change must establish an identity as a loyal member of the group and speak not as an outsider but as a member committed to the group's well-being. Second, the member should carefully observe the offending behavior and keep a record of how often it occurs and what the consequences are to the group. Armed with specific information and obvious concern for the good of the group, the member is ready for the next step, constructive confrontation.

The member should pick an appropriate time, indicate his or her concern with something that appears to be causing trouble for the group, state the specifics calmly and clearly, then ask whether other members share the concern. For instance, rather than saying, "We never get started on time and I'm sick and tired of it," the member should say instead: "For the past four meetings, we have started our work anywhere from 15 minutes to half an hour late. We seem to have a rule that we don't have to observe our announced starting time, which makes our meetings run late. Two of us have another committee meeting directly following this one, and for each of these late meetings we have missed the conclusion of our business. This means that we need to spend additional time at the next meeting bringing everyone up to date. Does anyone else share my concern?" If the norm was subconscious, it now has been brought to the attention of the group and becomes part of the surface agenda of the group where it can be discussed openly. If the member is wrong about the norm, the group can correct the perception without disparaging the concern. However, if the individual is right, the group will appreciate the concern and likely decide to change the norm. Even if the other members agree to a new norm, they may still need gentle reminders until the new behavior becomes habituated, part of "our way of doing things."

An example will clarify how one or more members can invoke change in a group's culture. A study group meeting in a small town library held weekly learning discussions to compare modern Protestant, Catholic, and Jewish theology. The study group had tried to be clear from the beginning that participants were there to come to an understanding of these three religious traditions. However, at times members forgot and attempted to convert one another. Discussion during these times would erupt into an uproar with several people talking or shouting at once. One particular evening one of us was present tape recording the group for a research project. Just after the meeting had formally adjourned, a member said to the study group, "You know, I'm really bothered by our tendency to all talk at once sometimes, and not listen to each other." He then turned to your author, Jack, and said,

"Jack, could some of us hear the recording you just made to see how we must sound to you?" When they heard themselves, there were groans: "Did we really sound as bad as that?" Members left the meeting in clusters of two and three, talking about what they had just realized. At the next meeting, the game of "uproar" again exploded, but this time a member said, "Remember the tape recording!" and order was resumed. There was no more interrupting for nearly an hour, and when it did occur, it lasted only several seconds before participants sheepishly shut up and offered apologies. The group had developed a new norm. Thus, although norms are usually developed generally without conscious intent, they are not fixed in stone and can be changed, with persistence, as the group's situation warrants. But always keep in mind a valuable lesson from structuration theory—any change in group interaction may have unforseen consequences.

DEVELOPMENT OF ROLE STRUCTURE

When they hear the term **role,** most people think of parts in a play or movie. Play scripts contain interlocking roles, each of which is a different character in the cast. Just as an actor plays different roles in different scripts, like Demi Moore as a Navy lawyer in *A Few Good Men,* a Puritan woman in *The Scarlet Letter,* and a mother-turned-stripper in *Striptease,* individuals enact many diverse roles in the numerous groups to which they belong. In one group the role might be *daughter* or *son,* in another *lead carpenter,* and in yet another *church treasurer.* A given individual might be a leader in one group and play a supporting role in another. The role a person enacts in any particular group is a function of that person's personality, abilities, and communication skills, the talents of the other members, and the needs of the group as a whole.

A particular role embraces a set of behaviors that perform some function for the group. There is a difference between a *behavior* and a *behavioral function.* At the individual level, every verbal or nonverbal act by a group member is a **behavior,** but at the group level, the function that behavior performs in the group system is called its **behavioral function.** For example, the joke Yukiko tells in a group is the *behavior.* However, Yukiko's joke can serve a variety of *functions,* depending on how she tells it, what else is happening in the group at the time, and so forth. Perhaps her joke relieves tension during an argument (a positive behavioral function), but perhaps it gets the group off track or makes fun of another member (negative behavioral functions). A behavioral function, then, is the effect of member behavior on the social structure (throughput) and task accomplishment (output) of the group. A member's role represents the cluster of behaviors performed by that member and the overall functions those behaviors perform for the group, just as an actor's role consists of all the lines and actions of the character in the play. Some functions are shared widely among group members (such as providing information or providing opinions), while others may become the exclusive domain of one member (such as keeping group records or joking to relieve tension).

Most small groups have certain *formal* roles, usually appointed or elected positions. A *chair* has the responsibility for calling meetings, planning agendas, and coordinating the work of the other members. A *secretary* is responsible for taking notes and distributing minutes of meetings. In these cases, the duties associated with a particular role are specified in advance, sometimes in writing. However, in most small groups members create and modify their own *informal* roles as the group progresses. Informal roles, also called *behavioral roles,* reflect the personalities, behaviors, and habits of the members in a particular group; they are not specified in advance but develop through the interaction among members.

Role Emergence

The informal role a particular individual plays in a small group is worked out in concert with the other members and is determined largely by the relative performance skills of the rest of the group members. This is accomplished primarily through trial and error. For example, Ty-isha may have a clear idea of how the group can accomplish its tasks; she will make attempts to structure the group's work: "I suggest we first make a list of all the things we need to do to finish our project." If no one else competes to supply that structuring function, and if the other members see that structuring behavior as helpful to the group, they will reinforce and reward Ty-isha's statements and actions: "Okay, Ty-isha that sounds like a good idea." This reinforcement, in turn, is likely to elicit more of those structuring behaviors from Ty-isha. On the other hand, if several members are also competent to structure the group's work, the group members collectively will reinforce the actions of the member they perceive to be the most skilled in this performance area. If Ty-isha is not reinforced as the group's "structurer," she will search for some other way to be valuable to, and valued by, the group. For instance, she may help to clarify the proposals of the other members ("In other words, are you saying that . . . ?") or become the group's critical evaluator ("I think there are two major flaws with that proposal."). *Every member needs a role that makes a meaningful contribution to the group.*

Because an individual's role depends on the particular mix of people in the group, that person's role will vary from group to group.

CONSIDER THIS

Think for a moment of all the groups to which you have belonged. Your role probably changed considerably through time as you changed, as new people were added to or left a group, or as the problem facing the group changed. Do you see any patterns to your role behavior?

A major principle of small group theory is this: *The role of each group member is worked out in the interaction between the member and the rest of the group* and continues to evolve as the group evolves. Thus, a well-organized person may end up leading one group and playing a supporting role in another, depending on the characteristics and competencies of all members relative to one another.

**Classifying
Group Roles**

Group researchers have developed a variety of systems for classifying group roles. Hare, in a 1994 historical review of research about group roles, recommends that group researchers begin to describe roles in terms that would be understood by the group members themselves.[18] One such system is the functional role classification system described by Benne and Sheats.[19] These researchers classified members' roles on the basis of the functions those roles performed for the group. They defined three main categories of behavior: task, maintenance (socioemotional), and individual. Task behaviors directly affect the group's task. Maintenance or socioemotional behaviors affect the relationships among members, thus indirectly affecting the task. Individual behaviors are self-centered behaviors that help neither the task nor the relationships, but function to satisfy the individual at the expense of the group.

Although Benne and Sheats's system was first described many years ago, recent research verifies its current usefulness as a classification system. Mudrack and Farrell, noting that there has been little direct empirical investigation into this system, conducted a study to determine how well this three-category system describes typical member behaviors from the perspective of the members themselves.[20] They found that the task, maintenance, and individual distinctions Benne and Sheats described hold up. Although their study suggested a five-category model as being most precise, the addition of the two factors (one was a task subcategory, the other a maintenance subcategory) actually did not measurably improve the usefulness of the model. Mudrack and Farrell concluded that the three-category system—task, maintenance, and individual—is fairly accurate.

To some extent, all classification systems oversimplify the situation by suggesting that a remark or nonverbal behavior performs only one function in a group; they are fluid and affect both dimensions. For example, assume Teresa says to Mona and Melvin, "I think you guys are bypassing each other, and you should listen more carefully." That statement, even though it focuses on the ways members are relating to each other (a socioemotional concern), also has a bearing on the task accomplishment of the group, especially if Melvin and Mona start paying better attention to each other. Moreover, Teresa's statement implies that she has the right to intervene with expert information about the group's process, which says something about her relationship to the group. Thus, although many researchers consider actions to be *either* task *or* relationship oriented, it is more accurate to say that an act may have considerable impact on *both* dimensions.[21] In fact, Mudrack and Farrell found that the gatekeeper role, a maintenance role we describe later, and the information-seeker role, a task role, straddled both categories.[22] Figure 7.2 depicts these two major dimensions and illustrates how individual acts can affect each dimension to a greater or lesser degree.

Task and social/relational impact of member behaviors.

FIGURE 7.2

• Specific act or behavior

Most researchers agree that both task and socioemotional needs must be met for a group to be effective. What follows is a list of behavioral functions, based on Benne and Sheats's classification, that groups need to achieve their goals. Figure 7.3 illustrates the roles three group members might enact using various combinations of the following behaviors.

Task functions affect primarily the task output of the group. Some of the most helpful, with statements that exemplify those functions, are:

Task Functions

Initiating and orienting: proposing goals, plans of action, or activities; prodding the group to greater activity; defining position of group in relation to external structure or goal. ("Let's assign ourselves tasks to finish before the next meeting.")

Information giving: offering facts and information, evidence, or personal experience relevant to the group's task. ("Last year, the library spent $12,000 replacing lost materials.")

Information seeking: asking others for facts and information, evidence, or relevant personal experience. ("Juan, how many campus burglaries were reported last year?")

Opinion giving: stating beliefs, values, interpretations, judgments; drawing conclusions from evidence. ("I don't think theft of materials is the worst problem facing the library.")

Clarifying: making ambiguous statements clearer; interpreting issues. ("So does 'excellent' to you mean that the report should be perfect grammatically?")

FIGURE 7.3   Roles of three members of a small group.

IDEA LEADER

DEVIL'S ADVOCATE

SOCIOEMOTIONAL LEADER

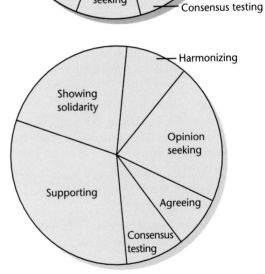

Elaborating: developing an idea previously expressed by giving examples, illustrations, and explanations. ("Another thing that Toby's proposal would let us do is . . .")

Evaluating: expressing judgments about the relative worth of information or ideas; proposing or applying criteria. ("Here are three problems I see with that idea.")

Summarizing: reviewing what has been said previously; reminding group of a number of items previously mentioned or discussed. ("So, by next week, Angie will have the research finished and Carl will have the charts done on the computer.")

Coordinating: organizing the group's work; promoting teamwork and cooperation. ("If Meagan interviews the mayor by Monday, then Joyce and I can prepare a response by Tuesday's meeting.")

Consensus testing: asking if the group has reached a decision acceptable to all; suggesting that agreement may have been reached. ("We seem to be agreed that we'll accept the counteroffer.")

Recording: keeping group records, preparing reports and minutes; serving as group secretary and memory. ("I think we decided that two weeks ago. Let me look it up in the minutes to be sure.")

Suggesting procedure: suggesting an agenda of issues, or special technique; proposing some procedure or sequence to follow. ("Why don't we try brainstorming to help us come up with something new and different!")

Maintenance functions influence primarily the interpersonal relationships of members. We think the following seven functions, with sample statements, are especially vital to task groups:

Maintenance (Relationship-Oriented) Functions

Establishing norms: suggesting rules of behavior for members; challenging unproductive ways of behaving as a member; giving negative response when another violates a rule or norm. ("I think it's unproductive to call each other names. Let's stick to the issues.")

Gatekeeping: helping some member get the floor; suggesting or controlling speaking order; asking if someone has a different opinion. ("Ruben, you look like you want to make a comment. Do you want to say something about the proposal?")

Supporting: agreeing or otherwise expressing support for another's belief or proposal; following the lead of another member. ("I think Joi's right; we should examine this more closely.")

Harmonizing: reducing secondary tension by reconciling disagreement; suggesting a compromise or new alternative acceptable to all; conciliating or placating an angry member. ("Jared and Sally, I think there are areas where you are in agreement, and I would like to suggest a compromise that might work for you both.")

Tension-relieving: making strangers feel at ease; reducing status differences; encouraging informality; joking and otherwise relieving tension; stressing common interests and experiences. ("We're getting tired and cranky. Let's take a ten-minute break.")

Dramatizing: evoking fantasies about people and places other than the present group and time, including storytelling and fantasizing in a vivid way; testing a tentative value or norm through fantasy or story. ("That reminds me of a story about last year's committee . . .")

Showing solidarity: indicating positive feeling toward other group members; reinforcing a sense of group unity and cohesiveness. ("Wow, we've done a great job on this!" or "We're all in this together!")

While the preceding functions are necessary to effective small group functioning, there is another category of functions detrimental to the group. They represent an individual member's hidden agenda.

Self-Centered Functions

Self-centered functions refer to those member behaviors that serve the performers' unmet needs at the expense of the group. We think the following three are especially harmful:

Withdrawing: avoiding important differences; refusing to cope with conflicts; refusing to take a stand; covering up feelings; giving no response to the comments of others. ("Do whatever you want, I don't care," or not speaking at all.)

Blocking: preventing progress toward group goals by constantly raising objections, repeatedly bringing up the same topic or issue after the group has considered and rejected it. ("I know we already voted, but I want to discuss it again!") It is *not* blocking to keep raising an issue the group has not really listened to or considered.

Status and recognition seeking: stage-hogging, boasting, and calling attention to one's expertise or experience when this is not necessary to establishing credibility or relevant to the group's task; game playing to elicit sympathy; switching subject to area of personal expertise. ("I think we should do it the way I did it when I won the 'Committee Member of the Year' award.")

This list is by no means exhaustive; it could be expanded considerably with such categories as *special interest pleading, advocating, confessing,* and similar harmful functions. Self-centered functions manipulate and use other members for selfish goals that compete with what the group needs.

Although researchers believe that both task and maintenance roles are essential to effective group functioning, task roles seem overly important to group members themselves, according to Mudrack and Farrell.[23] Members clearly recognize the contributions task roles make to the group effort, but they do not seem to value the contributions of the maintenance roles, nor did they devalue the individualistic roles. Mudrack and Farrell recommend researchers continue to study how members evaluate these categories of roles.

We cannot emphasize enough how important it is for you to understand the types of roles a small group needs and how you, as a group member, can perform appropriate roles for the group. Plas, writing about the importance of participatory management approaches in American industry, says:

> One of the keys to working well within teams is learning how to differentiate roles—process roles as well as task roles. Successful teams—no matter where you find them—are made up of individuals who know how to define roles for themselves and how to work with the roles that other team members have adopted.[24]

SUMMARY

1. A group's culture, including its norms and patterns of behavior, is formed through the process of structuration or how the verbal and nonverbal interaction among members both creates and maintains the group.

2. All groups must find ways to deal with their primary (interpersonal) and secondary (task-related) tensions.

3. Groups develop in stages, typically moving from the formation stage to the production stage, but members always need to deal simultaneously with socioemotional and task concerns, at all stages.

4. While formal rules may exist to govern some of the group's interaction, informal rules (norms) that guide members' behaviors evolve—sometimes unconsciously—with the tacit approval of the members themselves.

5. With their personal behaviors and skills, group members carve out roles in conjunction with other group members.

6. All groups need both task and maintenance functions to be performed, self-oriented roles detract from the group's purpose.

EXERCISES

1. Observe a small group during at least one discussion; take notes on what behaviors you observe and what norms these behaviors imply. Then, using the format that follows, record all the norms you infer from your observations by stating each as a rule of conduct for members. Try to identify at least 15 or 20 norms. Briefly describe the observed behaviors on which each norm is based. Finally, indicate whether you think the norm helped the group increase its output (+), had no effect on output (0), or reduced the group's output (−).

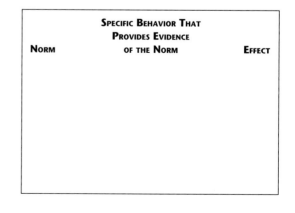

NORM	SPECIFIC BEHAVIOR THAT PROVIDES EVIDENCE OF THE NORM	EFFECT

2. Select a small group to which you have belonged since the beginning and which has met at least several times. Describe the phases in that group's development as best you recall them. What phases did you see? How did you know when the group left one phase and entered another? Did the phases overlap? Do your fellow group members recall the phases as you do, or differently?

3. Using the list of behavioral functions as a guide (pages 155–158), several observers should classify each remark made by each of several members of a group according to the functions. This gives you a tally of how often each person performs each function. How would you describe each member's role? Draw a role profile, similar to Figure 7.3, for each person, and label the informal role each performed.

BIBLIOGRAPHY

Ellis, Donald G., and B. Aubrey Fisher. *Small Group Decision Making: Communication and the Group Process.* 4th ed. New York: McGraw-Hill, 1990, chapter 5.

Feldman, Daniel. "Development and Enforcement of Group Norms." *Academy of Management Review* 9 (1984): 47–53.

Poole, Marshall S. "Group Communication and the Structuring Process." In *Small Group Communication: A Reader.* 7th ed. Robert S. Cathcart, Larry A. Samovar, and Linda D. Henman, eds. Dubuque, IA: Brown & Benchmark Publishers, 1996, 85–95.

NOTES

1. This story is a modified version of a case found in Marshall S. Poole, "Group Communication and the Structuring Process," in *Small Group Communication: A Reader,* 7th ed., eds. Robert S. Cathcart, Larry A. Samovar, and Linda D. Henman (Dubuque, IA: Brown & Benchmark, 1996): 89–91.

2. Marshall S. Poole, David R. Siebold, and Robert D. McPhee, "Group Decision-Making and the Structurational Process," *Quarterly Journal of Speech* 71 (1985): 74–102; Marshall S. Poole, David R. Siebold, and Robert D. McPhee, "A Structurational Approach to Theory-Building in Decision-Making Research," in *Communication and Group Decision Making,* eds. Randy Y. Hirokawa and Marshall S. Poole (Beverly Hills, CA: Sage, 1986): 237–64; and Poole, "Group Communication and the Structuring Process," 85–95.

3. Poole, "Group Communication and the Structuring Process."

4. Sunwolf and David R. Seibold, "Jurors' Intuitive Rules for Deliberation: A Structurational Approach to Communication in Jury Decision Making," *Communication Monographs* 65 (1998): 282–307.

5. Ibid., 303.

6. Ernest G. Bormann, *Discussion and Group Methods: Theory and Practice,* 3d ed. (New York: Harper & Row, 1990): 132–39.

7. David B. Barker, "The Behavioral Analysis of Interpersonal Intimacy in Group Development," *Small Group Research* 22 (February 1991): 76–91.

8. Bormann, *Discussion and Group Methods,* 139.

9. Robert F. Bales, *Interaction Process Analysis* (Reading, MA: Addison-Wesley, 1950).

10. William F. Whyte, *Pattern for Industrial Peace* (New York: Harper, 1951).

11. B. Aubrey Fisher and Randall K. Stutman, "An Assessment of Group Trajectories: Analyzing Developmental Breakpoints," *Communication Quarterly* 35 (Spring 1987): 105–24.

12. Bales, *Interaction Process Analysis.*

13. Henry M. Robert, *Robert's Rules of Order, Newly Revised* (Glenview, IL: Scott, Foresman, 1990): 471–521.

14. George C. Homans, *The Human Group* (New York: Harcourt Brace Jovanovich, 1950): 123.

15. Susan B. Shimanoff, "Coordinating Group Interaction via Communication Rules," in *Small Group Communication: A Reader,* 6th ed., eds. Robert S. Cathcart and Larry A. Samovar (Dubuque, IA: Wm. C. Brown, 1992): 255.

16. Shimanoff, "Coordinating Group Interaction."

17. Poole, "Group Communication and the Structuring Process."

18. A. Paul Hare, "Types of Roles in Small Groups: A Bit of History and a Current Perspective," *Small Group Research* 25 (August 1994): 433–48.

19. Kenneth D. Benne and Paul Sheats, "Functional Roles of Group Members," *Journal of Social Issues* 4 (1948): 41–49.

20. Peter E. Mudrack and Genevieve M. Farrell, "An Examination of Functional Role Behavior and Its Consequences for Individuals in Group Settings," *Small Group Research* 26 (November 1995): 542–71.

21. A. J. Salazar, "An Analysis of the Development and Evolution of Roles in the Small Group," *Small Group Research* 27 (1996): 475–503.

22. Mudrack and Farrell, "An Examination of Functional Role Behavior."

23. Ibid.

24. Jeanne M. Plas, *Person-Centered Leadership: An American Approach to Participatory Management* (Thousand Oaks, CA: Sage, 1996): 88.

From Individuals to Group: Fantasy and Cohesiveness

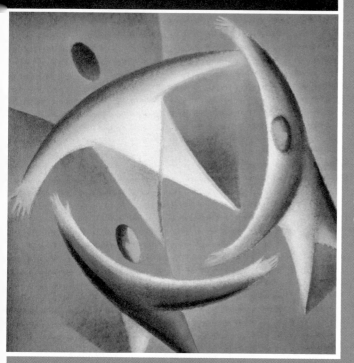

Central Message

In addition to norms and roles, a group's culture also comprises the communication network, status hierarchy, fantasy life, and degree of cohesiveness of the group, all of which are created by communication.

Study Objectives

As a result of studying Chapter 8 you should be able to:
1. Explain how the group's communication pattern creates its communication network and describe several common communication networks, including the effect each has on group outputs.
2. Explain how a status hierarchy forms and how status differences affect group process and output.
3. Describe how fantasy chains contribute to the formation of a small group's culture.
4. Explain cohesiveness and describe eight techniques for enhancing it in a small group.
5. Explain what *groupthink* is and the dangers it poses.
6. Explain what teambuilding involves and illustrate how it can be used to increase group cohesiveness.
7. Explain the theory of SYMLOG and illustrate how the SYMLOG method can provide insights about a small group's culture.

Key Terms

Cohesiveness
Communication
  network
Fantasy
Fantasy chain
Fantasy theme
Groupthink
Idiosyncrasy credit

Status
  Ascribed status
  Earned status
Symbolic
  convergence
SYMLOG
Teambuilding

When the U.S. women's soccer team won the World Cup championship in 1999, star player Mia Hamm said, "Everything I am I owe to this team."[1] By all objective measures, this team represented a stellar example of unity, trust, and teamwork. The cohesiveness and commitment of the members drove them to achieve outstanding individual effort. For example, starter Michelle Akers battled chronic fatigue syndrome and bad knees for a long time, yet she was one of the mainstays of the team. Shannon MacMillan, a starter on the 1995 women's team, came off the bench to score a goal against North Korea. But she didn't use her performance to lobby for a starting position. Instead, she said, "I'm going to do anything I'm asked for this team. My heart and soul is with it." Briana Scurry's save and Brandi Chastain's final kick past the Chinese goalie in the sudden death kick-off won the game for the United States; Chastain said about the kick, "I felt very confident. My team trusted me." According to assistant coach Lauren Gregg, after the 1995 1–0 loss to Norway, the humiliated women vowed never to let that happen again and talked constantly about what they could do, both individually and collectively, to win again. Clearly, this was a cohesive, productive team. What creates the kind of cohesiveness and teamwork that would cause a Mia Hamm, a sports star admired by many, to credit the team rather than herself for her performance?

Tony DiCicco, coach of the women's team, was largely responsible for molding the members, ranging from the quiet, intense Scurry to the gregarious, funny Julie Foudy, into the unified, high-performance team it became. DiCicco, who had previously coached men, took over the women's team in 1994. He learned quickly that the women responded well to challenges but poorly to chastisement, so he decided to employ a positive style. The postgame videos the women were shown did not include replays of their mistakes but included only their "best moves and winning decisions," a strategy DiCicco calls "catching them being good." Most of the women had been together for a long time, some since before the World Cup game in 1991, so they knew each other well. To increase trust, the motivational psychologist DiCicco hired had the team participate in a "trust walk," where blindfolded team members were led down a dangerous cliff by their teammates. She also created an individualized videotape for each player of her best moves and plays, set to music selected by the player herself. Although the tapes were designed to be viewed individually, team members eventually ended up sharing them and watching them together. The women performed exercises such as standing in a line while holding balloons between their bodies and trying to move in symmetry. DiCicco also had the women switch roommates at every stop to prevent cliques from forming. He was pleased when, upon giving the women a night off, they all chose to go out to dinner together.

There's no question that talent, ability, and individual initiative played a part in the team's success, but individual talent doesn't always translate into team performance, as we learned in Chapter 2. The women, with DiCicco's guidance, were able to create a culture of trust, unity, and support so the team could put all their talents together to win.

In this chapter we continue our study of group culture, focusing on how individuals come together to form a successful group with its own unique personality. There are two important points we want to emphasize again. First, all the elements of culture we discuss in this and the previous chapter are part of the throughput processes of the group that make it happen and are developed as members exchange verbal and nonverbal signals with one another, in other words, as members communicate. Second, these processes develop simultaneously. We talk about them one by one simply for clarity and convenience. Now we turn our attention to a group's communication networks, status hierarchy, fantasy life, and cohesiveness.

COMMUNICATION NETWORKS

A group's **communication network** is the pattern of message flow, or who speaks to whom during discussions. If Miguel calls on others one by one, they may develop the habit of not speaking until he calls on them. If Andrea speaks frequently, she may find others looking (literally) to her for some comment on each new issue. Infrequent interactants will find themselves increasingly ignored. A network of who speaks to whom emerges as a function of individual behaviors. The network may change as new problems arise that bring different members' specific knowledge or skills to the forefront, or as socioemotional concerns develop in the group. However, every small group is generally typified by one of the major network types described later.

Each type of network has strengths and weaknesses; none is universally better than any other. Whether a network facilitates problem solving depends on the task. For instance, usually a group of peers develops an all-channel network in which all participants are free to comment on a one-to-one basis with all others and to the group as a whole (see Figure 8.1). A wheel network is one in which all comments are directed toward one central person (usually the designated leader) who alone has authority to speak to the other members. A "Y," or hierarchical network, occurs when an autocratic leader speaks to lieutenants who in turn talk to subordinates. People at the ends of the Y rarely talk to the leader directly. Both the Y and wheel networks are more efficient for simple tasks, but in each, the central person is generally more satisifed with the communication and participation in the group than the more peripheral members. Another danger in these types of networks is that the central member may suffer from information overload and become frustrated or create a bottleneck hampering information flow. In addition, communication in restricted networks may break down into two or more private conversations during a group meeting.

On the other hand, the all-channel network, while slower when tackling complex problems, permits rapid communication among all members without having to get clearance from a central gatekeeping authority. Members are free to say what they want while ideas are still fresh in mind and pertinent. Communication flows freely; at least half the remarks are made to

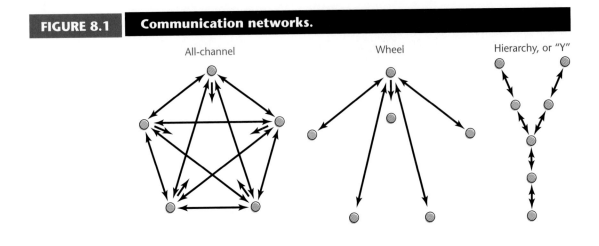

FIGURE 8.1 | **Communication networks.**

All-channel   Wheel   Hierarchy, or "Y"

group members as a whole and all members can hear and tune in to one-to-one or one-to-few comments. The all-channel network pays off in several ways. Morale is highest, and such groups tend to perform better on complex tasks when compared with restricted network groups. Even in all-channel groups, the flow of verbal messages may at times resemble a wheel or a hierarchy, such as during an emergency or under extreme time pressure.

STATUS HIERARCHY

Status refers to the relative importance, prestige, and power of a member in a small group. As roles emerge, each person is placed in a sort of pecking order or on a status ladder, like the one you saw emerge in the medical group in Chapter 7. Several advantages accrue to members of high status. High status is socially rewarding, so such members feel important and worthwhile. Other group members defer to them, grant them a disproportionate share of the group's attention, agree with their proposals, and seek their advice and opinions. People occupying formal, high-status roles (e.g., manager or CEO) may be given such tangible signs of status as large offices, private secretaries, and powers not granted to other members. Moreover, designated leaders, even of work teams and committees, are often given deference, support, and more eye contact.

Effects of status are numerous. High-status members talk more than low-status members and address each other more often than do low-status members, who address their remarks more often to high-status members than to each other.[2] Low-status members also send more positive messages to high-status members than to other low-status members, another reward of high status.[3] Low-status members are interrupted more and their comments are ignored more often than the comments of those with higher status. High-status members tend to talk more to the group as a whole, whereas low-status members express most of their comments to individuals (the classic Y network).

In addition to being granted a number of psychological or material rewards, high-status members are expected to meet certain responsibilities within the group. They are expected to work especially hard to accomplish the group's goals, and to uphold the group's norms. They may lose status by failing to fulfill the group's expectations, although they may be given additional leeway to bend the rules, called **idiosyncrasy credit,** that other members do not receive.[4] This means that, for members who have made an exceptionally valuable contribution to the group, certain rules can be bent. Recent research confirms this view. Estrada et al. found a high correlation between idiosyncrasy credit and leadership—the group members to whom others were willing to award idiosyncrasy credit also were perceived as leaders.[5] When this was the case, the group's performance was enhanced. However, they also found some low-performing groups in which idiosyncrasy credit was not related to group leadership. Estrada et al. speculate that in such groups the members' attention is diverted from the task.

Status within a small group may be *ascribed* or it may be *earned.* At first, before members know each other well and are sure what their respective contributions will be to the group, status is **ascribed** on the basis of each member's position outside the small group. It is based on such things as wealth, education, occupation, personal fame, or position in the group's parent organization. For example, a committee composed of a company CEO, the vice-president of manufacturing, a senior accountant, two employees from the marketing division, and a college student intern in marketing will initially have that order of ascribed status. However, status can also be **earned** or achieved based on a member's individual contributions to the group. The intern who conducts considerable research on behalf of the group and is a key contributor will have higher earned status than the senior accountant who completes no assignments. In some instances, the importance of variables that contribute to ascribed status, such as sex, appears to be shifting, as we noted in Chapter 5.

The most ideal group climate exists when relationships and relative status differences are somewhat flexible so that different members can become more influential as their particular knowledge and skills are pertinent to the issues or problems facing the group at any point in time. Wood found that paying undue attention to ascribed status differences negatively affected a group's ability to accomplish its task.[6] It is important to note that lower status does not mean *of little value.* Lower-status members are not necessarily unhappy in the group; cohesive groups value the contributions of each member, and each member knows it. Only when members say things like, "We could have done just as well without Morgan and Jolene on this committee," can we infer that lower status definitely means "inferior." More typically, everyone in the group might follow the lead of a normally quiet, low-status person who seems to have just the information or ability the group most needs at a given moment. That person might later slip back into a more usual low-profile position, but the contribution will have been noted and appreciated.

CONSIDER THIS

Sometimes a member's culture can affect that member's ascribed status in a group. Cultural variables such as ethnicity, sex, area of the country someone is from, and so forth, influence how others perceive you. What specific cultural variables can affect a member's status in the group and how might they affect other members' perceptions? Does that variable increase or decrease the member's status? What could you do if a cultural characteristic of yours is negatively affecting your group status? What could you do if you perceive that another member's group status is being affected by a particular cultural characteristic?

FANTASY THEMES

We have said before that a group's culture is produced by the interaction among group members. We discussed how roles and norms emerge as elements of a group's culture, but one of the most powerful ways in which group culture is created is through *fantasy*. Technically, **fantasy** refers to "the creative and imaginative shared interpretation of events that fulfill a group's psychological or rhetorical need to make sense of their experience and to anticipate their future."[7] Fantasy, in this sense, does not mean fictitious or unreal. It means that during certain periods of the group's interaction, rather than discussing events happening in the here-and-now of the group, the members are telling stories, relating past events, and sharing anecdotes that have a bearing *at the unconscious level* on the group's process. In other words, group members rarely set out consciously to establish the group's culture. Instead, they just talk. Some of that talk appears to be tangential to the group's real task, but in fact it meets psychological and rhetorical needs of the members.

When a group member says something not directly related to the present task of the group, that member has introduced a fantasy. This happens often during a discussion, with many fantasies going no further. However, sometimes group members pick up on the fantasy introduced by one group member and elaborate on it. Several members join the fantasy by adding their pieces to the story, in a kind of group storytelling. A fantasy that members elaborate on is called a **fantasy chain,** first described by Bales.[8] During a fantasy chain the speed of the interaction typically picks up, voices become louder, and a sense of excitement can be detected. The mood is electric. A fantasy chain may last from as little as half a minute to as much as half an hour. Eventually the chain peters out, often when one member pulls the group back on task. Fantasy chaining is a rhetorical tool for creating shared images of the group and its environment. In Chapter 3 we noted that communication is transactional; during fantasy chaining, group members transact, without preplanned intent, to create meaning for the group. This story-telling activity plays a crucial role in structuration of a group's culture.[9]

Fantasy chains develop in a fairly predictable way.[10] First, some form of ambiguity or uncertainty exists in the group. One member begins the fantasy by introducing a core image that somehow relates to the uncertainty. Other members spread that core image by adding their own elements to the fantasy, creating a group metaphor, rather than just an individual one. Finally, when the fantasy chain has ended, the group members have converged on a particular picture of the group's reality.

Fantasies are *about* something; the content of the fantasy is called the **fantasy theme.** Often, there is an obvious or *manifest* theme to the fantasy chain, and a *latent,* or below-the-surface theme that, when examined, reveals the culture, values, and norms of the group. Often, fantasies have heroes and villains, plot lines, and a well-developed ethical structure that gives moral or psychological guidance to a group. To interpret the latent meaning of a fantasy, Bales suggests looking for a sudden insight rather than trying to analyze the fantasy systematically.

Fantasy is rooted in the theory of **symbolic convergence,** which was articulated and developed by Bormann. Symbolic convergence theory acknowledges that humans are storytelling creatures who create and share meaning through talk.[11] *Convergence* refers to the fact that during interaction the private symbolic worlds of individuals often overlap, or converge. When that occurs, as it must to some extent in a group or there would be no group, meaning is shared; the symbolic, personal communication of two or more individuals constructs a shared reality that bonds the individuals, helps them discover how they feel about certain events, reveals shared values, and guides them to action. In other words, symbolic communication theory "accounts for the creation and maintenance of a group consciousness through shared motives, common emotional activity, and consensual meanings for events."[12] We will now turn from this fairly abstract discussion to several specific examples of how fantasy helps shape a group's reality.

CONSIDER THIS

Fantasy is one way groups create a common vision. In what other ways do you think groups create a common vision? What differences might there be between visions created through fantasy and visions created in other ways?

In the short and simple fantasy chain below, members of a student group are planning publicity for their annual Career Day seminar.[13] Chris asks Kevin what the previous year's group did for publicity:

Discussion	**Commentary**
Chris: Kevin, do you know what they did last time?	Chris asks a direct, task-relevant question.
Kevin: Yeah, somewhere I've got a list here. All they really did was put an ad in the school paper and then sent around this tacky memo to the faculty about a week ahead of time asking them to announce it in classes. It was embarrassing!	Kevin answers Chris, but introduces the fantasy about the "embarrassing" performance of last year's group.
Deirdre: I can't believe that's all they did!	Deirdre, animated, picks up on Kevin's criticism of the previous group.
Lori: It was John's fault—he didn't want to do *anything,* and the group didn't do anything!	Lori adds her part.
Tony: What a bunch of lazy wimps!	Tony contributes.
Chris: We've already done more than they ever did, and we've just gotten started.	Chris contributes, and adds the idea that *this* group has already done better than the last one.
Kevin: I know! We're going to look a lot better than they did!	Kevin adds to Chris's idea.
Lori: Okay, I like trashing those guys as much as you do, but we're really getting off track.	Lori stops the fantasy by getting the group back on track.

In this segment, the group starts out addressing its task directly, but quickly gets off task as members enjoy trashing the previous year's group. Kevin introduces the fantasy, with all group members participating in the fantasy chain until Lori, the group's designated leader, stops the chain and returns the group to its task.

What function has this fantasy served? The manifest theme of the fantasy is, "Last year's group did a rotten job of publicity." Remember, though, that fantasies help create shared meanings for the *present* group. In this sequence, trashing the previous group builds up the performance of the present group by comparison, as hinted at in Chris's comment, "We've already done more than they ever did." By saying what a lousy group the previous year's group was, this group is not so subtly saying, "We're so much better." The group is setting standards of excellence, establishing norms of professionalism missing in the previous group that motivate the members to do better. The following is an example from the church board introduced in Chapter 2. The group has been discussing routine matters when Marina initiates the fantasy:

Discussion	Commentary
Marina: I just noticed that spider plant in the corner. It's doing great! In fact, better than when it was in our living room!	Marina introduces the fantasy about the plant, apparently irrelevant to the group's task.
Sally: It really is healthy. Look at all the spider babies it's produced.	Sally picks up the fantasy and adds to it.
Norm: It seems to be happier here than when we had it at home. That peace lily in the corner looks pretty good, too.	Norm adds to the chain.
Sunni: You should see the plants in the sanctuary. They look so happy and healthy.	Sunni extends the fantasy to include the sanctuary plants as well.
Bill: Maybe we should bring in that half-dead shamrock in our kitchen. Do you think this environment would revive it?	Bill extends; his statement about the beneficial effects of the church environment hints at the meaning of this fantasy for this particular group.
Gary: It's all that tender, loving care!	Gary contributes.
Dick: They do look good, but we've got a lot to cover yet. Can we get back to the agenda?	Dick acknowledges, but brings the group back to its task.

The ostensible, or manifest, theme of this fantasy is how good the plants in the church look. The latent theme, which is not terribly disguised, is members' belief that they have helped create a positive, supportive atmosphere that is healthy for plants and, by extension, other living things (especially people). Thus, this particular fantasy chain reinforces the church board members' desire to do something important, life-giving, and good for the congregation. It also solidifies their commitment to the task.

Fantasies perform several functions for small groups. First, they help the members create the group's unique identity.[14] The two examples just discussed demonstrate that function. The student group helped define itself as an excellent, hard working, professional team by comparing itself favorably with the previous group. Church board members intensified their commitment to the job of establishing a new congregation and patted themselves on the back for creating a nurturing atmosphere.

Second, fantasies help a group deal with threatening or difficult information that members might feel reluctant to address directly. To illustrate, Morocco related the story of the first meeting of a research group whose student members believed their leaders were not providing them with enough direction.[15] One student recalled seeing a film about an experiment in which baby monkeys were deprived of maternal nurturing. The other members, who had seen the movie in school, began to contribute by adding details and developing a plot and dramatic images associated with the movie. The social and sexual development of the monkeys in the movie had been impaired by the lack of parental care, and this image served to symbolize the reality that these group members were *currently* experiencing. In essence, the group said, "The lack of attention and help on the part of the leaders will ultimately harm us."

Third, fantasies help direct a group's actions by subtly endorsing or condemning particular courses of action. For example, Putnam and her associates describe a contract bargaining situation between two committees, one of teachers and the other of administrators.[16] The administrators constructed a fantasy chain about one of the teachers, whose constant head nodding reminded them of a woodpecker or a toy bird bobbing up and down on a cup. Their fantasy theme created a shared image of the teachers as well meaning but inexperienced. Later during the bargaining situation, the teachers appeared to renege on a proposal they had earlier accepted. The administrators could have made a big deal of this by escalating the conflict, but the image of the teachers as inexperienced rather than unscrupulous led them to perceive the teachers' actions as an innocent mistake. This benevolent interpretation by the administrators gave the teachers latitude to err without derailing the bargaining process. The effect was to maintain good feelings all around. The fantasy, in part, inspired this outcome by molding the administrators' perceptions of the teachers' shortcomings.

Finally, fantasies can be entertaining and fun for the group. In the previous example, the administrators' committee kept itself happily entertained by imagining the teacher who nodded constantly as a woodpecker and a whirligig bird. Fantasies help groups exercise their imaginations and creativity. They are powerful shapers of a group's culture.

COHESIVENESS

Cohesiveness refers to the common bonds and sentiments that hold a group together. When a group is high in cohesiveness, the relationships among members are, on the whole, attractive to them; they have a high degree of "stick togetherness" and unity. Highly cohesive groups behave differently from less cohesive groups. They display more characteristics of primary groups than less cohesive groups.[17] They have higher rates of interaction. Members express more positive feelings for each other and report more satisfaction with the group, such as was demonstrated by the women soccer players choosing to go out to dinner together. In addition, cohesive groups exert greater control over member behaviors.[18] High cohesiveness is associated with increased ability to cope effectively with unusual problems and to work as a team in meeting emergencies. Production groups, if highly cohesive, can produce more than less cohesive groups, but may not do so if members are being influenced by intragroup norms for less production. Although results of individual studies have been mixed, two recent meta-analyses of cohesiveness research have found that, in general, highly cohesive groups are more productive.[19] The nature of the task influences the cohesiveness-productivity relationship.[20] If the task is one that requires a high degree of coordination and interdependence among members, with communication an essential factor in the group's task completion, then cohesiveness enhances productivity, such as was demonstrated by the women's soccer team.

There is an optimum level of cohesiveness beyond which performance decreases.[21] Whether or not a cohesive group is productive also depends on the degree to which members accept their task. Cohesive groups are productive only when the members have both high acceptance of organizational goals implicit in the group's task *and* a strong drive (motivation and enthusiasm) to complete the task.[22] This was certainly the case with the excellent teams studied by Larson and LaFasto.[23] However, groups that are highly cohesive but socially oriented rather than task oriented may end up accomplishing nothing.[24]

Highly successful and cohesive groups tend first to get acquainted and interested in each other as people. This type of self-disclosure increases cohesiveness, commitment to the task, and productivity.[25] Members can be heard saying, "I'm proud of our group, we really thrash out ideas until we arrive at the best, then we team up." However, high cohesiveness can also pressure members to conform to the majority or to high-status members' desires, which can result in a less-than-thorough critical evaluation of ideas, leading to what is called *groupthink*. Here we describe groupthink, including symptoms by which you can recognize it. In Chapter 10 we talk about how a designated leader can try to prevent it and we discuss the effects of groupthink on decision making in Chapters 12 and 13.

Cohesiveness provides real benefits to a group, but too much cohesiveness can create problems as well. When a group's balance is tilted toward maintaining cohesiveness and harmony rather than toward critical thinking, groupthink can result. **Groupthink,** a term coined by Irving Janis, occurs when a group, usually a highly cohesive one, allows the desire to maintain consensus to suppress confrontation and disagreement, so that the group produces decisions that are not carefully thought through.[26] Janis compared two decisions by President John F. Kennedy's National Security Council. The first, a disastrous one, occurred when the United States decided to invade Cuba at the Bay of Pigs shortly after Fidel Castro had established a communist government there. The second is considered a model of effective group decision

Cohesiveness and Groupthink

making; it was the 1963 decision to blockade Cuba when missile sites were discovered there and ships with nuclear warheads to arm them were photographed on their way from the Soviet Union. Janis was intrigued by the fact that essentially the same group of people made decisions of such divergent quality. He found the reason *not* in the individual decision makers' personalities or intentions, but in the *throughput processes* they used. Groups making effective decisions and proposing high-quality alternatives are willing to engage in open conflict, challenge one another's reasoning, and test all information and ideas for soundness. Janis found that Kennedy's advisers did not thoroughly test information before making the Bay of Pigs decision, which explains how such well-educated, intelligent individuals, in the face of evidence to the contrary, *as a group* allowed such a stupid decision to be made.

It is very important to note that just because a group decision turns out badly does not automatically mean the processes used to formulate the decision were influenced by groupthink. Recall what you learned from structuration theory: sometimes decisions go awry because of factors over which the group has no control or can't have known about. What makes a decision faulty because of groupthink is the failure to consider all the information available at the time of the decision in a thorough and unbiased way. The reason highly cohesive groups are particularly vulnerable to the groupthink trap is because that very cohesion induces a pressure for consensus, a fear that conflict signals a threat to the cohesiveness, and a general desire to keep everyone in the group together on a decision. This pressure to achieve consensus is particularly acute in groups experiencing time pressures and with leaders who have a preferred alternative that they attempt to promote.[27]

Groupthink manifests itself in the type of communication members exhibit. Cline compared the conversations of groupthink and non-groupthink groups and found several surprising differences.[28] Although levels of disagreement were similar in both sets of groups, the groupthink groups exhibited significantly higher levels of *agreement,* and these agreements were simple, unsubstantiated ones. Group members ended up making statements and agreeing with themselves. In contrast, the agreements exhibited in the non-groupthink groups were substantive in nature, with different speakers providing different evidence and lines of reasoning to support their assertions. Cline concluded that in groupthink, concern for positive relationships and cohesiveness overrides critical thinking.

Groupthink is a common phenomenon in government, business, and educational groups. It has been implicated in a number of disastrous policy decisions, including NASA's 1986 decision to launch the space shuttle *Challenger,* which exploded just after take-off.[29] It has also been linked to a number of clearly unethical decisions made in American business, including Beech-Nut's decision to market phony apple juice, E. F. Hutton's decision to kite checks, and Salomon Brothers' illegal bidding in Treasury auctions.[30] In all these decisions, group members had information that should have forewarned them of impending failure, but biases affected how they processed the information, and desire for harmony and cohesiveness sabotaged the decision-making process.

As we've said, not all poor decisions are attributable to groupthink. Aldag and Fuller advise us to consider the limitations of groupthink.[31] First, they note that such antecedents of groupthink as high cohesiveness and directive leadership do not inherently produce dysfunctions in a group. As we noted earlier, cohesiveness can be highly beneficial to a group and directive leadership that encourages members to be thorough and careful can counteract groupthink tendencies. These authors also point out that other elements, such as organizational politics, can skew decision making as well.

Several of their criticisms are supported by Mullen et al., whose meta-analysis of cohesiveness found that when other antecedent conditions are present in a group, cohesiveness can work either for or against the group.[32] Cohesiveness based on interpersonal attraction among members can produce the kinds of problems associated with groupthink, but cohesiveness based on commitment to the task has the opposite effect. The role of cohesiveness was also studied by Bernthal and Insko, who discovered that high socioemotional cohesiveness was most likely to produce groupthink symptoms, especially when it was paired with low task-oriented cohesiveness.[33]

The effects of cohesiveness can be magnified by the type of decision rule a group uses. Kameda and Sugimori studied group entrapment, which occurs when group members have already committed resources and energy to a particular course of action and stay committed to that course, even when serious problems arise.[34] When a group must decide unanimously instead of by majority rule, members' consensus-seeking communication behavior encourages them to develop rationalizations that commit them to a particular course. They talk themselves into a decision, and in order not to lose what they have already invested, they stick with that course. Kameda and Sugimori found that this is less likely to happen when unanimity is not a required condition, and postulate that a decision rule of unanimity would produce groupthink in the same way.

A revised model of groupthink that takes these and other factors into account has been proposed by Neck and Moorhead, who add the conditions of time pressures and the importance of the decision to the factors leading to groupthink.[35] These authors believe that two moderating factors, the role of the leader and how methodical the group's decision-making processes are, determine whether the antecedent conditions of cohesiveness, time, and importance will actually produce groupthink. The leader's behavior is particularly important. A leader with a closed communication style discourages member participation in decisions, discourages diverse opinions, states his or her opinions at the outset of a discussion, and does not emphasize the importance of making a wise decision. When groupthink conditions are present, this style is more likely to produce groupthink than an open style that encourages participation. We discuss the importance of methodical decision making further in Chapters 11 and 12.

Watching out for Groupthink

How can you recognize groupthink? The symptoms of groupthink identified by Janis and others fall into three main categories:

1. **The group overestimates its power and morality.**

    A group may be so optimistic that it overestimates the chances for its programs to succeed. Student groups in our classes sometimes have become so excited about creative activities they have developed for a classroom presentation that they ignore the rest of the presentation by saying, "The instructor will love it—it's more imaginative than anything else other groups have done." Unfortunately, the imaginativeness is sometimes the only part of their presentation we instructors love! In addition, the group may have such an unquestioned belief in the inherent morality of the group that the group ignores potential ethical questions that should be raised. For example, the group of men behind the burglary of the Democratic National Headquarters, which eventually led to the Watergate hearings and President Nixon's resignation in disgrace, believed that they had a morally determined duty to protect the American public by gathering intelligence to help the president.

2. **The group becomes closed-minded.**

    Either a high-status leader or the group has a preferred solution, and the group closes itself off to any information contrary to this preferred course of action. A group may also stereotype outside figures who disagree so it doesn't have to pay attention to what they might have to say. NASA officials were so biased in favor of launching that they ignored or devalued information provided by engineers who opposed the *Challenger* launch. In the Beech-Nut case, company officials wanted to buy apple juice at the lowest possible cost. The suppliers with the lowest juice prices were those most likely to be selling phony or impure juice. Beech-Nut officials, rather than demanding that *suppliers* prove their apple juice was pure, shifted the burden of proof to *their own research and development personnel* to prove that an inexpensive supplier's product *was not* pure before the company would switch to a different supplier. Beech-Nut stuck to this policy even when threatened by consumer lawsuits.

3. **Group members experience pressures to conform.**

    Pressure to conform manifests itself in a variety of ways. First, members censor their own remarks, exemplified in Figure 8.2. If you think everyone else in the group is in favor of a proposal, you will normally tend to suppress your own doubts and fears. Second, the group members have a shared illusion of unanimity, manifested by the amount of simple agreement discovered by Cline.[36] Because individuals do not express doubts openly, the members think they all agree. Consensus is assumed rather than obtained.[37] Third, a member who does venture a contradictory opinion is likely to experience direct pressure from the rest of the group to conform: "Why are you being so negative, Jim? The rest

Groupthink in action.

FIGURE 8.2

of us think it's a good idea." This makes it obvious to Jim that his disagreement is perceived as disloyalty. Also, the group may have a number of self-appointed *mindguards* who protect the group from mental threats, just as bodyguards do from physical threats. For example, a member who deliberately prevents dissonant information from reaching the group—by stopping outsiders from addressing the group, by failing to mention contrasting points of view contained in research materials, and so forth—acts as a mindguard, withholding all contradictory material from the group's consideration. Finally, in groups that adhere to strict status differences within the group, lower-status members are less likely to contradict higher-status members and will avoid issues they think may produce conflict.[38] These conformity pressures are especially dangerous when a group *must* achieve consensus. The need for consensus can lead to an "agreement norm," which curtails disagreement, ultimately causing the decision to suffer.[39]

Benefits of Cohesiveness

Although high cohesiveness can be associated with pitfalls such as group-think, cohesiveness can produce great results. A group that accomplishes its objectives, provides members with satisfaction in their participation, offers prestige in belonging, and is successful in competing with other groups is very attractive to its members. This can help produce highly committed and enthusiastic members who stay the course when problems arise and win world championships.

Cohesiveness is fostered to the extent that members know and like each other as individuals, by their frequency of interaction, and by the amount of influence each exerts on the group. In addition, some evidence suggests that cohesive groups cooperate in creating a dominant sensory metaphor as a group, and that cohesiveness can be monitored through metaphor.[40] For example, when a group is first established, various members indicate their understanding by saying, "I see," "I hear you," or "I grasp that." Each of these metaphors for "I understand" concentrates on a different sense—sight, sound, or touch. In cohesive groups, members tend to converge on a particular sensory metaphor. If the visual metaphor is "chosen," for example, members will all start saying, "I see," "I've got the picture," and "I've spotted a flaw." This happens below the level of conscious awareness and indicates that the members have influenced each other in subtle but significant ways.

Interestingly, open disagreement is more frequent in highly cohesive groups, probably because a climate of trust gives each member the security needed to openly disagree on issues, facts, and ideas.[41] On the other hand, if high-status members indicate that they perceive disagreement to be a personal affront and demand compliance, then cohesiveness may become groupthink and be maintained at the expense of high-quality decision making.

Cohesiveness, then, is generally desirable. To enhance cohesiveness, Bormann and Bormann suggest that a group should attend to seven items, to which we add an eighth:[42]

1. **Develop a group identity.**
   Talk about the group as *we*, not *you*. Develop nicknames for the group, insignia indicating membership, or mascots for the group.

2. **Build group traditions.**
   Encourage traditions and rituals, which give added meaning to the group's culture. Refer to past events with pride, and encourage the group to develop a rich fantasy life.

3. **Stress teamwork.**
   Members, especially designated leaders or high-performance members, should avoid talking about "my accomplishments." The team performance should come before individual glory.

4. **Get the group to recognize good work.**
   Encourage members to compliment and praise one another. Coach DiCicco talked about how one of his players, Michelle Akers, inspired him.[43] Low-status members, especially, need attention and recognition. Look for ways to support other members with their group work assignments, but also with non-group-related activities.

5. **Set clear, attainable group goals.**
   A long-term goal is easier to achieve if it is broken down into several short-term goals. In addition, goals should be challenging but not impossible to reach, because failure is demotivating.

6. **Give the group rewards.**
   Although many organizations reward individual performance, groups should be rewarded *as groups*. These can be tangible or intangible

rewards, including recognition dinners, public praise, letters of commendation, and so forth.

7. **Treat members like people, not machines.**

The efficient, highly oiled machine is *not* the best metaphor for the kinds of groups we have been discussing. People have human needs for warmth, affection, and esteem that should be recognized. Group work is not just about meeting control needs and task accomplishment, but meeting needs for inclusion and affection as well.[44]

8. **Support both disagreement and agreement.**

A norm of freedom of expression and openness should be maintained. Highly cohesive groups show more disagreement, with conflict encouraged, not repressed. Often, when conflicts are resolved, group members feel closer than ever and are more cohesive.

Sometimes a group needs something out of the ordinary to help it develop or improve its cohesiveness. *Teambuilding* is the current term for special programs designed to accomplish such goals. **Teambuilding** refers to any planned program of activities designed to enhance teamwork or improve a group's performance. In addition to enhancing cohesiveness, teambuilding activities can be used to improve group decision making, help members learn more effective ways of handling conflict, increase creativity, and improve communication skills and many other group throughput processes. Often, teambuilding activities occur during retreats that take groups out of their normal settings and encourage them to focus on the teambuilding topic.

Teambuilding

The best teambuilding programs are tailored to meet the unique needs of each specific group. For instance, the trust-building activity designed for the women's soccer team and the videotapes created for each individual player are examples of how good teambuilding is particularized for each individual team. This text provides a foundation for you to determine where to focus teambuilding activities for a particular group. The information provided in Parts 3 through 5, which deal with throughput processes and observation techniques, can be especially helpful as you decide where to focus your teambuilding activities.

Teambuilding activities can be effective and lasting. For instance, Carron and Spink found that a teambuilding program helped a very large group increase its cohesiveness.[45] Glaser described a three-day teambuilding retreat designed for department leaders of a fire management unit.[46] The teambuilding topics included communication skills, consensus building, and problem solving. Glaser found that, even three years later, members continued to report substantially improved teamwork.

A teambuilding session may be planned by a group's leader, one of the members, a subgroup within the group, or an outside consultant or facilitator. We have designed and facilitated many teambuilding sessions in our consulting work with a variety of groups, including union personnel, a large dental practice, departments within our respective universities, a construction company, and a church board, to name just a few. Some day you may be asked to plan a teambuilding session for one of the groups to which you belong. The following are suggestions for teambuilding planners.[47]

1. **Define the purpose of the teambuilding activity.**
   Teambuilding can potentially address dozens of topics. As a planner, be sure you know what the group's most pressing needs are and what you want the teambuilding to accomplish so you will select the appropriate activities to meet your goals.

2. **Take the group out of its usual setting.**
   Members can become distracted if they can be reached by the telephone, secretaries, co-workers, family members, and so forth. Taking the group away from its normal setting encourages members to concentrate on what the teambuilding is designed to cover.

3. **Have a plan, but be willing to let go of it.**
   As a teambuilding facilitator, it is especially important for you to have a clear picture of how you will start the process because that sets the tone for the entire teambuilding session. However, you may find that one activity is working particularly well at accomplishing the goals of the session, and that the group isn't ready to move on to the next planned activity. When that is the case, you must be flexible enough to let go of the larger plan and go with what is working. For instance, members of a group with whom one of us consulted seemed to be gaining a lot from their discussion of personality characteristics and learning styles. Your author quickly decided to eliminate one planned activity so the discussion could continue. Conversely, an activity you planned may be a bust or may not take as long as you had thought, so you must be ready with an alternative to keep the session moving.

4. **Help members recognize the strength in their own diversity.**
   Often, when team members work together day in and day out, they lose sight of the fact that diversity of skills and working styles can be a strength for any team. Instead, members get bogged down with the frustration and irritation of dealing with others whose styles are very different from their own. An important goal of many teambuilding activities is to remind members of the strengths they have. In a session one of us facilitated, members had been sniping at each other; the laid-back members thought others were too picky, and the perfectionist members called the others sloppy. An activity designed to illustrate both the strengths and weaknesses of each work style generated lively discussion and vocal appreciation on the part of both subgroups.

5. **Find ways to incorporate meaningful rituals and celebrations in the teambuilding activity.**
   A group's culture is formed not only by members' attention to the group's work. Rituals and celebrations, similar to the fantasies we discussed earlier, help create a rich culture, a shared sense of identity,

and high cohesiveness. For example, the church board described in Chapter 2 held a teambuilding retreat after new board members had been elected for the coming year. The board president, facilitator for this teambuilding activity, incorporated religious rituals into the retreat, including a symbolic communion service. While this type of activity might not be appropriate for a business organization, as a facilitator you should look for ways to weave rituals meaningful to the members into the teambuilding. For instance, some organizations conduct "roasts" of their top officials; these help build solidarity and cohesiveness among organization members.

CONSIDER THIS

If you had been Coach DiCicco and your team had lost in the 1995 World Cup, what would you have done to build the team back up? Why do you think DiCicco's methods worked? Think of a group that you belong to or that you know. What would you want teambuilding activities to accomplish for this group, and why?

Several of the processes we have discussed so far, especially group cohesiveness, can be depicted using SYMLOG, which is an acronym for the SYstem for the Multiple Level Observation of Groups. Developed by Bales, SYMLOG is both a theory and a methodology that permits a three-dimensional diagram to be constructed of a group.[48] Examples of such diagrams are provided in Figures 8.3 and 8.4. (Instructions for producing a simplified, SYMLOG-like diagram are included in the *Instructor's Manual*.) You can see, even without detailed information about SYMLOG theory, that the first group (Figure 8.3) is fragmented and polarized, but the second (Figure 8.4) is unified and cohesive.

SYMLOG theory rests on the assumption that behavior of each group member in a group can be classified along each of three independent dimensions: dominant versus submissive; friendly versus unfriendly; and task-oriented versus emotionally expressive.[49] SYMLOG may be used in one of two ways. With the scoring method, external observers score the verbal and nonverbal behaviors of members as they interact in real time. The rating method is easier, requiring no special training; external observers or group members themselves complete a 26-question rating scale evaluating each member's behavior. The results are tallied in a particular way so each member can be placed on the SYMLOG diagram.

Each of the three dimensions is represented by a pair of letters that anchor the pole positions. For example, *P* (positive) stands for *friendly* and *N* (negative) stands for *unfriendly* behavior. On the diagram, the more friendly a member is toward the other members of the group, the farther the circle is placed to the right. The more unfriendly members are located farther to the

SYMLOG: Depicting Cohesiveness

| FIGURE 8.3 | SYMLOG diagram of a noncohesive group. |

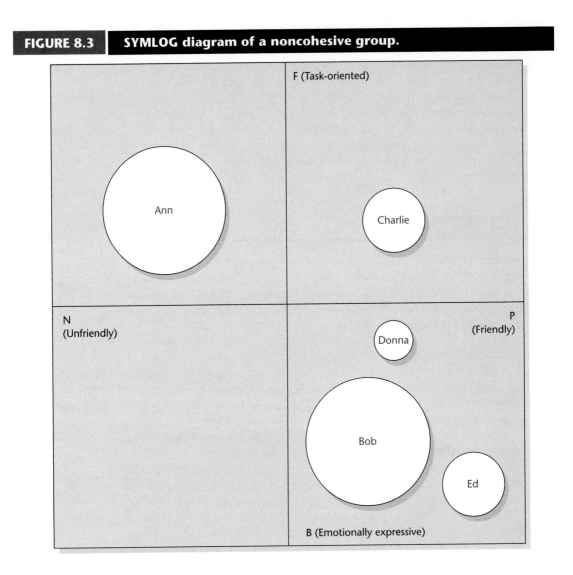

left. (In Figure 8.3, Ed is the most friendly and Ann the most unfriendly.) Task orientation is represented by *F* (forward); the more task oriented a member is, the closer he or she is to the top of the diagram. Emotional expressiveness is represented by *B* (backward); these members are closer to the bottom of the diagram. (In Figure 8.3, Ann is the most task oriented, and Ed the most emotionally expressive.) The third dimension is depicted by the size of a member's circle; dominant members have larger circles than submissive ones. (In Figure 8.3, Ann and Bob are the most dominant, Donna the most submissive.)

You can readily see that the group shown in Figure 8.3 is not cohesive. Ann is dominant, task oriented, and negative toward her fellow members.

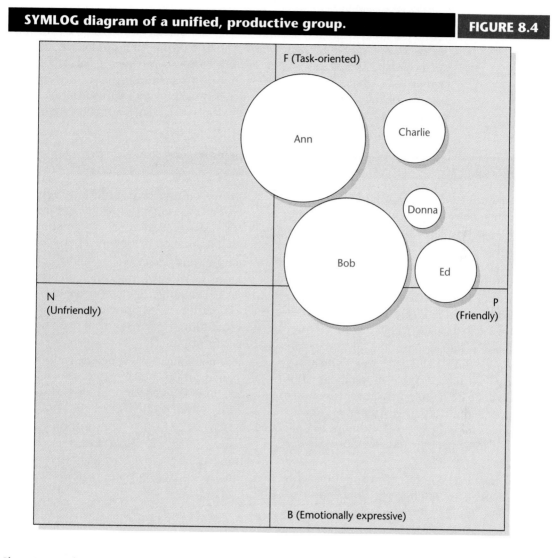

SYMLOG diagram of a unified, productive group. **FIGURE 8.4**

F (Task-oriented)

Ann

Charlie

Donna

Bob

Ed

N
(Unfriendly)

P
(Friendly)

B (Emotionally expressive)

She tries to dictate what happens in the group. Bob is dominant, but friendly and emotionally expressive, which gets the group off track frequently; almost certainly, Bob's behavior clashes with Ann's desire to stick to the task. Charlie, who is moderately dominant, task oriented, and friendly, is in the ideal position for a democratic, group-centered leader, but he's all by himself. Just by looking at the diagram you can tell that these people do not work well as a team. Members are dissimilar, they clash, there appears to be little cohesiveness, and there are wide variations in the degree of participation members exhibit.

The diagram in Figure 8.4 tells a different story. This group seems unified, with all members in the upper right-hand quadrant (which Bales calls the *decision-making quadrant*). Members are sufficiently task oriented to complete the group's assignment, but friendly enough toward each other that their interaction is probably harmonious. This is a picture of a productive and efficient group. As you can see, a SYMLOG analysis provides a "snapshot" of a group as a whole system whose component parts (the members) operate interdependently. SYMLOG is a particularly helpful tool to use during team-building activities because it so clearly displays the degree of cohesiveness.

SUMMARY

1. Communication shapes a group's communication network, which can be the wheel, the Y, or the all-channel network, which is ideal for a small discussion group.

2. A member's placement within the communication network and his or her role influences that member's status within a group. Ideally, members rely on earned rather than ascribed status within a group.

3. Fantasy is important to how groups create their culture. Fantasy chains, which are based on the principle of symbolic convergence that humans create meaning through their talk, help members create a shared reality, deal with uncomfortable information, and decide what actions to take.

4. Cohesiveness, the bonding between members, is another big contributor to group culture and generally helps increase a group's productivity, especially for tasks that require coordination and communication among members.

5. Groupthink can occur in highly cohesive groups that have low commitment to the task. Symptoms include a group's overestimation of its power and morality, closed-mindedness, and pressures to conform.

6. Teambuilding, or planned activities to enhance group performance, can increase group cohesiveness or address dozens of other group concerns.

7. SYMLOG, which is both a theory and a methodology, is a tool members can use to gain insight into how a group functions and to assess its level of cohesiveness.

EXERCISES

1. Observe a group (live or video) and, by yourself, rank the members according to the status you believe each has in the group. How much relative power and influence do you think each one has? Do you observe ascribed or earned status differences? If so, to what are they due? Then share your ranking with others in your class. How close were your rankings? What specific behaviors led you to rank the members as you did?

2. Tape record a group's interaction and listen to the tape later to identify fantasy themes.

(Listen especially for periods when the group seems excited and the energy level seems to pick up.) What function do you think the fantasy theme is serving for the group? What does it say about the group's shared reality?

3. Think of a group to which you belong or with which you are familiar. With a group of classmates, design a teambuilding activity for this group. First, decide what aspects of group discussion would be most beneficial for the group, then create activities you think would highlight these aspects.

BIBLIOGRAPHY

Bales, Robert F. *SYMLOG Case Study Kit.* New York: The Free Press, 1980.

Bormann, Ernest G. *Small Group Communication: Theory and Practice.* 3d ed. New York: Harper & Row, 1990, chapters 5, 7, and 8.

Clark, Neil. *Teambuilding: A Practical Guide for Trainers.* New York: McGraw-Hill, 1994.

NOTES

1. Information for this story was compiled from several sources. Most information came from Mark Starr and Martha Brant, "It Went Down to the Wire . . . and Thrilled Us All," *Newsweek,* July 19, 1999, 45–54, with additional information from Bill Saporito, "The New Dream Team," *Time,* July 19, 1999, 60–67, and David Leon Moore, "Goalkeepers: Don't Expect Any Handouts," *USA Today,* Friday, July 9, 1C–2C.

2. J. I. Hurwitz, A. F. Zander, and B. Hymovitch, "Some Effects of Power on the Relations among Group Members," in *Group Dynamics: Research and Theory,* 3d ed., eds. D. Cartwright and A. Zander (New York: Harper & Row, 1968): 291–97.

3. Dean C. Barnlund and C. Harland, "Propinquity and Prestige as Determinants of Communication Networks," *Sociometry* 26 (1963): 467–79.

4. E. Hollander, "Conformity, Status, and Idiosyncracy Credit," *Psychological Review* 65 (1958): 117–27.

5. Michelle Estrada, Justin Brown, and Fiona Lee, "Who Gets the Credit? Perceptions of Idiosyncracy Credit in Work Groups," *Small Group Research* 26 (February 1995): 56–76.

6. Carolyn J. Wood, "Challenging the Assumptions Underlying the Use of Participatory Decision Making Strategies: A Longitudinal Case Study," *Small Group Behavior* 20 (1989): 428–48.

7. Ernest G. Bormann, "Symbolic Convergence Theory and Communication in Group Decision Making," in *Communication and Group Decision Making,* eds. Randy

Y. Hirokawa and Marshall S. Poole (Newbury Park, CA: Sage, 1986): 221.

8. Robert F. Bales, *Personality and Interpersonal Behavior* (New York: Holt Rinehart and Winston, 1970): 105–8, 136–55.

9. Eric E. Peterson, "The Stories of Pregnancy: On Interpretation of Small-Group Cultures," *Communication Quarterly* 35 (1987): 39–47.

10. Catherine C. Morocco, "Development and Function of Group Metaphor," *Journal for the Theory of Social Behavior* 9 (1979): 15–27.

11. Bormann, "Symbolic Convergence Theory."

12. Linda L. Putnam, Shirley A. Van Hoeven, and Connie A. Bullis, "The Role of Rituals and Fantasy Themes in Teachers' Bargaining," *Western Journal of Speech Communication* (Winter 1991): 87.

13. This fantasy chain is a slightly expanded version of the one that occurs near the beginning of the leadership segment, part 1, of the videotape ancillary to this text, *Communicating Effectively in Small Groups.*

14. Morocco, "Development and Function of Group Metaphor," 15–27.

15. Morocco, "Development and Function of Group Metaphor."

16. Putnam, Van Hoeven, and Bullis, "The Role of Rituals and Fantasy Themes in Teachers' Bargaining."

17. David B. Barker, "The Behavioral Analysis of Interpersonal Intimacy in Group Development," *Small Group Research* 22 (February 1991): 76–91.

18. Harold L. Nixon II, *The Small Group* (Englewood Cliffs, NJ: Prentice-Hall, 1979): 74–76.

19. Charles R. Evans and Kenneth L. Dion, "Group Cohesion and Performance," *Small Group Behavior* 22 (1991): 175–86; Stanley M. Gully, Dennis J. Devine, and David J. Whitney, "A Meta-Analysis of Cohesion and Performance: Effects of Level of Analysis and Task Interdependence," *Small Group Research* 26 (November 1995): 497–520.

20. Gully et al., "A Meta-Analysis of Cohesion and Performance."

21. Lynne Kelly and Robert L. Duran, "Interaction and Performance in Small Groups: A Descriptive Report," *International Journal of Small Group Research* 1 (1985): 182–92.

22. Charles N. Greene, "Cohesion and Productivity in Work Groups," *Small Group Behavior* 20 (1989): 70–86.

23. Carl E. Larson and Frank M. J. LaFasto, *TeamWork: What Must Go Right/What Can Go Wrong* (Newbury Park, CA: Sage, 1989).

24. Wood, "Challenging the Assumptions."

25. Frederick G. Elias, Mark E. Johnson, and Jay B. Fortman, "Task-focused Self-disclosure: Effects on Group Cohesiveness, Commitment to the Task, and Productivity," *Small Group Behavior* 20 (1989): 87–96.

26. Irving L. Janis, *Groupthink: Psychological Studies of Policy Decisions and Fiascoes,* 2d ed. rev. (Boston: Houghton Mifflin, 1983).

27. Gregory Moorhead, Richard Ference, and Chris P. Neck, "Group Decision Fiascoes Continue: Space Shuttle *Challenger* and a Revised Groupthink Framework," *Human Relations* 44 (1991): 539–50.

28. Rebecca J. Welsh Cline, "Detecting Groupthink: Methods for Observing the Illusion of Unanimity," *Communication Quarterly* 38 (1990): 112–26.

29. Dennis S. Gouran, Randy Y. Hirokawa, and Amy E. Martz, "A Critical Analysis of Factors Related to Decisional Processes Involved in the *Challenger* Disaster," *Central States Speech Journal* 37 (1986): 119–35.

30. Ronald R. Sims, "Linking Groupthink to Unethical Behavior in Organizations," *Journal of Business Ethics* 11 (1992): 651–62.

31. Ramon J. Aldag and Sally Riggs Fuller, "Beyond Fiasco: A Reappraisal of the Groupthink Phenomenon and a New Model of Group Decision Processes," *Psychological Bulletin* 113, no. 3 (1993): 533–52.

32. Brian Mullen, Tara Anthony, Eduardo Salas, and James E. Driskell, "Group Cohesiveness and Quality of Decision Making: An Integration of the Groupthink Hypothesis," *Small Group Research* 25 (May 1994): 189–204.

33. Paul R. Bernthal and Chester A. Insko, "Cohesiveness without Groupthink: The Interactive Effects of Social and Task Cohesion," *Group and Organization Management* 18 (March 1993): 66–87.

34. Tatsuya Kameda and Shinkichi Sugimori, "Psychological Entrapment in Group Decision Making: An Assigned Decision Rule and a Groupthink Phenomenon," *Journal of Personality and Social Psychology* 65 (August 1993): 282–92.

35. Christopher P. Neck and Gregory Moorhead, "Groupthink Remodeled: The Importance of Leadership, Time Pressure, and Methodical Decision Making Procedures," *Human Relations* 48 (May 1995): 537–57.

36. Cline, "Detecting Groupthink." (FN 28)

37. Wood, "Challenging the Assumptions" 428–48.

38. Ibid.

39. Anne Gero, "Conflict Avoidance in Consensual Decision Processes," *Small Group Behavior* 16 (1985): 487–99

40. William F. Owen, "Metaphor Analysis of Cohesiveness in Small Discussion Groups," *Small Group Behavior* 16 (1985): 415–26.

41. Barker, "The Behavioral Analysis of Interpersonal Intimacy."

42. Ernest G. Bormann & Nancy C. Bormann, *Effective Small Group Communication,* 2d ed., (Minneapolis: Burgess Publishing Company, 1976), 70–76.

43. Bill Saporito, "The New Dream Team," *Time* (July 19, 1999): 60.

44. Ernest G. Bormann and Nancy C. Bormann, *Effective Small Group Communication,* 4th ed. (Edina, MN: Burgess, 1988): 74–76.

45. Albert V. Carron and Kevin S. Spink, "The Group Size-Cohesion Relationship in Minimal Groups," *Small Group Research* 26 (February 1995): 86–105.

46. Susan R. Glaser, "Teamwork and Communication: A Three-Year Case Study of Change," *Management Communication Quarterly* 7 (February 1994): 282–96.

47. Suggestions synthesized from Neil Clark, *Teambuilding: A Practical Guide for Trainers* (New York: McGraw-Hill, 1994); Glenn M. Parker, *Team Players and Teamwork* (San Francisco: Jossey-Bass, 1991); Glenn H. Varney, *Building Productive Teams: An Action Guide and Resource Book* (San Francisco: Jossey-Bass, 1989); and our own experiences.

48. Robert F. Bales and Stephen P. Cohen, *SYMLOG: A System for the Multiple Level Observation of Groups* (New York: Free Press, 1979). Space constraints prevent including a complete description of SYMLOG theory and methodology here; we refer readers who are interested in learning to construct a complete SYMLOG diagram for their groups to a workbook, *SYMLOG Case Study Kit,* R. F. Bales (New York: Free Press, 1980). The *Instructor's Manual* for this text includes instructions and necessary forms for completing a simplified, SYMLOG-like diagram so students can have a better idea of what SYMLOG can do.

49. Lynne Kelly and Robert L. Duran note that in some recent writings, Bales refers to the third dimension as acceptance versus nonacceptance of authority, which designation seems more appropriate when assessing group member values as opposed to behaviors; in "SYMLOG: Theory and Measurement of Small Group Interaction," in *Small Group Communication: A Reader,* 6th ed., eds. Robert S. Cathcart and Larry A. Samovar (Dubuque, IA: Wm. C. Brown, 1992): 39–52.

Perspectives on Leadership in Small Groups

9

Central Message

Small group leadership is an interactive phenomenon; it results from communicative behaviors appropriate to group task and relational goals, other members' behaviors, the context, and other contingencies.

Study Objectives

As a result of studying Chapter 9 you should be able to:

1. Define the concepts of *leadership, leader, leadership emergence,* and *designated leader.*
2. Explain the five sources of interpersonal influence (power) in a group and how they are involved in small group leadership.
3. Describe the process of leadership emergence.
4. Explain the three major approaches to small group leadership (traits, styles, and contingency approaches) and describe specific models included under each approach.
5. Name and describe seven communicative competencies important for small group leaders.
6. Explain how leaders and members are interdependent, and describe the LMX model.
7. Explain *distributed leadership* and why it is an appropriate model for small, task-oriented groups.

Key Terms

Autocratic leaders
Communicative competencies
Contingency approaches
Democratic leaders
Designated leader
Distributed leadership
Functions approach
Laissez-faire leaders
Leader
Leader-Member Exchange (LMX) model
Leadership
Leadership emergence
Power
Self-monitoring
Styles approaches
Traits approach

Jennifer, Robyn, Jiang, and Andreas comprise the broadcast advertising team in the corporate offices of a California-based retail company. Jennifer is the team's designated leader and their broadcast media buyer. Jiang, their promotions coordinator, is responsible for planning and directing promotional events, such as the back-to-school campaign, which coincide with the television and radio advertisements. He also makes sure that all of Jennifer's business records are kept up-to-date. Andreas, their production coordinator, assists Jennifer in writing, producing, and directing all television and radio commercials. Robyn, their broadcast advertising coordinator and Jennifer's administrative assistant, is primarily responsible for creating and maintaining working relationships with television and radio sales representatives. The company's quarterly profits are directly tied to successful media campaigns, which themselves are directly tied to how well this team works together.

Jennifer has been associated with the company for well over 20 years and is highly regarded in the advertising community. But everything does not always run smoothly for this broadcast advertising team. Although highly respected by her peers, Jennifer is a leader who must be in control of all tasks and the team's socioemotional environment. She tends not to let other members of the team make mistakes or create their own successes.

This leadership style poses problems for team members in a couple of areas. High turnover is common in this division. New employees are regularly being trained, often inadequately. New employees are never fully informed about their job responsibilities because Jennifer tightly controls the flow of information to them, but she is often too busy to work with them. Too often, they learn how and what they are supposed to do when they have been reprimanded by Jennifer for making a mistake. This creates resentment among the team and costs the company money for wasted time. Further resentment is created by her desire to control their socioemotional environment. For instance, if Andreas writes a poor advertising script, she expects one of his co-workers to tell him rather than convey the bad news herself. Yet this retail company is successful in part because the broadcast advertising group produces effective advertising. At what point is ineffective leadership considered a problem? Who is responsible for change? Is the character of a group solely determined by one person's behaviors? If you were an outside consultant what would you say to this division? These and other issues will be touched on in this chapter.

According to Larson and LaFasto, the final ingredient for effective group performance is team leadership, with the right person serving in the leadership role.[1] Because small groups are everywhere, you will certainly have your turn serving as a small group leader. This can be a source of self-esteem, recognition, and appreciation; it can also be a nightmare.

Much of the conventional wisdom about what makes a good leader is simply wrong. Many people hold oversimplified beliefs about effective leadership that interfere with their learning to function well as small group leaders. We hope this and the next chapter will dispel those beliefs, as well as help you discover the communication competencies you must develop to perform well as a leader.

In Chapter 9 we examine the concepts of *leader* and *leadership,* describe the process of leadership emergence, review historical and contemporary perspectives about leadership, examine the relationship between leaders and members, and develop an argument in favor of *distributed leadership* for most small task-oriented groups. In Chapter 10 we focus on the duties commonly expected of designated small group leaders in our culture and provide specific suggestions on how to perform them.

LEADERSHIP AND LEADERS

The terms *leadership* and *leader* have related but separate meanings. One refers to a process, the other to a person.

Most social scientists define **leadership** as interpersonal influence. The following definition by Hackman and Johnson reveals the importance of communication in the leadership process:

Leadership

> Leadership is human (symbolic) communication which modifies the attitudes and behaviors of others in order to meet group goals and needs.[2]

This definition incorporates two important implications. First, the use of the term *modifies* suggests that influence via communication, as opposed to physical coercion or other forms of force, is the heart of the process we term leadership. We aren't talking about an "attitude adjustment" through force, but through interaction and persuasion, human symbolic activity. Second, this definition implies that only influence directed toward accomplishment of a *group* goal can truly be termed *small group leadership.* Too many people equate leadership with power, but they are not the same. True, leadership involves power; however, other members of a group also control group interaction with their power resources.[3] What power resources might the members of the broadcast-advertising team have to pull off successful advertising campaigns while working for a superior with strong control issues?

The ability to influence stems from **power** that is derived from a particular source, or base. Leaders and followers transact to create a relationship based on perceived power. Leaders can influence the conduct of others to the extent they have power that is perceived and acknowledged by followers. The sources of power identified by French and Raven include reward, punishment, legitimate, referent, and expert.[4]

Sources of Influence (Power)

Leaders can *reward* followers by giving them both tangible and intangible items such as special attention, acknowledgment, compliments, personal favors, money, and material goods. Jennifer may come down hard on her broadcast-advertising team but she lets them leave early and gives the team free tickets to social events like concerts and baseball games. Leaders can also *punish* by withholding these same items. For example, the frown a leader may give a latecomer is a form of punishment. *Coercion* is a special form of punishment power that uses threats or force to "influence" others. Although good leaders may effectively use punishment (especially the fear of losing something important, such as belonging to the group or the respect of the others), they do not use hardball tactics to coerce or force compliance. Coercion breeds resentment, sabotage, and rebellion, which are not desirable small group outcomes. We do not consider coercion to be genuine leadership as we define it.

Legitimate power stems from a special position or role acknowledged by the followers. For instance, in a police task force, lieutenants are accepted as having the right to give orders to sergeants, who themselves may give orders to patrol officers. However, legitimate power includes only influence that is accepted as appropriate by followers. Thus, a committee chair does not have the right to tell members how to dress or wear their hair, although a supervisor might have such power.

Referent power is based on attraction or identification with another person. Some referent leaders have charisma that causes others to want to associate with them and imitate their behavior. For example, one of us skipped a class in high school because the referent leader of our small group of friends suggested it. Ideally, however, discussion leaders model positive behaviors for the other members to admire and emulate, such as listening, considering all sides of an issue, and keeping remarks orderly. The more leaders are admired and respected, the more members copy their behavior, and thus the greater their power to influence the group.

Expert power comes from what others believe a member knows or can do. For instance, if your group is responsible for producing a panel discussion for the rest of your class and you happen to be the only member who has ever participated in a panel discussion, you have expertise the others value, which gives you power in that particular group. The person with expert power is influential because he or she is perceived as having knowledge or skills vital to the group.

Usually a leader's power stems from more than one source. The more sources on which a person's power rests, the more that person has the potential to dominate a group. Conversely, the more these bases of power are distributed among members, the more likely verbal participation is to be shared, decision making to be collaborative, and satisfaction high. In other words, leadership can be provided by all members exercising their influence in service to the group goal. We expand on this idea later.

Leaders   The term *leader* refers to a person, or sometimes to a special position occupied by a person.[5] A leader in a small group is a person who influences the behavior of others through communication. We use the term *leader* to refer to three related types of individuals: a person who exerts influence toward achievement of a group's goal, a person who is perceived by the others as being a leader (influencer), and a person who has been appointed or elected to a leadership position (e.g., chair, team leader, coordinator, or facilitator). A person elected or appointed to a leadership position is called a **designated leader.**

Having a designated leader usually helps provide stability to a group. Numerous studies

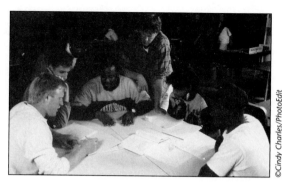

have shown that small groups with stable leadership are more effective in goal achievement than small groups that fail to settle issues about who is responsible for what. A group whose energy is siphoned off in a leadership struggle produces poor outcomes, dissatisfied members, and low cohesion.[6] In contrast, groups with designated leaders *accepted by the members* have fewer interpersonal problems and often produce better outcomes than groups without designated leaders.[7] The implication is clear: even in a group in which influence (and thus leadership) is widely shared, someone must coordinate the flow of communication and the work of the members.

Designated leaders greatly affect small groups.

Having the title *designated leader* gives someone legitimate power, but that person must still earn the respect and support of other members. A designated leader's behavior will be evaluated and may frequently be challenged by the members. If the designated leader's power rests solely on the legitimacy of the title, someone else with more broadly based power will likely emerge as a more influential informal leader.

Even though all members of a small group bear responsibility for the success or failure of the group, the designated leader shoulders special responsibility for the work of the group. As Stech and Ratliffe put it, both "group members and outsiders tend to hold the leader accountable for group beliefs, proposals, actions, and products."[8] This confers tremendous obligation on the designated leader to attend to how the group is functioning as a system and ensure that needed leadership services are provided. Not all leaders in a group are designated, however; many emerge over time. We now turn your attention to leadership emergence.

The process of **leadership emergence,** whereby one individual who starts out on an equal footing with other members but emerges to be perceived as the group's leader, has been charted by Aubrey Fisher, known for his focus on the communicative dynamics of small group decision making.[9] He developed his model (refer to Figure 9.1) from his own conclusions after listening to numerous hours of audiotaped small group interaction. The model is a description of member contention for leadership after one or more members make a move toward leadership.

Leadership Emergence

FIGURE 9.1	**A model of emergent leadership.**

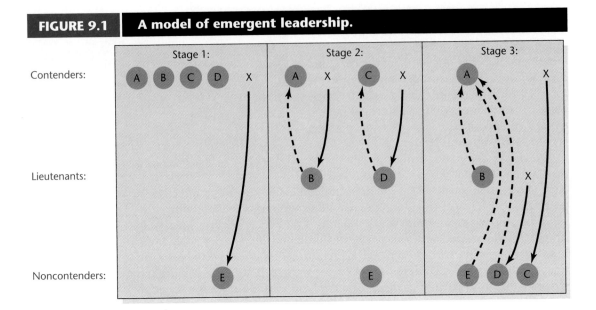

The three-stage model presumes that all members are potential candidates for leadership. Stage 1 is characterized by one or more members (see, for example, member E) falling from consideration almost immediately. Such members may perceive themselves as unable to lead or uninterested in leading for a number of reasons (e.g., too busy). Also, if some members exhibit behaviors others see as nonleaderlike (e.g., quiet, uninformed, or dogmatic) they will be eliminated.[10]

Stage 2 is characterized by the remaining members' bids for leadership being supported by other members. A and C are still in contention and enlist the help of B and D, who back out of contention but serve as lieutenants to A and C, respectively. Notice that two cliques or coalitions form around both A and C. Fisher noted that stage 2 can be lengthy, with verbal sparring typical. Eventually, one contender fails at her or his bid and drops out. The candidate that falls out of contention usually is too directive and communicatively offensive to others (e.g., talks too much, is manipulative).[11]

In Stage 3, A remains as leader and C falls out completely. Member E's support may or may not be important. If E's activity stays low, his or her support is not significant. However, if E becomes active, both A and C might vie for E's support because alliance with E could be extremely important to either one. Member D could also shift support to A during C's failed attempt to emerge as leader.

Fisher's model as depicted in Figure 9.1 is basic and can involve several variations. For instance, leadership emergence may involve only two stages. It can occur painlessly and quickly when only one member secures a lieutenant and the rest of the group follows along. Sometimes an early leader emerges who is later deposed, which causes the leadership emergence process to recycle back to stage 2. Finally, the leadership emergence process may not involve a stage 3 if the two contenders cooperate as coleaders.

You will note that while Fisher's model describes general processes based on the quantity and quality of communication, there is a sense that some personal characteristics (e.g., skills in verbalizing) are associated with who emerges as leader. In fact, it has been popular to explain leadership emergence by searching for the personal characteristics of the emergent leader.

Several recent studies of leadership have found a number of traits associated with leadership emergence. One of these is **self-monitoring,** discussed briefly in Chapter 6, which refers to individuals' abilities to monitor, in a given situation, both social cues and their own actions.[12] High self-monitors are sensitive to contextual cues, socially perceptive, and able to respond flexibly according to what seems needed at any given time. Zaccaro et al. found that more than half the variance of leadership emergence was explained by self-monitoring.[13] This was confirmed by Ellis and Cronshaw, who found that males who were high self-monitors emerged as leaders because they were better able to adapt their behaviors to fit the needs of the group.[14] However, this was not true for women, probably because female high self-monitors, who are sensitive to subtle clues, sometimes sense that their leadership behavior is perceived as inappropriate. They may then modify their actions to tone down that leadership behavior. These authors discovered that high self-monitors do in fact monitor social cues and are able to modify their responses; they are more likely to emerge as leaders across situations. However, low self-monitors, whose actions are motivated more by internal than external cues, can also emerge as leaders in situations in which they have favorable attitudes toward expressing leadership; they will not emerge as leaders if they hold unfavorable attitudes about leadership.[15]

Verbal style, together with the content of communication, also is associated with leadership emergence.[16] Consistent with earlier studies, Baker found that members whose communication style was quiet, tentative, or vague were perceived as uncommitted to the group and not knowledgeable about the group's task. These members were quickly eliminated as potential leaders because others did not believe they contributed ideas or helped organize the group. Those who did emerge as leaders made more attempts to suggest procedures for the group and thus helped to get the group organized. The emergent leader's participation profiles were high in procedure giving, moderate in idea giving, and low in stating opinions. Leaders' and members' styles were consistent in what Baker describes as mundane style: informal, unimaginative, ordinary. High-status members who were not leaders had a dramatic style

Personal Characteristics of Emergent Leaders

that, though unusual, was tolerated because of their perceived helpfulness to the group.

Years ago, biological sex was associated with group leadership in that males were more likely to emerge than females (for more about gender and sex and small group communication see Chapter 8). However, biological sex has not been a useful predictor of who will emerge as a leader in a group. Psychological gender, on the other hand, may be more useful. Regardless of sex, those individuals enacting a masculine communication style (i.e., independent, self-reliant, willing to take a stand) emerged more often as leader than those enacting feminine and nonandrogynous communication styles.[17] Generally, groups appear to choose leaders based on performance, most especially task performance. Hawkins observed mixed-sex groups and analyzed transcripts of their communication.[18] She found that task-relevant communication, not gender, was the factor that explained who emerged as leader. Furthermore, she found no significant differences in the amount of task-relevant remarks contributed by men and women. Sex, gender, and leader emergence are difficult processes to unravel. Shimanoff and Jenkins remind us that research, time and again, provides evidence that men and women lead equally well and group members are equally satisfied with both male and female leaders.[19]

This finding about the importance of task-focused communication is consistent with the findings of De Souza and Klein.[20] They hypothesized that the nature of the task would affect leadership emergence. They found that the type of task did not influence emergence, but that members' individual abilities to contribute to the task and their commitment to the group goal were associated with their emergence as leaders. They also discovered that groups with emerged leaders outperformed those without them. This latter finding is supported by Kurth, who found that group members themselves considered groups with emerged leaders more successful.[21]

Sometimes a group member will emerge as a leader even though the group already has a designated leader. Wheelan and Johnston followed four individuals identified by their peers as informal leaders in groups with formal leaders.[22] They found that the behavior of such leaders did not completely follow the behavior either of traditional emergent or designated leaders. Such individuals did talk more than most of their fellow members, but their talk was not more task-oriented, as is true with emergent leaders. Member leaders contributed more to the socioemotional aspect of the group, but not always in a positive way. They were more likely to challenge the designated leaders. They built coalitions with other members and generally displayed antiauthority positions. Wheelan and Johnston note that the presence of such members can have a substantial effect on the group's interaction but that too little is known about such members; they call for more research into informal member-leaders.

CONSIDER THIS

What does the process of leadership emergence tell you about how to *not* become a leader? The following rules, if followed, will probably result in low status and if followed well will get you out of being a leader.[23] Miss as many group meetings as possible. Say very little. Jump to be the group's secretary. Do what you are told. When you do contribute be dogmatic, verbally aggressive, and act like you know it all—do so early in the group's history. When you can, play the role of the joker. Finally, show a disdain for leadership. What other things can you do to make sure you are *not* a group's leader?

THEORETICAL APPROACHES TO LEADERSHIP

As with other social scientific phenomena, the study of leadership has moved from simplicity to complexity. In this next section, we present several of the most important approaches to the study of leadership. The most useful contemporary theories are based on models of communication. We urge you not to become rigidly attached to any one theory because all of them contain useful insights; moreover, new discoveries may simplify the complexity that currently exists.

Our discussion of leadership emergence has focused on communication characteristics, broadly, and specific personal characteristics often referred to as traits. A *trait* is a characteristic of a person. Some traits, such as eye color or height, are unchangeable; others, such as self-monitoring, are subject to some control. The **traits approach** to leadership examines how traits are related to leadership and assumes that leaders are more likely to have certain traits than other group members are. You just read how several traitlike characteristics have been associated with leadership emergence.

Traits Approaches

The earliest studies of leadership (from before the Christian epoch through the 1930s) assumed that people were collections of relatively fixed traits, with one leadership situation being much like another. Researchers who investigated leadership from this perspective looked for the trait or traits that distinguished leaders from followers. They believed that leaders were a special class of people who were born, not made. Social scientists used a number of personality measures in an effort to discover the traits of leaders. Some studies found that leaders tended to have higher IQs, and were taller, more attractive, and larger than nonleaders.[24] However, inconsistent results led scientists to reject the theory that leadership can be explained solely or even primarily on the basis of traits.

CONSIDER THIS

Despite our unsuccessful efforts to identify those traits that distinguish leaders from nonleaders, we still have fun playing with the physical characteristics associated with leaders, especially when we try to predict presidential elections. Did you know that male leaders brush their hair from the left (Al Gore brushes from the right)? Only 5 of 41 presidents have been left handed (all front-runners in the 2000 race are right handed). The taller presidential candidate enjoys a 3–1 advantage over other contenders (Bill Bradley is six-feet five-inches tall). And finally, some say "royal" blood is the best predictor in a presidential election; if elected, George W. Bush would be the most "royal" of any president.[25] What traits do you associate with leaders?

Modern trait approaches examine a variety of complex personality characteristics such as enthusiasm, verbal facility, creativity, critical thinking ability, self-confidence. Although they are labeled traits, they seem to represent behaviors that leaders perform rather than invariable, unchangeable characteristics. In short this approach, while intuitively appealing, has been less than helpful to us in our attempts to understand complex leadership processes. Personality characteristics are not easily measured and, most importantly, this approach does not help distinguish between good and bad leaders nor does it explain why leadership changes in a group.[26] Stogdill noted that "leadership is a relation that exists between persons in a social situation, and that persons who are leaders in one situation may not necessarily be leaders in other situations."[27]

We believe his conclusion that leadership is not a universal set of traits is valid; however, it seems equally clear that people with the ability to adapt their behaviors and who possess communication skills that help clarify the group's task and motivate other members will be influential in groups.[28] Foreshadowing our discussion of contingency approaches, we may say appropriate leader behaviors in a group are shaped by the needs of the group. A person with the ability to respond flexibly, whether that is a trait or behavior, will likely be influential in a group.

Styles Approaches

Styles approaches focus on the pattern of behaviors a leader exhibits in a group. Early style theorists attempted to discover whether there was one ideal style for small group leaders. More recent style theorists have looked at styles in relationship to member and task characteristics, suggestive of contingency approaches to leadership discussed later.

Considerable research has examined the behaviors of designated leaders classified as *democratic, autocratic,* and *laissez-faire.* Democratic leaders encourage members to participate in group decisions, including policy-making decisions ("What ideas do you have for organizing our task?"). Laissez-faire leaders take almost no initiative for structuring a group, but they may respond to inquiries from members ("I don't care; whatever you want to do is fine with me."). Autocratic leaders tightly control their groups, making assignments, directing all verbal interaction, and giving orders ("Here's how I've structured your task. First, you will . . ."). They ask fewer questions but answer more than democratic leaders, and make more attempts to coerce but fewer attempts to get others to participate.[29]

The autocratic and democratic styles of leadership described here correspond closely with the Theory X and Theory Y assumptions described by management theorist Douglas McGregor.[30] Theory X assumes that people don't like to work and must therefore be compelled by a strong, controlling leader ("boss") who supervises their work closely. In contrast, Theory Y assumes that people work as naturally as they play, and are creative problem solvers who like to take charge of their own work. Leaders who accept the assumptions of Theory Y behave democratically by providing only as much structure as a group needs, allowing members to participate fully in decision making and other aspects of the group's work.

Research findings have been consistent about the effects of leadership style on group output.[31] Democratically led groups are generally more satisfied than autocratically led groups; most people in our culture prefer democratic groups. Autocratic groups often work harder in the presence of the leader, but they also experience more incidents of aggressiveness and apathy. Democratic groups whose leaders provide some structure and coordination are better problem solvers and their members are more satisfied than those in laissez-faire groups without structure. Research continues into the complex relationship among leadership style, satisfaction, and productivity. A recent meta-analysis found a correlation between style and productivity only when the type of task was taken into account.[32] Democratic leadership is more productive in natural settings and, in laboratory settings, seems to produce higher productivity on moderately or highly complex tasks. The link between democratic leadership and satisfaction is not strong.

Although a leadership style that provides some degree of structure appears to be the most desirable for both productivity and satisfaction, several contingent factors (including cultural values) affect how much structure and control a particular group seems to need; that is, you cannot separate any one style from the situation leaders and followers find themselves in.[33] Even Jennifer, designated leader of the advertising team in our opening story, who typically engages in a controlling leadership style, finds herself adjusting to the situation and to the peculiarities she discovers in each new employee. We next consider contingency approaches.

All **contingency approaches** assume that group situations vary, with different situations requiring different leadership styles. These approaches explicitly acknowledge that factors such as members' skills and experience, cultural values, the type of task, and the time available affect the type of leadership likely to be effective. Contingency approaches acknowledge the complexity

Contingency Approaches

of small group systems, with all factors such as task, members, and environment affecting each other interdependently.

Not only do most current researchers accept contingency assumptions, but so do group members. Wood asked members of continuing small groups with task, social, and dual task-social objectives what they expected of designated leaders. Members expected different behaviors of the leaders depending on the group's focus, although a moderate degree of team spirit was expected by leaders of all types of groups.[34] Griffin found that the amount of structuring and directive behavior expected from supervisors depended on the level of growth needs of subordinates. People with high growth needs (i.e., who enjoy challenging jobs) most preferred participative, considerate supervisors, whereas employees with lower growth needs preferred more autocratic leadership.[35] A complex relationship was found among member needs, leadership style, and member satisfaction, giving credence to the general contingency hypothesis of leadership in small discussion groups.

Downs and Pickett also examined contingencies of leader style and member needs.[36] Groups of participants with high social needs were most productive with task-oriented procedural leaders and least productive with no designated leader. Groups of people low on interpersonal needs did equally well with designated leaders who provided task structuring only, with leaders who provided both task structuring and socioemotional leadership, and with no designated leader. Groups with some members high and some low in interpersonal needs performed somewhat better without a designated leader.

The contingency approach is also supported by Skaret and Bruning, who noted that satisfaction involves a complex interaction between leader behavior and work group attitudes.[37] The following traits of followers influence the type of leadership they preferred: degree of authoritarianism and dogmatism, need for achievement, and locus of control (whether one feels in control of one's own life or governed by fate).[38] From the research and theory surveyed, we can safely conclude that a discussion leader needs to be flexible, adapting to situational contingencies, but that in almost all situations a democratic structuring approach will be productive, or will at least not be counterproductive.

The Functions Approach

The **functions approach** is a subtype of contingency theory that assumes groups are most productive when specific functions are performed by leaders. The two major categories of functions are those that focus on interpersonal relationships (various writers call this *maintenance, socioemotional, social leadership,* or *initiating consideration*) and those concerned with the group's task (also called *initiating structure*). Examples of these kinds of functions were described in Chapter 7.

Several researchers have attempted to identify specific task and maintenance functions needed for effective leadership. One of the earliest category systems for studying behavioral functions was the Interaction Process Analysis developed by Bales.[39] Benne and Sheats identified a variety of task and maintenance functions they claim are productive for the group, along with a set of functions that are counterproductive.[40] Several of the Benne and Sheats functions are included in the lists in Chapter 7. More recently, Fisher identified four functions performed by leaders, whom he saw as providing a mediating function between group events and activities and the final outcome:

1. Leaders provide sufficient information, as well as the ability to process and handle considerable information.

2. Leaders enact a variety of functions needed within the group.

3. Leaders help group members make sense of decisions made and actions performed within the group by doing such things as supplying good reasons for those actions.

4. Leaders focus on the here-and-now, stopping the group from jumping to unwarranted conclusions or adopting stock answers too quickly.[41]

Another major function of leadership is captured in Weick's metaphor of *leader as medium*.[42] Task groups usually confront a variety of interpersonal and task obstacles that must be overcome. One of the most difficult is the need to reduce a vast amount of complex and often equivocal information to an understandable level. Goal achievement requires group members to devise a set of rules and procedures for narrowing the number of plausible interpretations so they can devise an appropriate course of action. Weick says the basic function of leadership is to assist the group in creating an organizing scheme of rules and procedures for problem solving. The leader is the medium, or mechanism, through which this is accomplished. As you saw from our story of the broadcast advertising team, their leader, Jennifer, does not do a very good job of helping her employees to narrow down plausible interpretations for any number of work tasks, especially their job responsibilities. She is a poor *medium*.

We view the functions approach as a contingency approach because two assumptions are implicit in the model. First, at different points in the group, different functions will be needed. For instance, *initiation* is needed to get the group started; *gatekeeping* is needed to facilitate participation, and so forth. Because of the unique combination of member skills, attitudes, behaviors, and so on, each group will require a different mix of functions. Second, the model suggests that any member of the group, not just the designated leader, can perform any of the functions. It assumes that the necessary functions must be performed by *someone* for the group to be effective, but not necessarily by the designated leader. This approach sets the stage for viewing group leadership behavior as a property of the *group,* and a function of the interaction between the person whose title is *leader* and the other members.

Fiedler's Contingency Model

Some contingency approaches assume that there are limits to leaders' abilities to adapt; in other words, people are relatively inflexible. Leadership behaviors are traitlike in that leaders have styles they prefer and use more effectively than other styles. Fiedler's contingency model of leadership reflects this view. He concluded that there are three factors upon which appropriate leader behaviors are contingent: leader-member relations, task structure, and leader position (or legitimate) power.[43] The central thesis of Fiedler's work is that individuals' personal needs and characteristics make them suited for leadership only in certain types of contingencies, so it is more productive to match prospective leaders to situations than to try to change the individual's style. This also implies that a group's leadership situation will remain relatively stable. Extensive application has been made of this theory in placing supervisory personnel. According to Fiedler, problem-solving groups are generally best served by democratic structuring leaders with concerns for people, rather than by autocratic or nonstructuring leaders. However, in other types of situations (for instance, during emergencies or in leading primary groups) a more autocratic or a more relationship-oriented style would be more productive.

Hersey and Blanchard's Situational Model

Other contingency approaches assume that people are flexible enough to adapt their behavior to meet the needs of many groups. Representative of this approach is the model of leadership adaptability and style developed by Hersey and Blanchard.[44] These authors postulate that leadership behaviors can be located along two dimensions, relationship orientation (giving socioemotional support) and task orientation (coordination efforts, instructions, advice and so forth). A leader can be high on one, both, or neither dimension. (Figure 9.2 illustrates these dimensions.) However, whether a leader is effective depends on his or her ability to adapt to the needs of the members at all points during the life of the group. For instance, a new group of inexperienced members needs more task but less relationship behavior from the leader until members understand their charge and objectives. As members become familiar with the task, the leader should begin to increase relationship behavior. Eventually task behavior can be reduced, and, at full member readiness, socioemotional support can be withdrawn, since the group's dependence on the leader is minimal. This model, which has not been widely tested empirically, implies that the leader must be able to analyze a group's situation and the readiness level of the members in order to provide the right amount of task instruction and socioemotional support. It also implies that a group's situation is not static, but changes throughout the life of the group.

Hersey and Blanchard's model places great faith in the leader's ability to adapt to the needs of the group. There is support for believing that many leaders are flexible, as the self-monitoring studies reported earlier suggested. Wood found, for example, that the discussion leaders she observed demonstrated behavioral flexibility. The comments of the designated leader varied depending on the stated purpose of the discussion and the previous success or failure of the committee. Leaders tended to compensate as needed, depending on what had occurred at previous meetings, by providing more or less structure. Wood noted, "The most important and obvious conclusion is that leaders of purposive discussions do engage in adaptive behavior."[45] Her results have been confirmed. Sorenson and Savage observed greater variety

Task and relationship needs of maturing groups. **FIGURE 9.2**

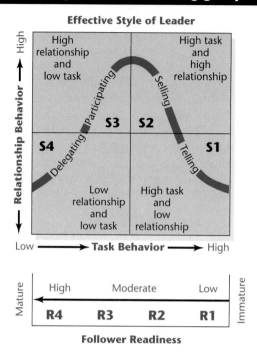

in the effective leaders' communicative styles than in those of ineffective leaders. In particular, leaders should attend to the degrees of dominance and supportiveness they exhibit.[46] Drecksell, too, found that leaders covered a wide range of functions, and their interaction was more complex than the interaction of other members.[47]

Chemers's *Integrative Systems/Process Model* is an example of another contingency model that assumes leaders can vary their behavior. Chemers's model reflects the complexity of a small group as a system; he assumes an interdependent relationship among all the possible input, throughput, and output variables of a small group.[48] Leadership in an open small group system involves interaction among inputs, including the leader's personal characteristics and competencies, cultural norms, situational contingencies, follower expectations and intentions, task variables, and the task itself. Process, or throughput, variables include leader/follower behaviors. Output variables include satisfaction, feedback, and group task performance. Because of its comprehensiveness, Fisher identified a problem with Chemers's model: "the number of variables that are potentially contingent on leadership and the possible combinations of those variables of situation, leader, and followers are virtually impossible to comprehend."[49] Thus, though theoretically sound, it is of limited practical value.

Chemers's Integrative Systems/Process Model

Communicative Competencies Approach

In an attempt to provide a model that acknowledges contingencies without overwhelming us with complexity, Barge and Hirokawa recently proposed a *Communication Competency Model of Group Leadership.*[50] The **communicative competencies** model is based on the assumptions that leadership involves behaviors that help a group overcome obstacles to goal achievement, that leadership occurs through the process of communication, and that communication skills (competencies) are the means used by individuals to lead small groups. This model maintains the task and relationship distinctions noted by many researchers, but provides an organizing scheme for the overwhelming array of facts and conjectures relating to group leadership. We consider it a contingency approach because it assumes that the actual context facing the leader and group is constantly shifting, so the task and relational communicative competencies needed vary from moment to moment. Group leaders must be highly flexible to draw from a personal repertoire of such competencies. We next direct your attention to the competencies we believe to be the most important to leadership and which we urge you to cultivate as personal skills.

COMMUNICATIVE COMPETENCIES OF EFFECTIVE DISCUSSION LEADERS

Knowing the behaviors and competencies that distinguish effective task group leaders can help you select a group's leader wisely and learn to be a better leader yourself. The following are specific communicative competencies exhibited by effective discussion leaders.

1. **Effective small group leaders are active communicators who encode ideas clearly and concisely.**

   Numerous studies have found emergent leaders to be high in verbal participation, although not necessarily the highest in a group.[51] Reynolds found that leaders maintained their influence by staying involved in group discussion and decision making.[52] But amount of talk alone is only a small part of verbal competency; Russell found that group leaders had higher levels of communicative skills than other members.[53]

   What are these skills? Lashbrook found that leaders were perceived as speaking more clearly and fluently than other members.[54] Facility in verbalizing problems, goals, values, ideals, and solutions characterizes effective discussion leaders. Barge and Hirokawa have theorized that the more complex the group's task, the more ambiguous the member roles, and the more negative the climate, the more important are the leader's communication skills.[55]

2. **Effective group leaders communicate a good grasp of the group's task.**

   Above all else, their communication behaviors reveal extensive knowledge about the task, skills for organizing and interpreting that knowledge, and an understanding of procedures that facilitate task accomplishment.

3. **Effective group leaders are skilled in mediating information and ideas supplied by all members.**

   Such leaders are especially competent in analysis of statements and in the kinds of critical thinking that lead to thorough evaluation and integration of information. They are good at providing structure to unorganized information, at asking probing questions to bring out pertinent information, and at evaluating inferences and conclusions drawn from information. They help all members focus on activities relevant to the group's goal.[56]

4. **Effective group leaders express their opinions provisionally.**

   Most Americans prefer their leaders not to express ideas dogmatically. Maier and Solem demonstrated that groups whose leaders suspended judgment and encouraged full consideration of minority viewpoints produced better solutions than did other groups.[57] Moreover, groups whose leaders withheld their opinions about solutions until later in a discussion produced more and better alternatives to a solution than groups whose leaders expressed their opinions early.[58] Groups prefer open-minded leaders.[59]

5. **Effective group leaders express group-centered concern.**

   From interviews with 90 successful leaders in various professions, Bennis and Nanus reported "there was no trace of self-worship or cockiness in our leaders."[60] Larson and LaFasto found that outstanding team leaders "articulate the team's goal in such a way as to inspire a desire for and eventual commitment to the accomplishment of the goal" and exhibit personal commitment to that goal in both words and deeds.[61] Furthermore, such leaders readily confront members who are more self- than group-centered.[62]

6. **Effective group leaders respect others when they speak.**

   Building on his studies of democratic leaders, Rosenfeld claimed that when ". . . people are equals with whom they work, the rewards and punishments are to be shared."[63] Such leaders are sensitive to nonverbal signals and the feelings these signify. Kenny and Zaccaro reported that leadership depends heavily on competencies in perceiving the needs and goals of members, then adjusting behaviors to these needs.[64] Effective discussion leaders are courteous.

7. **Effective group leaders share rewards and credit with the group.**

   As Fiedler and Chemers pointed out, "Leadership is an amazing ego-involving activity."[65] Leaders are often tempted to take credit for the accomplishments of the group and to consolidate their personal power. But effective leaders share as equals both within the group and when dealing with outsiders. They give credit to the group for accomplishments, and work to develop the leadership competencies of all members.[66] In short, effective leaders are skilled in communicating appreciation for efforts of members.

CONSIDER THIS

How does Jennifer, the leader of the broadcast-advertising group, violate these guidelines? How would you advise her, specifically?

THE RELATIONSHIP BETWEEN LEADERS AND FOLLOWERS

All contingency approaches assume an interdependent relationship between the communication behavior of the leader and the behavior, skills, preferences, and expectations of the members. In fact, although we discuss leaders and members separately, we do so only for convenience; leader-member behaviors form a unit, an interdependent system. Whether a leader's behaviors will be effective depends in large part on both the perceptions and behaviors of the other members.

Most people in our culture want their leaders to perform structuring behaviors, but to be considerate as well. Pavitt and Sackaroff found that experienced group members expected leaders to be enthusiastic and organized, and to encourage participation from all members as well as suggest procedures for the group.[67] This was confirmed by Ketrow, who found that a person who served as a procedural specialist was identified most often as a group's leader, and the task specialist was perceived as being most influential.[68] Infante and Gordon discovered that subordinates preferred a communication style they described as *affirming* (relaxed, friendly, and attentive) and low in verbal aggressiveness (attacks on others' self-concepts).[69]

One characteristic that may affect what members perceive and prefer is sex. Several studies suggest that women enact leadership differently than men, perhaps because members perceive different behavior as appropriate for men and women. Andrews found that although men and women had equal potential as leaders, women were uncomfortable calling themselves *leader* and preferred the designations *organizer* or *coordinator,* apparently because they perceived a stigma attached to the leader label.[70] This finding is supported by Owen, who noted that women distance themselves from the label of *leader.*[71] He also observed that women became leaders by outworking men in a group, and that they used more themes of cohesion. It is likely that women's leadership behavior is constrained by expectations of members. Watson found, for instance, that women who enacted a dominant approach were less influential than women who enacted a considerate approach to leadership, especially with males.[72] However, women gave dominant female leaders higher ratings of effectiveness, but, regardless of style, women liked female bosses less than men did. Watson suggests a problem-solving approach for female leaders that takes into account the difficulties women sometimes have in dealing with perceptions of others.

One model that has looked systematically at the nature of the interdependent relationship of leader-member behaviors and perceptions is the **Leader-Member Exchange (LMX) model,** which suggests that supervisory leaders develop different kinds of leadership relationships with different members, depending on leader and member characteristics. Members differ in the amount of *negotiating latitude* they are allowed by leaders; a member with a high negotiating latitude is given a great deal of leeway to design and perform his or her job, whereas a member with low negotiating latitude is not accorded such freedom by the leader. Generally, members with higher negotiating latitude are more satisfied and more committed to the organization or group. The members' degree of negotiating latitude is transacted through a reciprocal interaction process with the leader, whose impression of the member's capabilities helps determine in large part what degree of negotiating latitude will be permitted.[73]

McClane found support for an interaction between leader and member characteristics, with the best leader-member fit determined by congruence on the need for power.[74] Leaders with high power needs gave greater negotiating latitude to members with high power needs; likewise, leaders with low power needs gave greater negotiating latitude to members with low power needs. Characteristics such as sex, locus of control, and need for achievement were not related. Clearly, leaders with high power needs take a different approach to forming groups than leaders with low power needs; both types of leaders appear to be more comfortable with members who share their assumptions about the appropriate use of power. By extension, members are more likely to be satisfied with leaders who share their assumptions by rewarding them with higher negotiating latitude.

In a different study, McClane compared groups with wide variations in the amount of negotiating latitude and groups with little variation.[75] His results suggest that high differentiation (having some members with high negotiating latitude and some with little latitude in the same group) may have an undesirable effect on a group, particularly if the members accorded high negotiating latitude are seen as an elite core group with the rest feeling like hired hands.

The foregoing discussion is designed to remind us that neither the leader nor the members operate in a vacuum; instead, their interactions are shaped by each other. Models such as the LMX remind us that, even though we isolate leadership and treat it as an individual variable for study purposes, in fact it is a *system-level* variable that is a property of the group as a whole, not of the individual called the group's leader.

Leader-
Member
Exchange
(LMX) Model

THE CASE FOR DISTRIBUTED LEADERSHIP

We have said several times that small group leadership is the property of the group, not the individual who happens to hold the title of leader. We believe strongly that although a group's designated leader bears a lot of responsibility for coordinating and structuring the group's activities, all members can and should be equally responsible for the leadership of the group. The idea of distributed leadership explicitly acknowledges that the leadership of a group is spread among members, with each member expected to perform the communication behaviors needed to move the group toward its goal. A group that distributes leaderships is, in Hersey and Blanchard's terms, mature; the designated leader can largely withdraw from both task and relationship activity because the group members themselves are able to supply these for the group. Remember, a group may be able to function without a leader, but it cannot function without leadership. For example, Counselman reported on a group that had been active for 17 years without a designated leader.[76] Various leadership functions had been picked up by members of the group. The most important of these were providing structure, gatekeeping, setting group norms, and adhering to the group's task. We acknowledge that this is unusual; most groups can and should use the services of a designated leader. However, this case verifies the important point we made earlier about locus of leadership in a group: it belongs to the group.

Barge provided support for the distributed leadership concept when he compared two models of group leadership—one where the leader was an active, directive influence in the group; and a leaderless model, where all members engaged in the leadership process.[77] He discovered that the better predictor of group productivity was overall leadership activity, as opposed to the activity of the designated leader alone. In contrast to what we might expect, the more productive groups were not more controlling or directing. Instead of demonstrating a sender mode, the productive groups enacted a listener mode, reflecting a more contemplative approach with increased sensitivity to the environment and the other members. Barge concluded that while an individual leader's behavior may not necessarily help a group achieve its goals, the overall group leadership behavior does.

Gastil's studies of small group democracy also provide support for distributed leadership. Gastil says that democratic leadership distributes responsibility among members, empowers them by improving their general abilities and leadership skills, and helps the group in its decision-making process.[78] In examining factors that interfere with small group democracy, he notes that all the obstacles he identified were negatively related to comprehension and showing consideration for other members.[79] Listening, in other words, is potentially an important communication skill for members of groups with distributed, democratic leadership.

These findings affirm for us the concept we have of an ideal group. Most of the groups you belong to will have a designated leader, and we are not suggesting doing away with designated leaders. Instead, we invite you to consider what an ideal, responsible, mature group looks like. Even though the group has a designated leader, all members of ideal groups accept responsibility for their leadership. Members understand enough about the group process to know what functions are needed at what times, and they can supply those functions skillfully. Each member has, and acts on, a personal commitment to the group. Each member can step in to the leadership position and function effectively, with the support and contribution of the other members. Our concept of distributed leadership combines elements of several contingency approaches, particularly the functions and communicative competencies approaches. It assumes members are skilled at a variety of the task and interpersonal communication competencies needed for effective leadership. It also assumes that, along with the designated leader, other members can diagnose group needs and meet them appropriately. Once again, leadership is the property of the group, and all members are responsible for effective group leadership.

SUMMARY

1. Leadership was defined as a process of using human communication skills to help the group achieve its goal. Leadership is group–goal-oriented influence of one member on another, whereas the leader is a person who has been appointed, elected, or has emerged to fill a position (or role) of group leader.

2. The source of someone's ability to influence may be legitimate, referent, expert, reward, or punishment power. Coercion, a special form of punishment, is not considered an appropriate source of power in a group.

3. Leadership emergence can be captured in a three-stage model depicting how some members fall out of contention for leadership and others garner support.

4. Several approaches to the study of leadership were examined. Early traits approaches, which assumed that leaders were born rather than made, have been discredited. Styles approaches examine the effect of democratic, autocratic, and laissez-faire styles on such outcomes as productivity and satisfaction. Current con-

tingency approaches assume that there is not one ideal style suitable for all group situations.

5. Most contemporary researchers accept the contingency view of leadership. Important contingency theories we examined included Fiedler's, Hersey and Blanchard's and Chemers's models, the functions approach, and the communicative competencies approach.

6. Seven essential communicative competencies of effective group leaders were described.

7. Leadership is the property of the group, not just the leader. The behavior of each constrains and shapes the behavior of the other. The Leader-Member Exchange model was presented as an example of how leaders and members affect each other.

8. A distributed leadership model suggests that in an ideal and mature group members are as responsible for the productivity and effectiveness of the group as is the designated leader.

EXERCISES

1. In groups of four to six, discuss the following question for 15 minutes; then your group's spokesperson should report your conclusions to the rest of the class:

   "In addition to the communicative competencies listed in this chapter, what others do you think leaders of small task-oriented groups need, and why?"

2. Working alone, make a list of examples of small group leaders influencing followers through each of the five types of power. Share your examples with several classmates. Can you draw any tentative conclusions from your shared examples?

3. Think of an initially leaderless classroom group to which you have belonged. Did that group have an emergent leader? If so, describe the process you observed of how that

individual emerged as a leader. What traits and communication behaviors seemed related to this instance of leadership emergence?

4. Discuss the notion that different types of groups need different types of leaders. What contingencies can you identify that may have a bearing? From your experience, can you give examples of when a leader should have modified his or her behavior to fit the group needs? Do you think there is a best style of leadership to fit all situations?

5. In groups of four to six, discuss the strengths and potential drawbacks of using distributed leadership in a group. Assume you are a designated leader who wants all your group members to be responsible for the group. How would you go about introducing and implementing distributed leadership?

BIBLIOGRAPHY

Barge, J. Kevin, and Randy Y. Hirokawa. "Toward a Communication Competence Model of Group Leadership." *Small Group Behavior* 20 (1989): 167–89.

Bennis, Warren, and B. Nanus. *Leaders: The Strategies for Taking Charge.* New York: Harper & Row, 1985.

Cathcart, Robert S., Larry A. Samovar, and Linda D. Henman, *Small Group Communication: Theory*

and Practice. 7th ed. Dubuque, IA: Brown & Benchmark Publishers, 1996, section 7.

Hackman, Michael Z., and Craig E. Johnson. *Leadership: A Communication Perspective.* Prospect Heights, IL: Waveland Press, 1991.

Larson, Carl E., and Frank M. J. LaFasto. *TeamWork: What Must Go Right/What Can Go Wrong.* Newbury Park, CA: Sage Publications, 1989.

NOTES

1. Carl E. Larson and Frank M. J. LaFasto, *TeamWork: What Must Go Right/What Can Go Wrong* (Newbury Park, CA: Sage, 1989): 118.

2. Michael Z. Hackman and Craig E. Johnson, *Leadership: A Communication Perspective* (Prospect Heights, IL: Waveland Press, 1991): 11.

3. E. Hollander, "Leadership and Power," in *The Handbook of Social Psychology* 3, vol. II,

eds. G. Lindzey and Elliot Aronson (New York: Random House, 1985): 485–537.

4. John R. P. French and Bertram Raven, "The Bases of Social Power," in *Group Dynamics: Research and Theory,* 3d ed., eds. Dorwin Cartwright and Alvin Zander (New York: McGraw-Hill, 1981): 317.

5. Marvin E. Shaw, *Group Dynamics: Research and Theory,* 3d ed. (New York: McGraw-Hill, 1981): 317.

6. Ernest G. Bormann, *Discussion and Group Methods,* 2d ed. (New York: Harper & Row, 1975): 253–69; Nancy L. Harper and Lawrence R. Askling, "Group Communication and Quality of Task Solution in a Media Production Organization," *Communication Monographs* 47 (1980): 77–100.

7. E. P. Hollander, *Leadership Dynamics* (New York: Free Press, 1978): 13–16.

8. Ernest Stech and Sharon A. Ratliffe, *Working in Groups* (Skokie, IL: National Textbook Company, 1976): 201.

9. Donald Ellis and B. Aubrey Fisher, *Small Group Decision Making: Communication and the Group Process* (New York: McGraw-Hill, 1994): 203–6.

10. Ernest G. Bormann, *Small Group Communication: Theory and Practice,* 3d ed., (New York: Harper & Row, 1990) 205–14 and 291–92; John C. Geier, "A Trait Approach to the Study of Leadership in Small Groups," *Journal of Communication* 17 (1967): 316–23.

11. John C. Geier, "A Trait Approach to the Study of Leadership in Small Groups," 316–23.

12. M. Snyder, "Self Monitoring Processes," in *Advances in Experimental Social Psychology,* vol. 12, ed. L. Berkowitz (New York: Academic Press, 1979).

13. Stephen J. Zaccaro, Roseanne J. Foti, and David A. Kenny, "Self-Monitoring and Trait-Based Variance in Leadership: An Investigation of Leader Flexibility across Multiple Group Situations," *Journal of Applied Psychology* 76 (1991): 308–15.

14. Robert J. Ellis and Steven F. Cronshaw, "Self-Monitoring and Leader Emergence: A Test of Moderator Effects," *Small Group Research* 23 (February 1992): 113–29.

15. Steven F. Cronshaw and Robert J. Ellis, "A Process Investigation of Self-Monitoring and Leader Emergence," *Small Group Research* 22 (November 1991): 403–20.

16. Deborah C. Baker, "A Qualitative and Quantitative Analysis of Verbal Style and the Elimination of Potential Leaders in Small Groups," *Communication Quarterly* 38 (Winter 1990): 13–26.

17. Judith A. Kolb, "Are We Still Stereotyping Leadership? A Look at Gender and Other Predictors of Leader Emergence," *Small Group Research* 28 (1997): 370–93.

18. Katherine W. Hawkins, "Effects of Gender and Communication Content on Leadership Emergence in Small Task-Oriented Groups," *Small Group Research* 26 (May 1995): 234–49.

19. Susan Shimanoff and Mercilee M. Jenkins, "Leadership and Gender: Challenging Assumptions and Recognizing Resources," in *Small Group Communication: Theory and Practice,* 7th ed., eds. Robert S. Cathcart, Larry A. Samovar, and Linda Henman (Madison: WI: Brown & Benchmark, 1996): 327–44.

20. Gita De Souza and Howard J. Klein, "Emergent Leadership in the Group Goal-Setting Process," *Small Group Research* 26 (November 1995): 475–96.

21. Lita Kurth, "Democracy and Leadership in Basic Writing Small Groups," Paper presented at the Annual Meeting of the Conference on College Composition and Communication (March 1995).

22. Susan A. Wheelan and Frances Johnston, "The Role of Informal Member Leaders in a System Containing Formal Leaders," *Small Group Research* 27 (February 1996): 33–55.

23. Ellis and Fisher, *Small Group Decision Making: Communication and the Group Process,* 210–12.

24. Ralph M. Stogdill, *Handbook of Leadership: A Survey of Theory and Research* (New York: Free Press, 1974): 63–82; Marvin E. Shaw, *Group Dynamics,* 2d ed. (New York: McGraw-Hill, 1976): 274–75 and chapter 6.

25. "Predictions: If the Crown Fits . . . ," *Newsweek,* August 23, 1999 p. 8.

26. Ellis and Fisher, *Small Group Decision Making: Communication and the Group Process,* 182.

27. Ralph M. Stogdill, "Personal Factors Associated with Leadership: A Survey of Literature," *Journal of Psychology* 25 (1948): 64.

28. Charles Pavitt and Pamela Sakaroff, "Implicit Theories of Leadership and Judgments of Leadership among Group Members," *Small Group Research* 21 (1990): 374–92.

29. Lawrence B. Rosenfeld and Timothy B. Plax, "Personality Determinants of Autocratic and Democratic Leadership," *Speech Monographs* 42 (1975): 203–8.

30. Douglas McGregor, *The Human Side of Enterprise* (New York: McGraw-Hill, 1960).

31. Ralph K. White and Ronald Lippett, "Leader Behavior and Member Reaction in Three 'Social Climates'," in *Group Dynamics: Research and Theory,* 2d ed., eds. Dorwin Cartwright and Alvin Zander (Evanston, IL: Row, Peterson and Company, 1960): 527–53; William E. Jurma, "Effects of Leader Structuring Style and Task-Orientation Characteristics of Group Members," *Communication Monographs* 46 (1979): 282; Malcom G. Preston and Roy K. Heintz, "Effectiveness of Participatory versus Supervisory Leadership in Group Judgment," *Journal of Abnormal and Social Psychology* 44 (1949): 344–45; George Graen, Fred Dansereau, and Takau Minami, "Dysfunctional Leadership Styles," *Organizational Behavior and Human Performance* 7 (1972): 216–36; Norman R. F. Maier and Ronald A. Maier, "An Experimental Test of the Effects of 'Developmental' vs. 'Free' Discussions on the Quality of Group Decisions," *Journal of Applied Psychology* 41 (1957): 320–23; William E. Jurma, "Leadership Structuring Style, Task Ambiguity and Group Members' Satisfaction," *Small Group Behavior* 9 (1978): 124–34.

32. John Gastil, "A Meta-Analytic Review of the Productivity and Satisfaction of Democratic and Autocratic Leadership," *Small Group Research* 25 (August 1995): 384–410.

33. Ellis and Fisher, *Small Group Decision Making: Communication and the Group Process,* 184.

34. Julia T. Wood, "Alternative Portraits of Leaders: A Contingency Approach to Perceptions of Leadership," *Western Journal of Speech Communication* 43 (1979): 260–70.

35. R. N. Griffin, "Relationships among Individual, Task Design, and Leader Behavior Variables," *Academy of Management Journal* 23 (1980): 665–83.

36. Cal W. Downs and Terry Pickett, "An Analysis of the Effects of Nine Leadership-Group Compatibility Contingencies upon Productivity and Member Satisfaction," *Communication Monographs* 44 (1977): 220–30.

37. David J. Skaret and Nealia S. Bruning, "Attitudes about the Work Group: An Added Moderator of the Relationship between Leader Behavior and Job Satisfaction," *Group & Organization Studies* 11 (1986): 254–79.

38. M. L. Chemers, "Leadership Theory and Research: A Systems-Process Integration," in *Basic Group Processes,* ed. P. B. Paulus (New York: Springer-Verlag, 1983): 9–39.

39. R. F. Bales, *Interaction Process Analysis* (Cambridge, MA: Addison-Wesley, 1950).

40. Kenneth D. Benne and Paul Sheats, "Functional Roles of Group Members," *Journal of Social Issues* 4 (1948): 41–49.

41. B. Aubrey Fisher, "Leadership as Medium: Treating Complexity in Group Communication Research," *Small Group Behavior* 16 (1985): 167–96.

42. Karl Weick, "The Spines of Leaders," in *Leadership: Where Else Can We Go?,* eds. M. McCall and M. Lombardo (Durham, NC: Duke University Press, 1978): 37–61.

43. Fred E. Fiedler, *A Theory of Leadership Effectiveness* (New York: McGraw-Hill, 1967).

44. Paul Hersey and Kenneth Blanchard, *Management of Organizational Behavior: Utilizing Human Resources,* 7th ed. (New York: Prentice-Hall, 1996).

45. Julia T. Wood, "Leading in Purposive Discussions: A Study of Adaptive

Behaviors," *Communication Monographs* 44 (1977): 152–65.

46. Ritch L. Sorenson and Grant T. Savage, "Signaling Participation through Relational Communication: A Test of the Leader Interpersonal Influence Model," *Group & Organization Studies* 14 (September 1989): 325–54.

47. Gay L. Drecksell, "Interaction Characteristics of Emergent Leadership" (Unpublished doctoral dissertation, University of Utah, 1984).

48. Chemers, "Leadership Theory and Research: A Systems-Process Integration," 9–39.

49. Fisher, "Leadership," 203–4.

50. J. Kevin Barge and Randy Y. Hirokawa, "Toward a Communication Competency Model of Group Leadership," *Small Group Behavior* 20 (1989): 167–89.

51. Charles G. Morris and J. R. Hackman, "Behavioral Correlates of Perceived Leadership," *Journal of Personality and Social Psychology* 13 (1969): 350–61.

52. Paul D. Reynolds, "Leaders Never Quit: Talking, Silence, and Influence in Interpersonal Groups," *Small Group Behavior* 15 (1984): 411.

53. Hugh C. Russell, "Dimensions of Communicative Behavior of Discussion Leaders" (Paper presented to Central States Speech Convention, Chicago, April 1970).

54. Velma J. Lashbrook, "Gibb's Interaction Theory: The Use of Perceptions in the Discrimination of Leaders from Nonleaders" (Paper presented at the Speech Communication Association, Houston, December 1975).

55. Barge and Hirokawa, "Toward a Communication Competency Model."

56. Fisher, "Leadership," 205–7.

57. Norman R. G. Maier and A. R. Solem, "The Contributions of a Discussion Leader to the Quality of Group Thinking: The Effective Use of Minority Opinions," *Human Relations* 5 (1952): 277–88.

58. Lance E. Anderson and William K. Balzer, "The Effects of Timing of Leaders' Opinions on Problem-Solving Groups: A Field Experiment," *Group & Organization Studies* 16 (March 1991): 86–101.

59. Franklyn S. Haiman (From a paper given at the Speech Communication Association Annual Conference, Chicago, December 1984).

60. Warren Bennis and Burt Nanus, *Leaders: The Strategies for Taking Charge* (New York: Harper & Row, 1985): 57.

61. Larson and LaFasto, *TeamWork,* 121–23.

62. Ibid., 135.

63. Lawrence B. Rosenfeld, *Now That We're All Here . . . Relations in Small Groups* (Columbus, OH: Charles E. Merrill, 1976): 76.

64. D. A. Kenny and S. J. Zaccaro, "An Estimate of Variance Due to Traits in Leadership," *Journal of Applied Psychology* 68 (1983): 678–85.

65. Fred E. Fiedler and Martin M. Chemers, *Leadership and Effective Management* (Glenview, IL: Scott, Foresman, 1974): 5.

66. Larson and LaFasto, *TeamWork,* 126–27.

67. Pavitt and Sackaroff, "Implicit Theories of Leadership and Judgments of Leadership among Group Members."

68. Sandra M. Ketrow, "Communication Role Specializations and Perceptions of Leadership," *Small Group Research* 22 (November 1991): 492–514.

69. Dominic A. Infante and William I. Gordon, "How Employees See the Boss: Test of Argumentative and Affirming Model of Supervisors' Communicative Behavior," *Western Journal of Speech Communication* 55 (Summer 1991): 294–304.

70. Patricia Hayes Andrews, "Sex and Gender Differences in Group Communication: Impact on the Facilitation Process," *Small Group Research* 23 (February 1992): 74–94.

71. William Foster Owen, "Rhetorical Themes of Emergent Female Leaders," *Small Group Behavior* 17 (November 1986): 475–86.

72. Carol Watson, "When a Woman Is the Boss: Dilemmas in Taking Charge," *Group &*

Organization Studies 13 (June 1988): 163–81.

73. G. B. Graen and T. A. Scandura, "Toward a Psychology of Dyadic Organizing," in *Research in Organizational Behavior* 9, eds. L. L. Cummings and B. Shaw (Greenwich, CT: JAI, 1987): 175–208.

74. William E. McClane, "The Interaction of Leader and Member Characteristics in the Leader-Member Exchange (LMX) Model of Leadership," *Small Group Research* 22 (August 1991): 283–300.

75. William E. McClane, "Implications of Member Role Differentiation: An Analysis of a Key Concept in the LMX Model of Leadership,"

Group & Organization Studies 16 (March 1991): 102–13.

76. Eleanor F. Counselman, "Leadership in a Long Term Leaderless Group," *Small Group Research* 22 (May 1991): 240–57.

77. J. Kevin Barge, "Leadership as Medium: A Leaderless Group Discussion Model," *Communication Quarterly* 37 (Fall 1989): 237–47.

78. John Gastil, "A Definition and Illustration of Democratic Leadership," *Human Relations* 47 (August 1994): 953–75.

79. John Gastil, "Identifying Obstacles to Small Group Democracy," *Small Group Research* 24 (February 1993): 5–27.

Serving as Designated Leader

10

Central Message

A designated leader is expected to perform a variety of administrative, structuring, and developmental activities on behalf of the group. A democratic designated leader encourages members to enact a variety of leadership functions while serving as a completer for functions not being supplied by other members.

Study Objectives

As a result of studying of Chapter 10 you should be able to:
1. Articulate a personal philosophy of small group leadership that supports distributed leadership enacted by a group-centered, democratic leader.
2. Name the three major types of services expected of designated small group leaders and describe specific ways of providing them.
3. Produce written messages essential to the work of small secondary groups, including meeting notices and agendas, minutes, and reports to other groups and organizations.
4. Describe the ethical principles that guide group leaders.

Key Terms

Administrative duties
Agenda
Gatekeeper
Leader as completer
Liaison
Meeting notice
Minutes

The executive committee of a regional home health agency faced a critical task. The agency had decided to pursue Joint Review Commission accreditation. The application itself was lengthy and had to include an in-depth self-study, which was due in about a year. The problem, however, was that the executive committee had been meeting weekly for over six months without making any progress on the self-study. Celinda, the agency's director of operations and designated chair of the executive committee, was frustrated. She wanted the committee, all registered nurses who were department heads at the agency, to take ownership of the project, decide what would be contained in the various sections of the report, collaborate on gathering the data and information needed, and take responsibility for writing the report. Although the department heads *said* they wanted to work together on the report, they seemed listless at meetings and did only what Celinda specifically assigned them to do. They didn't seem to talk freely with one another or to exhibit the kind of open exchange of information necessary for completing such a massive task.

This health agency executive committee was in trouble. If things did not turn around, they would not meet the deadline for submitting the accreditation application. Celinda faced several obstacles, not the least of which was to get the executive committee members involved and committed to their task. One of the hardest jobs of a designated leader is to recognize there is a problem, diagnose the problem, figure out what actions to take, and implement change.

In Chapter 9 we explained that current theories of leadership focus on the leader's communication competencies, including the ability to perceive what a group needs and to adjust behavior accordingly. We supported the idea that leadership be appropriately distributed among members, who also benefit from improving their communicative competencies. However, developing these competencies can be a challenge; just because someone is designated as a group's leader does not automatically mean the group will receive the leadership services it needs. Thus, we cannot exaggerate how important it is for you to develop leadership competencies if you are to be effective either as a member or especially as a group leader:

> [T]he right person in a leadership role can add tremendous value to any collective effort, even to the point of sparking the outcome with an intangible kind of magic.[1]

Larson and LaFasto concluded that outstanding leaders begin by articulating a clear goal for the group in such a way that every member feels a desire for and commitment to that goal, and then developing a plan for achieving the goal that will ". . . unleash the energy and talents of contributing members."[2] This was the task facing Celinda. In this chapter we present specific suggestions to guide your performance as a designated leader, a kind of "leader's manual." We note again that it is appropriate for *all* members, not just the leader, to perform these duties as well. We first discuss general principles guiding the leader's relationship to the group as a whole, then explain the three major types of duties leaders are expected to perform for small groups in the United States, and finally present ethical principles important for small group leaders.

GROUP-CENTERED DEMOCRATIC LEADERSHIP

To reiterate a major theme from Chapter 9, we believe that leadership should be tailored to fit the specific situation facing the group. In some situations, such as with members who are inexperienced or unwilling, more controlling forms of leadership are appropriate, at least initially. In other situations, with highly experienced and capable members, a designated leader may not even be necessary. However, most situations will fall between those two extremes.

Our position is that the ideal form of leadership, at least according to the standards and values of American culture, is democratic leadership that recognizes the equality of all members by encouraging member participation in all group decisions. As Donald Petersen, the CEO whose leadership during the 1980s pulled Ford Motor Company from near-bankruptcy to profitability, said: "Employee involvement requires participative management. Anyone who has a legitimate reason, who will be affected by a decision, ought to have the feeling that people want to know how he or she feels."[3] This belief is a cornerstone of our political foundation, as is stated in the Declaration of Independence: "We hold these truths to be self-evident, that all men [sic] are created equal. . . ." We stress that this is the *ideal*. In group situations that do not seem to call for democratic leadership, then we believe the leader should exert the *least* amount of control necessary to help the group achieve its goal. Moreover, it is the leader's responsibility to work toward helping the members gain the experience, confidence, and skills they need so they can function effectively in a democratic group.

While it is true that certain situations call for other leadership styles, the kinds of task-oriented, problem-solving groups you will most often encounter call for democratic leadership. In a democratic relationship, attempts to coerce are perceived as unethical because they assume personal superiority and special rights on the part of the leader; they also chip away at the members' sense of self-identity. Attempts to coerce do not work because they eventually lead either to apathy or rebellion.

It may appear that we are contradicting ourselves when we say, "Be the type of leader a group needs, but be democratic." What we mean is that a leader should first recognize the group's current reality and serve the group as needed, while working toward achieving the ultimate goal of the ideal group, one in which members are committed, responsible, and mature; leadership services are distributed among all members; and any person could serve well as the designated leader.

FIGURE 10.1 | **The leader as "completer" of the group.**

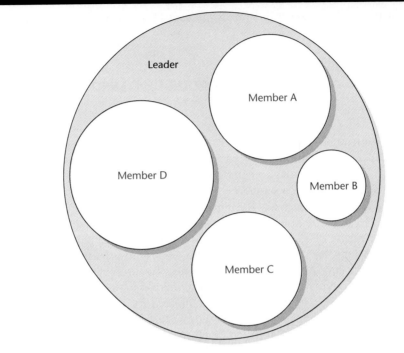

Leader as Completer If group members are capable enough to serve as the group's leader, what does that leave for the designated leader to do? The metaphor we suggest is that the members are the bricks and the leader is the mortar that binds them together, as shown in Figure 10.1. The bricks provide the support and substance of the group, but the mortar allows the whole group to hold its shape—completes the structure, so to speak. This concept of the **leader as completer,** as articulated by Schutz, suggests that ". . . the best a leader can do is to observe what functions are not being performed by a segment of the group and enable this part to accomplish them" or, if necessary, perform them.[4] Donald Ellis's study of leadership patterns confirmed this notion of stewardship.[5] His work suggests that leaders are not distinguished from other members by their performance of a set of specific behaviors. Instead, leaders vary their communication to each member, whereas the other members' communication behavior is consistent no matter whom they address.

This concept makes several demands on both the leader and the members. Members should be competent enough both to know what the group needs at any given time and to meet that need by saying and doing the right thing. For example, if the group has digressed, a member can, and *should,* jump in with something like: "I think we've gotten off track. Can we get back to the topic?" The leader, too, should be competent enough to recognize the need and be able to jump in *if someone else in the group has not already provided the needed leadership behavior.* This means that the leader is primarily a monitor or medium of the group's *process,* with the principle responsibility for maintaining a long-range perspective on the group's progress. To continue our executive committee story, Celinda not only concluded that she and the group needed help, she took action. In her case, she talked to her boss (the home health agency's director) and together they brought in two consultants (a university professor and licensed psychologist) to help the group over its impasse. Our model promotes *distributed leadership,* where everyone is ultimately responsible for the group.

RESPONSIBILITIES AND TECHNIQUES OF DISCUSSION LEADERS AND CHAIRS

Although being leader of a group can be time consuming, the designated leader's duties in a continuing group need not require much more effort and time than are expected of all group members, particularly if the group has developed along the democratic lines suggested. In fact, in groups of peers, leaders will *not* spend more time than the others if the other members view the job of organizing and carrying out the group's task as an activity to be shared by all members. For example, a group one of us belonged to discussed openly how leadership functions were to be distributed; one person was made responsible for calling meetings, a second for taking notes and having them distributed, and a third for soliciting items for the agenda from other members. During the discussion periods, the position of discussion leader rotated among members, as did the position of social chair. Ideally, every member can assume responsibility to supply whatever leadership services appear to be needed at any given time. This is the essence of effective discussion leadership, even though one person has been selected or has emerged as *the* leader. These responsibilities had somehow broken down in Celinda's executive committee and she *and* her group members had to find out why if they were to turn things around.

In Chapter 9 we presented information about contingencies that may affect the degree of control appropriately assumed by the designated leader. Contingency theory, which we support, requires leaders to be astute in their analyses of the group's situation and members' needs. Designated leaders, to function well as completers, must demonstrate tremendous flexibility to adjust their behavior to the needs of the group. Leaders can rely on group members to help them by periodic, *explicit* review of the group's procedures. Considering the following situational variables can help you optimize your leadership style:

1. **Group purpose and goals.**
   Learning, personal growth, and value-sharing groups need far less structure and control than secondary groups charged with recommending solutions to complex problems. In addition, specific procedures (brainstorming, buzz group procedures, problem census, nominal group technique, etc.) require considerable procedural control.

2. **Member expectations.**
   A designated leader will initially need to conform to what members expect of the role, but this can later be changed through explicit discussion of the leader's job and through development of the members' own leadership skills.

3. **Member skills and maturity.**

   As Hersey and Blanchard reported, members who are used to working together, who understand the task, and who are effective communicators need less leader control than inexperienced members or newly formed groups.

4. **Member involvement in the group's task.**

   When members perceive that the task is important to them personally, they will often resist tight procedural control by a leader. Leaders should try to help members realize the importance of the task and thus become involved. The members of the health agency's executive committee while publicly declaring they wanted to work together were not doing so and Celinda had to figure out why if she was to get them involved again.

CONSIDER THIS

You know a couple of things about the health agency's executive committee. The committee was composed of all registered nurses who were all department heads at the agency. In addition, they were struggling with an accreditation application which involves a self-study. They all believed their task to be an important step for the agency. It didn't seem as if there should have been a problem. What do you think their underlying problems might have been?

5. **The leader's skill and confidence.**

   Democratic leadership calls for skills in listening, organizing, summarizing, and timing that take a long time to develop. Leaders should remember that the other group members can serve as a resource; a leader who believes the group needs services he or she is not able to provide should ask for the help of the other members.

6. **The time factor.**

   If a decision must be made in a hurry, a group will welcome strict control of its procedures. When time is not limited, less leader control is needed.

   In problem-solving groups, the designated leader generally should focus primarily on task and procedural matters, secondarily on interpersonal relationship matters. There are three broad categories of services that designated leaders of such groups are expected to perform: administrative duties, discussion coordination, and group development. The advice we give about how to supply these services is based on research findings and the democratic philosophy we espouse. We suggest that each organization develop a manual of duties and responsibilities for its committees, task forces, and other small groups, including a statement of legitimate authority of the designated leaders. With such a manual, members' expectations will be much clearer and leaders will have guidelines to follow without having to guess at their duties.

Numerous **administrative duties** must be handled; the most important ones are planning for meetings, following up on meetings, maintaining liaison with other groups, and managing the group's written communication.

Administrative Duties

For small group meetings this famous adage holds: "To fail to plan is to plan to fail." Failure to plan wastes everyone's time and produces low-quality outputs. The following checklist can guide your planning for productive meetings.

Planning for Meetings

1. **Define the purpose of the meeting.**
   First, decide whether a meeting is necessary and wise. Do *not* call a meeting if other communication avenues (telephone, fax, e-mail, memo) will convey the message effectively, when there isn't time for participants to prepare adequately, when one or more essential people cannot participate, or when the issues are personal and better handled privately.[6]
   Define the purpose of the meeting clearly; don't have a meeting if there's no definite purpose for it. "To talk over our coming year as a committee" is *not* adequately defined as an objective, but "To establish an agenda of problems for committee actions during the coming six months" is clear. Be sure to formulate *specific* outcomes, such as a written report, list of recommendations, and so forth, to be produced from the meeting.

2. **Establish starting and ending times for the meeting.**
   Frequently, committees and study groups meet with strict time limits imposed by other concurrent meetings, class and work schedules, and other factors over which the group has no control. Even without such external time limits, ending times should be established. Running overtime will kill member involvement and attendance and is a barrier to operating democratically.[7] Setting an ending time encourages the group to use its time well. If the work cannot be finished, plan additional meetings.

3. **If special resource people are needed for the meeting, advise and prepare them.**
   Small groups frequently need to question specialists with unique knowledge and skills or experience. For example, the church board described in Chapter 2 invited church development specialists in to help board members organize activities to promote the growth of the church. Such invited resource persons need to know in advance what information to prepare and what to expect. Celinda and her boss had to brief the two consultants on the history of the group and their current perceptions of the group's problems. In this particular case, the consultants did not come to only one meeting but worked with the committee for six weeks.

4. **Make all necessary physical arrangements.**
   Has the meeting room been reserved? Are handouts, notepads, chalk, charts, and possibly beverages ready? Leaders should *think about* the selection and use of their meeting space. Among other things, members need to be able to see and hear other members, be able to view any audiovisual materials, and the room should comfortably fit the size of the

group. It should not be too large or else you run the risk of creating psychological distance between participants.[8]

5. **If needed, prepare a procedure by which the group can evaluate its process.**
Groups should periodically evaluate their throughput processes. Appropriate postmeeting reaction forms, described in Chapter 15, can be prepared to help do this.

6. **Notify members of the purpose or agenda, necessary preparation, and time and place of the meeting.**
The chair is responsible for seeing that members are notified and given ample opportunity to prepare for a meeting. In large organizations, this duty may be delegated to a staff person, such as professional secretary, but it is still the *responsibility* of the leader.

Following Up on Meetings   Two kinds of follow-up are needed: reminding group members of assignments to be sure they are completed and getting out necessary reports from the group to other groups or individuals. If adequate reports of minutes are kept, members can be reminded of routine assignments through these written records. Sometimes members agree to undertake special assignments. One member may agree to find bibliographic references, another to conduct a personal interview, and a third to procure copies of a relevant statute—all before the next meeting. The leader can make a brief phone call before the next meeting to ask tactfully whether the member encountered any trouble in completing the assignment; this serves as a gentle reminder and helps keep the group on track.

A chair often has to prepare and send letters, memoranda, formal reports, notices of group decisions, advice prepared by the committee, and so forth to appropriate people. This includes getting copies of minutes prepared and distributed, but more especially involves writing formal resolutions, sending advisory policy statements to administrative officers, calling and conducting a press conference, or carrying out whatever decisions for action the group has made. Although the group should decide what to do and who is to do it, the *who* is often the group's designated leader.

Liaison   A **liaison** serves as spokesperson for the group to other groups or to the parent organization; typically, this is the designated leader's job. In most organizations, the chairs of standing committees maintain necessary coordination among the small groups that compose the organization. Many organizations have regular meetings of division managers. Whenever you act as liaison, keep in mind that you represent *your group* rather than yourself.

Several specific occasions call for liaison. Many times two or more small groups must coordinate their work, such as when constructing a new building or producing a play. Occasionally committee chairs will be interviewed by public media. If you anticipate this happening, you can be prepared to answer reporters' questions. The chair's statements should accurately reflect the group's work, findings, and beliefs. Any statement that is biased toward one side of an internal group controversy will cause further friction and division within the group, and the leader will lose the trust of those members who feel misrepresented.

Although discussion involves mostly oral communicating, a group needs written messages and records to provide continuity from meeting to meeting; to remind members of their assignments; to confirm agreements and accomplishments; to provide legal documentation of attendance, decisions, and actions; to bring absentees up to date; and to inform the parent organization and others about what the group is doing. Although learning groups rarely keep records of meetings, problem-solving groups always should. Most committees are required to keep minutes of all meetings and to submit written reports to specified personnel. Even a single-meeting conference group needs a written record. For example, one of the authors belonged to a community theater for which the written record of an *ad hoc* personnel review committee provided evidence used in a lawsuit to support the theater's assertion that an employee was not fired arbitrarily. Lacking this record, the theater probably would have lost the suit.

Managing Written Communication for a Group

Four categories of written messages that contribute to small group leadership are personal notes, meeting records, meeting notices and agendas, and reports and resolutions.

Personal notes.   The typical conference room is pictured with note pads and pencils at each seat because taking notes focuses group members' listening so they aren't likely to lose sight of the group goal or switch subjects. When you take notes, don't try to record a transcript of the whole discussion. Instead, focus on keeping track, with just a key word or two, of the thrust of the discussion; notes should be detailed enough to prepare minutes or check the secretary's work. This helps you, as leader, summarize when needed, be sure no important concept or proposal is overlooked, and follow up between meetings to ensure that assignments are being completed. Examples of personal notes are provided in Figure 10.2.

If your instructor requires you to submit a case study of your group at the end of the semester or quarter, you can use personal meeting notes, in combination with a journal, to record the development of the group. For a thorough case study, record such matters as roles members seem to be developing, leadership behaviors, communicative successes and failures, and conflict management.

Group records.   All ongoing committees should maintain accurate and comprehensive **minutes** that serve as official records of the important content of meetings, especially of decisions made. Although the designated leader is responsible for seeing that minutes are recorded and distributed to members prior to the next meeting, that task may be delegated to a secretary or a volunteer from the group. Sometimes professional secretaries attend

| FIGURE 10.2 | A discussion leader's personal notes. |

October 4, 1991 --- Everyone present

<u>Discussion topic</u>: what topics should we include in our class
                    presentation on group polarization?

<u>Main criteria</u>:

    Judy & Bill --- to get an "A" info must be accurate
    Bart --- has to have practical application
    Bev --- Dr. Brilhart wants innovative presentation
    Everybody should have a part in presenting the topic to the class.

<u>Topics</u>

* Definition of group polarization (all agreed)
  Risky shift (Hal says can become a cautious shift w/ cautious
    members --- this term is outdated)

* Exercises to demonstrate when group takes risks + when it becomes
    cautious --- Judy says there's a bunch of these in a book she has

* Need to show how this applies in <u>real</u> life.

* Decisions Made
Assignments: Me (application); Judy & Bill (library research);
    Hal & Bev (exercises -- w/ Judy's book)

Next meeting --- Wed., October 11

meetings for the specific purpose of writing minutes, perhaps with the help of an audio recording. Even then, the leader is responsible for ensuring that the minutes are accurate.

Minutes are necessary for the efficient functioning of any group. Without such a written record, members often forget important information, fail to complete assignments, or argue about what was decided. For instance, the church board mentioned in Chapter 2 frequently referred to the minutes to recall what decisions members had made about various policies such as the rental charge for facilities, procedures for becoming a member, and so forth. The minutes prevented wasted time and unnecessary tension.

Minutes focus on the content, not the process of discussion. They are a summary record of all task-oriented information shared during the meeting, all ideas proposed as solutions, all decisions and how they were made (majority, consensus, consent), all assignments, and any plans or procedures for future action. Any special reports of procedures for future action should be attached to the minutes.

Minutes take the form of a special memorandum, though the format may vary depending on the origins and nature of the group, norms, and perhaps the history and bylaws of the parent organization. The written report of a task force or other *ad hoc* committee may take the form of a summary report, whereas standing committees (which typically consider more than one topic or problem per meeting) should number items of business in the order they were discussed. The minutes should be signed by the writer, with a copy sent to each member as soon as possible before the next meeting. This gives members a chance to check them for accuracy and correct them at the beginning of the next meeting. Figure 10.3 is an example of minutes from a student project group that dealt with only one major topic during its entire life.

The next example of minutes, shown in Figure 10.4, comes from the church board of Chapter 2. Notice that the format, suggested by Sally, the secretary, allows members to see immediately what items were considered and what actions were taken without having to comb through a lot of narrative.

Meeting notices and agendas. A notice of each meeting should be sent to all members in time to allow them to prepare for the meeting. A **meeting notice** is a memorandum that normally includes the following items:

1. Name of person to whom notice is sent.
2. Name and position of person sending notice and calling meeting.
3. When meeting will begin and end.
4. Where meeting will be held.
5. Purpose of meeting and specific outcomes to be achieved.
6. Agenda (if more than one item of business will be discussed) listing all problems or topics to be discussed.
7. Any relevant facts, reading sources, or other preparation members should make prior to meeting.
8. If this is a single-meeting group, conference, or first meeting of a new group, a list of all persons who will attend.

An **agenda** is a list of the items of business, topics, and other matters in the sequence they will be considered in the meeting. For a continuing group such as a standing committee or task force, usually the first item of business is the report of the previous meeting: should the minutes be approved as distributed or revised in some way? For a standing committee or board, the agenda might include a number of problems on which the group is working. For a task force, the agenda might be two or three questions about facts and

| **FIGURE 10.3** | **An example of minutes.** |

Report of Third Meeting of Polarization Instruction Group

Date of Meeting: Wednesday, March 12, 1997
Time and Place: 7:30–9:00 P.M. in Room 338, Craig Hall
Attendance: Bev Halliday, Inez Salinas, Terrell Washington, Bill Miklas, Judy Hartlieb

Report of Second Meeting
    Judy distributed copies of the report of the second meeting to all members. It was approved. It was decided that Judy would be responsible for recording and distributing reports of each group meeting.

Goals
    A suggested outline for problem solving presented by Terrell was followed. This led to a discussion of group polarization and to determining the actions to be taken involving the group's "problem."
    The group goals were identified as 1) understanding group polarization, 2) conducting a presentation with a class exercise on polarization for the class, and 3) each member being able to write a personal essay about the group experience.

Exercise Portion of Presentation
    After some discussion of the type of exercise to be used in the presentation, it was decided that Inez would be responsible for trying to locate a book with sample exercises that could be considered by the group at the next meeting. Bill will also have primary responsibility for this portion of the presentation and will see that copies of the test are produced and ready for the class. The other group members will individually brainstorm for exercise ideas, and further discussion of these will take place during our class meeting of Tuesday, March 18.
    Criteria for class exercises were discussed. It was concluded that the purpose of the exercise would be to demonstrate the phenomenon of group polarization at work. The exercise would be divided in such a way that each individual in the class would first take it alone and then with a small group, and see what shifts occurred.

Leader and Role
    The group determined that the leader would be responsible for developing agendas and outlines for future meetings and should serve as a overall controller and fill-in or backup person for other group members. Bev was selected by unanimous vote to fill this role as group leader.

Structure of Presentation
    A structure and time schedule of the presentation was decided on:

    5 minutes—Each member of the class takes the exercise individually.
    10 minutes—The class is divided into four groups, with four of our small group members serving as observers. Each group will determine how to solve the exercise problem.
    5 minutes—One member of our group will present a short report on group polarization research to the class. At the same time, the four observers will be finishing their notes regarding what happened in their respective groups.
    5 minutes—The four groups will each discuss what occurred in the group. The observer may start the discussion or serve as a guide/reference person, answering questions and giving insight into what happened with polarization in the group.
    5 minutes—The class as a whole will have the opportunity to share what was observed and experienced within the groups. The observers may again start the discussion and open the floor to any class member's contribution.

Additional Member Roles
    Bill agreed to present the five-minute oral report on polarization to the class.
    Terrell will be responsible for arranging meeting places and will serve as a backup to any member who might be absent.

Adjournment and Next Meeting
    The meeting adjourned at approximately 9:00 P.M. Further planning will take place on Tuesday, March 18, during class time.

Another example of minutes.   **FIGURE 10.4**

Board of Directors Meeting Minutes
April 16, 1997

Present: Bill Prior, Norm Kerris, Gary Sloane, Don Bowles, Sally Schultz (directors): Sunni Prior, Marina Kerris,
(invited guests); Jane Simmons, church secretary.

Call to order: Opening prayer was given by Sally. Minutes of the April 9 meeting were approved as presented.

Topic	Discussion	Actions/Recommendations
Attendance/ offering	120—Sunday, April 13 Total deposit—$1552.52 Building fund—$5858.00	
Founders Sun., May 18	Marina will attempt to get the SMSU Gospel Choir to sing for a 30-minute program. Covered dish supper to follow service. Jody (Hospitality Committee) in charge of set-up	
Adult Sun. School	Roy Hackman will be teaching from "Spiritual Economics" starting April 29.	
Rental of facilities	Ada Cole asked cost of renting sanctuary for a workshop; Discussion centered on cost of utilities/wear and tear	Norm moved, Don seconded, that we establish a policy of charging $30 per half day for all rentals. Passed.
Circle Suppers	Bill shared information about Circle Supper program; it has been very successful at the Columbia church. Discussion followed, and several names suggested to organize	Sally moved, Gary seconded, that we ask Jean Ames to coordinate; that we hold them monthly on second Saturday. Passed.
Search Committee	Marina reported we have 10 applications; search committee will telephone interview and ask 3 to come for a full interview.	

Meeting adjourned at 8:30 P.M. Don gave the closing prayer.

Respectfully submitted,

Sally Schultz

findings on the problem to which the task force was assigned. Figure 10.5 is
an example of a combined meeting notice and agenda.

When a member or subcommittee has conducted research for a group, a
written copy of the major findings should be distributed to all members. If
feasible, such a report can be included with the meeting notice and agenda.
The report might include tables, graphs, duplicated copies of text, lists, and
drawings. Likewise, prior to the meeting the report maker needs to prepare

FIGURE 10.5	**An example of combined meeting notice and agenda.**

Date: February 17, 1997
To: Curriculum Committee (Berquist, Bourhis, Galanes, Sneegas, Stovall, Sisco)
From: Christy Drale, chair
Re: Next meeting of the Curriculum Committee

The next meeting of the Curriculum Committee will be on Friday, February 21, from 1:00 to 3:00 P.M. in Craig 320.

AGENDA (by the end of the meeting we must have an answer for each of the following questions):

1. What will be the focus of our departmental assessment? (student outcomes, student perceptions, alumni perceptions, or something else?)
2. What areas of the department should be assessed?
3. Whom will we recommend as members of subcommittees to plan assessment procedures for each area decided under #2.

visual aids such as charts, diagrams, and graphs. Such a report can be incorporated into the minutes by mentioning it ("see attached") and stapling a copy to the official set of minutes.

Formal reports and resolutions. Many small groups must submit written reports of their work to a parent organization or administrator. Such reports may include findings, criteria, and recommendations. You probably have read about reports to the president by special task forces on such matters as air pollution, the quality of education, and health care financing. Reports of campus task forces are regularly mentioned in student newspapers. Corporations often have teams of scientists and engineers developing new products. The end product of these hundreds of hours of work is a written report, often accompanied by a brief oral report by the group's designated leader.

Although the designated leader is responsible for submitting the report, the actual writing is usually done by one or two members. A draft of the proposed report is sent to all members, inviting their suggestions for revisions and additions. The group then meets to discuss, amend, and eventually approve the draft report. The final version is signed by all members, copied, and submitted. Usually this type of report includes sections about the problem, a summary of findings, possible solutions considered, criteria used to judge these solutions, and the group's recommendations. Any or all of these may be headings for sections of the report.

If the final written report involves a resolution or main motion for the parent organization, the committee chair presents copies to all members of the organization and formally moves its adoption during the section of the assembly's agenda called *Reports of Committees*. The chair makes a brief persuasive speech and answers questions about the motion. Other members of the committee help in answering questions, and may make further supportive speeches. Formats for such motions can be found in any comprehensive manual of parliamentary procedure, such as *Robert's Rules of Order, Newly Revised,* or the organization may have its own special format for motions.

As you can see, management of written messages is an important part of a designated small group leader's work. Although good leaders enlist the help of members in performing these duties, they are the leader's ultimate responsibility. Clearly, good written and oral communication skills are necessary to function effectively as a leader.

Administrative duties of designated leaders precede and follow small group meetings. Now we consider what leaders are expected to do *during* actual meetings. In general, leaders should foster both creative and critical thinking about the task, while making the best possible use of members' time. The following guidelines will help you balance these broad goals.

Leading Discussions

Opening remarks should set the stage for the meeting by creating a positive atmosphere and helping focus the group on its task. They should be kept brief. Here are several guidelines:

Opening Remarks

1. Make sure members and guests have been introduced.
Groups are effective only when members feel free to participate. At a first meeting, an icebreaker or brief socializing activity can help members become comfortable with each other. Name tags may be provided. If guests are present, they should be introduced and their purposes made clear to the group.

Primary tension can hamper a group's decision making; sometimes a climate of trust or informality needs to be created or enhanced. You can suggest appropriate norms, such as to maintain confidentiality, to be respectful of each other, and to listen actively. When a new group meets for the first time, the designated leader should briefly describe his or her role and expectations of the other members. For example, all three of us have explained at the first meeting of committees that we would be facilitators and coordinators, but not make decisions for the group, argue for specific proposals, try to persuade the group to espouse a particular policy, or do more than a fair share of the group work.

Sometimes an unstructured period to let members get acquainted with each other's beliefs, values, backgrounds, and attitudes regarding the problem facing the group can help. This serves primarily a socioemotional function. The designated leader who senses such a need for ventilation and encourages it may later find the job of keeping talk organized and relevant much easier. The leader must balance the need for ventilation with the need for organization and should not let it go on too long. Look for signs that the group wants order.

CONSIDER THIS

Think of a problem you have dealt with in a group. Pretend that it is your responsibility to deliver the opening remarks for initiating a discussion of the problem. Write the introduction you would use.

2. **See that any special roles are established.**

   Will the group need a recorder in addition to the designated leader? Will the group have a member acting as a special observer? The group may choose to rotate such jobs so various members receive practice performing them.

3. **Briefly review or explain the specific purpose of the meeting, the specific outcomes that should be accomplished, and the group's area of freedom.**

   Members should have been informed of these by a meeting notice, but a brief reminder helps focus members on the task. In addition, there may be questions, so addressing them early may save time and prevent misunderstandings later.

4. **Distribute any handouts.**

   Handouts may include written materials from the parent organization or administrator, copies of findings, case problems, outlines to structure the problem-solving procedure of the group, and an explanation of a special discussion technique.

5. **Suggest procedures to follow.**

   You may want the group to plan a problem-solving procedure, or you may present an outline of questions for this purpose and ask the group to adopt or modify it. For an *ad hoc* problem-solving group, we suggest that you give each member a copy of an outline of questions to guide the group's problem-solving procedure, following the general procedural model explained in Chapter 11. Members should know whether decisions will be by consensus or majority vote. If rules for committees apply, members need to know them. If a special technique, such as brainstorming or the problem census, will be used, put the procedure on a chart or handout (these are discussed in Chapter 14).

6. **Ask a clear question to focus initial discussion on the first substantive issue on the agenda.**

   Your focus question may require a simple answer: "Tyrone, will you give us last week's sales figures?" Or it may need considerable discussion: "What do we think are the reasons for the drop-off in attendance?" In either case, the right question helps launch the group into the substantive portion of the agenda. Questions are discussed in more detail in Chapter 11.

Once the group members are oriented toward both each other and the task, the leader can help the group function efficiently by adding structure to the group's deliberations. The following suggestions will assist you. *Structuring Discussions*

CONSIDER THIS

Stop and do not read further yet. Think back to the group discussions you have been involved in. What were the most significant problems in these discussions? What were the best qualities of these discussions? Now, read on and see if the following suggestions touch what you believe to be the best and worst aspects of group discussions.

1. **Keep the discussion goal oriented.**
   Be sure all members understand and accept the goal. If a digression occurs, bring the discussion back on track with statements such as: "How will this help us achieve our goal?" or "What does that have to do with what we were discussing?" Topic switching is common, so you'll need to be on constant guard against it. When an irrelevant topic crops up or someone jumps ahead in the problem-solving procedure, you can usually reroute the discussion with a comment such as: "We seem to have gotten off track. Let's finish our discussion of how serious the parking shortage is before talking about why it exists." A procedural outline in the hands of all members helps keep the discussion goal oriented and orderly.

2. **Summarize each major step in problem solving and each major decision.**
   Before the group goes to the next issue or agenda item, be sure members have achieved closure on the current issue, with each member having the same understanding of what was decided. You can do this by summarizing, asking whether the summary is adequate, and then checking to see whether the group is ready to move on: "So, we've decided that building a tunnel under National Avenue will be too costly and probably will not solve the jaywalking problem, right? [Pause to verify understanding.] Now, are we ready to go on to the next item, the overhead bridge? [Pause again to give people time to respond.]" This kind of summary helps members make the transition to the next topic. When group members start to repeat each other, suggest that agreement seems to have been reached and that the group may be ready to move on to the next question. To summarize and make transitions competently, you will need to keep complete personal notes.

3. Help the group cover all items on its agenda.

To complete your agenda, you will have to watch both the time and the discussion format. First, watch the clock; nothing is more frustrating than running out of time before you have a chance to discuss an issue important to you. Members often get so involved in the discussion that they lose track of time, so it's up to the designated leader to monitor this: "We are only on our third agenda item, with 15 minutes left. Are we ready to wrap this topic up, or would you rather deal with the remaining agenda items at a special meeting next week?" (But also remember the pitfalls of being a time-oriented listener, which we discussed in Chapter 3; balance is the key.)

4. Bring the discussion to a definite close.

This should be done no later than the scheduled ending time for the meeting, unless all members consent to extending the time. The conclusion can include a summary of all progress the group has made, a statement of how the reports of the meeting will be distributed to members, assignments for follow-up and implementation, commendations for a job well done, or an evaluation of the meeting to improve the group's future interactions. The designated leader may ask the recorder for help in reviewing assignments made to members and decisions agreed to by the group.

Equalizing Opportunity to Participate

While you are keeping verbal interaction organized and goal directed, you also need to ensure that everyone has an equal opportunity to speak, with no one stagehogging or withdrawing. There are several things you can do to produce such equality:

1. Address your comments and questions to the group rather than to individuals.

Unless you want to elicit a specific item of information or respond directly to what a member has said, speak to the group as a whole. Make regular eye contact with everyone when you ask questions, especially with less talkative members.

2. Make sure all members have an equal opportunity to speak.

You may have to act as **gatekeeper,** regulating who will speak next so that everyone has a fair, equal chance. Eye contact can show you expect the less talkative members to speak. Looking at those who talk a lot encourages them to talk more and may further discourage quiet members. We suggest you make a visual survey of the entire group every minute or so. If you see a nonverbal sign that a silent member has something to say, you can help that person get the floor: "Pieta, did you want to comment on John's proposal?" or "Pieta, you seem concerned about John's proposal. Would you share your concerns with us?" That opens the gate to Pieta without putting her on the spot if she has nothing to say. Sometimes reticent members can be assigned roles that *require* their participation. For instance, someone might be asked to investigate an issue and report to the group, or be asked to serve as *devil's advocate,* which forces participation. If you know a member is well informed but has not spoken out, try encouraging participation without forcing: "Selim, I think you studied that issue. Could you give us any information about it?"

Controlling compulsive, dominating, and long-winded members is often more difficult than encouraging quiet members. Some people repeatedly interrupt and drown out the voices of others. Highly verbal people can be valuable, but verbal monopolizing must be controlled for the sake of the group. The following techniques are listed from the most subtle to the most direct:

a. When feasible, seat talkative members where you can seem to overlook them naturally, and try not to make eye contact when you ask a question of the group.

b. When a windbag has finished one point, cut in with a tactful comment, such as, "How do the *rest* of you feel about that issue?" to suggest that someone else speak.

c. Suggest a group rule that each person make one point, then give up the floor to others, and that no one interrupt or drown out another speaker (except when the leader does so on behalf of the group).

d. In private, tactfully ask the excessive talker to help you encourage quiet members to speak: "Your ideas have been very helpful to the group, but I'm concerned that, because you are so articulate, others feel intimidated about participating. How can you help me get Susan and Juan to contribute to the discussions more often?"

e. Have an observer keep a count of how often or how long each member speaks, and report the findings to the group. If a serious imbalance is apparent, the group can decide what to do.

f. As a last resort, ask the person to control talking or leave the group: "While your ideas are excellent, your constant talking prevents other members, whose ideas are equally good, from contributing. This hurts both group morale and decision making. For the sake of the group, if you will not control your talking, I think you should leave the group."

3. Listen with real interest to what an infrequent speaker says, and encourage others to do the same.
Nothing discourages a speaker more than a lack of listening. Yet the evidence is clear that most people ignore comments from a member who previously has said little. Leader intervention can help an infrequent speaker get a fair hearing.

4. Avoid commenting after each member's remark.
Some designated leaders fall into this pattern unawares, producing a wheel network of verbal interaction. Other leaders do this to overcontrol

the group. Listen, speak when you are really needed, but don't become the constant interpreter or repeater of what others say.

5. **Bounce requests for your opinions on substantive issues back to the group.**

Many people have a tendency to accept uncritically what a leader says (as in the phenomenon of *groupthink,* discussed in Chapter 8 and later in this chapter). Under most circumstances, you will encourage both creative and critical thinking by members if you withhold your opinions until others have expressed theirs. When you do offer an opinion, give it as only one point of view to be considered, not as the *right* interpretation. When you are asked "What do you think we should do?" you might reply "Let's see what other members think first. What do the rest of you think about . . . ?"

6. **Remain neutral during arguments.**

If you get heavily involved in an argument, you will lose the perspective needed to be a completer and mediator, to summarize, and to perform all the other communicative behaviors of a good leader. When you realize evaluation is needed, point that out and ask others to provide it. At most, act as a devil's advocate for a point of view that otherwise would not be considered. Of course, you are always free to support decisions as they emerge or point out that members have overlooked a major issue or possible negative outcome, thus encouraging critical thinking.

Stimulating Creative Thinking

Groups are potentially more creative than individuals, but often group outputs are mediocre or worse. Sometimes creativity must be stimulated deliberately. Leaders can do several things to encourage creativity:

1. **Defer evaluation and ask group members to do the same.**

The main idea behind brainstorming, described in Chapter 14, is to defer evaluation of ideas until members have no more ideas to suggest. Evaluation stifles creativity; who wants to suggest an idea that will get shot down? If you want to stimulate creativity, you (and the other members) must establish a safe climate where people feel safe to propose innovative suggestions. When a group member criticizes a suggestion, gently remind that person of the "defer evaluation" rule.

2. **Try brainstorming and other creativity-enhancing techniques.**

This suggestion extends the first. Brainstorming not only requires deferred judgment, it also encourages members to be playful with their own and others' ideas, to use others' ideas as a springboard, and to invent wild and crazy suggestions that may turn out to be useful. In addition, Chapter 14 contains other techniques designed to disable the logical part of the mind temporarily so that the creative mind can emerge.

3. **Encourage the group to search for more alternatives.**

When no one seems to be able to think of any more ideas, you can ask an idea-spurring question: "What *else* can we think of to . . . ?" or "I wonder if we can think of five more ways to . . . ?" Often, the most creative ideas are ones that pop up after the group thinks it has exhausted its possibilities.

4. **One at a time, ask how each component of a solution or item might be improved.**
   For instance, you might ask "How could we improve the appearance of . . . ?" or "How could we add to the strength of . . . ?"

5. **Watch for suggestions that might open up whole new areas of thinking, then pose a general question about the new area.**
   For example, if someone suggests putting up signs in the library that show the cost of losses to the users, you might ask "How *else* could we publicize the costs of losses to the library?"

After a group has done its creative thinking, it must then subject the various options to rigorous evaluation before it reaches a final position. All information and options should be subjected to critical evaluation, but sometimes groups develop norms of overpoliteness or conformity to the opinions of high-status members. In such cases, as with groupthink, members may be reluctant to criticize or find flaws with others' ideas. Following are ways to encourage good critical evaluation without evoking unmanageable secondary tension.

Stimulating Critical Thinking

1. **If the group gets solution-minded too quickly, suggest more analysis of the problem.**
   This is a common problem and a major source of faulty decision making. Chapter 11 presents a systematic method for helping a group focus on problem analysis.

2. **Encourage members to evaluate information.**
   For example:
   a. To check the relevance of evidence you might ask: "How does this apply to our problem?" or "How is that like the situation we are discussing?"
   b. To evaluate the source of evidence you might ask: "What is the source of that information?" "How well is Dr. So-and-so recognized in the field?" or "Is this consistent with other information on the subject?"
   c. To check on the credibility of information you might ask: "Do we have any information that is contradictory?"
   d. To encourage thorough assessment of a group member's suggestion you might ask: "How will implementing that solve our problem?" or "How will the students (union members, secretaries, neighborhood residents, etc.) react to that suggestion?"
   e. To test a statistic you might ask how it was derived, who conducted the study, or how an average was computed.
   f. Bring in outside experts to challenge the views of the group.

3. **See that all group members understand and accept all standards, criteria, or assumptions used in making judgments.**

   For example, you might ask: "Is that criterion clear to us all?" "Does everyone agree that using our professional association's guidelines is a good idea?" or "Do we all accept that as an assumption?"

4. **See that all proposed solutions are given a thorough testing before they are accepted as final group decisions.**

   Encourage the group to apply the available facts and all criteria. Be especially careful to consider possible harmful effects of all proposed solutions. You may want to remind members of the dangers of groupthink (see Chapter 8).

   a. Ask questions such as the following to encourage thorough evaluation:

   Do we have any evidence to indicate that this solution would be satisfactory? Unsatisfactory?

   Are there any facts to support this proposal?

   How well would that idea meet our criteria?

   Would that proposal solve the basic problem?

   Is there any way we can test this idea before we decide whether or not to adopt it?

   What negative consequences might this proposal produce?

   b. Ask members to discuss tentative solutions or policies with trusted people outside the group.

   c. One or more members can be asked to take the role of critical evaluator or devil's advocate so that all ideas are challenged and everyone has a chance to air doubts.

   d. Divide the group into two subgroups under different leaders to evaluate all alternatives, then rejoin to iron out differences.

   e. Before reaching a binding solution with far-reaching consequences, hold a "second chance" meeting at which all doubts, ethical concerns, or untested assumptions can be explored.

Preventing Groupthink   We have contended that the designated leader of a group has a dual responsibility for building team spirit while at the same time doing everything possible to ensure full evaluation of all information and ideas presented to the group. In Chapter 8 we talked about groupthink, a dysfunctional group process that occurs when this balance is thrown off. We showed you how to recognize signs of groupthink in your group. Here, we offer some suggestions for combating the tendency toward groupthink and for helping the leader perform the difficult balancing act.

1. **Assign the role of critical evaluator to each member or establish a subgroup to serve that capacity.**

   Each member must feel responsible for helping the group achieve the best possible solution. For instance, Kroon et al. found that making members collectively accountable for the group decision counteracted two antecedents of groupthink, the group's insulation and the leader's promotion of a preferred alternative, especially in male groups.[9] However, just *saying* this to the members will not make it happen. Group leaders must make sure by their actions that critical evaluation is more important than apparent harmony or deference to the leader's position. Leaders must learn to *welcome* criticism of their own ideas and proposals, thereby modeling for the other members a willingness to be influenced by reason and evidence.

The group may want to structure the devil's advocate process, discussed earlier, by officially appointing an individual or a subgroup with the specific charge of poking holes in the group's favored option. If members know that a group member has been assigned the devil's advocate role for a particular decision, they are more likely to view the criticisms as useful and as being part of her or his job and less likely to take them personally.

2. **Leaders should refrain from stating their preferences at the outset of a decision-making or problem-solving session.**

One of the major forces leading to the Bay of Pigs decision was President Kennedy's own referent power.[10] Kennedy's advisors admired and respected him so much that they were reluctant to criticize his ideas. Even leaders who do not have Kennedy's charisma have significant power stemming from the sources discussed in Chapter 8. Anderson and Balzer found that when a leader expresses an opinion early during a discussion, the group generates significantly fewer alternatives, which are less likely to be adopted by the group.[11] It is typical for members to defer to the wishes of a designated leader. This impairs the decision-making process that, at its most effective, is based on an exhaustive search for options and vigilant appraisal of them.

3. **Leaders can establish two or more independent subgroups to work on the same problem.**

The rivalry of subcommittees may spur them to a greater effort on behalf of the full committee. Each subcommittee is likely to think of ideas, solutions, and possible consequences the other subgroup failed to consider. The clash between competing subgroups often sparks creative and novel solutions and highlights potential flaws.

4. **Leaders should take whatever steps are needed to prevent insulation of the group.**

Sometimes a group can be so cohesive it fails to consider that others may perceive situations differently. A committee to which one of us belonged developed a sweeping proposal to alter the undergraduate curriculum. Group members had worked together for an entire year, carrying each other along on their enthusiasm and commitment. However, because they were so caught up in their own shared vision, they failed to consider some implications of their proposal for other faculty, who greeted the recommendations with dismay. The group had become insulated from external opinion.

Leaders can take several steps to offset insularity. They can encourage members to get feedback on tentative proposals from trusted associates outside the group, then report back to the group. Had the faculty committee done this, it would not have been surprised at the proposal's reception. Leaders can also arrange for outside experts to discuss their views with the group, thereby helping to ensure a broadly based foundation for making the decision.

5. **Leaders can use available computer technology to encourage thorough problem solving.**

There are many computerized group support systems now available, ranging in cost, that are designed to keep a group focused on its task. These systems permit members to react anonymously so the effects of strong leadership and status differences are minimized. In some systems, members' evaluative comments can be displayed on an overhead computer screen for everyone to see simultaneously. This discourages digression and encourages thoroughness. Miranda found that, even when a group is predisposed to groupthink, *group support systems prevent groupthink* and promote effective decision making.[12] We describe some of these group support systems in more detail in Chapter 14.

Fostering Meeting-to-Meeting Improvement

A group doesn't achieve its ultimate goal by chance. After each meeting, the designated leader should assess in what ways it could have been improved and especially how well the meeting's goals were accomplished. That, then, suggests a road map for improving future meetings. Here are specific suggestions:

1. **Determine how the meeting could have been improved.**
The leader should assess whether the group's purposes were clearly communicated and whether members agreed on the goals. Was the entire agenda covered in timely fashion? Was the meeting well structured? Did members stay on the topic, for the most part? Was the thinking both creative and critical, at appropriate times? Were the members allowed to digress too often? Not enough? Did the leader take on too much of the responsibility for conducting the discussion, thereby depriving members of valuable experience? Were there any members who talked too much? Not enough? After answering these and other questions, the leader should plan strategy for the next meeting.

2. **Determine the most important changes to be made at the next meeting and adjust behavior accordingly.**
After examining all the areas where improvements could be made, the leader should select two or three of the most potentially harmful areas and concentrate on improving those. If the agenda was half completed, the leader should keep better track of time and allow fewer digressions at the next meeting. If one or two members monopolized the floor, the leader should plan ways to curtail their participation. The leader can

then share the plan with the members: "Last week, we accomplished only half the items on our agenda. This week, I'm going to pay more attention to our time, and I'll be stepping in more often to help us stick to one issue at a time. I'd appreciate your help with this, too."

Developing the group involves two fundamental processes: helping the group evolve into an effective team, and helping the individual members grow to their potentials so distributed leadership can work effectively. In Chapters 7 and 8 we explained how a collection of individuals develops into a group with a unique culture of communication patterns, norms, role structure, and throughput procedures. Earlier in this chapter we talked about the importance of the leader helping develop the group members' maturity level so they can increasingly assume the leadership of the group. Most members do not start out knowing how to do this; being an effective group member requires communication skills that are developed with practice. The leader can greatly facilitate the growth of the individual members.

Developing the Group

An important job for the leader is to develop the members' leadership skills, including the members' abilities to assess the group's throughput processes and suggest appropriate changes. Here are several suggestions:

Helping Individuals to Grow

1. **Encourage members to assess the group's processes and suggest appropriate changes.**
   Sometimes the impetus for group growth can be supplied just by asking the group to examine itself and ask "How are we doing?" Periodic self-assessment is a characteristic of outstanding teams.[13] There are several ways for the leader to build self-assessment into the group's processes. For instance, a short period of evaluation could end each meeting, spurred by the questions: "How well do you think our meeting went today?" and "How might we make our next meeting more productive?" The answer to the second question led the church board in Chapter 2 to rearrange its agenda so that "new business" would be discussed early in the meeting, before group members became tired and uncreative.

   Another suggestion might be to designate someone as a process observer to share observations with the group, break into the conversation to point out something that appears to be hampering the group, suggest communicative techniques and procedures the group has overlooked, and give evaluative comments when the discussion has concluded. The job of process observer may be rotated among members, so everyone gets practice observing and assessing.

   Another suggestion might be to bring outside consultants in to assess the group and offer suggestions for improvement. This is what Celinda did for the health agency executive committee. Outside consultants can also act as process observers.

2. **Model the behavior you want others to adopt.**

   As designated leader, you can model group-centered, thoughtful, responsible behavior. Be sure to examine your own attitudes when a group you chair is doing poorly; your own behavior can do a lot to promote teamwork and develop the trust needed for collaboration. Encourage others to evaluate your suggestions, and react open-mindedly and nondefensively to others' criticisms.

3. **Give members practice at performing needed group duties.**

   Suggest ways in which group members can serve the needs of the group. For instance, rotate the job of recorder so several members get practice. Give members the chance to report on their areas of expertise to the group and to perform special tasks for the group. Let members substitute for you as discussion leader or liaison to other groups. Don't jump in right away when you see that the group needs something; give the other members a chance to respond before you do.

Establishing and Maintaining Trust

True collaboration (literally, "working together") is possible only when members trust each other. Larson and LaFasto found that interviewees from outstanding teams almost always mentioned *trust* when asked about their group's climate: "Trust is one of those mainstay virtues in the commerce of mankind. It is the bond that allows any kind of significant relationship to exist between people. Once broken, it is not easily—if ever—recovered."[14] Analysis of their data shows four components of trust: honesty (no lies, no exaggerations); openness (a combination of open-mindedness and willingness to share); consistency (predictability, dependability); and respect (treating others with fairness and dignity). After six weeks of observation and interviews with all the executive committee members, the consultants concluded that lack of trust in Celinda and each other was their *key* problem. Part of their reluctance to work on the self-study stemmed from fear of problems the self-study might expose. Did you guess their problem correctly?

The following suggestions can help you establish and retain a climate of trust:

1. **Establish norms, based on ethical principles, that build trust.**

   Communication that builds trust is based on three important ethical principles: working to understand others, communicating to enhance others' identities and self-concepts, and behaving like a responsible group member. Specific behaviors that promote trust are listening actively, encouraging others to explain themselves, helping others with assignments or tasks, maintaining confidentiality, getting assignments done when promised, making sure you understand someone's position before disagreeing, and making others feel free to disagree without being treated as weird or politically incorrect.

2. **Confront trust violators and other problem members.**

   Two of the most common complaints are that groups tolerate members who put self over group and that designated leaders fail "to confront and resolve issues associated with inadequate performance by team members."[15] If repeated efforts by you and other members to improve things are unsuccessful, it is far better to remove offenders from the group than to allow trust to erode and group energy to be deflected into destructive avenues.

3. **Be a principled leader.**

Larson and LaFasto suggest that effective team leaders exemplify the kind of group-centered leadership we have described.[16] Principled leaders put the needs of the group ahead of their individual needs and behave in ethical ways consistent with the group's norms. For instance, they do not say they want group participation, then squash members' attempts to participate. Good group leaders have a vision of the group's future, which they convey clearly; they inspire members to work toward that vision. They show personal commitment to the team's goals. Moreover, they work to expose the talents of the other members. Leaders create leaders by giving members the experience and latitude they need to act with self-confidence. Although Celinda was pained to learn that not only did committee members not trust each other, they also did not trust *her,* she did not respond defensively, but instead supported the committee in their efforts to identify their fears, establish a time line, and assign responsibilities to each member.

Establishing a climate of trust will do more than anything else to develop cooperation and teamwork among members. In addition to having clear, inspiring goals and trust, there are specific things a designated leader can do to promote teamwork:

Promoting Teamwork and Cooperation

1. **Speak of "us" and "we," rather than "I" and "you."**

The leader should convey, verbally and in every other way, that he or she is a full-fledged, committed member of the group. The designated leader also should ask what it means if another member consistently refers to the group as "you."

2. **Create symbols of group identification.**

A sense of unity can be fostered by inside jokes, shared fantasies, logos, a name for the group (for example, a particularly effective advertising agency committee called itself the "Can Do Committee"), slogans, T-shirts, and so on.

3. **Watch for and challenge any hidden agenda item that seems to conflict with group goals.**

If you suspect a hidden agenda item is interfering with group functioning or goal achievement, promptly bring this to the attention of the group: "Jusuf, you have rejected every suggestion the group has proposed without examining it fully. As a result, members are becoming frustrated and angry. Is there something going on that we should know about?" Avoidance makes such problems worse.

4. **Share all rewards with the group.**

Designated leaders often receive praise from authority figures of a group's parent organization. Wise leaders give credit to the group. They comment about what the group has done, express pride in being a part of the group, and acknowledge the service of all members.

5. **Keep arguments focused on facts and issues, not personalities.**

Step in at once if any member starts an attack on another's personality, ethnicity, or character. However, recognize also that members may have strong feelings about some issues, so don't squelch expressions of feeling, as long as those expressions do not denigrate others.

6. **Don't let the discussion get so serious that members cannot enjoy themselves.**

Humor may help reduce the tensions generated when people work hard together at the job of hammering out ideas. Good task leaders may have trouble with humor. Lee observed, for instance, that many of the most efficient leaders lacked human warmth, but groups need *both* efficiency *and* satisfying interactions.[17] He suggested that taskmasters relax and allow digressions, which can relieve secondary tension. As leader, you want to let the group chain out fantasies that enrich its life and contribute to establishing shared beliefs and values. The result of such tension-relieving activity is more concerted effort by group members in the long run. If you are not skilled at tension release, enlist the help of members who are. Bring the group back to task after the joke is over or the fantasy has chained out.

7. **When a group seems to be deadlocked, look for a basis on which to compromise.**

Perhaps you can synthesize parts of several ideas into a consensus solution or suggest a mediation procedure, such as the *principled negotiation procedure* described in Chapter 13. However, to do so you must have been even-handed as the leader, remaining somewhat detached from the fray, while listening, observing, and maintaining perspective.

ETHICAL PRINCIPLES FOR GROUP LEADERS

As we have suggested, the leader's behavior should serve as a model for members to follow. As Hackman and Johnson said, "Responsible leaders maintain the highest possible standards of ethics."[18] These authors suggest several principles for leaders that we believe are relevant for small groups:

1. **A leader should not intentionally send deceptive or harmful messages.**

Not only should leaders tell members the truth, they should hold *truth* to be an appropriate standard for the group's decision making. To us, this means ensuring that *all* relevant information, whether it supports the leader's position or not, is presented to the group and that the group evaluates all information in an unbiased, fair way.

2. **A leader should place concern for others above concern for personal gain.**
   This means that a leader should not take advantage of the power of the leader position for personal gain or advantage. Good leaders do not use insider information for *personal* gain. Hidden agendas, whether belonging to the leader or members, should not be allowed to interfere with the needs of the group. Moreover, as we have mentioned previously, leaders should refrain from actions that might harm the self-esteem of members.

3. **A leader should respect the opinions and attitudes of members and allow members the freedom to consider the consequences of their actions.**
   This principle supports democratic, group-centered leadership that encourages equal opportunity for all to participate. It also supports our preference for distributed leadership and acknowledges how important it is for leaders to develop the capabilities of members.

CONSIDER THIS

You have tried to create a group culture which promotes distributed leadership. However, one member consistently refuses to carry out his responsibilities; he always has a reason why something is not done. You very much want to create a group culture in which all members can consider the consequences of their own actions. You have even, purposely, not done the work for this member to show what happens when work is not completed on time. The problem is that you face a deadline and the project report must be turned in soon. What do you do? When is enough, enough? Where do you draw the line?

4. **A leader should stand behind members when they carry out policies and actions approved by the leader and the group.**
   Ethical leaders support members who carry out the plans of the group and the leader. They do not save their own skins by leaving group members hanging.

5. **A leader treats members consistently, regardless of sex, ethnicity, or social background.**
   Members are valued for their contributions to the group. Ethical leaders minimize external status differences to encourage participation by all.

6. **A leader should establish clear policies that all group members are expected to follow.**
   Group procedures and rules are clearly understood, and ethical leaders follow the same rules and norms that members are expected to follow.

As with other desirable behaviors, the leader should model ethical behavior that will serve as a standard for members to follow. By doing so, the leader will help create a climate of trust and a spirit of cohesiveness.

SUMMARY

1. Good leaders provide the degree of coordination and structure appropriate to the group's situation, yet ideally encourage group members to mature so they can assume distributed leadership of the group. The leader acts as a completer, providing essential group services not provided by other group members.

2. Outstanding designated leaders articulate group goals clearly, adhere to high standards of performance, and promote equality among group members.

3. In the United States, group leaders are expected to provide administrative services, facilitate discussions, and help the group develop.

4. Designated group leaders should establish a climate of trust by modeling for the other group members the ethical principles presented.

EXERCISES

1. Based on your most recent experiences in group discussions, make three lists: (1) your most important strengths as a discussion leader; (2) your most serious weaknesses; and (3) the steps you plan to take to add to your strengths and to reduce your weaknesses.

2. Think of leaders of small groups to which you have belonged and discuss the following with class members:
   a. Who was the worst leader? List the specific characteristics and behaviors that led to your judgment.
   b. Who was the best leader? List the specific characteristics and behaviors that led to your judgment.
   c. Which of the above behaviors were most important in distinguishing between the two?

3. Split the class in half. One half will serve as observers and the other as discussants; later, they will switch roles. The discussants should form groups of four or five, with approximately equal numbers of observers per group. Each group should select a designated discussion leader and a case problem or question of interest (for instance, how to improve the quality of undergraduate education at your college, how to reduce cheating, etc.). The observers should be prepared to observe the leader's behavior and answer the following questions:
   a. What functions did the leader perform? How effective was each? How appropriate?
   b. At what points during the discussion did the leader fail to supply some needed leadership service? Did someone else step in to provide it? What was the effect on the group?
   c. Overall, how effective was the leader?

4. After a meeting of five or six members of your class or of your project group, each member should write the minutes for the meeting. Exchange your minutes with those written by all other members of the group; compare, then see if you can agree as a group on an official report of the meeting.

5. In groups of four to six, discuss the ethical principles suggested for group leaders. Make a list of other principles by which you think group leaders should abide. Share your lists with the class.

BIBLIOGRAPHY

Cathcart, Robert S., and Larry A. Samovar, eds. *Small Group Communication: A Reader.* 6th ed. Dubuque, IA: Wm. C. Brown Publishers, 1992, especially section 8.

Fisher, B. Aubrey. "Leadership: When Does the Difference Make a Difference?" In *Communication and Group Decision-Making.* Randy Y. Hirokawa and Marshall S. Poole, eds. Beverly Hills, CA: Sage Publications, 1986, 197–215.

Hackman, Michael Z., and Craig E. Johnson. *Leadership: A Communication Perspective.*

Prospect Heights, IL: Waveland Press, 1991, especially chapters 6 and 7.

Larson, Carl E., and Frank M. J. LaFasto. *TeamWork: What Must Go Right/What Can Go Wrong.* Newbury Park, CA: Sage Publications, 1989.

Schwarz, Roger M. *The Skilled Facilitator: Practical Wisdom for Developing Effective Groups* (San Francisco: Jossey-Bass, 1994).

Tropman, John E. *Making Meetings Work: Achieving High Quality Group Decisions.* Thousand Oaks, CA: Sage Publications, 1996, part 2.

NOTES

1. Carl E. Larson and Frank M. J. LaFasto, *TeamWork: What Must Go Right/What Can Go Wrong* (Newbury Park, CA: Sage, 1989): 118.

2. Larson and LaFasto, *TeamWork,* 121–23.

3. Donald E. Petersen, cited in "Management Digest," a special advertising section of *Newsweek* (March 5, 1990): 19.

4. William C. Schutz, "The Leader as Completer," in *Small Group Communication: A Reader,* 3d ed., eds. Robert S. Cathcart and Larry A. Samovar (Dubuque, IA: Wm. C. Brown, 1979): 400.

5. Donald G. Ellis, "Relational Control in Two Group Systems," *Communication Monographs* 36 (1979): 153–66.

6. Michael Z. Hackman and Craig E. Johnson, *Leadership: A Communication Perspective* (Prospect Heights, IL: Waveland Press, 1991): 129.

7. John Gastil, "Identifying Obstacles to Small Group Democracy," *Small Group Research* 24 (February 1993): 5–27.

8. Roger M. Schwarz, *The Skilled Facilitator: Practical Wisdom for Developing Effective Groups* (San Francisco: Jossey-Bass, 1994).

9. Marceline B. R. Kroon, David van Kreveld, and Jacob M. Rabbie, "Group versus Individual Decision Making: Effects of Accountability and Gender on Groupthink," *Small Group Research* 23 (1992): 427–58.

10. Irving L. Janis, *Groupthink: Psychological Studies of Policy Decisions and Fiascoes,* 2d ed. (Boston: Houghton-Mifflin, 1983).

11. Lance E. Anderson and William K. Balzer, "The Effects of Timing of Leaders' Opinions on Problem-Solving Groups," *Group & Organization Studies* 16 (1991): 86–101.

12. Shaila M. Miranda, "Avoidance of Groupthink: Meeting Management Using Group Support Systems," *Small Group Research* 25 (February 1994): 105–36.

13. Larson and LaFasto, *Teamwork,* 130–31.

14. Ibid., 85.

15. Ibid., 136.

16. Ibid., 118–29.

17. Irving J. Lee, *How to Talk with People* (New York: Harper & Row, 1952): 158–60.

18. Hackman and Johnson, *Leadership: A Communication Perspective,* 205.

EFFECTIVE PROBLEM SOLVING IN THE SMALL GROUP

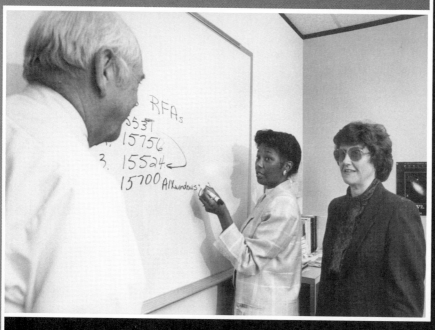

© Gary Conner/PhotoEdit

Problem solving is the reason most secondary groups exist. Because problems solved by groups affect us all, we need to understand how to maximize the effectiveness of the problem-solving process in groups. Part 4 describes the nature of problem solving, provides vital information to improve group decision-making processes, and explains how you can use conflict to enhance group problem solving and decision making.

Problem-Solving Discussion

Central Message

Problem solving is most effective when a group explores the problem thoroughly and generates a variety of possible solutions, which members then evaluate on the basis of their possible consequences. Following an appropriate adaptation of the general Procedural Model of Problem Solving helps a group do this.

Study Objectives

As a result of studying Chapter 11 you should be able to:

1. Analyze the undesirable present situation, the obstacles, and the goal of any problem.
2. List the characteristics any problem has and explain their importance when developing a procedural outline for group problem solving.
3. Plan procedural outlines for the group's problem-solving process to ensure that no step crucial to the quality of the solution is overlooked.
4. Understand the importance of being clear about the criteria or standards by which the group will judge possible solutions.
5. List the five components of the general Procedural Model of Problem Solving (P-MOPS), explain the importance and nature of each step, and be able to adapt the model for discussing any sort of problem.
6. Use the Single Question format to help a group engage in the vigilant interaction necessary to arrive at the best possible solution to a problem.

Key Terms

Acceptance requirements
Area of freedom
Charge
Cooperative requirements
Criteria
Decision making
Intrinsic interest
Intuitive problem solvers
Obstacle
Population familiarity
Problem
Problem questions
Problem solving
Procedural Model of Problem Solving (P-MOPS)
Single Question format
Solution multiplicity
Solution questions
Structure
Systematic problem solvers
Task difficulty
Technical requirements
Vigilant Interaction Theory

In a tragic accident on his honeymoon, Tyrell Washington, a 24-year-old African American man, dived into a swimming pool and broke his neck at C4. Paralyzing him from the neck down, with minimal movement in his right hand. After surgery, Tyrell was transferred to a rehabilitation hospital in a large city two hours from his home, where several experts collaborated to help with his care. Weekly "plan of care" meetings were held to confer about Tyrell's care. The meetings were run by a medical doctor with a specialty in spinal cord injuries, and attended by two nurses assigned to this wing, a psychologist, a medical social worker, an occupational therapist, and a physical therapist. Each provided a unique perspective on each patient.

At one particular meeting, when Tyrell had been at the rehabilitation hospital for five months, his primary care nurse noted that he had lost two pounds during the previous week; although this weight loss was not immediate cause for alarm, the nurse asked the others if they had observed anything unusual going on with Tyrell. The psychologist supported her, saying that the patient exhibited signs of depression and had made statements such as, "It would have been better for everybody if I'd drowned," which indicated that he did not accept his physical condition. The physical therapist noted that Tyrell's physical range of motion in his arms and legs had improved, but at their last session, he had seemed to be fatigued and asked to end the session early. The social worker added that Tyrell's family was worried about finances; Tyrell's disability insurance would not pay for all the modifications he would need to the house he and his wife had bought before their wedding and his mother was particularly concerned about what he'd be able to do when he left the hospital. His job with a regional trucking company provided excellent benefits but depended on his physical ability and strength to do the job. He wasn't trained to do anything else.

Because the family lived two hours away, after the initial crisis of his injury, family members, including his wife, came to see him only on weekends, so he was alone most of the day. The occupational therapist said Tyrell had not shown interest in using any of the assistive devices, such as a toothbrush holder, designed for quadriplegics. After further discussion about Tyrell's physical and emotional condition, the doctor decided that providing him with a mild antidepressant would be warranted, and the psychologist and social worker decided to work together to identify resources to help improve Tyrell's ability to cope with his situation and his future. The group went on to discuss the next patient.

Although groups usually surpass individuals in solving complex problems, the adage "To fail to plan is to plan to fail" is even more true for group problem solving than for individuals' complex endeavors. All too often, authorities assume that if they assemble a group of intelligent, knowledgeable individuals, effective problem solving will result automatically. Unfortunately, this is not the case. Not only do problem-solving group members need to have expertise about the problem, as did the group in our opening story, they also need to know how to proceed *as a group* to be sure all aspects of the problem have been examined. For high-quality solutions, groups must attend to *both* information and the process of problem solving; indeed, without the latter they may not even be able to complete their assignments. For example, a group of principals and teachers Wood observed for more than a year were unable to complete their task. Their expertise was sufficient, but the group members lacked essential group problem-solving skills.[1] If the doctor in Tyrell's hospital hadn't made it possible for other medical specialists to provide relevant information, and if he hadn't listened to that information, Tyrell's problem might easily not have been addressed.

CONSIDER THIS

The group charged with overseeing Tyrell's care represented diverse experts in health care. What contribution to the whole did each person make? Were all the relevant parties represented at the meeting? Is there anyone else you think should have been represented at the meeting?

When asked how they solve problems, most people will say something like "get the facts, weigh the alternatives, and make a decision." That's not a bad procedure, though incomplete, but extensive observation reveals that both individual and group problem solving is usually more haphazard.[2] The problem-solving groups Berg observed changed themes on average every 58 seconds, often without completing discussion of the issues or themes raised.[3] In the typical problem-solving discussion, someone mentions a problem, someone else suggests a way to solve it, the group briefly discusses the idea, and then it is adopted or something else is proposed, perhaps with brief periods of discussing the problem itself. Groups often flit from idea to idea, until time begins to run out and a decision is made quickly with no plans to implement it.

As you might imagine, this haphazard procedure is unlikely to produce an adequate solution to a complicated problem, such as how to reduce the cost of health care or increase the literacy of the adult population of the United States. Vital elements of the problem may be neglected, innovative thinking is unlikely, and evaluation is not thorough. Organizing problem-solving discussions helps groups balance participation, improve reflectiveness, coordinate group members' thinking, and establish important ground rules for proceeding.[4] A systematic procedure is needed to solve complex problems effectively.

Chapter 11 will help you understand the importance of *procedures* information and in problem solving. We differentiate problem solving from decision making, analyze the major dimensions that problems have, and present two general but flexible models for efficient and effective group problem-solving discussions.

PROBLEM SOLVING AND DECISION MAKING

Many writers use the terms *problem solving* and *decision making* synonymously, but we want you to distinguish clearly between them, for there is a major difference. **Decision making** refers to the act of *choosing* among options that already exist. **Problem solving** is a more comprehensive, multistep procedure through which a group develops a plan to move from an unsatisfactory state to a desired goal. Problem solving usually requires a group to make numerous decisions; it also involves *creating* or *discovering* alternatives, not just choosing among them. Thus, decision making is one part of problem solving. An example may clarify this difference. A task force in Springfield, Missouri, was charged with solving the problem of what to do with solid waste. The group needed to make a number of decisions in the course of identifying the city's various options and developing a plan for the handling of solid waste. In contrast, a committee charged with selecting from three possible sites the best location for a solid waste materials recovery facility is strictly a decision-making group. We discuss decision making in detail in Chapter 12.

EFFECTIVE PROBLEM SOLVING

The present chapter will show how you can make group problem solving effective. First, we define the concept of "problem" and the components common to all problems. Then we explain the conditions that must exist for group problem solving to be effective.

Problem   A **problem** is a discrepancy between what actually is happening and what *should* be going on. All problems have three major components: an existing situation that is undesirable, a goal or desired state, and obstacles to reaching the goal, as shown in Figure 11.1. Understanding the general character of these three components is essential to planning problem-solving procedures.

1. **Undesirable present situation.**

   Unless someone is dissatisfied with the way things are, no problem exists; a problem, then, is in part a matter of human awareness and feelings. For example, imagine that a club to which you belong has gradually been losing members, but no one has felt anything was wrong. But at your next regular meeting the secretary points out that you do not have a quorum needed to conduct business. Someone else says your continued existence as an organization is threatened. *Now* you feel concerned that the situation is unsatisfactory. Recognition of this undesirable present situation is the beginning of a problem for you.

2. **Goal.**

   The perception of an unsatisfactory situation usually suggests a goal (a desired situation), even if it's at first vague. In our example, you can

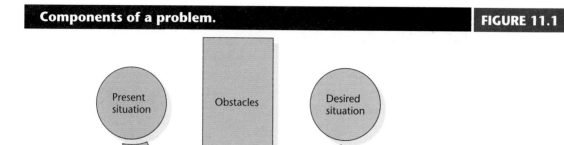

Components of a problem. **FIGURE 11.1**

already say that you want to increase your membership and attendance at meetings so your organization can survive. You might soon be able to state the goal precisely: "To increase membership by 50 percent and double attendance at meetings."

3. **Obstacles.**

An **obstacle** is anything that interferes with reaching the goal. Lack of information, inadequate funds or equipment, and a lack of needed skills would be obstacles, as would anything that must be changed, removed, or overcome. In our example, one immediately obvious obstacle is the lack of information about why membership and attendance have been dropping.

Problem solving is the procedure undertaken to arrive at a solution, including both a plan for arriving at the goal and the actual execution of the plan. Then, if the solution does not achieve the goal, further problem solving will be needed.

Obviously, a problem-solving plan must suit the specific characteristics of the actual problem. What are these characteristics? In his classic synthesis of group dynamics, Shaw described five characteristics of problems that small groups tackle: *task difficulty, solution multiplicity, intrinsic interest, cooperative requirements,* and *population familiarity.*[5] To these we add *acceptance requirements, technical requirements,* and the group's *area of freedom.* Only the most general steps in the problem-solving procedures will be the same for all problems.

Task difficulty refers to the problem's complexity, hence the effort, knowledge, and skill needed to achieve the goal. Groups generally are asked to tackle complex problems, those for which a number of different perspectives must be considered, not simply to choose among equivalent alternatives. For instance, consider recent government task forces assigned to recommend

Problem Characteristics

improvements in the American health care system, reduction of the budget deficit, or improvement of learning levels of high school graduates—problems beyond the capacity of any single person. Solving these problems is more complex than recommending an acceptable theme for a junior–senior prom.

Solution multiplicity refers to the number of conceivable or feasible alternatives for solving the problem. To illustrate, there are usually only a few useful ways to get from your residence to your classroom, but there are innumerable ways to decorate your living room. Structured procedures like *brainstorming* have long been available to help us think of more possible alternatives when solution multiplicity is even moderately high.[6]

Intrinsic interest was defined by Shaw as "the degree to which the task in and of itself is interesting, motivating, and attractive to the group members,"[7] reminding us of Larson and LaFasto's finding that outstanding teams had clear, elevating goals. Berkowitz found that, when group members were highly interested in their task, they preferred sharing in control of the group's procedures, but they preferred strong procedural control by a discussion leader when interest was low.[8] Our experience verifies this finding: if interest is high, members at first want to express opinions and feelings and will resist strict procedural control. After they have vented their feelings, procedural control of the problem-solving procedure is more likely to be accepted.

Ideally, groups would discuss only intrinsically interesting problems. In actuality, people are assigned to committees that deal with a variety of problems, some of little interest to them. If this is the case, members should discuss it openly and either change their attitudes or request that some other group tackle the problem.

The phrase **cooperative requirements** means the degree to which coordinated efforts are essential to satisfactory completion of a task. Increased complexity requires members to talk to each other, share information, and cooperate, in short, to be competent communicators.

The **population familiarity** dimension is the level of members' knowledge about and previous experience with the task. It is no surprise that groups with experienced members tend to perform better than groups with inexperienced ones.[9] When population familiarity is low to start, the problem-solving procedure should concentrate on analysis of the problem. But sometimes very knowledgeable people become smug and unwilling to think of new approaches. Then procedures to increase innovation may be essential.

The acceptance requirements dimension refers to the extent to which a proposed solution must be acceptable to people whom it will affect. Legislation enacted to solve public problems has often backfired when acceptance requirements were overlooked. A task force recently created a planning and zoning ordinance for a county near where Jack, one of the authors, lives, but citizen groups, while acknowledging a need for some such law, refused to accept it. The United States has experienced epic struggles over laws controlling alcohol, marijuana, and driving. Sometimes a group must give heavy consideration to the acceptability of a solution, other times little or none.

How problem characteristics affect the procedure for group problem solving.	**FIGURE 11.2**

PROBLEM CHARACTERISTIC	ADAPTATION OF PROBLEM-SOLVING PROCEDURE
1. Intrinsic interest is high.	A period of ventilation before systematic problem solving.
2. Task difficulty is high.	Detailed problem mapping; many subquestions.
3. Solution multiplicity is high.	Brainstorming.
4. Cooperative requirements are high.	A criterion step, creating and ranking explicit criteria.
5. High level of acceptance is required.	Focus on concern of people affected when evaluating options.
6. High level of technical quality is required.	Focus on evaluating ideas, critical thinking; perhaps invite outside experts to address group.
7. Population familiarity is high.	Focus on criteria and creation of multiple options.
8. Need only one or a few stages of the problem-solving process.	Shorten procedure to only steps required.

The **technical requirements** characteristic of a solution refers to whether it must be technically feasible or match some standard of technical excellence. For instance, U.S. automakers have had to rethink their procedures for quality control of their products, and some have done so with great success. The Food and Drug Administration has technical standards of both safety and effectiveness that all proposed new drugs must pass.

A group's **area of freedom** refers to the amount of authority given the group, which is either implied or stated in a *charge* to a group. A **charge** is an assignment given to a subordinate group by a parent organization or person with authority to do so. A charge specifies what a group is to do, including an area of freedom that defines the extent of the group's authority. Group members need to be clear about and accept both the charge and area of freedom.

For example, an advertising team charged with creating an ad campaign for a sports car and with recommending the television stations for the advertising spots is exceeding its area of freedom if it actually purchases the spots without permission.

Considering each of the problem characteristics just described will help you determine the appropriate procedure for solving a problem. Discussing all these variables should be done by members very early, especially if the problem is a complex one requiring numerous meetings, so that an appropriate plan or outline can be devised that takes all aspects of the problem into account. The plan will then include research inputs needed, the discussion process for the group, and implementation of the final result, as suggested by Figure 11.2.

ORGANIZING PROBLEM-SOLVING DISCUSSIONS

Procedures and communication for group problem solving have been investigated by social scientists in many fields, especially during the last half of the 20th century. From their findings we present a group of guiding principles for any discussion of complex problems by small groups, a general procedural format that can be adapted to virtually any problem, and an alternative procedure that allows a group preferring a looser structure to generate its own unique procedure without serious danger of lapses in critical thinking.

Vigilant Interaction Theory

Vigilant Interaction Theory (also called *Functional Theory*) states that the quality of a group's performance depends directly on the quality of the group's interaction.[10] If members are thorough and careful (i.e., vigilant) in how they think and talk about the problem, then the outcome is likely to be of higher quality than if they are not. Based on earlier work by Gouran that linked critical thinking and communication to high-quality inferences,[11] Vigilant Interaction Theory suggests a group address four general issues before making the final decision about how to solve a problem. These four issues are the core of Vigilant Interaction Theory:

1. "Is there something about the current state of affairs that requires improvement or change?"
2. "What do we want to achieve or accomplish in deciding what to do about the problem?"
3. "What are the choices available to us?"
4. "What are the positive and negative aspects of those choices?"[12]

These four issues are also the heart of the general Procedural Model (P-MOPS) we present in the next section of this chapter. Productive groups usually take up these issues in a more or less organized sequence, though the sequences may vary from discussion to discussion.[13] The single biggest error by groups that reach faulty solutions is *omission* of one or more of these steps, or failure to be thorough in discussing them. Both laboratory studies of group problem solving using college students and a field study of committees in a large utility company support Vigilant Interaction Theory. The study of the committees in the utility corporation found empirical support for the hypotheses relating all four major steps in vigilant problem-solving interaction to the quality of the groups' final recommendations for improving health of employees.[14] Vigilant Interaction Theory, because it focuses on how competent *communication* is related to the quality of group decisions and solutions, remains a fruitful area for future research.[15]

In summarizing research on the relationship between the quality of group interaction during problem-solving discussion and the quality of the final solutions reached, Hirokawa said:

> It should be clear at this point that effective group decision making usually does not happen by accident. In most cases, a group is able to make a high-

quality choice because the system of reasoning that it employed in arriving at a final choice was characterized by: (1) proper understanding of the problematic situation, (2) appropriate choice-making objectives, (3) accurate evaluation of the positive and negative qualities of available choices, and (4) warranted utilization of high-quality information in arriving at a final decision.[16]

Even when groups have the needed resources of valid information and member thinking skills, they may still do poorly if knowledgeable members lack persuasive skills (communicative competence) or hold back on information and arguments because of personal likes and dislikes of other members. Communicative competence and focus on the group task are essential to high-quality outcomes. Focus on the task and vigilant interaction can both be facilitated by proper discussion structure.

Using some systematic procedure for problem solving is generally a good idea, as we have argued. Some people tend to be **intuitive problem solvers** who size up a situation, then arrive at a solution without consciously following any perceptible procedure. They jump to a solution instinctively, often with an "Ah-ha!" reaction. We all experience intuition, and intuitive insights can be valuable. For example, a scientist struggling with a problem may have a sudden insight that points to the solution or a feeling about the way to proceed. However, as valuable as intuition is, we should not rely on it alone to solve problems. Those scientists who experience intuitive flashes still must test and critically evaluate those insights to determine whether they will work or to refine them so they can be used. So it is with groups; using intuitive solutions is fine—so long as group members have thoroughly evaluated those solutions before adopting them.

Systematic problem solvers, on the other hand, think their way through a set of logical steps, a structure of problem solving like the Vigilant Interaction issues investigated by Hirokawa. There are many different types of structured processes groups can use, and many are based on philosopher John Dewey's *reflective thinking* model of how individuals make decisions. Some versions of this are sometimes given the title *standard agendas*. All are designed to help groups organize their problem solving so that no important steps are neglected.

Some of the advantages of structuring group problem solving have been presented earlier in this chapter. There are others. For instance, Scheidel and Crowell found that uninstructed groups tended to spiral considerably from discussing problem issues to problem solutions, a sequence called "reach-testing."[17] Observers rate the quality of such discussions lower than discussions organized with the structure of reflective thinking or Vigilant Interaction.[18] Even low task-oriented participants rate structured discussions higher than those in which the designated leader fails to help organize the problem-solving procedure.[19] In a study by Brilhart, participants following a highly structured problem-solving procedure made a greater proportion of statements relevant to the issue of problem solving than when the leader did not clearly guide the group through such a structure.[20] Poole concluded that following a structured

The Need for Structure

procedure often provides logical priorities and reminds discussants of some-thing they forgot to do (such as analyze the problem thoroughly) in an earlier stage of problem solving.[21] So long as the logical priorities are incorporated into a sequence (e.g., problem analysis before proposing solutions), no one structure appears consistently to surpass others. In a study by Brilhart and Jochem, the quality of final decisions reached by groups following three differ-ent problem-solving structural outlines was not significantly different (though a significant proportion of the participants preferred one of these structures).[22] That no one structure produced superior final decisions was confirmed in ex-periments reported by Bayless and Larson, but Larson did find that using *no* structural pattern for problem solving produced definitely inferior solutions.[23]

Some theorists have argued that following a systematic linear procedure is not normal for small groups; however, the groups they observed had not been trained either in problem solving or in group procedures. Trainers in business and industry invariably have recommended teaching corporate personnel such procedures as a necessity before instituting participative management tech-niques such as quality circles or self-managed work teams. In a recent article, three researchers associated with a corporation in which numerous scientists conduct research and development in small teams argued forcefully for a highly systematic, structured format of problem solving by trained scientists to prevent the kinds of mistakes often attributed to "random error." These writers say that the epitome of discovery is to "methodically gather and analyze all the available data about an observable phenomenon. Contrary to what many are teaching, systematic problem solving is *not* a rigid set of specific techniques or a single prescribed discussion format . . . [but] a matter of effective group *communication* and data *handling*."[24] The high degree of structuring helps keep the attention of the group focused by using pointed questions to which specific answers are sought, though the group may need to start discussion less rigidly. In fact, group participants themselves seem to want methods and procedures to help groups function more effectively, according to Broome and Fulbright.[25] They found that experienced group participants who were more representative in terms of age and professional status than typical college stu-dents identified methodological deficiencies as significant barriers to effective group problem solving. These participants wanted tested procedures to help them deal with complex problems more productively.

Recent research by Hirokawa supports the importance of using system-atic procedures. In one study, the groups with the highest-quality decisions used a vigilant decision-making procedure and engaged in second guessing, or retrospective questioning of previous choices.[26] In another study, Hiro-kawa found that it was not so much the particular procedure groups used that determined the quality, but whether certain important functions were performed.[27] That is, for effective group problem solving, groups must thor-oughly and accurately understand the problem, must have a variety of ac-ceptable alternatives, and must evaluate each alternative carefully, especially assessing the negative consequences that might result from each alternative. Groups that do this, regardless of the particular decision-making technique used, perform better than those that don't. However, consistent with Larson's findings, using *any* procedure is more effective than using none because systematic procedures help ensure that the critical functions are attended to.

Hirokawa found that differences in decision quality are linked directly to how well groups satisfy these and other decision functions such as understanding the requirements for an acceptable choice.[28] He also found that assessment of positive and negative qualities is important at different stages of a group's deliberation. For instance, effective groups first seem to spot the serious defects when they initially screen alternatives. Once they find an alternative that appears to be free of fatal flaws, they switch strategies and begin to detail the positive aspects of the alternative. Hirokawa says, "instruction needs to move away from discussion procedures and formats (e.g., 'standard agendas') and more toward the effects or consequences of those procedures and formats."[29] He views group problem solving as a complex interplay among a variety of individual-level and group-level variables that include members' cognitive and psychological characteristics, their personal motives and communication skills, decision rules under which the group operates, the relationships among the members, and the communication patterns of the group.[30]

The question remains whether individuals who rate low in critical thinking tests and low in preference for procedural order can be taught to accept and follow such systematic problem-solving procedures to advantage. The evidence indicates they can. Further, none of us appears to be purely intuitive or systematic as problem solvers; in terms of a currently popular theory, we have both left and right brain hemispheres that can function in problem solving. How much of our approach to problem solving is genetically determined and how much is learned from parents, teachers, and colleagues is open to question. But Nisbett and Ross successfully taught subjects to replace simplistic intuitive strategies (which led to many errors in problem solving) with formal structural and statistical procedures used by scientists.[31] Sternberg demonstrated that impulsive people, who did poorly in solving problems on IQ tests, could be taught to proceed more systematically and successfully.[32]

Systematic problem-solving procedures help groups clarify *criteria* for an effective solution. **Criteria** are the standards against which available options must be judged, and group members must agree on criteria before a solution is adopted. Theorists have long argued about whether and when a problem-solving discussion should include a step during which the group talks about, proposes, and decides on specific explicit criteria. Some textbooks have argued that reflective thinking requires deciding on criteria as part of the problem analysis, or at least before talking about solutions. Other theorists have argued that criteria should be discussed explicitly, but only after having accumulated all the possible solutions first. Still others say little about criteria. Evidence provides no simple, single answer to the questions of whether and when to discuss criteria during group problem solving. In the first study to address this question, Brilhart and Jochem found that the quality of final decisions was not affected by *when* criteria were discussed

Discussing Criteria

or by whether discussion of criteria was a separate step in the problem-solving outline the group used. However, significantly more of the participants preferred to discuss criteria *after* brainstorming rather than discussing them before brainstorming or not explicitly discussing them at all.[33]

Both Poole and Hirokawa have suggested that the actual sequence may not matter so much as the intellectual content of problem discussion (i.e., Vigilant Interaction Theory). Criteria may not need to be discussed explicitly if they are well known. Hirokawa et al. explored the importance of *evaluation clarity* in applying criteria. Evaluation clarity is high when criteria are clearly presented to the group as part of the charge or the presentation of the problem and are understood by all members. Evaluation clarity is low when standards are not presented to the group, are fuzzy, or are not understood alike by all members. In their experiment, Hirokawa et al. asked students to select one of several alternative punishments for a student guilty of plagiarism. Some groups were given explicit criteria; others were not told on what basis to evaluate the possible punishments. These authors concluded that "when evaluation clarity is high, group decision performance is only weakly related to the establishment and utilization of evaluation criteria. However, when evaluation clarity is low, group decision performance is strongly correlated with a group's efforts to establish and utilize appropriate evaluation criteria."[34]

The previous studies suggest that when criteria are already well known and shared in advance of a group's problem-solving discussion, it is not necessary to discuss them. However, when there is no advance convergence among members on criteria for an effective solution (i.e., evaluation clarity is low), explicit discussion about criteria will probably improve solution quality. We think that it is a real leadership service to determine whether criteria are explicitly understood and agreed upon and, if not, to get the group to state criteria as clearly as possible before extensively evaluating alternatives. Further, if the problem is high in solution multiplicity, we recommend delaying discussion of criteria until *after* listing possible solutions. When options are few or technical demands are high, it may be wise to discuss criteria as part of the problem analysis unless they have been presented unequivocally as part of the charge or problem statement to the group.

CONSIDER THIS

Do you think the criteria for Tyrell's care (in our opening story) are likely to have been clear to all the medical professionals collaborating on his care? Is it likely that each professional might have perceived the problem differently? If you had been the doctor in charge of the meeting, what could you have done to clarify criteria and make sure the medical professionals were using the same criteria? Is it likely that Tyrell's wife or his minister would use the same criteria?

The research reported and analyzed above suggests that systematic procedures can help groups use members' critical thinking skills and knowledge to advantage, thus arriving at better solutions to complex problems. We are now ready to consider a structural model that helps members incorporate Vigilant Interaction Theory into their problem-solving discussion.

P-MOPS: A GENERAL PROCEDURAL MODEL OF PROBLEM SOLVING FOR STRUCTURING PROBLEM-SOLVING DISCUSSIONS

As we have repeatedly pointed out, the effectiveness of a specific problem-solving procedure is affected by contingencies of problem characteristics, member experiences, member traits and preferences, corporate culture, and so forth. Effective problem solving requires that such key issues be dealt with thoroughly. Trying to find a way to offset the human tendency to be guided by internal states more than by what others say and do in problem-solving discussions has led us to the development of a general **Procedural Model of Problem Solving (P-MOPS).** The acronym P-MOPS has a double purpose: it helps us remember the full name of the model, and in punlike fashion indicates that the purpose of the model is to help groups "mop up" all the details or logical necessities for high-quality problem solving. We say that this is a *general* procedural model because while it provides a systematic structure based on both scientific method and Vigilant Interaction Theory, it can be adjusted to all the contingencies faced by groups solving all kinds of problems.

The following are the major basic steps in P-MOPS:

 I. Problem description and analysis: "What is the nature of the problem facing the group?"
 II. Generation and elaboration of possible solutions: "What might be done to solve the problem we've described?"
 III. Evaluation of possible solutions: "What are the probable benefits and possible negative consequences of each proposed solution?"
 IV. Consensus decision: "What seems to be the best possible solution we can all support?"
 V. Implementation of the solution chosen: "How will we put our decision into effect?"

This model assumes that the leader, perhaps with the help of all members, has formulated a written outline containing specific questions about all subissues the group must consider to be sure that no important contingency will be overlooked. P-MOPS, then, is not a rigid recipe or mathematical formula, but a guide that can be tailored to help you consider logically the vital issues involved in complex problem solving. After we present an explanation of each step in P-MOPS, we will show you two adaptations of the P-MOPS procedure and give you tips for its use.

I. What is the nature of the problem facing us?
   Early in the discussion the group needs to focus most talk on the details of what is unsatisfactory, what led to the undesirable situation, what is

ultimately desired, and what the obstacles to that goal might be. First, if the group has been given a charge, members need to be sure they understand and agree on their charge. For instance, instructors frequently assign group projects in small group communication courses. That assignment is a charge. If you have such an assignment, make sure all members of your project group understand the charge as intended by the instructor. Second, be sure you are clear about the form your output is to take: a panel discussion presented to the class? a video or film presentation? a written recommendation designed to solve a campus or local problem? Can you explain how you will be graded: as a group, as individuals, or by some combination of both? Will each member be required to write a case study analyzing your group? If so, what format must the paper follow? Will you need to keep a journal of group activities, or some other record?

Important principles for guiding the investigation and discussion of the nature of your problem/goal include:

A. Focus on the problem before thinking about how to solve it. What would you think if you drove your rough-running car into a garage and the service manager immediately said, "You need new valves in your engine," without so much as looking under the hood? Most of us would drive away as quickly as possible. A competent technician, after questioning you about how the car was acting, might attach an engine analysis computer before making a tentative diagnosis. Just so, one of the most common failings in group problem solving is getting solution-centered before thoroughly diagnosing the problem. Writers concerned with business groups have noted this tendency and the potential harm it can cause.[35] Time spent in this step often saves headaches later, while fudging on problem analysis leads to such outcomes as unnecessary conflict, wasted time, and solutions that don't work.

B. State the problem in the form of a single, unambiguous *problem question,* not a *solution question.* **Problem questions** focus on the undesired state of affairs and the goal, whereas **solution questions** suggest a solution, a means of arriving at the goal, and thus tend to short-circuit the thinking of discussants to that one solution. Examples of both types of questions can be seen in Figure 11.3.

C. Map the problem thoroughly. Think of the problem as an uncharted area with only vague boundaries. To map the problem, the group must gather key information about the problem such as *who, what, why, when, how long, where, how, how serious, what limitations,* and *what feelings.* Participants must *share* all they know about the situation: facts, complaints, conditions, circumstances, factors, happenings, relationships, effects, and so forth. They may discover that they need to learn a lot more before proceeding with a plan of action, so then they must answer such questions as, "How will we get the information we need?" and "Who will look up what?"

Solution versus problem questions. **FIGURE 11.3**

SOLUTION QUESTIONS

How can I transfer a man who is popular in his work group but slows down the work of other employees in the group?

How can we increase the publicity for our club's activities so attendance will be increased?

PROBLEM QUESTIONS

How can I increase the work output of the group?

What can we do to increase attendance at our club's activities?

Maps of a problem before and after discussion. **FIGURE 11.4**

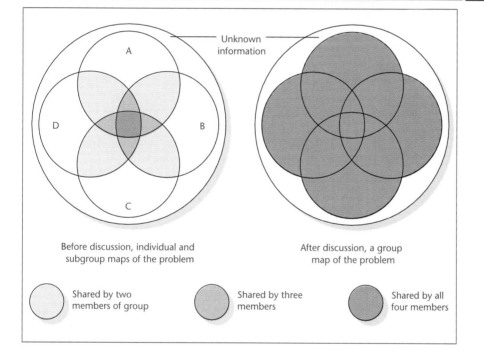

Before discussion, individual and subgroup maps of the problem

After discussion, a group map of the problem

Shared by two members of group

Shared by three members

Shared by all four members

Figure 11.4 illustrates the mapping of the problem, before and after information is gathered, shared, and interpreted. The large circle represents all that could be known and understood about the problem. Each of the members—A, B, C, and D—comes to the initial meeting with some information and opinions about it, a unique personal map represented by the four inner circles. Some information is shared by two members, some by three, and a small amount by all four. And some useful information is not yet known to *any* member. Once the members have discussed the problem freely and shared all the information they have, the group map looks like the second large circle, much closer to the "real" problem.

One of the greatest obstacles to such problem-centered thinking is a member (especially if this is a designated leader) who comes to the group with the problem already solved in his or her own mind. The presenter of a problem must set preconceived solutions aside; mutual influence is a hallmark of teamwork in group problem solving.

D. Be sure the group members agree on criteria, as we discussed earlier. In addition to establishing standards by which group solutions must be judged, criteria also express the values shared by group members. Two people with different values will use different criteria to evaluate options, and therefore can arrive at very different solutions.[36] Recall the Rubenstein study (see Chapter 5) of Arab and American students who were asked whom they would save; *all* Arabs chose the mother, but *none* of the Americans did. In this case, Arab and American values supported widely divergent criteria for evaluating the decision (i.e., whom to save). Unless agreement exists about criteria, consensus on a solution is unlikely.

Criteria must be ranked or prioritized. Be sure to give highest priority to criteria that *must* be met. Ideas can then be rejected if they do not meet *absolute* criteria, and those that remain can be ranked on how well they meet *relative* criteria (see Figure 11.5). Moreover, criteria should be stated as quantitatively as possible; criteria like "efficient" are too abstract to be measurable, but may help a group arrive at standards of "efficiency" that can be measured.

E. Be sure all members understand the group's area of freedom alike. Any policy solution must be evaluated from the standpoint of the charge.

During the first step of the P-MOPS model, an outlined series of questions can guide the group's description and analysis of a complex problem. The questions in Figure 11.6 are suggestive; such questions must be tailored to the specific problem and asked in the explicit language of that problem. Everyone should be encouraged to ask any and every question he or she feels needs an answer before planning a strategy to overcome all obstacles between the group and its goal.

II. **What might be done to solve the problem?**

If you try panning for gold in an Ohio stream, you probably won't make any money. You *might* succeed in finding gold in a stream in Arizona, Colorado, or California. As this analogy suggests, if there are no good ideas in the list being considered by a group, the solution recommended or adopted will fail to achieve the goal or may even make the situation worse. It is crucial in step II that a group have as many ideas as it can find and invent so it can choose the best, or, if necessary, can redefine the goal and problem. Also, you would not want to have nuggets wash

Absolute versus relative criteria to guide plans for a club's annual picnic. **FIGURE 11.5**

ABSOLUTE (*must* be met)	**RELATIVE** (*should* be met)
Entertainment must not cost over $400.	Location should be convenient, that is, within 30 minutes' driving time for all members.
Must be enjoyable to members and their families. (*Enjoyable* means: provide a variety of activities designed to appeal to people ranging in age from 3 to 80.)	Facilities should be comfortable, for example, shelter in case of rain, electrical outlets, hot and cold running water, restroom facilities, and so on.

Questions to guide problem analysis. **FIGURE 11.6**

What does this problem question mean to us?
What is our charge and area of freedom?
What is unsatisfactory at present?
  Who (or what) is affected?
  When, where, and how?
  How serious do we judge the problem to be?
  How long has the problem existed?
  Do we need to gather any additional information to assess the nature and extent
    of the problem adequately?
What conditions have contributed to the problem?
  What appear to be causative conditions?
  What precipitated the crisis leading to our discussion?
What exactly do we hope to accomplish (the goal, desired situation)?
  What obstacles to achieving the desired goal exist?
What information do we need before we can find a satisfactory solution?
  What additional subquestions must we answer?
  How might we find answers to these subquestions?
  What are the answers to these subquestions?
How can we summarize our understanding of the problem to include the present and
  desired situation and causal conditions?

out of your gold pan or lose track of a briefly mentioned idea that could turn out to be part of the best solution to a complex problem. Good technique prevents losing nuggets; *writing down each idea proposed as a solution* (preferably where everyone can see it and not forget it) will prevent losing ideas. A couple of principles can improve the group's success at finding and inventing solutions:

A. Defer judgment during discussion while collecting and inventing proposals. This is the heart of the technique called "brainstorming" presented in Chapter 14. Judgment stifles creative thinking and increases apprehension about others' responses to ideas. When solution multiplicity is low, or when thorough exploration of the problem leads to a sudden insight into a solution, group members should still make an effort to think of other possible solutions, perhaps by asking "What else *might* we do?" If nothing else is uncovered, the solution should still be evaluated thoroughly against all available criteria, and especially for possible negative consequences. The proposed solution may be refined and improved considerably through such critical thinking/discussion.

B.   Often during this part of the problem-solving procedure, a participant will think of some detail of the problem that ought to be explored more fully, a sort of "Let's examine that rock again—it might have gold in it." The group will then need to cycle back to further mapping of the problem, and *should* do so instead of doggedly pursuing still further solutions at the moment just for the sake of following procedure. The group can pick up where it left off after it has backtracked to investigate and clarify the problem further, and will be better informed for making an intelligent choice among solutions. Such second-guessing is characteristic of effective problem-solving groups.[37]

CONSIDER THIS

Using the first two steps of the P-MOPS procedure, how would you analyze Tyrell's problem, in our opening case? What are the possible options the team might consider for dealing with the problem? Can you see the connection between how you define the problem and how you think about handling it?

III.   What are the probable benefits and possible negative consequences of each proposed solution?

Once the problem has been thoroughly analyzed, with alternatives accumulated and criteria clearly understood by all members, the group is ready to evaluate the alternatives. For group problem solving to work optimally, pros and cons of each solution must be explored. Members must all have achieved convergence on explicit criteria if evaluation clarity is to occur. If not done previously, the first substep in this stage of group problem solving is to establish criteria. Every member must feel free to express opinions openly and honestly, without being attacked personally or attacking anyone else, for the group to achieve the best possible outcome.

Norms that promote critical examination of issues are desirable:

A.   Evaluation should be viewed as a cooperative venture, a team effort to prevent mistakes.

B.   Feelings, ideas, opinions, and even hunches should be shared openly and evaluated without any reflection on the person who expresses them. Anonymous computer messages may be a way to support this norm in groups experiencing power struggles.

C. Members should insist on exploring assumptions and implications of every idea, especially the potential negative consequences. Ideally, the person who proposed an idea will *invite* such critical evaluation.

D. Personal attacks and *ad hominem* remarks are unacceptable as substitutes for evidence and argument. Sensitivity to others' feelings and insensitivity to criticism of one's own ideas is called for. Ascribed status differences based on corporate positions, wealth, education, race, or any criterion other than relevant knowledge should play no part in evaluation discussion.

E. Members should often paraphrase what they think are the positions, feelings, and values of those with whom they disagree, always in a mood of inquiry—"Am I right about what you have just said?"

F. New issues should be raised or a challenge offered to an idea only when there is enough time to discuss the question thoroughly, not just before time to adjourn. If this happens, schedule another meeting to delay the final decision.

G. Trickery, bargaining, manipulation, deception, pressure to concur, and other breaches of communicative ethics are unacceptable. If noticed by any member, such unethical conduct should be pointed out at once and rebuked.

IV. **What is the best possible solution we can all support?**
If a decision seems to have emerged during evaluation of alternatives, the discussion leader should test for consensus. If everyone now agrees with one solution, the group is ready for the final stage of a complete problem-solving cycle. If two or more alternatives are still under consideration, the group should discuss such consensus-building questions as:

Which solution seems most likely to be accepted and supported by all persons affected by it?

Is there some compromise solution we can all accept as being likely to achieve our objectives without creating new problems?

Could we combine parts of our remaining ideas to create a solution we can all accept?

Once the group has decided which solution to recommend or adopt, the stage has been set for the final phase of this problem-solving discussion: implementation.

V. **What will we do to put our solution into effect?**
Unfortunately, many groups arrive at policy decisions or solutions with no plans for putting them into effect. For example, a committee charged with making a recommendation to a parent organization needs to decide who will make the report, in what form, and with what support from the entire group, and perhaps plan a campaign to prepare the general membership to accept the suggestion. A construction crew may need to acquire raw materials and schedule construction time.

Competent leaders see that a group has worked out all necessary details of implementation, or that doing so has been assigned to someone. At this point the group should decide on answers to such questions as:

Who will do what, when, and how?

Do we need any follow-up evaluation of how well our solution is working? If so, how will we do that?

PERT, described in Chapter 14, is a helpful procedure for planning implementation of a multistep solution.

You can see that the general Procedural Model of Problem Solving is flexible by design and can be adapted to fit almost any problem. In many cases the charge to a group will involve only some phases of the total problem-solving procedure: the group is to recommend several options, but not choose one; the group is to prepare an extensive investigation and analysis of the problem, but make no recommendations; the group is to implement a policy previously decided by another group. In such instances, only the relevant stage of P-MOPS would be used.

However you tailor P-MOPS to fit your problem, help group members remember the P-MOPS issues by putting the P-MOPS outline in plain view of all members (through a visual display or a handout) and charting the group's progress. For instance, as members complete their description and analysis of the problem, their findings can be posted on newsprint, wall boards, or on a computer display. This helps keep members focused on the *group* goal instead of diverting to personal agenda or social items. In one study on an early version of P-MOPS, students preferred to have the procedure in front of them on a chart rather than just having the leader explain the procedure or announce each new question or step as the group came to it.[38] Kelly, Jaffe, and Nelson insist that the progression of a discussion be made visual to a group, perhaps with flipcharts, as it moves through steps.[39] In a recent article about how computers can be used to help groups solve complex problems, Broome and Chen note that two of the best uses of computer technology are for displaying ideas graphically and recording them as the group proceeds.[40] Whatever procedural outline you use, P-MOPS or something else, we recommend visual display of the steps in the procedure and of the group's progress.

We have made the point several times that providing some structure to decision making generally improves decision-making quality. However, rigidly adhering to any system or structure can be counterproductive, so whatever structure or procedure you use, be careful not to use it in such a lock-step way that you harm the decision-making process. Pacanowsky notes that certain kinds of complex problems, called "wicked" problems, are particularly difficult to solve using overly structured procedures.[41] Wicked problems are those with no known format for finding a solution. The group may be at the point of generating solutions when someone realizes that the problem has been defined wrongly and suggests recycling to an earlier step in the problem-solving process. Your procedures, whatever they are, should be flexible enough to allow for this, especially for complex problems.

Leader's procedural outline for a club's annual picnic.   **FIGURE 11.7**

PROBLEM QUESTION: What should be done to improve student parking at Southwest Missouri State University?

I. What is the nature of the problem students encounter with parking at SMSU?
   A. What is the scope of our concern with student parking?
      1. Do any terms in the question need to be clarified?
      2. What authority do we have?
      3. Do we need to determine the authority and duties of departments involved with campus parking?
   B. What is now unsatisfactory about student parking?
      1. What have we found to be unsatisfactory?
         a. Have any studies been done?
         b. What complaints have students been making?
      2. Does any other information exist about student parking that we need to consider?
   C. What goals does the committee hope to achieve by changes in parking that we need to consider?
   D. What obstacles may stand in the way of improving parking for students?
      1. What do we know about what is causing the problem(s) we've described?
      2. How much interest do involved persons have in this problem?
      3. What limits are there on resources that might be needed?
         a. Funds?
         b. Space?
         c. Personnel?
         d. Other?
      4. Are there any other obstacles to changing student parking?
   E. How shall we summarize the problem(s) with student parking at SMSU?
      1. Do we all perceive the problem the same?
      2. Should we subdivide the problem?
         a. If so, what are the major subproblems?
         b. In what order shall we take them up?
II. What solutions to the student parking problem(s) we've described are possible?
III. What are the relative advantages and disadvantages of each proposed solution?
   A. Do we need to further clarify our criteria?
   B. What are the advantages and disadvantages of each proposal?
      1. Might any have unacceptable negative consequences?
      2. How effective might each be?
      3. How well does each meet our other criteria?
IV. What do we agree to recommend to the proper authorities as a solution to the student parking problem?
V. How will we make our recommendations for improving student parking?
   A. To whom will our recommendations be given?
   B. In what format will we make them?
      1. Written?
      2. In person?
      3. Other, or a combination?
   C. Do we need to plan any follow-up?
   D. Who will do what, when, and how?

The following two figures show you how P-MOPS can be tailored to address complex or simple problems. Examples of two leaders' outlines modifying P-MOPS are presented in Figures 11.7 and 11.8. In Figure 11.7, the outline deals with all the complexities of parking on an urban campus.[42] From the outline, you can see how major criteria were arrived at and used to evaluate proposals.

FIGURE 11.8	Leader's procedural outline for a brief problem-solving discussion.

I. What sort of written final exam should we have for our class?
   A. How much authority (area of freedom) do we have?
   B. What facts and feelings should we take into account as we seek an answer to this question?
II. What are our objectives (criteria) in deciding on the type of exam?
   A. Learning objectives?
   B. Grades?
   C. Type of preparation and study?
   D. Fairness to all?
III. What types of written final exam might we have?
IV. What are the advantages and disadvantages of each?
V. What will we recommend as the form of our written exam?

Figure 11.8 is a leader's simple outline for structuring discussion of a problem for which few solutions were possible and discussion time was limited.

THE SINGLE QUESTION FORMAT: A LESS HIGHLY STRUCTURED FORMAT

In the event a group chooses not to use some adaptation of P-MOPS, perhaps because members are low in preference for procedural order, it is still essential for discussion to be critically vigilant to be sure of arriving at the best solution possible. As designated leader, you could ask the group to apply a procedure created by Larson, which was based on a series of studies by another researcher of how successful problem solvers reasoned.[43] When using this **Single Question format,** early in the discussion the group must decide on the issues that need to be dealt with, how to answer these questions, and then proceed to do so. The list of questions provides structure to the discussion and should ensure that the major concerns of Vigilant Interaction Theory are met. Here is the format developed by Larson:

I. What is the single question that, when answered, means the group knows how to accomplish its purpose?
II. What subquestions must we answer before we can answer the single question we have formulated?
III. Do we have sufficient information to answer the subquestions with confidence?
   A. If "yes," what are our answers? (Then go to V.)
   B. If "no," the group continues to IV or adjourns to look for answers.
IV. What are the most reasonable answers to the subquestions?
V. If our answers to the subquestions are adequate, what is the best solution to the problem?

The church board to which you were introduced in Chapter 2 used a version of the Single Question format to develop the church's first annual budget.

An example of the Single Question problem-solving procedure.   **FIGURE 11.9**

I. What is the single question . . . ?
    What is the most environmentally benign, politically acceptable, and economically feasible way to dispose of solid waste from Springfield and surrounding counties?

II. Subquestions
     In what ways could the solid waste of the Springfield area be disposed of? How much will each feasible method of waste disposal cost the citizens of Springfield and surrounding counties?
     What will facilities and start-up cost?
     What will continuing operation cost?
     Will the method generate enough revenue to pay its costs?
     What might be harmful effects of each method of disposal?
     What effects will each method have on water, air, land, and components of the environment?
     What health hazards might each method create?
     What problems might we have in getting voters to accept each method?
     What group or groups are likely to oppose each method?
     How well has this method been accepted elsewhere?
     How workable is the method?
     What personnel or training would be required?
     What has its dependability been elsewhere?
     How long will this method serve Springfield?

III. The task force engaged in extensive research efforts, including paying consultants, hiring an engineering consulting firm, and making several trips to observe facilities used by other cities.

IV. The task force recommended that a MERF (Materials Recovery Facility) with composting and limited landfill usage be recommended to voters. After an extensive information campaign involving newspapers, public forums, and broadcast media, voters approved the MERF concept. City council passed an ordinance requiring that residents not be allowed to send waste materials to private facilities to ensure generation of a sufficient amount of revenue to operate the MERF. A coordinator of the project has been hired, and a firm has been contracted with to build and operate the MERF.

Because the church was new, it had no past financial history on which to rely for budgetary information. The *single question* was, "What will be our annual budget for fiscal year 2000?" Board members knew that if they could estimate the costs of fixed expenses and the money needed by each committee, they would have a good idea of the annual budget. Thus, the subquestions asked: "What will be the individual budgets for all the subcommittees?" and "What will be our fixed expenses?" Since members did not have the information available at the initial budget meeting, they adjourned so the treasurer could meet with the committee heads to get the needed information. When all the individual subquestions were answered, the broad single question was answered as well.

You will notice that this format calls for a thorough analysis of the problem, then a search for any missing information, followed by construction of a solution based on findings and interpretations of the group. A final step, not mentioned by Larson in his original article, would be, of course:

VI. How will we put our decision into effect?

An example of an initial outline that might have been created by a group following the Single Question format is shown in Figure 11.9. Such an outline is a product of the first part of the discussion, and it keeps being refined and added to as the group's investigations and discussions proceed toward their goal. Every member must have a copy of the questions as they are generated, answers as they are provided, and an agenda for each meeting. Using this format calls for close teamwork and decision making by consensus.

SUMMARY

1. Decision making involves choosing among alternatives. Problem solving entails creating or discovering the alternatives. Every problem includes an unsatisfactory situation, a desired goal, and obstacles that must be surmounted in order to reach the goal.

2. The problem-solving process should be tailored to fit the problem's specific characteristics: task complexity, degree of solution multiplicity, intrinsic interest, cooperative requirements, population familiarity, level of technical requirements, acceptance requirements, and the area of freedom.

3. Groups need some structure in the problem-solving process to ensure that no important step is overlooked. No single sequence is better than all others; any

structure is better than none at all. All sequences should conform to Vigilant Interaction Theory.

4. Whether and when the group should explicitly discuss criteria for evaluating proposed solutions depends on whether evaluation clarity is high or low.

5. The Procedural Model of Problem Solving (P-MOPS) is a general procedure that includes problem description and analysis, a search for and evaluation of alternatives, a decision, and an implementation plan. It can be modified to suit any problem, from simple to complex.

6. The Single Question format is a less structured alternative that simply asks members to agree on key subissues before reaching the overall solution.

EXERCISES

1. Select a problem you are concerned about, write it as a problem question, then analyze it into the three major components described in Chapter 11. Use the following format:

Problem question—

What is unsatisfactory about the current situation—

Goal (desired situation)—

Obstacles to achieving goal—

2. Select a problem affecting all members of the class, such as the type of final exam or some campus or community issue in which all class members have a high level of interest. Write a paper in which you analyze this problem on each of the variables below. Give a rating number and a brief explanation of why you gave this rating for each variable.

    Task difficulty—(from high = 10 to low = 1)
    Solution multiplicity—(scale of 10 to 1)
    Intrinsic interest—
    Cooperative requirements—
    Population familiarity—
    Acceptance requirements—
    Technical requirements—
    Area of freedom—

3. As a class, select two problems for study: one should have a high level of solution multiplicity, one a low level. Each class member will write a leader's outline for structuring a group discussion of each problem, adapting P-MOPS to the characteristics of the problem. Compare outlines in small groups of four or five students each; then as a group write one outline for organizing discussion of each problem.

4. Choose a problem now faced by your school or community, then use the Single Question format to create a sequence of questions and subquestions for guiding a vigilant problem-solving discussion of the problem. Compare outlines or sets of questions in small groups, then combine into one outline that contains all issues group members agree should be explored before deciding on a solution.

5. View a videotape of a problem-solving discussion (for instance, one of the groups in the previous discussion might have been recorded with a camcorder). Either as an entire class or in small groups, evaluate the vigilance, structure, omissions, and productivity of the discussion. Point out specific instances when the discussion might have been improved and when member behaviors clearly contributed to the quality of the group product.

BIBLIOGRAPHY

Cathcart, Robert S., Larry A. Samovar, and Linda D. Henman, eds. *Small Group Communication: Theory and Practice.* 7th ed. Dubuque, IA: Brown & Benchmark, 1996, section 3.

Hirokawa, Randy Y., and Marshall S. Poole, eds. *Communication and Group Decision-Making.* Beverly Hills, CA: Sage Publications, 1986, 81–111.

Larson, Carl E., and Frank M. J. LaFasto. *Teamwork: What Must Go Right/What Can Go Wrong.* Newbury Park, CA: Sage Publications, 1989.

Shaw, Marvin E. *Group Dynamics.* 3d ed. New York: McGraw-Hill, 1981, chapter 10.

Worchel, Stephen, Wendy Wood, and Jeffry A. Simpson, eds. *Group Process and Productivity.* Newbury Park, CA: Sage Publications, 1992.

NOTES

1. Carolyn J. Wood, "Challenging the Assumptions Underlying the Use of Participatory Decision-Making Strategies: A Longitudinal Case Study," *Small Group Behavior* 20 (1989): 428–48.

2. Irving L. Janis and L. Mann, *Decision Making: A Psychological Analysis of Conflict, Choice and Commitment* (New York: Free Press, 1977); Irving L. Janis, *Groupthink: Psychological Studies of Foreign-Policy Decisions and Fiascoes,* 2d ed. (Boston: Houghton Mifflin, 1983).

3. David M. Berg, "A Descriptive Analysis of the Distribution and Duration of Themes Discussed by Task-Oriented Small Groups," *Speech Monographs* 34 (1967): 172–75.

4. Susan Jarboe, "Procedures for Enhancing Group Decision-Making," in *Communication and Group Decision Making,* 2d ed., eds. Randy Y. Hirokawa and Marshall Scott Poole (Thousand Oaks, CA: Sage, 1996): 345–83.

5. Marvin E. Shaw, *Group Dynamics.* 3d ed. (New York: McGraw-Hill, 1981): 364.

6. See, for example, John K. Brilhart and Lurene M. Jochem, "Effects of Different Patterns on Outcomes of Problem-Solving Discussions," *Journal of Applied Psychology* 48 (1964): 175–79; Ovid L. Bayless, "An Alternative Model for Problem-solving Discussion," *Journal of Communication* 17 (1967): 188–97; and Sidney J. Parnes and Arnold Meadow, "Effects of 'Brainstorming' Instruction on Creative Problem-Solving by Trained and Untrained Subjects," *Journal*

of Educational Psychology 50 (1959): 171–76.

7. Shaw, *Group Dynamics,* 364.

8. Leonard Berkowitz, "Sharing Leadership in Small Decision-Making Groups," *Journal of Abnormal and Social Psychology* 48 (1953): 231–38.

9. James H. Davis, *Group Performance* (Reading, MA: Addison-Wesley, 1969).

10. Randy Y. Hirokawa, "Communication and Group Decision-Making Efficacy," in *Small Group Communication: A Reader,* 6th ed., eds. Robert S. Cathcart and Larry A. Samovar (Dubuque, IA: Wm. C. Brown, 1992): 165–77; Randy Y. Hirokawa and Kathryn M. Rost, "Effective Group Decision Making in Organizations: Field Test of the Vigilant Interaction Theory," *Management Communication Quarterly* 5 (February 1992): 267–88.

11. Dennis S. Gouran, "Inferential Errors, Interaction, and Group Decision-Making," in *Communication and Group Decision Making,* eds. R. Y. Hirokawa and M. S. Poole (Beverly Hills, CA: Sage, 1986): 93–111.

12. Hirokawa and Rost, "Effective Group Decision Making," 4.

13. Randy Y. Hirokawa, "Group Communication and Problem-Solving Effectiveness II: An Investigation of Procedural Functions," *Western Journal of Speech Communication* 47 (1983): 59–74; Marshall S. Poole and Joel A. Doelger, "Developmental Processes in Group Decision-Making," in *Communication and Group Decision Making,* eds. Hirokawa and Poole (Newbury Park, CA: Sage, 1986): 35–61.

14. Hirokawa and Rost, "Effective Group Decision Making," 20–22.

15. John F. Cragan and David W. Wright, "The Functional Theory of Small Group Decision Making: A Replication," *Journal of Social Behavior and Personality* 8 (1993): 165–74.

16. Hirokawa, "Communication and Group Decision-Making Efficacy," 165–77.

17. Thomas M. Scheidel and Laura Crowell, "Developmental Sequences in Small Groups," *Quarterly Journal of Speech* 50 (1964): 140–45.

18. Dennis S. Gouran, Candace Brown, and David R. Henry, "Behavioral Correlates of Perceptions of Quality in Decision-Making Discussions," *Communication Monographs* 45 (1978): 62; William E. Jurma, "Effects of Leader Structuring Style and Task Orientation Characteristics of Group Members," *Communication Monographs* 46 (1979): 282–95.

19. Jurma, "Effects of Leader Structuring Style."

20. John K. Brilhart, "An Experimental Comparison of Three Techniques for Communicating a Problem-Solving Pattern to Members of a Discussion Group," *Speech Monographs* 33 (1966): 168–77.

21. Marshall S. Poole, "Decision Development in Small Groups II: A Study of Multiple Sequences in Decision Making," *Communication Monographs* 50 (1983): 224–25; "Decision Development in Small Groups III: A Multiple Sequence Model of Group Decision Development," *Communication Monographs* 50 (1983): 321–41.

22. Brilhart and Jochem, "Effects of Different Patterns," 177–78.

23. Bayless, "An Alternative Model for Problem-solving Discussion," 188–97; Carl E. Larson, "Forms of Analysis and Small Group Problem Solving," *Speech Monographs* 36 (1969): 452–55.

24. Charles M. Kelly, Michael Jaffe, and Gregory V. Nelson, "Solving Problems," *Research Management* 30 (1987): 20–23.

25. Benjamin J. Broome and Luann Fulbright, "A Multi-Stage Influence Model of Barriers to Group Problem Solving: A Participant-Generated Agenda for Small Group Research," *Small Group Research* 26 (February 1995): 25–55.

26. Randy Y. Hirokawa, "Why Informed Groups Make Faulty Decisions," *Small Group Behavior* 18 (1987): 3–29.

27. Randy Y. Hirokawa, "Discussion Procedures and Decision-Making Performance,"

Human Communication Research 12 (1985): 203–24.

28. Randy Y. Hirokawa, "Group Decision-Making Performance: A Continued Test of the Functional Perspective," *Human Communication Research* 14 (1988): 487–515.

29. Hirokawa, "Discussion Procedures and Decision-Making Performance," 221.

30. Randy Y. Hirokawa and Dierdre D. Johnston, "Toward a General Theory of Group Decision Making: Development of an Integrated Model," *Small Group Behavior* 20 (1989): 500–23.

31. Richard Nisbett and Lee Ross, *Human Inference: Strategies and Shortcomings of Social Judgment* (Englewood Cliffs, NJ: Prentice-Hall, 1980).

32. Robert J. Sternberg, "Stalking the IQ Quark," *Psychology Today* 13 (September 1979): 42–45.

33. Brilhart and Jochem, "Effects of Different Patterns," 179.

34. Randy Y. Hirokawa, John G. Oetzel, Carlos G. Aleman, and Scott E. Elston, "The Effects of Evaluation Clarity and Bias on the Relationship between Vigilant Interaction and Group Decision-Making Efficacy" (Paper presented at the Speech Communication Association convention, Atlanta, November 1991).

35. For example, see Kelly, Jaffe, and Nelson, "Solving Problems"; Norman R. F. Maier and R. A. Maier, "An Experimental Test of the Effects of 'Developmental' vs. 'Free' Discussions on the Quality of Group Decisions," *Journal of Applied Psychology* 41 (1957): 320–23; and Randy Y. Hirokawa, "Group Communication and Problem-Solving Effectiveness: An Investigation of Group Phases," *Human Communication Research* 9 (1983): 291–305.

36. Moshe F. Rubenstein, *Patterns of Problem Solving* (Englewood Cliffs, NJ: Prentice-Hall, 1975): 1–2.

37. Hirokawa, "Why Informed Groups Make Faulty Decisions," 3–29.

38. Brilhart, "An Experimental Comparison of Three Techniques."

39. Kelly, Jaffe, and Nelson, "Solving Problems," 22.

40. Benjamin J. Broome and Minder Chen, "Guidelines for Computer-Assisted Group Problem Solving: Meeting the Challenges of Complex Issues," *Small Group Research* 23: (1992): 216–36, especially 228.

41. Michael Pacanowksy, "Team Tools for Wicked Problems," *Organizational Dynamics* 23 (Winter 1995): 36–51.

42. Used with permission of Greg Gravenmeier, student in Jack Brilhart's class.

43. Carl E. Larson, "Forms of Analysis and Small Group Problem-Solving," *Speech Monographs* 36 (1969): 452–55; this format has also been presented in several small group texts.

Decision Making in Small Groups

12

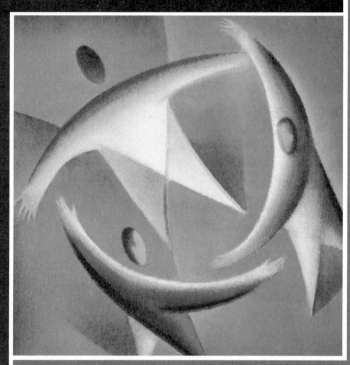

Central Message

The extent to which a group employs critical thinking has a major influence on its decision-making processes and ultimate decision quality.

Study Objectives

As a result of studying Chapter 12 you should be able to:

1. Describe the relative advantages and disadvantages of group and individual decision making.
2. Explain the group polarization effect.
3. Understand the differences among decisions made by a leader, by majority vote, and by consensus, including the advantages and disadvantages of each procedure.
4. Explain five procedural guidelines for making group decisions by consensus and the reasons for these guidelines.
5. Describe the phases groups often experience during decision making and explain several factors that may influence these phases.
6. Describe the factors that contribute to effective decision making.
7. Describe five common fallacies that inhibit critical thinking and explain how they interfere with a group's decision making.

Key Terms

Ad hominem attack
Assembly effect
Conjunctive tasks
Consensus decision
Critical thinking
Disjunctive tasks
Fact
Fallacy
False dilemma
Faulty analogy
Group polarization
Inference
Majority decision
Overgeneralization
Phasic progression

Decision making is one of the central activities of small groups. Decision making means choosing among two or more alternatives and engages both rational and nonrational thinking processes. Consider, for a moment, the decision-making process of burglars when deciding whether or not to rob a particular house. Biron and Ladouceur interviewed 25 young, male burglars who operated primarily within their own neighborhoods.[1] They discovered that burglars engage in a rational decision-making process during which they consider several criteria before they burgle a house. In general, the burglars they interviewed considered the site, the potential value of the goods to be stolen, and the ease of disposing of those goods. They asked themselves a series of questions, such as, "Are neighbors able to see the house and observe potential burglar activity?" "Are there bushes that can hide the burglars from view?" "Is there a dog protecting the property?" and "Does the house appear to be unoccupied?" These are quite appropriate criteria to use for the decision about which house to burgle. In addition, the decision-making process usually requires decision makers to discover and evaluate information about their particular choice options before making a decision, and the burglars in this study showed a high degree of creativity in seeking information about potential targets. For instance, they called the business offices of professionals such as doctors and lawyers to learn of their vacation plans so they could maximize their chances that the houses they planned to rob would be vacant.

Like the rest of us, burglars describe themselves as rational decision makers, but Cromwell et al. found that most burglaries are crimes of opportunity and that burglary is less rational than the burglars would like to think.[2] Burglars attend to two types of cues in "deciding" what house to burgle. Gain cues, which pertain to the value of the goods the burglar is likely to gain, actually play a fairly small part in the decision-making process because, as one burglar noted, all houses have something worth stealing. Risk cues, which pertain to the likelihood of getting caught, are much more salient when burglars cruise a neighborhood to scout potential targets. A house that is unoccupied, not easily seen by neighbors, and accessible (e.g., without deadbolts and alarms) makes an attractive, opportunistic target.

Interestingly, two-thirds of burglars work as members of groups. As we shall see later in this chapter, decision making, even among burglars, involves both cognitive and psychological information processing, both of which are affected by participation with others. Decision making in groups changes the decision-making process.[3]

In the course of solving a problem, groups must make a number of decisions, both trivial and important. Every group task—from deciding whether or not a defendant is guilty and selecting the appropriate punishment to choosing an employee benefits package—requires at least one and probably several decisions. This need to make decisions in concert with others demands that we understand how to optimize the group decision-making process. Failure to understand this process produces disasters, such as the poor decision in 1986 to launch the shuttle *Challenger,* which exploded shortly after take-off.[4]

We are competing with societies—Japanese, Chinese, South Korean—that are more skilled than we at collective decision making. We dare not remain complacent. Furthermore, we cannot work effectively in small groups without understanding their processes and dynamics.[5]

In the last chapter we described the comprehensive group problem-solving process. Here, we narrow the focus to the decision-making process, with a focus on improving group decision making.

GROUP VERSUS INDIVIDUAL DECISION MAKING

Group decisions made through discussion are usually superior to individual decisions or to averaging individual decisions.[6] They are even better, usually, than decisions made by members who are especially knowledgeable about a problem.[7] This is because group members can compensate for each other's weaknesses, with each member having unique information that complements the others' information.[8] Group members can spot each other's errors, recognize truth, and process more information than individuals can.[9] The higher the quality of a group's inputs and throughput processes are, the better the group's decisions.

Groups frequently achieve an **assembly effect** in which the decision is qualitatively and quantitatively superior either to the best individual judgment of any member or to the average of the judgments of all the members. This is a kind of synergy that occurs in the operation of the small group as a system—the whole becomes greater than the sum of its parts. Two recent studies found evidence of the assembly effect.[10] However, synergy is achieved only when group members interact and work *interdependently* on the task; groups whose members work independently do not achieve this result.[11] For example, if group members complete individual assignments on their own and later compile their individual products into the final group product without discussing each member's individual work *as a group,* then that group will probably not achieve an assembly effect.

Several input and throughput factors affect group decision quality, especially the type of task, the abilities of the members, and the type of communication among members. For example, groups have been found superior on **conjunctive tasks,** where each member possesses information needed to solve a problem but no one member has all the needed information. However, groups are not superior at **disjunctive tasks,** which require little or no coordination, often enabling the most expert member working alone to produce a correct answer.[12] Often, groups do both—they cycle between conjunctive and disjunctive tasks and must know when to switch from individual to group decision making. Pacanowsky, for instance, notes that teams can be

Factors Affecting Decision Quality

more efficient when members can work individually, then pool their insights to create a team-designed solution.[13] Ideally, members recognize which type of task they are working on and which type of decision making would be most suitable.

The abilities of the members is another input factor that affects decision quality. Gruenfeld and Hollingshead discovered that members with high *integrative complexity*—the ability to engage in highly complex reasoning processes—produced group interaction that was more complex and better able to incorporate diverse viewpoints into the ultimate decision, particularly on conjunctive tasks.[14] Similarly, Scudder et al. found that when members are predisposed to process information cognitively—that is, they have a high *need for cognition*—decision quality is affected positively.[15] Laughlin et al. discovered that overall decision-making performance was hurt by weaker members, whose impaired abilities to reason and hypothesize correctly affected the entire group.[16] Salazar et al. also found that group potential, as defined by individual member abilities, is a "powerful determinant of group decision performance."[17] All these authors recommend further investigation into the relationship of member abilities and group potential to decision quality.

Communication among members, a group's essential throughput process, is an important factor affecting decision quality. Verbal interaction itself, not just a summing of individual members' perceptions or opinions, contributes to the increased decision quality that groups usually exhibit.[18] Salazar et al. note that communication is perhaps even more important than originally thought, particularly task-relevant communication.[19] Communication that was goal directed, with issues handled systematically and where assertions were documented, were associated with increased decision quality. These authors offer these findings as support for Functional Theory (i.e., Vigilant Interaction Theory) described in the previous chapter. Their findings are consistent with those of Scudder et al., who discovered that groups whose members carefully assessed their options produced better decisions.[20]

It is clear from these and other studies that *both* input *and* throughput factors affect decision-making quality. Hirokawa proposes that input and throughput factors interact, each assuming greater importance in certain circumstances.[21] He suggests that when task "unfavorableness" exists (i.e., when the task is complex, there are multiple acceptable choices, the criteria are not obvious, and the information processing necessary to complete the task is high), then the throughput process of communication will have a greater effect on decision quality.

In addition to affecting decision quality, group involvement in decision making increases the acceptance of a decision.[22] Coch and French demonstrated that when workers have a voice in changing a work procedure, they are more productive and loyal than when the change is imposed on them.[23] As Block and Hoffman wrote, "the effectiveness of gaining members' commitment to change through use of group decision is unquestioned."[24]

As effective as group decision making can be, it is not automatically superior to individual decision making. It takes more time, sometimes one or two members can dominate a discussion, and occasionally the fact that other people are present can push an otherwise well-informed discussant further in a particular direction than he or she would normally go. Burleson, Levine, and Samter found that, although 8 of 10 groups that produced consensus decisions had better decisions than the individual members acting alone, 2 of the 10 produced worse decisions.[25] Wood observed several factors that impede effective decision making, including members who do not possess needed skills and information or make conscientious efforts to acquire them from outside sources, and members whose social needs prevent them from attending to the task.[26] Poor operating procedures, especially failure to provide the kind of structure and coordination needed to accomplish the task and failure to test for consensus, hurt decision quality. Finally, adherence to ascribed status differences impaired open and honest communication, which prevented critical thinking. As we discussed in Chapter 8, cohesiveness *and* performance norms influence decision quality. Miesing and Preble discovered that groups that were very cohesive and had high performance expectations performed better.[27] Hirokawa found that groups that approached decision making systematically made better decisions than groups that did not.[28] On the other hand, Gouran found that group interaction sometimes promoted collective inferential error if members accepted unusual cases as representative, passively accepted specialized knowledge, and created hypothetical stories that had no basis in fact.[29]

We can sum up the meaning of all this research comparing the quality of individual versus group decision making this way: groups are usually superior in making decisions about how to solve discussion-type problems, depending on the members' abilities, the type of task, how high their norms are for quality (performance), whether they have sufficient cohesiveness to enforce such norms, how systematic and organized their problem-solving procedures are, and how skilled and determined the group members are at arriving at valid conclusions based on sound evidence.

If assembling a group decision is sometimes a good choice but sometimes a poor one, how can you know whether to ask a group or an individual to make any particular decision? Vroom says that the decision to ask a group to make a decision should be based on analysis of three dimensions.[30]

1. The quality or rationality dimension concerns whether one decision is likely to be clearly better than another. There is one best way, for example, to assemble a swing set, but many different acceptable ways to plan a party.

2. The leader must determine how important it is that the decision be accepted by group members. Some decisions, particularly those which affect members' jobs or daily lives, may appear perfectly sound but will not work if group members do not accept them.

3. The group must have time to engage in discussion, for group decision making is considerably more time consuming than individual decision making. Therefore, a series of trade-offs is involved when an organization or authority elects to let a group make a decision.

GROUP POLARIZATION

The central point of group decision making is that members influence each other. Such influence can produce the **group polarization** tendency, sometimes called the risky or cautious shift, which refers to the finding that group members often make decisions that are more extreme (either more risky or more cautious) than the individual group members' initial preferences.[31] In other words, group members push themselves *further* in a particular direction than where they initially started. Two explanations have been proposed for this.[32]

The *social comparison theory* (SCT) suggests that as members get to know each other's values, they want to appear "correct" and may exaggerate opinions in the direction they believe the group values positively. For example, if you are mildly liberal politically and you are in a group that seems to value liberal thought, then you might be tempted to exaggerate how liberal you are. Thus, if the group or cultural norm favors risk (as with many business decisions in our culture), the group will shift toward risk; if caution is the cultural norm (as with a decision affecting a child's life), the group shifts toward caution.

The second explanation for group polarization is the *persuasive arguments theory* (PAT), which says that the number, salience, and novelty of arguments in a particular direction persuade members to move in that direction. Thus, if members favor risk (or caution), there will be more and stronger arguments presented in favor of risk (or caution); the persuasive power of these arguments shifts the group in that direction.

Studies have found some support for both SCT and PAT. Whether SCT or PAT better explains choice shift in a specific group may depend on conditions within the group. For example, Hale and Boster found that as the task became more ambiguous, SCT seemed to explain shifts better, but as task ambiguity decreased, PAT made more sense.[33] Kaplan and Miller learned that the type of task mattered; SCT explanations prevailed for tasks requiring judgment, but PAT explained the choice shifts better for intellective tasks that had correct answers.[34]

Cromwell et al.'s study of burglars, mentioned earlier, finds support for the concept of group polarization and confirms that both cognitive and emotional factors come into play during group decision making.[35] Burglars themselves believe they take more risks when working with others, but the evidence suggests otherwise. When rating targets, burglars are actually fairly conservative in their ratings of risk. Cromwell et al. found that rating targets in groups seems to increase the burglars' abilities to respond to risk cues as one burglar may point out risks the others miss. For example, in one group of three burglars, two rated a particular house a 6 (with 10 the lowest risk), but the third burglar, a woman, pointed out that the time was nearly 3 PM, school would soon be out, and many children were likely to be playing nearby. The burglars reassessed the risk as 2.

At the same time, burglars working together apparently increase each other's excitement and egg each other on. In the same study, Cromwell et al. found that burglars in groups were more likely to go on multiple burglary sprees, hitting multiple targets, something that individual burglars did not and would not do. These findings about burglar risk and caution, which seem incompatible, can be reconciled as follows. Burglars deciding to commit a crime experience high rates of arousal, which is influenced by the presence of others. This social facilitation effect can lead to increased risk taking. However, assessing a particular site for degree of risk is actually a low-arousal state and requires information-processing skill, which seems to be helped by the presence of others. Thus, both cognitive and psychological factors appear to be involved in decision making and both are affected by the participation of others. It is interesting to note that one of the major advantages for group decision making—that several heads are better than one—is distinctly helpful during the information-processing phase of decision making.

Thus, decision making can be impaired or improved by the particular norms and arguments that prevail in a group, a lesson learned from structuration theory in Chapter 7. Being aware of these normal group tendencies can help group members guard against bias in decision making.

CONSIDER THIS

Have you ever made a decision in a group that was worse than a decision you would have made alone? What were the factors operating on you that inhibited you from helping the group make a better decision? Similarly, have you ever made a decision in a group that was better than a decision you'd have made alone? Why was the group decision superior? What factors seemed to contribute most to the better decision?

METHODS OF DECISION MAKING IN GROUPS

Groups may use a number of different methods to make decisions. The three most common are by the designated leader, by majority vote, and by consensus. Each can be appropriate, depending on the situation.

Decision Making by the Leader

Sometimes a designated or emergent leader will think the problem through alone and announce a decision, or will consult with the group and then announce the decision. Group members are then given instructions for executing the decision. The resulting solution may or may not be a high-quality one, but other outcomes of such control by the leader may be resentment, lowered cohesiveness, halfhearted support for the decision, and unwillingness to contribute to subsequent decisions. Members may even sabotage the decision. We once observed a group of faculty members who became furious that their designated leader had made an important decision without consulting them. They called a special meeting to overturn his decision. After discussing their options, they proceeded to make *exactly the same* decision he had made. Clearly their distress was not about the *content* of the decision—it was about the *process* and their belief that the leader had disenfranchised them.

Decision Making by Majority Vote

Making a **majority decision** through voting by a show of hands, saying *aye,* or with written ballot is probably the procedure used most often to settle a difference of opinion in democratic groups. On the plus side, everyone has an equal opportunity to influence the decision by speaking, each vote counts equally, and the decision is reached more quickly than if the group's norms require a consensus decision. Majority voting resolves conflicts by the numerical power of the majority. Of course if the vote is unanimous, consensus has been achieved. But usually the vote is split, with minority members (losers) sometimes doubting that their ideas have been understood fully and treated fairly. People in a minority may even remain silent for fear of being ridiculed for opinions that deviate from the majority opinion. Not only does the quality of the decision sometimes suffer, but the group may also experience lowered cohesiveness and commitment to the decision. When a group's bylaws *require* that a vote be taken, the group may want to discuss an issue until consensus has been reached, then vote to confirm it "legally."

Decision Making by Consensus

A **consensus decision** is one that all members agree is the best that everyone can support. It may be, but is not necessarily, the alternative most preferred by all members. When a true consensus has been reached, the output is usually a superior-quality decision, a high level of member satisfaction, and acceptance of the result. However, reaching consensus may take much more time than other procedures. Furthermore, unanimity—the state of perfect consensus in which every group member believes that the decision achieved is the best that could be made—is not at all common. Sometimes a true consensus cannot be achieved, no matter how much time is spent in discussion. Certain personality traits, values, and other characteristics of the members affect a group's ability to achieve consensus. For example, Beatty found that groups with members similar in decision-rule orientation were more likely to achieve consensus.[36] Three common decision-rule orientations are attempts to minimize losses (a conservative, pessimistic approach), attempts to maximize gains (a risk-taking, optimistic approach), and the maximum expected utility approach (an attempt to derive the highest average payoffs no matter whether a pessimistic or optimistic future is envisioned). Beatty noted that the degree of comfort members felt with the decision was more important in achieving consensus than the quality of the decision itself. Groups with members whose decision-rule orientations were similar had an easier time achieving consensus. Thus, more than just the merit of the decision is involved when a group strives for consensus.

CONSIDER THIS

Imagine two different groups of burglars, one with members whose decision rules attempt to minimize losses and another whose rules attempt to maximize gains. Can you envision how these two different orientations could affect their joint decision making? To the burglars, what might be the advantages and disadvantages of each approach?

Consensus may be superficial when some members accommodate to other higher-status members, including "experts" who express their opinions with exceptional force, a designated leader, or a large majority. Gloria, one of the authors, once completed "Lost on the Moon," a group decision-making exercise in which the group is asked to rank the utility of several items, in a group of electrical and mechanical engineers who appeared to have a great deal of expertise on technical matters. She readily conceded to these experts. Interestingly, her individual ranking of the items was better than the group's ranking, but compliance to the perceived expertise of the engineers deprived the group of this member's reasoning. Even though it may be uncomfortable to be the group's opinion deviate, do not suppress your opinions.

Conflict is likely in the course of arriving at consensual decisions. Expect it and welcome it, particularly the type of constructive argument that enhances critical thinking. Use your best active listening and reasoning skills. In the next chapter we present specific suggestions to help you manage conflict.

CONSIDER THIS

Each type of decision making is appropriate under certain circumstances. Which types of decisions do you think a leader should make, or under what kinds of circumstances do you think it is all right for a leader to make a decision for a group? Which decisions are necessary to reach by consensus? Which by majority vote?

Suggestions for Achieving Consensus

The process of reaching consensus gives all members an opportunity to express how they feel and think about the alternatives, and an equitable chance to influence the outcome. Consensus depends on active listening so that all important information and points of view are understood similarly by all discussants. A consensual decision is often synergistic, with the group producing something superior to the members' individual ideas because alternatives are clarified and tested in the process of working toward consensus. Here are some discussion guidelines outlined by Hall for making consensus decisions:

1. Don't argue stubbornly for your own position. Present it clearly and logically, being sure you listen to and consider all reactions carefully.

2. Avoid looking at a stalemate as a win–lose situation. Rather, see whether you can find a next best alternative acceptable to all.

3. When agreement is reached too easily and too quickly, be on guard against groupthink. Don't change your position just to avoid conflict. Through discussion, be sure that everyone accepts the decision for similar or complementary reasons and really agrees that it is the best that can be reached.

4. Avoid conflict-suppressing techniques, such as majority vote, averaging, coin tossing, and so forth. Although they prevent destructive interpersonal conflicts, they also suppress constructive substantive arguments.

5. Seek out differences of opinion, which are helpful in testing alternatives and evaluating reasoning. Get every member involved in the decision-making process. The group has a better chance of selecting the best alternative if it has a wider range of information and ideas.[37]

PHASIC PROGRESSION DURING DECISION MAKING

In Chapter 7 we described how groups experience a formation phase and a production phase as they develop from a collection of individuals into a group. Several people have observed that groups also cycle through relatively predictable phases or stages during the process of decision making and problem solving. Bales and Strodtbeck were among the first to identify this **phasic progression.**[38] During the *orientation* phase, members orient themselves to the task and to one another, if they do not already know each other. In the *evaluation* phase, they decide what they collectively think about the problem or decision. Finally, during the *control* phase, the group has reached enough socioemotional maturity for members to concentrate on completing their task. For each new problem they confront, groups will tend to cycle through all three of these stages, returning to an orientation stage for a new problem once a decision has been reached about a previous problem.

More recently, Fisher observed that experienced decision-making groups pass through four phases as they work toward deciding among a group of alternatives.[39] These phases are orientation, conflict, decision emergence, and reinforcement. They can be identified by the kinds of interactions that occur in each.

Orientation.   During the orientation phase, members develop a shared understanding of their task, the facts about available options, and how to interpret them. Signs of disagreement are minimal; ambiguous and favorable remarks are common. This makes sense because, when group members are uncertain about the facts or concerned about how others will perceive them, they will be wary of making strong statements of disagreement that might offend another member. In this early stage, a member is more likely to say, "Well, that idea sounds like it might work, but maybe we should take time to think about it some more," than to say, "That's not going to work at all—we're going to have to try a lot harder if we are to come up with a decent solution." The first remark is ambiguous and tentative, the second is unambiguous and definite.

Conflict. During the conflict phase, members offer initiatives, take stands, disagree, offer compromises, argue for and against proposals, and generally discuss ideas in a more open manner than during orientation. Ambiguous remarks fall to a low level in this phase, but disagreeing and agreeing remarks are common. For instance, Selena says, "I think we should get more information about the impact this might have before we proceed much further." Andrew replies, "Naw, we have all the information we need right now to decide." Then Tina supports Selena: "I agree with Selena. We need to know a lot more or we might really mess things up." Members argue for and against proposals, with most people taking sides. Wishy-washy behavior disappears as opinions are expressed clearly and forcefully.

Decision emergence. For a group to achieve its goal, it must move, somehow, from a position where each member argues a particular point of view to a position where members are willing to be influenced by one another. This movement coincides with the reappearance of ambiguity in the group. Whereas the earlier ambiguity served as a way of managing primary tension, now it helps resolve secondary tension by allowing the members to back off from staunchly held positions and save face at the same time. It would be hard on a member's self-image to switch suddenly from "I think we should accept the first proposal" to "I think we should reject the first proposal." A transition is needed; the ambiguity provides this transition, which allows the member to move from "I think we should accept the first proposal" to: "*Maybe* you are right. There might be some problems with the first proposal that I hadn't considered. Let's look at it more closely before we decide." Members move gradually toward a common group position. Near the end of this phase a consensus decision will emerge, sometimes suddenly. The members will usually know when this point is reached, and they will all indicate support for the decision. (If this does not occur, then it is appropriate for the group to resolve its disagreement by majority vote.)

Reinforcement. After a group has accomplished its primary objective, it doesn't just immediately move on to a different problem or disband. Members will reinforce each other and themselves for a job well done. They will say such things as, "Wow, it took a long time but we got some really important things done," or "I really like the proposal. It's going to work beautifully," or "I'm proud of us for coming up with this. You guys are super, and this has been a rewarding experience." Members pat each other on the back and reinforce the positive feelings they have toward the decision and toward each other. This good feeling will carry over to the next meeting.

Fisher believed that unless some outside factor (like severe time pressure) interferes with the group's natural decision-making process, these phases will follow each other in a predictable way, although the proportion of time spent in each phase may vary from decision to decision. It is important to recall, however, that he studied interaction in previously developed groups that had already passed through their formation stage.

As we noted in Chapter 11, Poole and his associates found that groups take a variety of paths to problem solving. Poole's investigations have called into question the idea that most groups experience exactly the same phases, in the same order.[40] Group decision making is more complex than unitary sequences suggest. A number of factors influence not only what phases groups experience but also in what order the phases occur.[41] For example, some groups experience long, drawn-out conflict phases with little socioemotional integration after the conflict. Others experience lengthy periods of idea development with no overt conflict. Poole's contingency model of group decision making describes three types of factors that affect phasic progression: objective task characteristics, group task characteristics, and group structural characteristics.[42] *Objective task characteristics* include such factors as goal clarity and potential impact of the decision. For example, if the group's goal is clear at the beginning of the process, members may be able to shorten the orientation phase. *Group task characteristics* include such factors as time and population familiarity. Members are more likely to spend extra time orienting themselves to the task and arguing the merits of various options for a novel task that is unfamiliar to them than they are for a familiar one. Finally, *group structural characteristics* refer to how members of the group work together and include such factors as cohesiveness, conflict, and history. Members who have experienced divisive conflict may either run away from potential arguments in the group or may approach group meetings with their defenses up and boxing gloves on. As you can see, group decision making is complicated, with numerous factors potentially influencing phasic progression.

Note that there is a distinction between the phases that occur during a decision-making cycle and those that occur during the development of a group. These two processes operate in conjunction with each other and can readily be synthesized. Throughout its entire life, a group must deal simultaneously with process and production concerns. In Chapter 7 we described the two developmental phases, formation and production, that groups typically experience. Within each of these broad phases, a group makes a variety of decisions and may solve more than one problem. For instance, early in the formation phase of development the group may need to decide who will

Decision making within the development of a small group.   FIGURE 12.1

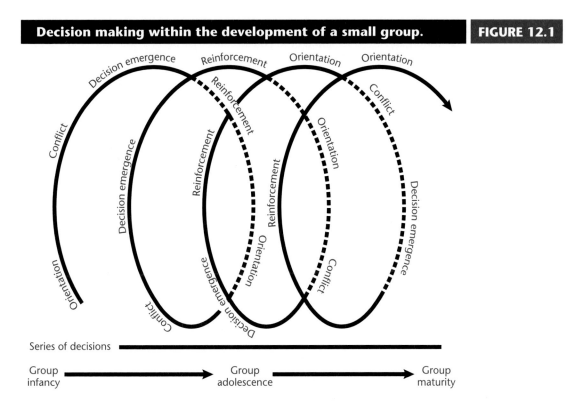

take notes, whether its decisions will require consensus or whether majority vote will suffice, how much information it must gather, how members will address each other, and so on. In the production phase it must investigate the problem, generate ideas, decide which of several alternatives is best, how the final report will be written and by whom, to what extent members are satisfied with the group's work and what can be done if they are not, and so forth. (Note, too, that both process and production decisions must be made in *all* stages of a group's development.)

Fisher's work provides the information needed to link the group's development stages with its decision-making stages. For each new major decision a group faces, members must orient themselves to each other and to the group's new task, argue for and against the various options available, *decide* something, and achieve some sort of closure through reinforcement of the decision. Thus, from our review of the important previous work on phasic progression and from our own experience, we envision a group cycling repeatedly through phases like those Fisher described while moving gradually forward from early formation to full and efficient production at the same time solving one or more problems. This movement is captured in the spirals of Figure 12.1. This back-and-forth spiral movement is typical of many continuing groups. Scheidel and Crowell observed the spiral-like progression of a group's problem-solving process and noted that a group does not move in a clear, unbroken line toward a decision.[43] This spiral-like effect has been observed by other researchers. Sabourin and Geist described the collaborative nature of group decision making as a process in which group members build on each other's proposals.[44] Fisher and Stutman also observed the messy, but ultimately progressive, nature of the spiral model.[45] It may be especially helpful for members high in preference for procedural order to know that such messy cycling between problem analysis to a decision and solution discussion is normal; they can better endure the frustration they feel when groups do not move in an orderly linear sequence from problem analysis to solution implementation. After all, only when they are *not* engaged do troops march in steady, straight lines!

EFFECTIVE GROUP DECISION MAKING

There are certain steps a group can take to help ensure that it has made the best possible decision. In the following guidelines, we have synthesized the key elements of the problem-solving process that directly relate to decision-making effectiveness:

1. **Make sure members understand the problem clearly.**

   If members do not see the problem clearly, a group may choose a decision that attacks symptoms instead of causes or that will not work as well as another option. Groups that clearly understand the choice-making situation select more wisely and avoid conflicts based on lack of similar maps of the problem.

2. **If members do not already understand the criteria for evaluating the decision, they should be discussed openly.**

   Criteria, as we explained in Chapter 11, are those standards that must be met when choosing any option. For example, if the parent organization for your group has said you must stay within a prescribed budget, your eventual decision must satisfy this criterion, so you need to agree on that.

3. **Evaluate all the options, using your established criteria, on the basis of both positive and negative consequences.**

   The most effective groups are able to anticipate possible negative consequences and thereby eliminate the worst options right off the bat. Think of all the things that can go wrong with each option, assess how serious each consequence could be, then thoroughly examine the positive aspects of each alternative. Make your final selection based on *both* evaluations.

4. **Select one option, tentatively, and "second guess" your choice.**

   The most effective groups do not simply choose to get things over with. They continue to cycle back over issues previously covered as they encounter new information or think of other things that are pertinent. Once you have made a tentative choice, go back over your choice as a group, reevaluating your information, reasoning, and assessment. In so doing you may be able to make further improvements in your chosen alternative.

CONSIDER THIS

It is easy to shortchange the decision-making process, and that may be perfectly acceptable under certain circumstances. Under what circumstances, or for which types of decisions, do you think it is all right to shortchange the decision-making process? For which decisions should you *never* shortchange the process? Can you give specific examples?

The final recommendation for improving the quality of group decisions is so important that we have chosen to devote a separate section to discussing it. *Group members who want to ensure that their decisions are the best that can be made must employ critical thinking skills at each step in the decision-making process.*

CRITICAL THINKING AND THE QUALITY OF GROUP DECISION MAKING

Critical thinking is the systematic examination of information and ideas on the basis of evidence and logical or probable reasoning, rather than intuition or hunch. Unfortunately, many groups do not encourage critical thinking skills. Meyers et al. found that group arguments in undergraduate groups consisted of simple assertions almost half the time and that members seldom cited rules of logic or used criteria as standards.[46] In this section we focus on how you can evaluate the evidence and reasoning that link information and ideas.

Critical thinking is the responsibility of *all* group members, but sometimes a group may appoint a member as its *critical advisor.*[47] We have sometimes referred to this person as a *devil's advocate;* others call this member a *reminder.* A member so designated is responsible for critically evaluating the ideas brought before the group after considering many of the ideas and guidelines we have presented. Criticism is constructive and ought to encourage other members to participate in the critical thinking process. Ideally, groups rotate this role among members so that the criticism is more likely to be associated with the role and not the particular member. Groups that use this role are less likely to do such things as allow one member to dominate the discussion or make faulty assumptions, thus improving the quality of their decisions.[48]

Information—facts, ideas, opinions, data—is the raw material from which a group's decision is made. A group's final decision can be only as good as the

Evaluating Information

information inputs used by the group. It's essential for a group to evaluate information for accuracy, credibility, and relevance to the group's decisions.

Distinguishing between Facts and Inferences   It is especially important to distinguish between facts and inferences, opinions, and preferences. Often, group members state opinions as though they were facts, thus leading other group members to accept what may be erroneous conclusions.

A **fact** can be verified as *true* or *false*. If false, it is not a fact. Facts either exist or do not exist; they are not open to argument. A *statement of fact* is a declarative statement that describes an observation of some event. "It is raining outside" is a statement of fact. The event (the rain) is described and the statement implies how someone could verify its accuracy (e.g., by looking out the window). It is a *true* statement if it accurately describes observed events (e.g., it really is raining). Present events are relatively easy to verify. If the statement of fact refers to a past event, that past event must have actually been observed by somebody. However, since the past event is not presently available to the group for verification, only statements about it can be verified. For example, we ourselves cannot verify that George III occupied the throne of England in 1773, but we can verify that records indicate he was king. If several independent sources report the same information as fact, you can be more confident than if it comes from only one source.

An **inference** is an opinion that goes beyond what was actually observed; it makes a leap from a fact to a conclusion based on that fact. A *statement of inference* is a declarative statement that contains an opinion, preference, or conclusion. For example, "The Springfield metropolitan area is growing rapidly" is a statement of inference that goes beyond the *fact* that the area's population was 207,204 in the 1980 census and 243,300 in the 1990 census. *Rapidly* is a relative term; whether we choose to accept this inference as valid depends on what we compare the growth rate to: average growth rate for metropolitan areas in the United States, average growth rate for Missouri metropolitan areas, recent growth rate for areas of similar size, and so on. An inference *is arguable.* The following benchmarks and examples will help you distinguish statements of fact from statements of inference or opinion:

Statements of Fact	Examples:
Are limited to description;	The population of greater Springfield recorded in the 1990 census was 243,300.
Can be made only *after* observation;	On June 3, 1993, John (Jack) Brilhart owned two horses.
Are as close to certain as humans can get;	The university library's catalog contained 2,437,532 volumes on July 8, 1996.
Only a limited number of facts exist.	After instituting lotteries, three states reduced their tax rates.

**Statements of Inference
and Opinion**

Go beyond what was
observed directly;

Can be made at any time
without regard to
observation;

Can be made by anyone,
observer or not;

Entail some degree of
probability, inferential risk,
or uncertainty;

An unlimited number can
be made about anything.

Examples:

Springfield is growing rapidly.

Jack Brilhart likes horses.

The heart of a good university is its
library.

We should legalize gambling to reduce
the state tax.

Factual-type statements, including statistics or the results of surveys, need to be evaluated carefully for dependability. Surveying is a sophisticated operation and must be done correctly or the results can be misleading, especially if surveys are based on other than random or scientific sampling. The questions and who asks them can make a big difference in the results.

*Evaluating
Survey and
Statistical Data*

Ask the following questions when evaluating statistics: Who commissioned the study? How were the data gathered and analyzed? How were questions phrased? You may need the help of an expert to evaluate and interpret statistical data properly, especially if you are basing an important conclusion on those data.

When first introduced to the differences between facts and opinions, some students act as if statements of opinion are less valuable in a discussion. Hardly so! Facts themselves are not arguable but provide the basis for discussion and debate. Groups must deal not only with what has been verified but also determine priorities of values, ethics, goals, and procedures acceptable to all. Members make inferences about what will probably happen *if* they adopt each possible alternative. For example, facts regarding AIDS and how it is spread are fairly well known, but what a particular board of education will *do* about it depends on the values, opinions, and judgments about policies that will be acceptable to the community.

*Evaluating the
Sources and
Implications of
Opinions*

Opinions are not all equal, although all people have an equal right to express their opinions. Opinions *can* be evaluated for their validity and appropriate use of fact. First, consider the source of the opinion.

1. Is this person (or other source) a recognized expert on the subject? How do other experts in the field regard this person? If their opinions are different, how might this be explained?

2. Does the source have a vested interest that might have influenced the opinion? For example, a flood victim, insurance agent, politician, and

taxpayer will have different opinions about whether government should reimburse victims of natural disasters for all their losses.

3. How well does the source support the opinion with documented evidence? Is the evidence well organized, with supporting statistics and tables and clear reasoning?

4. How consistent is this opinion with others expressed by the source? If not consistent, is there an acceptable explanation for the person's inconsistency?

Second, consider the implications of the opinion. To what further conclusions does it lead, and are these acceptable to the group? For example, a writer may argue that outlawing private ownership of handguns would protect us from accidents and murderers. What are the implications of this statement? That dangerous devices should not be allowed in the hands of citizens at large? That only nonessential dangerous tools that could potentially be used as murder weapons should be restricted? That eventually all potential murder weapons should be restricted? Another writer may argue that anyone with no felony record should be allowed to use a handgun after demonstrating competence in handling it safely and correctly. What are the implications of that opinion? That only convicted felons use handguns to kill another person? That most accidents would be prevented if people knew how to handle guns safely? That handguns are useful to many people? The point is that when a group decision depends on opinions, it is most important to test these opinions, especially for what they assume and imply.

CONSIDER THIS

> After the school shootings in Littleton, Colorado, many people said that watching violent television was the cause of the violence in schools, such as at Littleton, or that lack of gun control was the cause of the violence. Arguments were made for censoring television or for enacting stricter gun control laws. How valid do you think these arguments are?

Evaluating the information available to the group is only the first element of critical thinking. It is equally important to evaluate how both information sources and group members reason from this information.

Evaluating Reasoning

Critical thinking requires that conclusions (including decisions) be based on both sound evidence and clear, valid reasoning that connects information with conclusions in an appropriate and defensible way. Once you have evaluated the information (raw data), you must also look at how speakers and writers reason from that information. Are their conclusions logical and plausible, based on appropriate reasoning from information that is offered in support? Here is where *group* decision making can be clearly superior to individual decision making, because one member is usually able to spot a flaw or a reasoning error, called a **fallacy,** that another member missed. Several common fallacies observed in group discussions include overgeneralizing, making *ad hominem* attacks, suggesting inappropriate causal relationships, posing a false dilemma, and making faulty analogies.[49]

An **overgeneralization** is a conclusion that is not supported by enough data. Because something is true about one or a few instances or persons, it is said to be true of all or most instances or persons of the same type. For example, when a person concludes that because *some* college students have defaulted on their government-guaranteed loans, *most or all* college students are irresponsible, that person has overgeneralized. Generalizations are not automatically wrong. After all, that is what statistics do—help us generalize appropriately from a relatively small sample to a large population. The problem occurs when we *over*-generalize. To test generalizations, ask whether evidence other than personal testimony is being offered to support the generalization. Ask how many cases the generalization is based on, and whether the cases are typical of the phenomenon they are supposed to represent. Try to determine whether the sample offered is biased in any way.

Overgeneralizing

An ***ad hominem* attack** is a statement that attacks a person instead of pointing out a flaw in the person's argument. The attack diverts the group's attention so members debate the merits of the person rather than the position he or she has taken on the issue. *Ad hominem* attacks may be explicit ("You can't trust women or minorities to evaluate affirmative action laws fairly!") or veiled ("Why do you think someone like that could help our group?"). In any case, they are a subtle form of name-calling. Determining the credibility of the person supplying information is important, but *ad hominem* attacks do not help evaluate credibility—they condemn individuals on the basis of characteristics irrelevant to the validity of opinions or accuracy of information they provide. And they do *not* help evaluate the arguments advanced by the person for or against some proposal.

Ad Hominem
Attacks

Sometimes people assume that because two events are related or occurred close to each other in time, one must have caused the other. Establishing accurate causal connections is complex and difficult, even using statistical procedures. Common sense suggests that events usually have multiple and complex causes. To suggest that one single event causes another almost always oversimplifies a relationship among numerous variables. For example, we recently overheard a newscaster say that, because female graduates of women-only colleges were more likely to serve on the boards of Fortune 500 companies than graduates of coeducational schools, attendance at women's colleges probably "caused" greater career achievement. This is a preposterous statement! Numerous factors influence career achievement. Many women's colleges are both highly selective and expensive; their

Suggesting Inappropriate Causal Relationships

students are often bright, grew up in families who own or are connected to Fortune 500 companies, and can afford to attend expensive schools. Attendance at women-only colleges may indeed provide women with greater opportunities for engaging in leadership activities. More likely, native ability and family connections "cause" both attendance at women-only colleges and career achievement. Whenever group members see causal connections being posited, they should look for other reasons why the events might be linked. Only when alternative explanations have been eliminated should a causal connection be accepted as probably true, and then only tentatively.

False Dilemmas   A **false dilemma** poses an either–or choice that implies, wrongly, that only two options or courses of action are possible. For example, either the university builds a new parking lot *or* students have to walk miles to get to class. Either sex education is taught by the parents *or* by the schools. Each of these statements ignores the fact that other options exist to accomplish both goals. The university could provide a shuttle bus service to transport students from faraway parking lots, schedule classes early or late to alleviate parking crunches at certain times, or set up a car-pooling service to improve the parking situation. Children can be taught sex education by their parents; their teachers; their ministers, priests, or rabbis; committees composed of teachers and parents working together; teams of clergy and parents; and so forth. The either–or choices offered in both cases obscure the fact that many other options are possible—in other words, the "dilemma" is false. Just because a writer or speaker does not offer you alternatives should not blind you to their existence. Whenever you are offered an either–or choice, we encourage you to look for additional options or to think in terms of *degree* rather than *good or bad, effective or ineffective,* and so forth.

Faulty Analogies   A **faulty analogy** is a comparison that asks us to stretch a similarity too far. Comparisons help us understand issues more vividly, but all comparisons have limitations. Author Gloria's orange house cat may look and act like a tiger, but he does not eat ten pounds of meat per day and cannot hurt you if he jumps on your lap. We have heard many students complain (we have even complained ourselves!): "You can't really learn how to be a public relations professional in college. It would be like trying to learn to swim from a book, but never getting in the water." At first glance, this remark hits home with those of us who know that there indeed are limitations to what you can learn in school. Examining the analogy more closely, however, reveals that many classroom activities and assignments prepare students for professional practice. Public relations majors practice writing for a variety of audiences, learn principles of graphic design and use them to design materials for a variety of clients, put together dynamic oral presentations, write up job specifications and budgets for proposed projects, and so on. All these are activities that public relations professionals carry out in professional practice. Whenever you hear an analogy being offered as an argument, ask yourself three things: (1) What two things are being compared? (2) How are they similar? And, more important, (3) How are they different? That is, where is the comparison inaccurate? Always ask, "Is the conclusion warranted by *this* analogy?"

The fallacies we have just presented are among the most common, but by no means are they the only ones you will encounter. The important thing is for you and your fellow group members to be alert to mistakes in reasoning so you will not be led by faulty reasoning to make poor decisions.

SUMMARY

1. Group decisions are usually better than those made by individuals, but this depends on several factors, including the type of task, the abilities of the members, whether group norms support high or low production, and the decision-making procedures used. Ideally, groups achieve an assembly effect, that is, the group's decision is superior to the summative effect of all the individual members' decisions. Group decisions are warranted when the decision must be accepted by the members, when there is a quality (i.e., not-one-best-solution) component, and when members have time to deliberate thoroughly.

2. Group decision making entails not only rational but other psychological processes which can lead to a group polarization effect, or the tendency of people in groups to adopt more extreme solutions.

3. Group decisions can be made by the designated leader, by majority vote, or by consensus. Consensus is facilitated by viewing the group decision as a cooperative rather than competitive process and using disagreements to stimulate creative thinking.

4. To help achieve valuable consensus, don't be stubborn, avoid win–lose thinking, be on guard against groupthink, don't use conflict-suppressing techniques, but instead value differences of opinion that improve group outcomes.

5. Groups often pass through predictable phases during decision making. Bales and Strodtbeck identified three (orientation, evaluation, and control) and Fisher identified four (orientation, conflict, decision emergence, and reinforcement). Recent researchers, such as Poole, suggest that the types, lengths, and sequence of phases, depend on several group and individual factors.

6. Several factors can improve group decision making: defining the problem carefully, agreeing on criteria, thoroughly evaluating the positive and negative characteristics of all the options, second-guessing the tentative choice and, most important, thinking critically.

7. Not only the information available to the group but also the reasoning and logic that link that information to conclusions must be carefully evaluated. Members should be especially watchful for common fallacies that impair reasoning, such as overgeneralizing, *ad hominem* attacks, making inappropriate causal links, posing a false dilemma, and making faulty analogies.

EXERCISE

Read the following case problem, then break into groups of five or six and come to a consensus decision. Use the following questions to guide your postdecision evaluation:

1. What problems in choosing did your group have?
2. What seemed to cause these problems?
3. Do you think you made the best choice? Why or why not?
4. What guidelines can you write to apply what you learned?
5. What did you learn from this exercise?

Scholarship Awards Committee

You comprise a Scholarship Awards Committee at State University. A special trust fund was established by an anonymous donor to award one full-tuition scholarship per year, renewable for three years, to a person with demonstrated need for financial assistance, a reasonable expectation of success as a student, and who is unlikely to attend college if not granted some form of aid. There are no other conditions attached to the award except that a student committee must select the winner from a list of applicants supplied by the admissions office. Admissions has given you a list of five eligible applicants and said no other information can be given to you. Who will receive the scholarship? You can award only one scholarship.

Duane, age 16, a white student from a middle-class family, finished high school in three years. He says he rushed through because he could not have tolerated another year of the bull. His mother, a widow with two younger children to support, can work only part time in her field as a registered nurse. Duane's high school grade average was 3.0. University tests predict a 2.6 college grade point average in a science curriculum and 3.1 in nonscience. His mother is determined that Duane should be a physician. Duane says he is not sure of what job or profession he wants. He has some emotional problems; a psychiatrist he has seen recommends college because he thinks Duane needs "an intellectual challenge."

Carla, age 17, is a Hispanic student with very high recommendations from the small town high school where she earned a 3.8 grade average. In her senior year she became engaged to Luis, a long-distance truck driver, who wants her to get married at once and forget college. She is known to have spent a few nights with him on a cross-country trip to haul grain. Your university predicts she will earn 2.6 in science and 3.3 in a nonscience program. She says she wants to become a social worker "to help work with migrant children in California." The priest where she attends church says she has a fine mind, but he predicts she will marry and drop out even if she starts college. Her parents are uneducated (less than high school), hard working, law abiding, and very poor.

Melissa, age 26, is an African American divorcee with a seven-year-old son. She had a 2.8 grade average in high school "because I goofed around," but tests predict a 2.9 in science and a 3.6 in nonscience at your university. She says she wants to become an English instructor, "in college if I get lucky, or at least in high school." She was a beauty contest winner at 18, but says she is bitter toward men and will never remarry. She gets no child support or other family assistance. Her present boss, a dress shop owner, gives her a good character reference but predicts she will marry rather than finish college.

Sam, age 19, is an African American student who was offered several football scholarships, but they were withdrawn when an auto accident injured his legs. He can get around well but cannot compete in athletics. His high school grade average was barely passing, but entrance test scores predict a 2.5 average in science and 3.0 in a nonscience curriculum. His father, a day laborer, says he can contribute nothing toward a college education for Sam. Sam says he is determined to become a football coach, though he has been advised that may be difficult without a college playing record.

Chou (Joe), age 27, escaped from China after he lost his right hand during the Tiananmen Square massacre. Orphaned as a youngster, he was brought to this country by a local church organization from Hong Kong. He spoke no English when he arrived in the United States, but now is competent. He earned his GED while he lived with the church's minister and wants to become a computer programmer. The university predicts a 3.0 average in science and a 2.8 in a nonscience program. He is limited in his ability to support himself through manual labor; because he cannot work his way through school, he needs financial assistance.

BIBLIOGRAPHY

Browne, M. Neil, and Stuart M. Keeley. *Asking the Right Questions: A Guide to Critical Thinking.* 3d ed. Englewood Cliffs, NJ: Prentice-Hall, 1990.

Cromwell, Paul F., Alan Marks, James N. Olson, and D'Aunn W. Avary. "Group Effects on Decision-Making by Burglars." *Psychological Reports* 69 (1991): 579–88.

Hirokawa, Randy Y. "Discussion Procedures and Decision Making Performance: A Test of a Functional Perspective." *Human Communication Research* 12 (1985): 203–24.

Isenberg, Daniel J. "Group Polarization: A Critical Review and Meta-Analysis." *Journal of Personality and Social Psychology* 50 (1986): 1141–51.

Mennecke, Brian E., Jeffrey A. Hoffer, and Bayard E. Wynne. "The Implications of Group Development and History for Group Support System Theory and Practice." *Small Group Research* 23 (1992): 524–72. Provides a thorough, current review of group development literature.

Walton, Douglas N. *Plausible Argument in Everyday Conversation.* Albany, NY: State University of New York Press, 1992.

NOTES

1. Louise L. Biron and Carol Ladouceur, "The Boy Next Door: Local Teenage Burglars in Montreal," *Security Journal* 2 (1991): 200–204.

2. Paul F. Cromwell, James N. Olson, and D'Aunn W. Avary, "How Residential Burglars Choose Targets: An Ethnographic Analysis," *Security Journal* 2 (1991): 195–99.

3. Paul F. Cromwell, Alan Marks, James N. Olson, and D'Aunn W. Avary, "Group Effects on Decision-Making by Burglars," *Psychological Reports* 69 (1991): 579–88.

4. Dennis S. Gouran, Randy Y. Hirokawa, and Amy E. Martz, "A Critical Analysis of Factors Related to Decision Processes Involved in the *Challenger* Disaster," *Central States Speech Journal* 37 (1986): 119–35.

5. Joseph D. Anderson, "Working with Groups: Little-Known Facts That Challenge Well-Known Myths," *Small Group Behavior* 16 (1985): 267–83.

6. Jay Hall, "Decisions, Decisions, Decisions," *Psychology Today* 5 (November 1971): 51–54, 86–87; Jay Hall and W. H. Watson, "The Effects of a Normative Intervention on Group Decision-Making Performance," *Human Relations* 23 (1970): 299–317.

7. Irving L. Janis, *Groupthink: Psychological Studies of Policy Decisions and Fiascoes,* 2d ed. (Boston: Houghton Mifflin, 1983).

8. Mark F. Stasson and Scott D. Bradshaw, "Explanations of Individual–Group Performance Differences: What Sort of 'Bonus' Can Be Gained through Group Interaction?" *Small Group Research* 26 (May 1995): 296–308.

9. Patrick R. Laughlin, Scot W. VanderSteep, and Andrea B. Hollingshead, "Collective versus Individual Induction: Recognition of Truth, Rejection of Error, and Collective Information Processing," *Journal of Personality and Social Psychology* 61, no. 1 (1994): 50–67.

10. Brant R. Burleson, Barbara J. Levine, and Wendy Samter, "Decision-Making Procedure and Decision Quality," *Human Communication Research* 10 (1984), 557–74; Herm W. Smith, "Group versus Individual Problem Solving and Type of Problem Solved," *Small Group Behavior* 20 (1989): 357–66.

11. Patricia M. Fandt, "The Relationship of Accountability and Interdependent Behavior to Enhancing Team Consequences," *Group & Organization Studies* 16 (1991): 300–312.

12. Herm W. Smith, "Group versus Individual Problem Solving and Type of Problem Solved," *Small Group Behavior* 20 (1989): 357–66.

13. Michael Pacanowsky, "Team Tools for Wicked Problems," *Organizational Dynamics* 23 (Winter 1995): 36–51.

14. Deborah H. Gruenfeld and Andrea B. Hollingshead, "Sociocognition in Work Groups: The Evolution of Group Integrative Complexity and Its Relation to Task Performance," *Small Group Research* 24 (August 1993): 383–405.

15. Joseph N. Scudder, Richard T. Herschel, and Martin D. Crossland, "Test of a Model Linking Cognitive Motivation, Assessment of Alternatives, Decision Quality, and Group Process Satisfaction," *Small Group Research* 25 (February 1994): 57–82.

16. Laughlin et al., "Collective versus Individual Induction."

17. Abran J. Salazar, Randy Y. Hirokawa, Kathleen M. Propp, Kelly M. Julian, and Geoff B. Leatham, "In Search of True Causes: Examination of the Effect of Group Potential and Group Interaction on Decision Performance," *Human Communication Research* 20 (June 1994): 529–59.

18. Burleson et al., "Decision-Making Procedure and Decision Quality."

19. Salazar et al., "In Search of True Causes."

20. Scudder et al., "Test of a Model."

21. Randy Y. Hirokawa, "The Role of Communication in Group Decision-Making Efficacy: A Task-Contingency Perspective," *Small Group Research* 21 (May 1990): 190–204.

22. M. L. Chemers, "Leadership Theory and Research: A Systems-Process Integration," in *Basic Group Processes,* ed. P. B. Paulus (New York: Springer-Verlag, 1983), 19–20; Randy Y. Hirokawa, "Consensus Group Decision-Making, Quality of Decision and Group Satisfaction: An Attempt to Sort Fact from Fiction," *Central States Speech Journal* 33 (1982): 407–15.

23. Lester Coch and John R. P. French, Jr., "Overcoming Resistance to Change," *Human Relations* 1 (1948): 512–32.

24. Myron W. Block and L. R. Hoffman, "The Effects of Valence of Solutions and Group Cohesiveness on Members' Commitment to Group Decision," in *The Group Problem Solving Process,* ed. L. Richard Hoffman (New York: Prager, 1979), 121.

25. Burleson et al., "Decision-Making Procedure and Decision Quality," 557–74.

26. Carolyn J. Wood, "Challenging the Assumptions Underlying the Use of Participatory Decision-Making Strategies: A Longitudinal Case Study," *Small Group Behavior* 20 (1989): 428–48.

27. Paul Miesing and John F. Preble, "Group Processes and Performance in Complex Business Simulation," *Small Group Behavior* 16 (1985): 325–38.

28. Hirokawa, "Consensus Group Decision-Making," 407–14; Randy Y. Hirokawa, "Why Informed Groups Make Faulty Decisions: An Investigation of Possible Interaction-Based Explanations," *Small Group Behavior* 18 (1987): 3–29.

29. Dennis S. Gouran, "Inferential Errors, Interaction, and Group Decision-Making," in *Communication and Group Decision-Making,* eds. R. Y. Hirokawa and M. S. Poole (Beverly Hills, CA: Sage, 1986), 93–111.

30. Victor H. Vroom, "A New Look at Managerial Decision-Making," *Organizational Dynamics* (American Management Association, 1973), 66–80.

31. Marvin E. Shaw, *Group Dynamics,* 2d ed. (New York: McGraw-Hill, 1976), 70–77.

32. Daniel J. Isenberg, "Group Polarization: A Critical Review and Meta-analysis," *Journal of Personality and Social Psychology* 10 (1986): 1141–51.

33. Jerold L. Hale and Franklin J. Boster, "Comparing Effects-Coded Models of Choice Shifts," *Communication Research Reports* 5 (1988): 180–86.

34. Martin F. Kaplan and Charles E. Miller, "Group Decision Making and Normative versus Informational Influence: Effects of Type of Issue and Assigned Decision Rule," *Journal of Personality and Social Psychology* 53 (1987): 306–13.

35. Cromwell et al., "Group Effects on Decision-Making by Burglars."

36. Michael J. Beatty, "Group Members' Decision Rule Orientations and Consensus," *Human Communication Research* 16 (1989): 79–96.

37. Hall, "Decisions, Decision, Decisions."

38. Robert F. Bales and Fred L. Strodtbeck, "Phases in Group Problem-Solving," *Journal of Abnormal and Social Psychology* 46 (1951): 485–95.

39. For a complete summary of Fisher's work on decision-making phases, see B. Aubrey Fisher and Donald G. Ellis, *Small Group Decision Making: Communication and the Group Process,* 3d ed. (New York: McGraw-Hill, 1990), especially chapter 6.

40. Marshall Scott Poole, "Decision Development in Small Groups I: A Comparison of Two Models," *Communication Monographs* 48 (1981): 1–24; "Decision Development in Small Groups II: A Study of Multiple Sequences in Decision Making," *Communication Monographs* 50 (1983): 206–32; and "Decision Development in Small Groups III: A Multiple Sequence Model of Group Decision Development," *Communication Monographs* 50 (1983): 321–41; M. S. Poole and Jonelle Roth, "Decision Development in Small Groups IV: A Typology of Group Decision Paths," *Human Communication Research* 15 (1989): 322–56; and "Decision Development in Small Groups V: Test of a Contingency Model," *Human Communication Research* 15 (1989): 549–89.

41. Poole, "Decision Development II" and "Decision Development III."

42. Poole and Roth, "Decision Development V."

43. Thomas M. Scheidel and Laura Crowell, "Idea Development in Small Discussion Groups," *Quarterly Journal of Speech* 50 (1964): 140–45.

44. Teresa C. Sabourin and Patricia Geist, "Collaborative Production of Proposals in Group Decision Making," *Small Group Research* 21 (1990): 404–27.

45. B. Aubrey Fisher and Randall K. Stutman, "An Assessment of Group Trajectories: Analyzing Developmental Breakpoints," *Communication Quarterly* 35 (1987): 105–24.

46. Renee A. Meyers, David R. Siebold, and Dale Brashers, "Argument in Initial Group Decision-Making Discussions: Refinement of a Coding Scheme and a Descriptive Quantitative Analysis," *Western Journal of Speech Communication* 55 (Winter 1991): 47–68.

47. Joann Keyton, *Group Communication: Process and Analysis* (Mountain View, CA: Mayfield, 1999): 63.

48. Beatrice Schultz, Sandra M. Ketrow, and D. M. Urban, "Improving Decision Quality in the Small Group," *Small Group Behavior* 17 (1995): 521–41.

49. Much of the following information is distilled from M. Neil Browne and Stuart M. Keeley, *Asking the Right Questions: A Guide to Critical Thinking,* 2d ed. (Englewood Cliffs, NJ: Prentice-Hall, 1986).

Managing Conflict in the Small Group

13

Central Message

If properly managed, the inevitable conflict during a small group's deliberations can improve problem solving and decision making by providing a variety of perspectives that promote critical thinking.

Study Objectives

As a result of studying Chapter 13 you should be able to:

1. Define conflict, and explain both the positive and negative effects it can have on a group.
2. Describe a member who is an *innovative* or *opinion deviate* and explain how such a person can help a group improve its decision making.
3. Describe the four types of conflict that typically occur in small group interactions.
4. Describe the distributive (win–lose) and integrative (win–win) orientations and five specific conflict management styles typically used to manage small group conflict.
5. Describe the ethical standards needed for dealing with conflict.
6. Explain the principled negotiation procedure for helping a group resolve conflict.
7. Explain three alternative methods for breaking a deadlock when negotiation fails, and describe a mediation procedure a group can use if it is deadlocked.
8. Explain the goals of the Common Ground approach to managing conflict and describe its basic rules for dialogue.

Key Terms

Accommodation
Affective conflict
Avoidance
Collaboration
Common Ground dialogue
Competition
Compromise
Conflict
Deviate

Distributive approach
Inequity
Integrative approach
Principled negotiation
Procedural conflict
Substantive conflict

One of the most enduring and intractable conflicts in American society in the past 30 years has been the conflict over abortion between pro-life and pro-choice proponents. This conflict has generated intense, often vicious debate and even violence because the two sides are so far apart on this issue. Or are they? In recent years, the grassroots organization Common Ground Network for Life and Choice has been sponsoring small group discussions, community forums, and seminars designed for joint participation by pro-life and pro-choice individuals.[1] Common Ground started when B. J. Isaacson-Jones, a pro-choice advocate in St. Louis and administrator for an abortion clinic, read a newspaper article by one of her archenemies, pro-life lawyer Andrew Puzder. The article said that even if it was unlikely the two sides would give up their positions, surely they could work together to help impoverished women and their children. Isaacson-Jones and Puzder started meeting and found that they did, in fact, share common concerns. Their initial conversations have spawned discussions throughout the country at which pro-choice and pro-life individuals work together to discover their areas of agreement. Groups have been active in Buffalo, Davenport, Minneapolis, St. Louis, Washington, D.C., Cleveland, and elsewhere.

Common Ground organizers note that they are not trying to force the two sides to compromise. Instead, they visualize the discussions as the intersection of two overlapping circles; each of the circles remains whole, but each fully supports the ideas contained in the overlapping part—the common ground. In one typical format, participants meet in small groups of two pro-lifers, two pro-choicers, and one facilitator, who establishes the ground rules. Common Ground groups are learning groups, not debating societies. Participants are to speak honestly, respectfully, and personally rather than as a representative of a group; they should not try to get the other side to give up its positions. Sometimes, before discussion begins, the participants complete questionnaires the way they think people from the opposite side would complete them. Each side holds misconceptions about the other: pro-choice individuals learn that pro-lifers prefer collaborative instead of authoritarian decision making and pro-life individuals learn that pro-choicers believe that abortion is violent and is not appropriate as a birth control method.

In their small groups, facilitators ask participants to talk about who their heros are and to share why they hold their respective positions about abortion. Active listening is a hallmark of the Common Ground process; whenever a pro-lifer speaks, a pro-choicer is asked to paraphrase until the original speaker is satisfied, and vice versa. Surprisingly, the two sides agree on and support a number of goals they are willing to work on together, including encouraging men and women to be sexually responsible, fostering equality for women, reducing teen pregnancies, supporting and funding adoption as a choice, and working to remove the conditions that lead women to seek abortions. The two sides have realized that they can work together without abandoning any of their own individual values or beliefs. The organizers hope that finding common ground can encourage discovery of nonviolent and positive solutions to difficult societal problems.

Pick up any popular general interest magazine and you will probably see an article about how to get along at work, at home, with friends. Sometimes, what you read may give you the impression that conflict should be avoided at all costs! The truth is that whenever individuals come together in any sort of social context, disagreement and conflict are inevitable. Trying to avoid conflict is futile and unwise.

CONSIDER THIS

Think about times when you thought you had nothing in common with someone you perceived as an adversary. Sometimes you may have had heated conversations and at other times you did what you could to avoid *any* conversation. What were some of the things participants in Common Ground found they could agree on and thus act on together? Imagine a group of pro- and anti-affirmative action individuals participating in a Common Ground project. What might they find they have in common?

Americans are ambivalent about conflict. Along with values that stress agreement and "getting along," we say "stick to your guns." We have trouble reconciling the benefits of *both* harmony and conflict. Other cultures do not experience this tension to the same degree. For example, the same Chinese word means both *crisis* and *opportunity.* Eastern cultures, in particular, see such apparently opposing concepts as harmony and conflict as yin and yang, sides of the same coin. Americans, too, must learn to appreciate the value of them both in human relationships so that agreement *and* disagreement can contribute positively to a group's interaction.

In small groups, conflict is an integral part of problem solving and decision making. It is a natural byproduct of trying to come to some agreement about an issue or problem. Each member will perceive the situation in a slightly different way, have different values, priorities, and preferences. These variations in perceptions and beliefs are brought out into the open during discussion. If a group's goal is simply for members to understand each other, these differences can remain unresolved. But if a group's goal is to solve a problem or make a choice, divergent opinions must be reconciled.

Conflict is necessary to effective decision making and problem solving. Why bother to ask a group to solve a problem if you don't think that several heads are better than one? By involving a group, you tacitly acknowledge the value of diversity, the same diversity that guarantees conflict. Conflict *should* occur during group problem solving; if it doesn't, the group members aren't taking advantage of their diversity. Failure to express disagreement and avoiding discussion of conflict-producing issues leads directly to ineffective problem solving and poor decision making.[2] For the group to receive the full benefit of the collective judgment of its members, the members must be willing to disagree, point out errors, and even argue.

Although too much conflict can hurt a group or even destroy it, our experience has been that groups of students err in the direction of too little rather than too much conflict. Most of our students are afraid of disagreement and prefer groups with little or no conflict.[3] The more conflict members experience, the more negatively they view the group experience.[4] For that reason, this chapter stresses the benefits of conflict. We explain how to distinguish beneficial from detrimental conflict and how to manage conflicts to produce the best possible decision or solution.

A DEFINITION OF CONFLICT

A variety of definitions exists for **conflict,** ranging from something that occurs when individuals have reached an impasse[5] to a state of genuine difference.[6] We choose Hocker and Wilmot's definition:

> *Conflict* is an expressed struggle between at least two interdependent parties who perceive incompatible goals, scarce resources, and interference from the other party in achieving their goals.[7]

This definition embodies several implications that are consistent with a *communicative* focus on conflict in small groups.

First, the notion of conflict as an *expressed struggle* indicates that conflict involves communicating. While a group member may *feel* internal distress, this distress becomes interpersonal conflict *only when it is expressed,* whether verbally or in such subtle ways as not making eye contact or shifting nervously in one's chair.

Second, parties to a conflict must have an interdependent goal such that it is impossible for one person to attain the goal and not the others. Some groups have understanding of diverse points of view as their goal. In such groups, members do not have to coordinate their beliefs and efforts to agree on a solution. However, many secondary groups must produce something—a report, a proposal, a set of recommendations—that *all* group members must agree to. Such group members are interdependent; one cannot achieve the goal without the others. Therefore, they must find ways of reconciling diverse perspectives and beliefs affecting the decision. For example, Edd may detest Desha's views about what is appropriate treatment of laboratory animals, but that won't matter much unless both are in a group that is charged with recommending a university policy regarding treatment of laboratory animals; for the group to succeed fully, Edd and Desha must reconcile their views enough to collaborate on a policy each can support. Thus, the interdependence group members experience is accompanied by interference. Edd's disagreement with Desha interferes with Desha's having her way, and vice versa. This interference may take the form of Desha trying to persuade the other group members to accept her view, Edd trying to undercut Desha's credibility within the group, or Desha sabotaging Edd's car so he will miss an important meeting.

Third, this definition suggests a number of things over which people conflict, such as goals and scarce resources, to which we add values, beliefs, and ways of achieving goals. We have observed numerous student groups whose members disagree on group goals. Maria's goal is to earn an A for a group presentation to the class, but Garry's goal is to do just enough to earn a C. Their divergent goals will cause a problem for the group. In contrast, assume that both Maria and Garry want to receive an A for the presentation, but Maria prefers to involve the class in an exercise followed by discussion, while Garry prefers to show and discuss a movie. In this instance, they agree on the goal but differ on the best course of action to reach the goal. Or, suppose that Edd believes that humans are superior to all other forms of life, which makes it appropriate for laboratory animals to serve human needs, but Desha values all animal life forms equally. This fundamental difference in values may make it impossible for their group to reach consensus on a policy regarding laboratory animals. You can probably tell from these examples that some conflicts, such as those over values and goals, are harder to resolve than others. In a group, the more alike members are with respect to basic values and beliefs, the easier it will be for the group to achieve consensus, yet their similarity may also reduce their creativity.

Fourth, parties to a conflict must *perceive* that they are in conflict. This perceptual dimension is a very important one. There is nothing that automatically labels a situation as *conflict;* instead, conflict depends on how people perceive the situation. For instance, if Thomas disagrees with a proposal you have made, you have a *choice* about how to perceive Thomas's disagreement. You can say, "What a jerk! What makes him think he can do any better!" In this case, you have framed his disagreement as a conflict. However, you could also have said, "I wonder why Thomas disagrees? Maybe there's something in my proposal that I forgot to consider." In this latter case, you have framed his statement of disagreement as a possible attempt on Thomas's part to improve and strengthen your proposal. Thus, perception defines a situation as a conflict.

Perception of a situation is closely associated with emotions and behavior. To illustrate, your feelings can range from mild distress to out-of-control rage, depending on how you perceive the situation. If you think Thomas is a jerk for disagreeing with you or believe he disagreed just to make you look bad in some way, you will feel furious. Furthermore, you may be tempted to seek revenge or escalate the intensity of the conflict. On the other hand, if you perceive Thomas's disagreement to be motivated by a desire to strengthen your idea, then you may be only mildly hurt at his criticism, or even pleased that he cared enough to give your idea such a careful reading. In this latter case, you will behave cooperatively toward Thomas and collaborate to improve the proposal, not try to escalate the conflict. Thus, no perception of conflict, no conflict.

Your perceptions, emotions, and behavior merge with the other person's perceptions, emotions, and behavior to form an interactive system. Remember, you can't be in a conflict situation alone; your behaviors affect other people, as theirs affect you. Suppose you decide Thomas is a jerk, so you rip his criticism of your proposal to shreds. That will certainly affect Thomas, who may now conclude that *you* are a jerk who just can't take constructive criticism. Thomas may now decide to escalate the conflict or try to destroy your credibility within the group. On the other hand, if you indicate to Thomas that you genuinely want to know more about his criticism and the reasons for it, he may decide you are an enlightened, cooperative group member whom he can trust and on whose good judgment he can rely. This may lead him to seek your opinions, support, and ideas in the future. Thus, your perceptions, emotions, and behavior form a feedback loop with the other person's perceptions, emotions, and behavior; each element affects each other element, and none operates independently, as is shown in Figure 13.1. Changing one of the elements will automatically change the others.

Positive and Negative Outcomes of Conflict

Communication scholars concur that conflict has both beneficial and harmful outcomes.[8] We mentioned earlier that without the kind of conflict that comes from a critical examination of an issue, a group is unlikely to make a good decision, but we also have pointed out that conflict can be harmful. We will now examine some of these positive and negative effects.

Benefits of Conflict

Conflict can affect group decision making, teamwork, and satisfaction. Here are several potential benefits of conflict:

1. **Conflict can produce better understanding of both issues and people.**
   We often assume that most people see things as we do and feel as we do, and are often surprised to discover otherwise. When students discover others holding differing opinions on an issue, Smith, Johnson, and Johnson found that they become uncertain about their own positions, seek actively to get more information about the issue, are able to take the perspective of the other students, and are better able to retain information, both about their own position and those of other people.[9] Franz and Jin discovered that, during the first half of a meeting, disagreement fosters learning about the issues.[10] Without this disagreement and kicking issues around, creativity and problem analysis and understanding are shortchanged.

2. **Conflict can increase member motivation.**
   People who do not care will not expend any energy disagreeing about an issue. However, when group members participate in a conflict episode they are actively involved with the issue. They are interested, excited, and pay close attention, so they learn more about the issue. A student in one of our classes could not accept a statement by a fellow

Perceptions, emotions, behavior, and interaction in a conflict.   **FIGURE 13.1**

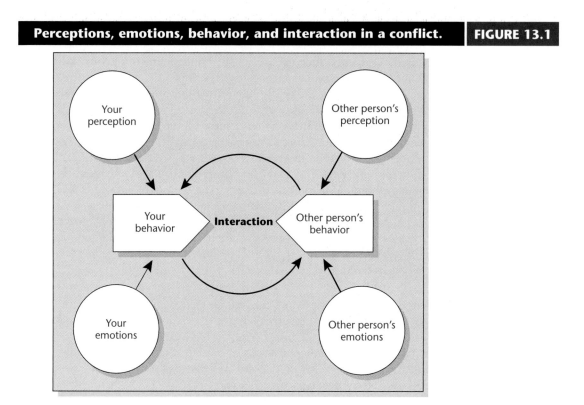

group member that nonverbal signals were more potent than words in conveying meaning. Unable to resolve the issue to his own satisfaction, he investigated the issue by using library and personal resources, and discovered the validity of the statement. His search provided some excellent examples the group was able to use in its class presentation— all because he got into an intellectual argument.

3. **Conflict can produce better decisions.**
   This outcome is the goal of good *group* problem solving. Through conflict, you discover first that others disagree, then *why* they disagree. You find flaws in reasoning, holes in arguments, factors that other members failed to consider, or implications that were ignored. Thus you help the group prevent mistakes. One of us belonged to a campus staff charged with developing a plan for cutting costs at a commuter campus. The developer of the plan recommended closing the snack bar at 5 PM. Another member of the staff pointed out that closing at 5 PM would leave many evening students who came to the campus directly from work without food service and might eventually lead to a drop in enrollment. After considerable debate, the committee decided to provide expanded vending machine service, which would accomplish the goal

of cutting personnel and utility costs, but not leave the evening students without food.

4. **Conflict can produce greater cohesiveness among group members.**
   When a group experiences and resolves conflict successfully, the members learn that the ties holding the group together are strong enough to withstand disagreement. Most of us who have had serious arguments with significant others can recall the closeness we feel after we have "made up." Instead of driving us apart, the conflict serves as a catalyst to strengthen the bonds between us. So it is with groups. The early disagreement Franz and Jin observed produced eventual understanding and consensus later.[11] The twin outcomes of task success and interpersonal tolerance can increase group cohesiveness. For example, in the food service example, staff members felt so good about the final outcome and so positive about each other's willingness to listen to opposing arguments that they adjourned for lunch together in a spirit of camaraderie.

Negative Effects of Conflict   Although conflict can be beneficial, we all have seen how harmful it can be. If you have ever said to yourself after a group meeting, "I'll be glad when this project is finished; I hope I never have to work with these people again," you have experienced some of the harmful effects of conflict. These include hurt feelings, lowered cohesiveness, and even group dissolution. One of us had a recent group discussion course end with one group very disappointed in their group experience and each other. Group members were so upset that some of them told friends not to take a group discussion class because people will just end up hating each other.

1. **Conflict can cause bad feelings among group members.**
   Most of us do not like to have others disagree with us. This is particularly true when others not only disagree with an idea or proposal we give, but appear to devalue us as people. Their remarks appear caustic, even hostile. This type of perceived attack causes hard feelings. Members may be silent for fear of an attack, thereby depriving the group of valuable information and opinions. (We discuss later how you can deal with such an attack.) Moreover, even a conflict over issues and ideas can be carried on so long that it increases tension and wears group members down to the point where they dread coming to meetings.

2. **Conflict, especially if it involves personal attacks or is carried on too long, can lower group cohesiveness.**
   If you believe that others in a group do not value your contributions, you will not be eager to spend time with that group. If you have a choice, you will spend your time with other groups that seem to value you more. Prolonged conflict and attacks on one's self-concept loosen the bonds of attraction and cohesiveness, which can cause members to reduce the effort they put forth to achieve the group's objectives.

3. Conflict can split a group apart.

A member who believes a group dislikes his or her ideas, but finds support in other groups, will usually leave the group in which the conflict occurs. Conflict that goes on too long and too intensely tears members apart. One of us once observed a friendship group split up over a political issue. One side believed that busing was an appropriate way to achieve racial equality; the other side disagreed. The two sides did not simply have an intellectual disagreement; they began to impugn each other's good will, ability to reason, and commitment to democratic values. Unkind things were said, a rift occurred, and the group died.

CONSIDER THIS

How do you know when a conflict has become personal? What specific behaviors in conflict episodes do you perceive as personal? What happens to you when you perceive the conflict has gotten personal? What do you do to escalate a conflict? Are conflicts about certain topics or with certain people more prone to "meanness?" Why?

Expressing Disagreement in a Group

Many people are reluctant to express opinions that differ from a group's majority opinion because expressing such disagreement may cause such a person to be seen as a deviant member by the rest of the group. (This is especially true in other cultures, such as in Asian ones.) A **deviate** is a member who is viewed by the other members as substantially different in some *important* way from the others. Two common types of group deviates are members who do not participate and members who express incompatible views about the issues and test opinions of the group.[12] The second type is more likely to be involved in overt disagreement or conflict in a group. While the deviate's role may be uncomfortable, it is a potentially valuable one for a group. Reluctant as you may be to express a deviant opinion, ethically you should do it for the good of the group. However, you do not want to rebelliously block or withdraw. Instead, you want to be an *innovative* or *opinion deviate,* someone who disagrees with a proposed action or decision of the group but who is strongly committed to the group and its goals.

Sometimes it is very hard for an opinion deviate to influence a group. Lindskold and Han found that it was nearly impossible for a single conciliatory member to influence a nonconciliatory group.[13] Thameling and Andrews also found that opinion deviates exerted little influence.[14] Other group members responded more emotionally to deviates than to conforming group members. A sex bias has been observed: members responded more cooperatively to male than to female deviates. Group members appeared to *perceive* male deviates as bright and well informed, and showed a willingness to work with them by asking for evidence, questions, additional information, and so forth; however, they were more likely to *perceive* female deviates as arrogant or overly confident. These researchers suggest that an individual who wants to express a deviant opinion do so cautiously and carefully. If you first develop solid group credentials of loyalty and commitment, other members will trust your motives when you deviate from a majority opinion.

However, even with all these caveats about the difficulty of being an opinion deviate, this kind of disagreement is valuable to the group, particularly for groups in the United States and other Western cultures. Valentine and Fisher found that innovative deviance accounted for one-fourth of group interaction, serving a critical thinking function.[15] What task roles from Chapter 7 might be associated with opinion deviance? Innovative deviance in the form of contradiction, challenging statements by other members, continuing a disagreement started by others, or agreeing with an assertion someone else had attacked was particularly helpful in the group's conflict and decision emergence phases. Furthermore, most innovative deviance occurred immediately prior to consensus, supporting the notion that conflicts can contribute to consensus. Social skill is important, too. Covey found a high correlation between social skill and the use of verbal reasoning in conflict resolution, as well as a negative correlation of social skill with verbal aggression and physical violence.[16] The quality of the argument matters, also. Garlick and Mongeau discovered that argument quality was the only factor that allowed a minority subgroup to influence majority attitudes.[17] Thus, deviant opinions, skillfully and sensitively expressed, can help a group make better decisions.

Types of Conflict

As we have already shown, conflict in and of itself is neither necessarily helpful nor harmful to a group. What matters is what the conflict is about, how it is initiated, and how it is managed. Before we examine several types of conflict that can occur within a group and discuss the potential effects of each, we present a description of conflict in a group of students charged with selecting speakers for their university's Speaker Series.[18] Every major type of conflict occurred in this group.

The Speaker Committee—Kevin, Lori, Chris, Deidre, and Tony—had met several times, but made little progress. Kevin either missed meetings or came late; the others were angry with him. The committee couldn't agree on anything. They argued about whether they should select entertaining or educational speakers, whether they should book one major speaker or several lesser-known ones, whether they should decide by consensus or majority vote, and, most of all, what they should do about Kevin. Occasionally, one of the members would ask a question that encouraged the others to examine their decision and the criteria by which to make their decision, and occasionally a member would make a suggestion that received widespread support. In general, though, they exhibited many problems in managing their conflicts. The conflicts in this group of students illustrate the four types of conflict described as follows.

Substantive conflict, also called *intrinsic* conflict, is task-related conflict such as disagreement over ideas, meanings, issues, and other matters pertinent (intrinsic) to the task of the group.[19] It involves *what* the group should do. Substantive conflict is the basis for effective decision making and problem solving in a discussion group. It is the vehicle by which ideas, proposals, evidence, and reasoning are challenged and critically examined, doubts are brought into the open, and the group works together to find the best solution. Opinion and innovative deviance described earlier are usually substantive in nature. In our example, the Speaker Committee debated whether an entertaining or educational speaker would be a better choice. The ensuing argument helped members clarify the purpose of the Speaker Series and presented good reasons for considering each type of speaker.

Substantive Conflict

Affective conflict, also called *extrinsic* conflict, is conflict that originates from interpersonal power clashes, likes and dislikes unrelated to the group's task.[20] It represents the *who* in small group conflict and is generally detrimental to the efficient functioning of any group. For example, Speaker Series committee members Lori and Kevin did not like each other and missed no opportunity to disagree or belittle each other. When Kevin said he preferred to schedule an entertaining rather than an educational speaker, Lori said, "I could have expected that from you. Let's not learn—let's party!" This statement revealed that Lori personalized the conflict with Kevin. Her dislike compounded the effects of disagreement over work procedures and ideas. She rarely failed to make sarcastic comments to Kevin throughout the meeting. Such conflict is both difficult to resolve and exceedingly harmful to the group.

Affective Conflict

Although the origin of this type of conflict is difficult to pin down, our observations of numerous groups suggest that much of it is rooted in one person's acting as if he or she is superior, and another member's refusal to accept this difference in status or power. Most of this "I am superior, more important, more knowledgeable" signaling is nonverbal, projected by subtle patterns of vocal tones, postures, and head/body angles. Much of what is called interpersonal conflict emerges from a struggle for position and power. Recent research has indicated that group members are able to differentiate between personalized (affective) and depersonalized (substantive) conflict, and that the type of conflict affects group consensus.[21] Because affective conflict can impede resolution of substantive issues, Fisher and Brown recommend disentangling relationship and substantive goals and pursuing them independently.[22] Doing so gives the parties a chance to resolve their substantive differences, even though they may never change their feelings about each other. We talk later about how you might do that.

Procedural conflict is a type of substantive conflict over the procedures a group should follow in working toward its goals. Disagreement is about the *how* of group interaction. For instance, members of a group may disagree

Procedural Conflict

about whether they should make decisions by consensus or whether majority rule will suffice. In our Speaker Series Committee, Lori proposed splitting up the money available to the committee and letting each person select whatever speaker he or she wanted with his/her share of the money as the most efficient way of deciding the issue. But Deidre pointed out that if every person chose the same type of speaker, the series would be boring. The group then realized the value of consensus decision making. This disagreement over *how* the group made its major decisions is a clear example of procedural conflict. The difference of opinion expressed by Deidre and Lori helped clarify the issue.

Procedural conflict is sometimes used to mask affective or substantive conflict. Putnam notes that it can occur because members genuinely disagree over procedures, but it also can be used to withdraw from another substantive conflict by forcing a vote or otherwise regulating the group's work.[23] Although procedural conflict may seem to be a straightforward difference over how the group should accomplish something, it may be rooted in differing member needs for structure versus freedom. Members high in needs for procedural order are more comfortable with linear procedures than members who prefer less structured procedural order.

CONSIDER THIS

Reflect back on our discussion of listening preferences in Chapter 3 and learning styles in Chapter 6. Using your understanding of these preferences and styles, describe how might they produce different kinds of substantive, affective, and procedural conflict in a group.

Conflict over Inequity

One of the most prevalent sources of conflict in the groups we have observed is perceived **inequity** in the group: group members do not seem to have equal workloads and/or do not make equal contributions to the group. Inequity reduces satisfaction with the group and is associated with high levels of conflict.[24] In our Speaker Series Committee, Kevin's work and contributions to the group were perceived as inadequate. Although Lori rode Kevin the hardest about his lack of commitment to the group, Chris, Deidre, and even Tony mentioned Kevin's lack of follow-through and failure to complete assignments for the group. When Kevin was late again, Chris said, "I'm tired of waiting for the jerk. Let's get started," and later Deidre directly confronted Kevin by listing his behaviors that indicated lack of commitment to the group ("You've missed two of the last four meetings, and were late to the ones you did come to."). Kevin's perceived inequity of effort within the group had created serious conflict between him and the other members. Kevin's continued lack of commitment to the group also contributed to Lori's strong feelings of dislike and her constant needling. She scrutinized his contributions more closely than those of the other members and criticized Kevin for statements that she accepted from other people. For example, both Tony and Kevin wanted an entertaining speaker, but Lori singled Kevin out for ridicule about wanting to party more than learn. Because of his inequity of performance, he was being required to measure up more perfectly to the group's performance norms than the others.

Although we describe these four types of conflict as though they are distinct, they are not mutually exclusive. One type can easily lead to another. Frequently two or more types blend. In our example this was most clearly seen with Lori, whose dislike of Kevin combined with Kevin's inadequate contribution to the group and his disagreement with her position (Kevin wanted an entertaining speaker, but Lori wanted an educational one). All these conflicts united to intensify Lori's dislike. Lori looked for things over which to be angry with Kevin. She was probably the most relieved member when Kevin eventually left the group.

MANAGING CONFLICT

We hope we have convinced you of the value of innovative, opinion deviance and substantive conflict during small group problem solving. Conflict is inevitable when people meet in groups. Avoiding it *circumvents the very reason for engaging in group discussion*—that the thinking of several people is likely to be more valid and thorough than the thinking of one person acting alone. Both the attitudes of group members involved in a conflict and the procedures they use to manage the conflict affect the outcomes. Using further examples of the Speaker Series Committee, we discuss both attitudes and procedures that facilitate productive conflict.

Basic Approaches Toward Conflict Management

Most people have a basic attitude or approach toward managing conflict, either *distributive* or *integrative*. The **distributive approach,** also called a *win–lose* attitude, assumes that what one person gains is at another's expense. Thus, there can be only one winning side; the other or others are losers. In the Speaker Committee Tony and Kevin wanted to choose an entertaining speaker and Deidre and Lori wanted an educational one. The distributive orientation assumes that only one faction can win. *Either* Tony and Kevin get their entertaining speaker, *or* Lori and Deidre get their educational one. Whichever wins, the other side loses.

The **integrative approach** assumes that there is some way to manage the conflict so all parties can end up winners; in other words, the main concerns of all parties can be integrated into a solution in which all involved receive what is most important to them. Someone with an integrative orientation would assume that a speaker could be found who is *both* entertaining *and* educational; thus, both factions can win. This approach has also been called a *win–win* attitude.

A group may not be able to integrate the concerns of *all* members into its final solution or decision. Perhaps members' values are so divergent they cannot be merged, or maybe resources are so scarce that needs cannot be fully met. In such cases, perhaps partial integration—*compromise*—is the best that can be achieved. However, even if a group does not develop a fully integrative solution, it certainly will not develop one if members begin with the premise that integration is impossible. Common Ground projects all over the United States show us that even groups made up of members with deeply polarized viewpoints on an issue can find ways to integrate their efforts. Without an integrative orientation, members will not expend their energies to develop creative solutions but will spend time quarreling about the merits of one proposal over another in an attempt to win rather than find the best solution possible.

Conflict Management Styles

Your perception of the conflict situation is a major determinant of how you are likely to deal with the conflict.[25] Elements of the situation include your perceptions about whether the conflict is repetitive, the degree to which you and the other party have mutual goals, how certain you are about how to solve the problem, whether you believe the other party is the source of the conflict, and the degree of negative feelings you have for the other. These combine to influence your desire to cooperate. The specific management style you choose is likely to be a product both of how cooperative and how assertive you are, as illustrated in Figure 13.2.[26]

While no conflict style is always best, some conflict styles are perceived as more appropriate in certain circumstances. Canary and Spitzberg found, for example, that the topic of the conflict interacted with gender of the participants to influence perceptions of both effectiveness and appropriateness.[27] We recommend a contingency view in which the most productive way for settling a conflict depends on time pressures, distribution of information and skills, group member values and needs, and other input variables. While each conflict style is appropriate under certain circumstances, having an integrative orientation is always acceptable in problem-solving discussions.

Avoidance

The **avoidance** style is a passive approach in which a participant expends no energy discussing or exploring options. The member who disagrees but says nothing is avoiding conflict. Sometimes called *nonconfrontation,* conflict avoidance reduces satisfaction in groups.[28] Such passive behavior is appropriate only when the problem is unimportant and the risks of making a poor decision are slight. For example, a committee to which one of us belonged was asked to develop a decorating plan for a student lounge/study area. The art instructor on the committee recommended a color scheme not particularly appealing to the chemistry professor on the committee. The students liked the colors, so the chemistry professor kept his objections to himself. He reasoned that because he spent so little time in the lounge, color did not matter much to him.

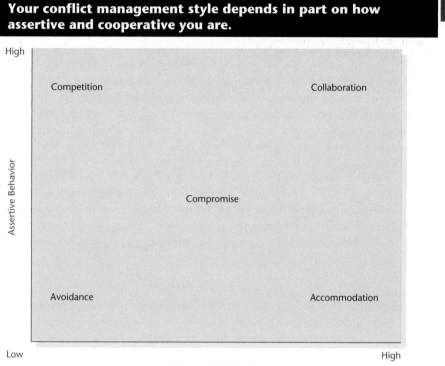

Your conflict management style depends in part on how assertive and cooperative you are.

FIGURE 13.2

Accommodation, also called *appeasement,* is a highly cooperative but passive approach that occurs when you give in to someone else. It may occur when the issue is not important to you, or when the relationship is more important to you than the outcome. For instance, in the Speaker Series Committee, after a brief discussion about educational versus entertaining speakers, Tony said, "I can go along with an educational speaker. I just want to avoid this arguing." Tony wanted to accommodate in order to end the arguments. Accommodation is appropriate only when the issue is relatively unimportant to you or the other person's needs are genuinely more important to you, but don't accommodate just to end a fight, for the resentment you carry around with you may eventually poison the relationship anyway.

Accommodation

Competition is a highly aggressive, uncooperative style in which one person tries to win over another. Sometimes called *dominating* or *forcing,* competition is appropriate when you have strong beliefs about something and you perceive that other approaches will not allow your needs to be acknowledged or accommodated. However, competitive approaches can damage relationships and may end up doing more harm than good. In the Speaker Series Committee, Lori and Kevin competed. Lori threatened to quit the group

Competition

if only entertaining speakers were chosen, and Kevin told Tony not to accommodate so readily because he, Kevin, had plenty of good arguments left in support of entertaining speakers. Both statements imply that the speaker will do whatever is necessary to get his or her way.

Collaboration

Collaboration, also called *negotiating* or *problem solving,* is a cooperative and assertive style that stems from an integrative attitude. It encourages all parties to a conflict to work together in searching for a solution that meets everyone's needs. In the Speaker Series Committee, Deidre suggested that the committee look for a speaker who was both entertaining and educational. In doing this, she assumed that both important needs of the factions could be met without either faction having to give up anything, that each faction's "must have" point could be accommodated. Collaborative solutions can be ideal because all members of groups that arrive at collaborative solutions believe they have won without the others' having lost. However, collaboration often takes more time than other approaches and certainly takes more energy.

Compromise

A **compromise,** also called a *shared outcome,* assumes that each party to the conflict will have to give up something in order to gain something more important. In the Speaker Series Committee, Chris suggested a compromise when he said, "Maybe we can get two speakers, less expensive, one educational and one entertaining." Each faction would have to agree to give up the idea of bringing in one very well-known speaker. Thus, compromises entail some losses for both parties. For this reason, we recommend attempting to find a collaborative, fully integrative solution when the decision is important to all group members, one in which each member will be responsible for implementing the outcome and the group is not pressed for time.

However, we think compromise should *not* be considered a dirty word! When collaborative resolution is impossible or takes more time than is available, a compromise is a desirable and ethical outcome, especially if each group member feels that what he or she had to give up is fair in comparison with what others had to give up.

Expressing Disagreement Ethically

Ethical behaviors in conflict situations are those that promote the beneficial outcomes of conflict (e.g., greater understanding of issues, increased cohesiveness) while minimizing the destructive outcomes (e.g., hurt feelings, personal attacks). The following suggestions will help members behave with integrity and sensitivity during conflicts:

1. **Do express your disagreement.**
   We have already noted that not confronting disagreements can reduce satisfaction with the group, and failure to express honest disagreement circumvents the decision-making and problem-solving process in a group. By not speaking up when you disagree, you deprive the group of

potentially valuable information. In a sense you deceive, because your silence suggests that you agree.

2. **Stick with the issue at hand.**

   Kreps suggests that when you disagree, you should deal directly with the issue under discussion. Do not bring up side issues or allow hidden agenda items to motivate you.[29] To do so is as unethical as to use irrelevant emotional stories to arouse support.

3. **Use rhetorical sensitivity in expressing your disagreement.**

   Be sensitive and perceptive enough to select words that will not connote negative images. Especially do not try to push others' emotional buttons. This means monitoring the effects of your statements on others and adjusting as appropriate. Use persuasion, not threats, to make your points.[30] Being rhetorically sensitive also means you'll follow the next ethical guideline.

4. **Disagree with the idea but do not ever criticize the person.**

   Express disagreement so that it does not devalue the person with whom you disagree. Members of groups with norms for expressing conflict cooperatively and integratively are more satisfied with the group's process and outcome than members of groups with norms for competitive and distributive (win–lose) expression of conflict.[31] Thus, "One flaw in your proposal to shut down the snack bar is that it does not consider the food service needs of evening students" is far superior to "You inconsiderate bozo! What are the evening students supposed to do?" Above all, no name calling or personal attacks!

5. **Base your disagreement on evidence and reasoning.**

   Kreps notes that disagreements should be reasonable and substantive, based on evidence and reasoning.[32] They should not be based on rumor, innuendo, unsubstantiated information, or emotionalism. If you have no evidence or your reasoning is shown to be potentially faulty, *agree* instead of quarreling. As much as possible, keep the conflict issue-based. This has the added advantage of being more likely to be persuasive.

6. **React to disagreement in a spirit of inquiry, not defensiveness.**

   Alderton and Frey believe that group members' reactions to argument are more important than the arguments themselves in creating group polarization.[33] If someone disagrees with you, do not react defensively as though you had been attacked personally. Keep your mind open to others' ideas, evaluations, and suggestions. Listen actively to your fellow member's remarks. Be certain that the person disagreeing has understood your position correctly, then clarify any misunderstandings, and work together to search for the most effective solutions. In this way you can make conflict work *for* rather than *against* the group. This may not be easy! But it will benefit the group and you will have a clear conscience.

7. **If someone persists in attacking *you*, stay calm and speak reasonably.**

   One of the biggest challenges a group member has is to respond to a personal attack by another. The worst thing you can do is let another's attacks intimidate you into being silent! Instead, confront the attacking member calmly and reasonably, explaining how you feel and what you want the other to do: "I resent your personal attacks, and I think they are inappropriate. I am willing to listen to your objections, but I want you to stop your attacks now." If the attacker was caught up in the heat of the moment, he or she may apologize and calm down. If your initial confrontation doesn't succeed, ask for the *group's* intervention: "Do we all think personal attacks are unacceptable behavior?" The other members, who probably are as uncomfortable as you, will now be encouraged to support you in confronting the attacker.

8. **Use an integrative rather than a distributive approach to solving the conflict.**

   Assume that there is a way to satisfy, at least partially, the important needs of all parties to the conflict. Use your energy to search for alternatives that integrate all parties' needs, not to destroy the other party. Act in ways that improve, not damage, the relationship. Remember that a solution satisfying all parties will be more lasting than one leaving one party feeling disgruntled or mistreated. Also, consider the ethics of a person who gains pleasure from beating another in a way that damages the *group!*

No matter how skilled at expressing disagreement and how ethical, group members can still crash on the rocks of conflict if their procedures for handling it are poor. We have selected six procedures for managing stubborn conflicts, in order of preference.

Negotiating Principled Agreement

A task-oriented group experiencing a conflict must move toward resolution for the group's goals to be accomplished. There are a variety of techniques designed to help groups resolve conflict. We especially like the *principled negotiation* procedure because it is consistent with all the ethical principles we have outlined above and is an extremely effective procedure that helps a group negotiate consensus from initially divergent points of view. As described by Fisher and Ury, **principled negotiation** is an all-purpose strategy that encourages all participants in a conflict situation to collaborate by expressing their needs and searching for alternatives that meet those needs.[34] It is called "principled" because it is based on ethical principles that encourage users to remain decent individuals and not act in ways that will damage the relationship among them. It puts the integrative approach into action.

Principled negotiation is an efficient and fair way to develop a solution meeting the legitimate needs of all parties; therefore, it is likely to produce lasting solutions. Tutzauer and Roloff say the guidelines in the principled negotiation procedure are consistent with their discoveries about communication behaviors that produce integrative outcomes.[35] They found that exchanging information, asking questions instead of making demands, and foregoing rigid, inflated positions helped bargainers attain integrative outcomes. *Appropriate communication techniques alone* helped bargainers attain integrative outcomes regardless of their initial orientations. In addition, this type of negotiation will not harm the relationship among participants and frequently improves it. We particularly like it because it recognizes the major elements that enter into conflict—perceptions, emotions, behaviors, and interaction among individuals—and acknowledges that each must be considered.

The following description of principled negotiation shows how a group can incorporate the communication principles presented throughout this book, including such concepts as rhetorical sensitivity, active listening, and integrative conflict management, into a practical, effective technique for managing conflict. The group leader, an outside consultant, or members themselves can use the procedure. Here are the four steps:

1. **Separate the people from the problem.**

   In most conflicts, the content of the disagreement becomes tangled with the relationship among the participants. Each should be dealt with directly and separately. All parties should be given the opportunity to explain, without interference, how they perceive the conflict and how they feel about it. Parties should share perceptions as they try to put themselves into each other's shoes. If emotions run high, allow them to be vented. Do not overreact to emotional outbursts, but listen actively and show by your actions as well as your words that you care about the needs of the other members with whom your interests conflict. The goal is not to become bosom buddies with the other party to a conflict (although that may happen), but to develop a good working relationship characterized by mutual respect.[36]

2. **Focus on interests, not positions.**

   When group members stake out certain positions ("I insist that we have an educational speaker!"), they become attached to those *positions* rather than the original *needs* the positions were designed to meet. For example, we discussed earlier the committee that debated closing the food service facility at 5 PM. One side's position was that the snack bar must be closed, but the other side's position was that the snack bar must be kept open. These two positions are incompatible, and there is no way to reconcile them—in their present form, one must win and one must lose. However, when group members started to explore the *interests* behind the positions (the desire to save money and the desire to meet needs of evening students), then an avenue opened whereby both parties could have their desires met by finding a way to do *both simultaneously*—provide the students with food without raising costs by expanding the vending service. Rigidly adhering to the initial positions would have precluded the discovery of this solution. Support for this comes from Innami, who discovered that when members stick to their positions, decision quality is impaired, but when they exchange facts and reasons, decision quality improves.[37] Moreover, high-quality arguments are more persuasive and overcome the influence of such factors as status differences.[38]

3. **Invent options for mutual gain.**

The previous example illustrates how a new option, expanded vending service, was created that had not been apparent when the conflict started. We earlier have suggested separating the invention process from the decision process, and employing techniques like brainstorming. Negotiators should assume that the interests of all parties can be integrated into the group's final solution. The same committee that debated food service options for evening students also discussed how evening students could be served by the bookstore.[39] The evening student advisor on the committee noted that the campus bookstore was open in the evenings only during the first week of the quarter. Many evening students who drove directly to campus from work could not arrive early enough for the bookstore's regular hours, and so were unable to exchange books, purchase supplies, or even browse. The advisor proposed that the bookstore hours be extended to 8 PM every evening. The campus budget officer objected strongly, noting that the proposal would result in cost increases for personnel salaries unlikely to be recovered by purchases made by evening students.

The positions adopted by each person represented attempts to meet the legitimate needs of two important groups: the evening students and the budget watchdogs. However, through open discussion focused on the interests (not the positions) of each, a solution was invented that incorporated both sets of needs. The bookstore would remain open two evenings per week throughout the quarter, and would start business later in the morning the rest of the week. The total number of hours of bookstore operation was the same, so costs were not increased, but the distribution of the hours changed to meet the needs of more students.

4. **Use objective criteria.**

Negotiations will be perceived as fairer if objective criteria *agreed upon by all parties* are established as the standard for judging alternatives. Group members will profit from establishing such criteria at the beginning of any problem-solving session, but they should *insist* on it in prolonged conflicts because such criteria make negotiation less likely to be a contest of wills and more likely to be settled upon principle instead of pressure. This is an egalitarian approach in that much of the battle for dominance is removed from the negotiation process. For example, many people use the *Bluebook* to determine a fair price for used cars. You may want $5,000 for your 10-year-old Nissan Sentra, and your buyer may want to pay only $100. However, if both of you agree that the *Bluebook* is an appropriate standard and it indicates that a fair price is $1,500 to $2,000, depending on model and condition, this narrows the negotiating range between you and makes reaching agreement more likely.

In another example, the United Way organization of a major midwestern city nearly disintegrated as a result of arguments over which agencies should receive money. Finally, the *ad hoc* committee established a set of cost accounting procedures enabling each agency to determine how many people could be served for what amount. These procedures then served as relatively objective criteria for United Way to use in determining which agencies to fund.

Sometimes, despite a group's best intentions, even principled negotiation fails to bring about consensus, or a group is operating under a time deadline that forces members to use other methods.

Settlements derived through negotiation by the group itself are preferable to solutions imposed by someone else because they tend to be more acceptable to all members. The first two of the four alternatives presented in the following section involve the group in breaking a deadlock. However, sometimes a group simply is not able to break a deadlock. In that case, when a decision *must* be made, the designated leader has the two remaining options.

When Negotiation Fails: Alternative Procedures

If a seemingly irreconcilable conflict emerges over goals or alternatives, the leader might suggest the following procedure, which is an abbreviated form of that used by professional mediators for apparently deadlocked negotiations between a union and management. The procedure represents a last-chance group attempt to arrive at an acceptable decision without resorting to third-party arbitration. If this procedure fails, other alternative procedures can be taken to resolve the conflict issue without producing consensus. Two-sided conflict is assumed for simplicity.

Mediation by the Designated Leader

1. Presentation of Alternatives

   a. A proponent of side 1 presents exactly what the subgroup wants or believes and why. Other members supporting the position may add clarifying statements, arguments, evidence, and claims, but proponents of side 2 can say nothing.

   b. Side 2 can now ask for clarification, restatements, explanations, or supporting evidence, but may not disagree, argue, or propose any other alternative.

   c. A spokesperson for side 2 is now required to explain side 1's position to the complete satisfaction of all other group members, both side 1 and side 2. (Note the similarity to active listening presented in Chapter 3.) Only when this person has restated side 1's proposal and supporting arguments to everyone's satisfaction is the group ready to advance to the next step.

   d. Side 2's position is now presented by a spokesperson. Exactly the same procedural rules apply as during presentation and clarification of side 1's position.

2. Charting Alternatives

   a. The designated group leader now writes both positions on a chalkboard or large poster and underneath lists pros (benefits, advantages) claimed by its proponents and evidence advanced in its support. Under the heading cons the leader should list any disadvantages, possible harmful effects, or evidence advanced against the alternative. An example of such a chart is shown in Figure 13.3.

   b. When all positions have been charted, the group may want to see whether there is unanimity about any of the statements on the chart. What, if anything, do members agree upon?

3. Search for Creative Alternatives

   a. The designated leader reviews all elements of common ground shared by all group members, such as shared interest in solving the problem, shared history of the group, and so forth, then urges group members to seek a win–win resolution, an alternative all could accept. The leader may propose such a solution, or

   b. The designated leader asks members to compromise and create an alternative that meets the minimum requirements of both sides.

4. Resolution occurs when and if a consensus or compromise alternative is adopted.

If this procedure is successful, some time should be spent by group members discussing the procedure itself, how they feel about the group and each of the other members, and how the group can manage future conflicts. Generally, when the previously described procedure is followed out of a sincere desire to resolve the conflict, the group will find at least a compromise and will develop increased cohesiveness and team spirit. Lacking a consensus or compromise, other procedures will be needed to reach a decision.

Voting   *Voting* is one such alternative procedure. Naturally, some members are bound to dislike the outcome, but voting may be a necessary step in overcoming an impasse. You may recall the example presented earlier of a faculty subcommittee's presenting a sweeping proposal to the full faculty committee, only to be met with dismay instead of enthusiasm. After repeated attempts to develop an integrative solution failed, the committee took a vote to decide the issue. One danger with voting is that the group may arrive at premature closure on an issue. Be especially careful, if this is the option you select, that the group really is deadlocked.

Forcing   Another option is *forcing*. Here, the leader breaks the deadlock and decides on behalf of the group. For example, in the U.S. Senate the presiding officer can break a tie. As with voting, several members are likely to be disappointed, but in instances in which an outside group, parent organization, or legitimate authority demands a report or when the group faces a deadline, a leader may have little choice.

| **Example of a chart of pros and cons.** | **FIGURE 13.3** |

*How might accidents be reduced on National Ave?
Construct an overpass*

Pro
Would eliminate
   accidents, if used
Would not impede
   traffic flow
Would not take long
   to complete (compared
   to underground tunnel)

Con
Would be expensive
Students might not
   use it (inconvenience)
People might throw
   things at cars
   below

Third-party arbitration occurs when the group brings in an outside negotiator to resolve its differences. This typically happens with joint labor–management disputes and some court-related cases. Arbitrators often have the power to resolve issues any way they please, from deciding entirely in favor of one party to splitting the difference between them. Sometimes, just the threat of bringing in a third-party arbitrator is enough to force conflict participants to negotiate with each other in good faith. Usually, all parties to the conflict end up feeling dissatisfied. Thus, third-party arbitration should be proposed only when the leader believes the group has reached an impasse and the cost of continuing the conflict, including resentment and the possibility of destroying the group, will exceed the cost of arbitration. Of course, group members must agree to such a resolution procedure.

Third-Party Arbitration

Sometimes, no resolution about a group's issue is possible, but that does not automatically create a hopeless situation. Even when members cannot agree on basic values or goals, they often can find some areas where they do agree, as with the *common ground approaches* we now discuss.

We began this chapter with a story about Common Ground groups. These kinds of projects have sprung up all over the country.[40] Their purpose is to seek alternative ways to ease tensions surrounding highly contentious and divisive public issues (e.g., abortion, affirmative action, animal testing, biogenetics, bilingual education, immigration). A unique characteristic of these efforts is their common goal: they do not seek to solve the issue or mediate a compromise. Rather, they attempt to create a safe place for dialogue to occur between deeply divided individuals in the hope of finding common ground, thereby easing tensions and perhaps reducing violence. In addition, they attempt to discover and use areas of genuinely shared values between these individuals constructively, something often hidden in contentious debate. **Common Ground dialogue** is a process of constructively managing socially divisive conflict.[41]

Common Ground Approaches

You will notice that Common Ground small groups, in their attempt to manage their conflict, are different from those we have focused on in this chapter. We have dealt with groups whose members must manage conflict in their attempts to come to some agreed upon resolution. Common Ground groups are created with the sole purpose of finding a way to bridge highly divisive viewpoints that can result in violence. So these group members enter their groups already knowing they do not agree and their purpose is not to solve their differences or mediate a compromise. All the above procedures for managing failed negotiation assume a goal of resolution; common ground dialogue does not. Yet you will see some, if not all, of the same ethical principles in the rules guiding Common Ground dialogue.

Chasin and Herzig have described several behavioral patterns which occur when individuals get caught up in chronic conflict or stalemated controversy.[42] Often those on one side will not listen to those on the other side; individuals become entrenched in their positions. Questions one side asks the other side clearly have ulterior motives. Members of either side tend to see the members of the other side as all alike. This happens in part because, when confronted, people do minimize their internal differences to appear "together" on the issue. Members of both sides tend to blame the other side for the problem, refuse to see their role in the problem, mind-read the other side, and remain closed-minded about the other side. Attempts by either side to begin a process of conciliation are perceived as propaganda ploys. Finally, members of both sides believe there is value in sticking with the struggle in spite of outsider efforts to break the deadlock. You will see in the following rules of Common Ground dialogue attempts to overcome these behavioral patterns in the pursuit of common ground.

The following is one kind of Common Ground dialogue model applied to the topic of abortion, as in our opening case. You will see that the process is far more involving than you might have expected after reading our case study. This model is comprised of a total nine steps.[43] Facilitators ensure that both sides of the issue are equally represented and the sessions are held on neutral ground.

Recruitment of Participants

1. Potential participants are identified through informal networks and activist publications, after which Common Ground coordinators make telephone invitations. During these conversations, potential participants are filled in on the Common Ground procedures and answer questions.

2. Follow-up letters are sent to those wishing to participate. The letter details the kind of dialogue that will be facilitated and includes a chart of the dialogue rules. This chart explains the difference between dialogue and debate. Recruits are also given questions to think about before the meeting.

Pre-meeting Activity

3. Prior to the actual common ground dialogue session, participants get acquainted at an informal dinner. They may *not* talk about abortion and may share whatever they wish about themselves as long as they do not

reveal which side of the abortion issue they are on. You can see here that the purpose of this step is to help these individuals see each other as *people,* not positions. Sometimes they are also asked to fill out questionnaires the way they think someone from the other side would complete them.

4. Participants are assigned seats next to someone on the other side of the issue. They are then reintroduced to the dialogue rules and they are asked verbally to agree to them. They must maintain confidentiality, avoid interrupting each other, use respectful speech (e.g., "pro-choice" not "anti-life"), and give each member the right to "pass" if they do not want to respond to a question or comment.

Establishing the Ground Rules for the Dialogue

5. The facilitators share with the group their observations of the informal dinner interaction. They point out how much members of each side are in fact more different from each other than the other side assumed.

6. Three questions are asked of each member. After a question is read, each member responds in order while everyone else remains attentive and silent. The questions invite members to share a personal experience related to abortion, give what they believe to be the heart of the matter, and identify any gray areas in the abortion issue.

Rules during the Dialogue

7. Once all three questions are processed, participants are encouraged to ask questions of each other. Participants are encouraged to ask genuine questions of curiosity, not rhetorical ones with hidden agendas. They are reminded not to attempt to persuade but to focus on the member present. "They" and "them" are discouraged so that they do not act as representatives of one side. Active listening is facilitated during discussion.

8. When the dialogue begins to wind down, the facilitators move to end the session. They ask two questions in the same format as the three in step 6. Each member is asked to reflect on what she or he did or didn't do to make the dialogue go as it did. And members are asked to share parting thoughts.

9. A couple of weeks later, participants are telephoned. They are asked to offer any suggestions for improving the model and how they have taken and will take their experience into their daily lives.

Follow-Up

Common Ground dialogue models such as this one are another way to manage failed negotiations and in this case chronic conflict. This model outlines only the general procedures and does not begin to touch on the many rules which guide the actual dialogue. Each step, when applied in actual dialogue, involves extensive mediation by facilitators so that participants can "hear" each other and safely learn where they have common ground. Then, this discovery is used to promote more positive outcomes and possible joint projects by the participants (e.g., reducing teen pregnancy, funding and supporting adoption as a choice) while allowing them to "agree to disagree."

CONSIDER THIS

Review the nine steps and identify the principles for expressing disagreements ethically. Then ask yourself how each step tries to encourage the principle.

SUMMARY

1. Conflict occurs when interdependent parties perceive incompatible goals, scarce resources, and interference in achieving their goals and express this struggle outwardly. It has perceptual, emotional, behavioral, and interactional dimensions.

2. Although conflict can cause bad feelings, lower cohesiveness, or even group disintegration, it can also stimulate member involvement and understanding, increase cohesiveness, and produce better decisions. An opinion or innovative deviate expresses disagreement and may cause or experience discomfort, but contributes to critical thinking.

3. Types of conflict include substantive (task-oriented), affective (over personality and power differences), procedural (over how the group operates), and inequity (over unequal workloads or contributions by members). One type can lead to another in an actual conflict situation.

4. A distributive orientation to managing conflict assumes winners and losers, but an integrative orientation assumes the possibility of a win–win solution. Degree of cooperation and assertiveness underlie the five common conflict management strategies of avoidance, accommodation, competition, collaboration, and compromise.

5. Ethical principles governing appropriate conflict-managing behavior include expressing one's views sensitively, focusing on the issues, and expressing the disagreement but not attacking another person. Disagreements should be based on substance, not innuendo. Members should respond nondefensively, with a spirit of inquiry, and remain open-minded to contradictory ideas. Finally, members should avoid fight-to-the-death conflict resolution strategies.

6. Group members should try to use procedures such as the principled negotiation procedure that are ethical and help parties find solutions satisfactory to all.

7. If a group cannot achieve consensus, other options include mediation by the leader or voting. Forcing or third-party arbitration, where someone decides for the group, are a last resort.

8. Common Ground dialogue can be used to discuss polarizing public issues, such as abortion, by helping participants discover genuinely shared values that can lessen tension and violence.

EXERCISES

1. Select a group to which you now belong. Try to remember all the recent conflicts or disagreements experienced by the group. On paper, briefly describe each conflict, indicate what type it was, and explain how it was settled. Use the following format:

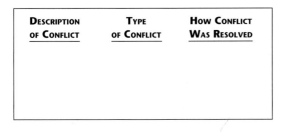

DESCRIPTION OF CONFLICT	TYPE OF CONFLICT	HOW CONFLICT WAS RESOLVED

2. Think of an extended conflict you observed or were involved in. Analyze it according to the perceptions-emotions-behavior-interaction model.
    a. How did each element of the model affect each other element?
    b. What was the relationship of the conflicting parties to each other at the beginning of the conflict episode and at the end?
    c. What do you conclude about conflict from this?
    d. Would you do anything differently if you were faced with the same situation again?
3. Select a controversial issue for your class about which there are two or more contrasting positions. Form into discussion groups of four or five so that at least two people initially are on each side of the issue. Two classmates should serve as observers for each group of discussants. Discuss the issue and attempt to come to some consensus. Observers should note and report on the following:
    a. What was said about the issue?
    b. How were disagreements expressed?
    c. Were there any ways that disagreement could have been expressed more

appropriately? (The observers should pay particular attention to the effect on the receiver of the disagreeing remarks.)
4. Your class should split into dyads with one nonparticipating observer per dyad. One dyad partner should play the role of quality control manager and the other that of production manager in a manufacturing plant. Assume the production manager wants to get the quality control manager to reject fewer items so that production can be increased. Half the groups should be instructed to negotiate with a distributive orientation and half with an integrative one. Observers should note and report exactly what was said in attempting to settle the conflict and what appeared to be the effect. Discuss how you felt in your particular situation. Were there any consistent differences in the feelings of the participants in the two assigned orientations? What did you learn from this activity?
5. Select a controversial public issue with at least two sides. In groups or dyads, explain how you would use the principled negotiation procedure to help the competing sides resolve their differences:
    a. Imagine how people from each side feel about the situation and what their perceptions might be of themselves and people from the opposite side.
    b. First, describe the positions of each side. Then determine what might be the needs or interests behind the positions.
    c. Determine whether there are any interests that might be compatible, and brainstorm options that bring these common interests together.
    d. Determine whether there are any objective criteria that could be used to help the parties resolve their conflict, and show how these criteria might be used.
    Discuss your findings and suggestions as a whole class. What did you learn by using the principled negotiation procedure?

BIBLIOGRAPHY

Cathcart, Robert S., Larry A. Samovar, and Linda D. Henman. *Small Group Communication: Theory and Practice.* 7th ed. Dubuque, IA: Brown & Benchmark, 1996, section 4.

Fisher, Roger, and William Ury. *Getting to Yes: Negotiating Agreement Without Giving In.* New York: Penguin Books, 1983.

Hocker, Joyce L., and William W. Wilmot. *Interpersonal Conflict.* 3d ed. Dubuque, IA: Wm. C. Brown Publishers, 1991.

Putnam, Linda L. "Conflict in Group Decision Making." In *Communication and Group Decision Making.* Randy Y. Hirokawa and Marshall Scott Poole, eds. Beverly Hills, CA: Sage Publications, 1986, 175–97.

NOTES

1. The primary sources for this case study are Leslie Wirpsa, "Listening Key as Foes Seek Common Goals: Abortion Activists Find Hospitality Helps Melt Barriers," *National Catholic Reporter* (June 28, 1996): 5; and Frederica Mathewes-Green, "Pro-life, Pro-Choice: Can We Talk?" *The Christian Century* (January 3, 1996): 12–15. Other articles providing supporting information are Gene Warner, "Rev. Schenck Joins Common-Ground Camp on Abortion," *The Buffalo News* (March 23, 1999): 4B; Benjamin J. Hubbard, "Room Exists for Discussion on Abortion," *Los Angeles Times* (January 24, 1998): B10; Melodee Hall Blobaum, "Genuine Dialogue Can Bridge the Gap," *The Kansas City Star* (February 20, 1999): 2; and Barbara Brotman, "Both Sides of Abortion Issue Seek Detente; Daylong Session Finds Common Ground," *The Plain Dealer* (December 1, 1998): 6F.

2. Carolyn J. Wood, "Challenging the Assumptions Underlying the Use of Participatory Decision-Making Strategies: A Longitudinal Case Study," *Small Group Behavior* 20 (1989): 428–48.

3. Victor D. Wall, Jr., Gloria J. Galanes, and Susan B. Love, "Small, Task-Oriented Groups: Conflict, Conflict Management, Satisfaction, and Decision Quality," *Small Group Behavior* 18 (1987): 31–55.

4. Kathleen M. O'Connor, Deborah H. Gruenfeld, and Joseph E. McGrath, "The Experience and Effects of Conflict in Continuing Work Groups," *Small Group Research* 24 (August 1993): 362–82.

5. M. R. Shakun, "Formalizing Conflict Resolution in Policy-Making," *International Journal of General Systems* 7 (1981): 207–15.

6. Gordon L. Lippett, "Managing Conflict in Today's Organization," *Training and Development Journal* 36 (1982): 67–75.

7. Joyce L. Hocker and William W. Wilmot, *Interpersonal Conflict,* 3d ed. (Dubuque, IA: Wm. C. Brown, 1991): 12.

8. Morton Deutsch, "Conflicts: Productive and Destructive," *Journal of Social Issues* 25 (1969): 7–41; Kenneth W. Thomas, "Conflict and Conflict Management," in *Handbook of Industrial and Organizational Psychology,* ed. M. Dunnette (Chicago: Rand McNally, 1976): 890–934; Louis B. Pondy, "Organizational Conflict: Concepts and Models," *Administrative Science Quarterly* 12 (1976): 296–320; Brent D. Ruben, "Communication and Conflict: A System-Theoretic Perspective," *Quarterly Journal of Speech* 64 (1978): 202–12; J. Guetzkow and J. Gyr, "An Analysis of Conflict in Decision-Making Groups," *Human Relations* 7 (1954): 367–82; and E. P. Torrance, "Group Decision-Making and Disagreement," *Social Forces* 35 (1957): 314–18.

9. Karl Smith, David W. Johnson, and Roger T. Johnson, "Can Conflict Be Constructive?

Controversy versus Concurrence Seeking in Learning Groups," *Journal of Educational Psychology* 73 (1981): 654–63.

10. Charles R. Franz and K. Gregory Jin, "The Structure of Group Conflict in a Collaborative Work Group during Information Systems Development," *Journal of Applied Communication Research* 23 (May 1995): 108–27.

11. Franz and Jin, "The Structure of Group Conflict."

12. Sue D. Pendell, "Deviance and Conflict in Small Group Decision Making: An Exploratory Study," *Small Group Behavior* 21 (1990): 393–403.

13. Svenn Lindskold and Gyuseog Han, "Group Resistance to Influence by a Conciliatory Member," *Small Group Behavior* 19 (1988): 19–34.

14. Carl L. Thameling and Patricia H. Andrews, "Majority Responses to Opinion Deviates: A Communicative Analysis," *Small Group Research* 23 (1992): 475–502.

15. Kristin B. Valentine and B. Aubrey Fisher, "An Interaction Analysis of Verbal Innovative Deviance in Small Groups," *Speech Monographs* 41 (1974): 413–20.

16. Mark K. Covey, "The Relationship between Social Skill and Conflict Resolution Tactics" (Paper presented at the annual convention of the Rocky Mountain Psychological Association, Snowbird, Utah, 1983).

17. Rick Garlick and Paul A. Mongeau, "Argument Quality and Group Member Status as Determinants of Attitudinal Minority Influence," *Western Journal of Communication* 57 (Summer 1993): 289–308.

18. The conflict described in the following episode and used as the extended example here is segment 2 of the videotape ancillary to this text, *Communicating Effectively in Small Groups* (Dubuque, IA: Wm. C. Brown, 1991).

19. Guetzkow and Gyr, "An Analysis of Conflict," 367–82.

20. Ibid.

21. Roger C. Pace, "Personalized and Depersonalized Conflict in Small Group Discussions: An Examination of Differentiation," *Small Group Research* 21 (1990): 79–96.

22. Roger Fisher and Scott Brown, *Getting Together: Building a Relationship That Gets to Yes* (Boston: Houghton-Mifflin, 1988): 16–23.

23. Linda L. Putnam, "Conflict in Group Decision Making," in *Communication and Group Decision Making,* eds. Randy Y. Hirokawa and Marshall Scott Poole (Beverly Hills, CA: Sage, 1986): 175–96.

24. Victor D. Wall, Jr., and Linda L. Nolan, "Small Group Conflict: A Look at Equity, Satisfaction, and Styles of Conflict Management," *Small Group Behavior* 18 (1987): 188–211.

25. R. H. Kilmann and K. Thomas, "Developing a Forced-Choice Measure of Conflict-Handling Behavior: The MODE Instrument," *Educational and Psychological Measurement* 37 (1977): 309–25.

26. Hal Witteman, "Analyzing Interpersonal Conflict: Nature of Awareness, Type of Initiating Event, Situational Perceptions, and Management Styles," *Western Journal of Communication* 56 (Summer 1992): 248–80.

27. Daniel J. Canary and Brian H. Spitzberg, "Appropriateness and Effectiveness Perceptions of Conflict Strategies," *Human Communication Research* 14 (1987): 93–118.

28. Hal Witteman, "Group Member Satisfaction: A Conflict-Related Account," *Small Group Behavior* 22 (1991): 24–58.

29. Gary L. Kreps, *Organizational Communication,* 2d ed. (New York: Longman, 1990): 193.

30. Fisher and Brown, *Getting Together.*

31. Gloria J. Galanes, "The Effect of Conflict Expression Styles on Quality of Outcome and Satisfaction in Small, Task-Oriented Groups" (Unpublished doctoral dissertation, Ohio State University, 1985).

32. Kreps, *Organizational Communication.*

33. Steven M. Alderton and Lawrence R. Frey, "Argumentation in Small Group Decision-Making," in *Communication and Group Decision Making,* eds. Randy Y. Hirokawa and Marshall Scott Poole (Beverly Hills, CA: Sage, 1986): 157–73.

34. Roger Fisher and William Ury, *Getting to Yes: Negotiating Agreement Without Giving In* (Boston: Houghton-Mifflin, 1981; Penguin Books, 1983).

35. Frank Tutzauer and Michael E. Roloff, "Communicative Processes Leading to Integrative Agreements," *Communication Research* 15 (1988): 360–80.

36. Fisher and Ury, *Getting to Yes.*

37. Ichiro Innami, "The Quality of Group Decisions, Group Verbal Behavior, and Intervention," *Organizational Behavior and Human Decision Processes* 60 (December 1994): 409–30.

38. Garlick and Mongeau, "Argument Quality and Group Member Status."

39. A version of the discussion about this issue is depicted on the ancillary videotape, *Communicating Effectively in Small Groups* (Dubuque, IA: Wm. C. Brown, 1991). Segment 3 depicts an ineffective discussion, and segment 4 shows an effective discussion where this major issue of bookstore hours is resolved.

40. The information in this section is taken from Trophy R. Olson, " 'Common Ground' Discourse as a Way to Mediate in the Abortion Issue: An Interpretive Analysis" (Unpublished master's thesis, California State University, Fresno, 1997).

41. S. Roth, L. Chasin, R. Chasin, C. Becker, and M. Herzig, "From Debate to Dialogue: A Facilitating Role for Family Therapists in the Public Forum," *Dulwich Centre Newsletter* 2 (1992): 41–48.

42. R. Chasin and M. Herzig, "Creating Systematic Interventions for the Sociopolitical Arena," in *The Global Family Therapist: Integrating the Personal, Professional and Political,* eds. B. Bernina-Gould and D. Hillboe DeMuth (Needham, MA: Allyn & Bacon, 1993): 32–69.

43. This is the Public Conversations Project model. See Olson, "Common Ground Discourse," 47–52.

GROUP DISCUSSION AND OBSERVATION TECHNIQUES

© Jeff Hunter/Image Bank

Individuals skilled in a variety of group problem-solving techniques are valued and sought-after members of any organization. So are people who can observe a group discussion, analyze the process, spot problems, and provide appropriate recommendations for improvement. The final two chapters provide information and techniques to help you put your understanding of small group communication to work for the benefit of any group or organization to which you belong.

Special Discussion Techniques and Methods

14

Central Message

Special techniques can be used to improve the regulation of discussion, enhance problem-solving effectiveness, and improve overall teamwork in organizations. For any of these techniques to be effective, all members must understand the procedure and may need specialized training.

Study Objectives

As a result of studying Chapter 14 you should be able to:
1. Use the guidelines for committees in *Robert's Rules of Order*.
2. Explain how problem census and RISK techniques can help uncover problems; describe the procedures for each technique.
3. Explain how focus groups and buzz groups can generate information for a variety of uses, and describe the procedures for each technique.
4. Plan and lead brainstorming and synectics sessions to enhance group members' creativity.
5. Explain and use the Program Evaluation and Review Technique .
6. Describe the purpose and procedure for conducting the Nominal Group Technique.
7. Explain what quality circles and self-managed work groups are, how they work, and what is necessary for either method to be productive.
8. Describe such electronic support mechanisms as teleconferencing and Group Decision Support Systems, and explain how groups can benefit from them.

Key Terms

Brainstorming
Brainwriting
Buzz group session
Focus groups
Group Decision Support Systems (GDSS)
Nominal Group Technique
Problem census

Program Evaluation and Review Technique (PERT)
Quality circle
RISK technique
Self-managed work groups
Synectics
Teleconferences

A university music department had experienced a number of problems over the years, including faculty members' lack of support for one another and lack of clarity about their vision for what kind of department they perceived themselves to be. Should they model themselves after music conservatories, where students focus intensely on music to the exclusion of other studies, or should they encourage their students to receive a broad general education that includes many other courses besides music?

The dean of the college where the department was housed led the department in a day-long retreat to get faculty focused in a particular direction. He utilized a number of group techniques to accomplish this. After some ice-breaker exercises to remove apprehension and inhibitions, he used a modification of the nominal group technique to help the group identify what their main issues were and how they might address them. The faculty members were first asked to identify, in writing, the most problematic 8 or 10 issues they perceived within the department, and they had to state the problems in a positive way. For instance, they couldn't say, "Faculty meetings are a waste of time because we never know what we're going to be talking about." Instead, they had to restate the issue positively: "Our faculty meetings would be more productive if we had an agenda published in advance and we stuck to the agenda." Once all issues had been posted for everyone to see, the dean led faculty in a discussion of them and they made decisions about what they would do.

The dean also used the nominal group technique variation to identify the department's considerable strengths. After all the issues and problems had been categorized into five or six main themes, he used a variation of the buzz technique to ensure that all the members of this large department participated. The large group was broken into five smaller groups of 4 or 5 members, each of which worked on a particular departmental issue. Unlike the typical buzz technique, the groups were given an hour to work through their particular theme and report to the department as a whole. At the conclusion of the retreat, the department had a plan for the year which all members supported, had functioning committees established to work on particular issues, and felt much better about themselves and their future as a department than they had in a long time.

It has been estimated that there are over a million nonprofit organizations in the United States. There are thousands of governmental groups at all levels: local, county, state, and regional. In 1992, there were over 11 million meetings in the United States *every day!* Imagine the number today. You probably belong to about six organized groups and these do not include the many informal groups you belong to.[1] Think about all the techniques these groups use daily, such as the ones used by the dean and the music department. In Chapter 14 we shift our focus from small group communication theories and processes to specific group formats and techniques. We have included a variety of techniques that were developed for small groups that are components of larger organizations. These techniques can be modified or combined to serve specific group or organizational purposes. The dean in our story modified the nominal group technique and buzz groups to suit his purpose.

REGULATING GROUP DISCUSSION

Appropriate group regulation gives each participant an equal opportunity to speak and ensures that decisions are made democratically. The larger a group, the more important it is to have formal procedures to regulate interaction so order can be maintained. Many organizations and large assemblies have adopted *Robert's Rules of Order, Newly Revised* as their parliamentary code.[2] Robert also includes a code of rules for board and committee meetings of organizations. When an organization adopts *Robert's Rules of Order,* the committees of that organization are bound to use Robert's rules for committees, which are much less formal and detailed than the parliamentary rules that govern large meetings. These rules make it unnecessary (and undesirable) for members to keep uttering "question," "point of order," or "I move to table the motion."

The bylaws of a parent organization may have special rules governing committees; if at any point these contradict what Robert says, the bylaws prevail. Chairs of committees need to know the organization's bylaws and, if the organization has adopted a parliamentary manual, what that manual says about committee procedures.

We have summarized Robert's rules for committees below for three reasons: first, because Robert is the parliamentary authority adopted by most American organizations; second, so you can know how to act in committees covered by *Robert's Rules;* and third, so you can use these rules properly if you are in the formal role of chair.

Administrative Matters

1. The chair of a committee may be selected in one of three ways: appointed by the parent organization, selected by the committee members, or the first person named to the committee is automatically the chair.

2. A committee meets on call of its chair or any two members.

3. A quorum (minimum number of members needed for the committee to take any legal action) is a simple majority of committee members, unless specified otherwise by the parent organization.

4. Formal reports of committees should contain only what was agreed to by a majority of those present at a regular and properly called (notice given to each member) meeting at which a quorum was present. Usually the chair makes formal reports from a committee in writing, but reports of less formal action or works in progress may be given orally to a parent organization.

5. If a committee has been unable to reach consensus and a minority of its membership wants to make a report or recommendation to the parent organization different from that of the majority, it is usually permitted to do so as soon as the "majority" committee report has been made. This is not a *right* of a committee minority, but during debate under parliamentary rules the members who did not agree with the majority

may speak their opposition. However, no one has the right to allude to what happened during the committee's private discussions unless the entire committee has agreed that this is to be permitted.

Responsibilities of the Chair

6. The chair is responsible for records of the committee but may delegate the work, or a separate secretary position may be created. The chair is still responsible for supervising this process.

7. Unlike *presiding* officers, committee chairs can take stands on issues without leaving the chair position. They can also make motions and vote on all questions, as can all other members of the committee. (In some large committees, it may be decided that the chair will act as if in a large assembly; if so, the chair should do so *at all times,* refraining from participating in the substance of a discussion and voting only to create or break a tie.)

Discussing, Making Motions, and Voting

8. Members do not need the formal recognition of the chair to speak, but may speak whenever they want *so long as they do not interrupt others.*

9. Many of the motions required in an assembly are irrelevant. A member can discuss virtually anything informally in committee sessions, so there is no need for points of order, motions to table, or matters of personal privilege. In short, the bulk of what is called *parliamentary law* is obstructive to committee meetings.

10. Motions do not need a second. A motion is a proposal for the group to take some action.

11. There is no limit to how many times a member can speak on an issue, and motions to limit or close discussion are *not* permitted.

12. Informal discussion is permitted with no motion pending. In a parliamentary discussion, members cannot discuss an issue without a motion, but in a committee meeting no motion is needed until *after* the discussion has indicated that consensus or majority decision has been achieved.

13. A majority of those actually voting is required before any decision can be made. Usually a vote is taken to confirm a decision already sensed by the group. "Straw" (nonbinding) votes can be taken at any time to determine whether a majority or consensus exists before a binding vote is taken. The leader might say, "I think we have consensus on this. Would all who favor the proposal please raise your right hand?"

14. No motion is needed to record a vote. When a proposal is clear to all members, a vote can be taken and the outcome recorded as a decision.

15. The chair can ask if all members consent or agree with an idea or proposal. If no one objects, the decision is made and reported in the minutes. For example: "It was decided by consent that Jean and Bob should draft a resolution to present at the next meeting of the club."

16. A motion to reconsider a previous vote can be made at any time, with no limit to how many times a question can be reconsidered. Unlike in a parliamentary body, even a person who voted with the losing side can move to reconsider. Thus, a person who was absent or did not vote can ask for reconsideration of a previous decision if the action has not yet been carried out.

17. Motions can be amended in committee, but this is best done informally. If time is available, it is preferable to decide changes by consensus rather than by voting.

In summary, few rules of order and precedence are required in committees of organizations that have adopted *Robert's Rules of Order*. Voting is done to show that a legal majority supported a decision, not to shut off discussion. Any issue within the freedom of the committee can be presented for discussion at any time, and discussion can be quite informal and as lengthy as needed.

In the only study of its kind, Weitzel and Geist examined the use of parliamentary procedure in community groups.[3] While much has been written about parliamentary procedure, no one has explored how using *Robert's Rules of Order* actually affects group decision making. In Chapter 11, we described Vigilant Interaction Theory, which states that the quality of a group's final product is related to the quality of the communication during problem solving and the degree of vigilance a group employs. Weitzel and Geist wanted to know the relationship between group vigilance, the use of parliamentary procedure, and effective problem solving in real versus experimental groups. What they discovered may surprise you.

They found that the community groups did not display a sophisticated understanding of parliamentary procedure even if members thought they were "experts." Few of the groups selected a parliamentarian, many produced and approved slipshod minutes, and motions often went unseconded and were generally handled in a less than sophisticated manner. But does this mean their communication was terrible and group satisfaction was jeopardized? No. These groups used *Robert's Rules of Order* only when they needed to and their problem-solving communication did not appear to suffer from their selective use of the rules. Weitzel and Geist concluded, from this initial research, that there was no evidence that the quality of the groups' communication was impaired by what some might consider inept use of parliamentary procedure.

What does this mean to you? Do not memorize *Robert's Rules of Order* and go into a group thinking they are essential to effective problem solving. Following *Robert's Rules of Order* does not ensure vigilance. The community group members were concerned more about getting their business done than with strict adherence to parliamentary procedure. When parliamentary procedure *is* used, it does help provide a systematic process of problem solving and decision making while protecting group member interests. Thus, to ensure a good decision, groups should use good judgment rather than mechanically or blindly following a particular set of rules.

GROUP TECHNIQUES FOR INCREASING PROBLEM-SOLVING EFFECTIVENESS

In this chapter we present a selection of small group techniques for improving organizational effectiveness. Knowing when and how to apply these techniques will enhance your value to your group or organization. All the techniques we have selected may be tailored for specific contexts or purposes by modifying them or combining them with other techniques. If you decide to use any of them, make sure you or the group coordinator explains the procedures carefully before the group tries them. Providing participants with a handout or chart will help.

We have classified these techniques by their major function: identifying problems, generating information, enhancing creativity, and improving problem solving within organizations. However, most fulfill more than one function.

Identifying Problems

People closest to a problem (such as cooks and waiters in a restaurant, teachers in a school, or production workers in a factory) are often more aware of difficulties and problems than managers are. The following two techniques help bring out the individual perceptions of *all* individuals in an organization. Making such perceptions widely available can help prevent costly or life threatening events later on.

The Problem Census

The **problem census** is a "posting" technique used to identify important issues or problems. It is particularly useful for building an agenda for future problem-solving meetings or discovering problems encountered by organization members. A university department where one of us worked periodically conducted a problem census that developed into an agenda for a series of future meetings. The census first identified the list of problems, then different faculty members assigned themselves to research and present an outline of each of the problems for eventual problem solving by the committee. The following are the steps for conducting a problem census:

1. Seat the group in a semicircle facing a chart or board.
2. Explain the purpose of the technique, which is to bring out all problems, concerns, questions, or difficulties any member would like to discuss.
3. The leader then asks each participant, in round-robin fashion, to present one problem or question. This continues until all problems have been presented.
4. The leader posts each problem as it is presented by writing it clearly on the chart or board. The leader must accept totally whatever is presented, never challenging or disagreeing, but asking for clarification or elaboration as needed. Often, the leader can distill a long problem statement into a concise phrase, but should always ask the speaker if the distillation is accurate before posting it. Each filled page of the chart is

fastened to the wall for all to see. (A computer display for doing this is available in some organizations.)

5. The group now establishes a priority order for the entire list, usually by having members vote for their top three or four choices. *All* the problems are retained on the agenda; voting just prioritizes the list.

6. The group may now find that some of the questions can be answered or solved at once by other members to the satisfaction of the presenter. Such questions are removed from the list.

7. Each remaining problem is dealt with in turn, based on the number of votes it received, at this or subsequent meetings. Some issues may call for a factual presentation by a consultant, some may be handled by a brief lecture, and some by distributing printed material. Other problems will require extensive analysis and discussion by the entire group or an *ad hoc* subcommittee.

The RISK Technique

Once a group has decided on a solution, that solution has to be evaluated carefully. Recall that earlier we talked about second-chance meetings where members can raise last-minute doubts, and we reported Hirokawa's research showing that one crucial function a group should perform is evaluation of negative consequences.[4] The **RISK technique** is designed specifically to allow an organization to assess how a proposed change or policy might negatively affect the individuals and groups involved.[5]

A special task force or selected committee of affected employees can use the RISK procedure to benefit not only themselves but the entire organization. Suppose the CEO of an organization has tentatively decided to restructure a particular department. The CEO could then ask members of that department to participate in a RISK session to identify possible problems (RISKS) that the proposed restructuring might cause. Minor concerns can then be dealt with immediately, and possible major problems can be identified and perhaps resolved before they occur. More important, if the proposed plan has a *fatal flaw,* the CEO may decide not to implement it. There are six basic steps in the RISK technique:

1. The leader presents the proposed solution or change in detail, and asks members to think of any risks, fears, or problems with the proposal.

2. Members may either brainstorm as a group to generate problems, or may first work individually using the brainwriting procedure described later.

3. The problems are posted in round-robin fashion on a chart or board. Once this has been done, members should study the list and add to it any additional concerns that occur to them. It is *absolutely imperative* that the leader be nonjudgmental. If members feel threatened they will not reveal their real concerns. Don't rush this process—often the risks felt to be most serious by some members will be voiced after a considerable lull.

4. After this initial meeting, all risks are compiled into a master list and circulated to all participants, who are asked to add anything else that occurs to them.

5. At a second meeting, additional risks felt by any member are added to the master list. Then members discuss each risk one by one. They decide whether each is serious or is one that can readily be resolved and removed from the list. Members should be encouraged to share their feelings—fears, doubts, concerns—during this interaction.

6. The remaining risks are processed into an agenda and handled the same way as items from the problem census. If the risks cannot be resolved, the proposed plan should be seriously reconsidered and either modified or discarded.

Generating Information and Ideas

Organizations and groups need information for a variety of purposes. The following two procedures are all-purpose techniques that enable group and organization members to provide information about a number of matters that can later be used in numerous ways.

Focus Groups

Long used in advertising and marketing research, **focus groups** enable an organization to identify problems, interests, concerns of employees and the general public, potential markets, and possible directions for innovation. Focus groups engage in unstructured or loosely structured discussion about a topic presented to them by a facilitator, who often simply announces the topic and lets group members respond freely in whatever way they choose. This free-association discussion is usually tape-recorded for later content analysis. Focus groups are often used to discover what customers look for in a product or how they may react to possible name or design changes. President Clinton and other politicians are well known for their use of focus groups to discover what voters think about certain issues. They also have provided information about employee morale, patients' feelings about how they were treated in a medical center, student reactions to the effectiveness of an advisement center, and so on.

The uses of focus groups can be quite varied. For example, one of us recently served on a focus group for a lawyer preparing to take a major product liability case to court. In front of two focus groups, he briefly presented both sides of the case by sharing the major evidence and arguments from both sides. After he finished, the focus groups went into separate rooms to talk about the evidence while videocameras recorded the discussion. The focus groups did not have to come to agreement; instead, members were encouraged to talk freely about what was and was not convincing about the evidence. Later, the lawyer and his staff analyzed the videotaped discussion to determine where their case was strong, where it needed bolstering, and what the major issues would be from a potential jury's perspective. They were then much better able to sharpen and focus their arguments during the actual trial, which the lawyer eventually won.

A **buzz group session** is used to organize a large meeting into many small *Buzz Groups* groups that work concurrently on the same question. This permits all participants in the large group to become actively involved in the discussion. Purposes may be to generate questions for a speaker or panel, to identify problems or issues, to compile a list of ideas or possible solutions, and generally to stimulate personal involvement and thinking by members of a large assembly. For instance, one of us participated with 500 educational leaders in Kentucky who met to work out techniques for promoting a Minimum Foundation Program for public education in that state. Organizers sought a favorable vote of taxpayers in a special election to support a state tax for local schools based on need. This meant higher taxes and a flow of money from wealthier to poorer districts. Several times the buzz group technique helped identify specific local problems, inexpensive advertising and promotional techniques, arguments for the program, and so forth. Although the conference was large, every attendee participated actively in discussion, and enthusiasm and involvement were remarkable. The college dean in our chapter-opening story used a modified version of a buzz group session to ensure participation by all members. The procedure is as follows:

1. The chair presents a target question—as concise, limited, and specific as possible—to the entire assembly, which may be seated in rows in an auditorium or at small tables. The question should be displayed on a blackboard or handout for all to see. The following are examples of such questions:

> What techniques could be used to publicize the Minimum Foundation Program to citizens of each county or city?
>
> What new projects might local unions undertake to help members with social problems?
>
> What are the arguments for (or against) a Materials Recovery Facility (MRF) for Springfield?

CONSIDER THIS

Now that you have some idea of the sorts of target questions a chair can pose to a group in a buzz group session, think of some questions that the dean in our opening story could have presented to the music department to get them started.

2. Divide the large group into work groups of six by seating them at small tables or, if in a large auditorium, by counting off by three in each row. Then have alternate rows turn to face each other as shown in Figure 14.1. Each group should be given a copy of the target question on an index card.

FIGURE 14.1   **Buzz group seating in an auditorium.**

3. Appoint a recorder-spokesperson for each group based on seating by saying something like: "The person sitting in the forward left-hand seat will be its recorder. The recorder should write down on the card *all* ideas presented, then have the group rank-order them." Assistants should then pass out blank cards.

4. Ask each group to record as many answers to the target question as it can think of in five minutes. Spend one minute evaluating the list to decide whether any items should be eliminated and in what order to present them. Thus, discussion occurs in groups of six members for six minutes. This procedure is sometimes called *Phillips' 66* because it was developed and popularized by J. Donald Phillips, former president of Hillsdale College in Michigan, who served as consultant for the Kentucky Conference.

5. When the five minutes are up, warn the groups and allow an extra minute if all seem involved. Then, ask each group to evaluate and rank-order its list.

6. At this point you may do any of several things, depending on group size and overall meeting plan:

   a. Collect the cards and edit them to eliminate duplications. Make a tally of the number of times each item was listed. Duplicate and distribute the total list to the entire group at a subsequent meeting or present it to some special group for processing.

   b. Ask each recorder to report orally from his or her seat, in round-robin fashion, one new item from the card as a secretary records all items on a chart or board in front of the room. Process the list as above or according to the problem census technique described earlier.

   c. Have each recorder present the complete list to the speaker or panel.

This versatile technique has many variations. For example, groups may have more than six minutes and may even follow a brief outline provided by the leader.

Enhancing Group Creativity

Sometimes, innovation is a group's or organization's main goal. In order for groups to maximize their creativity, they must be allowed to function in an environment in which judgment is eliminated and linear thinking is replaced by holistic, intuitive thinking. Later, at a more appropriate time, critical think-

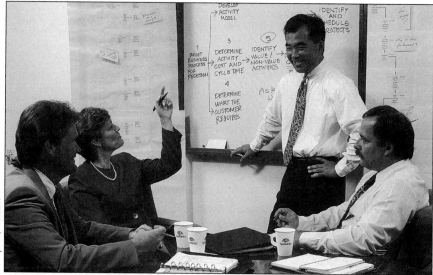

Brainstorming produces many possible solutions to a problem.

ing is reintroduced to evaluate the creative ideas generated by the group. The following techniques help a group enhance its creativity.

The **brainstorming** technique was developed by an advertising executive who recognized the need for imagination and a spirit of playfulness for successful advertising campaigns.[6] In order for the group's creativity to be released, members must feel safe in a nonthreatening environment that is free of judgment.[7] Because critical evaluation kills creativity, the main principle behind brainstorming is "no evaluation" during the brainstorming process. Evaluation of the ideas takes place *after* the group has listed as many ideas as possible. Brainstorming is widely used wherever solution multiplicity is needed. It has been used to solve thousands of problems in such diverse industries as banking, engineering and design, marketing, medicine, decorating, programming, education, government, and food science (to name a few). Brainstorming can be used in conjunction with other techniques; it is often used as the second step in the general Procedural Model of Problem Solving. The basic procedure has four steps and involves four major rules:

Brainstorming

1. **The group is given a problem to solve.**

   The problem can vary from quite specific (What shall we name our new soft drink?) to highly abstract (How can we improve living conditions in the residence halls?).

   Problems for brainstorming should have high solution multiplicity, and group members may engage in some preparation prior to brainstorming. In one recent case with which the authors are familiar, a team brainstorming names for a new pudding first ate some of the pudding, then talked about its taste and what it reminded them of in an unstructured focus group discussion. Then they brainstormed more than 500 possible names!

2. **Members of the group are encouraged to generate as many solutions as possible.**

Four general guidelines are followed during this period of brainstorming:

a. *No evaluation is permitted.* This means that no criticism of, laughing at, or other negative reactions to any idea are permitted. Trying to think imaginatively while being critical is like trying to accelerate with one foot on the gas pedal and one on the brake.

b. *Quantity is sought.* The more ideas listed, the better. If there is a lull in ideas the facilitator must encourage more by asking the group to think of ways to modify previously listed ideas, add a few more, or consider other characteristics of the problem.

c. *Innovation is encouraged.* Members are asked to provide unusual ideas, even those that seem wild and crazy at first mention. Remember, every new idea was unique at its inception.

d. *Hitchhiking is encouraged.* Members are asked to build on or modify ideas presented by other members of the group. A member with a hitchhiked idea snaps his or her fingers for immediate attention to get the idea charted at once.

3. **All ideas are charted so the entire group can see them.**

The facilitator writes the ideas on large sheets of plain paper, then posts the sheets along the walls so everyone can see the ideas. (Computer displays are now available for this.) Looking at the posted ideas often triggers new ideas. The sheets can later be used to write the report of the meeting.

4. **All ideas are evaluated at a different session.**

After the brainstorming technique has been used to generate a long list of possible solutions, critical thinking is used to evaluate each idea, possibly to modify or improve on some of them, or to select for the solution or policy only those ideas that meet essential criteria such as feasibility, effectiveness, and acceptability. Sometimes a different group evaluates the suggestions. If the same group does the evaluating, it should take a break, even if only a short one.

Staying nonjudgmental is not easy! Members have a natural tendency to comment about the suggestions: "That sounds great!" or "That's a goofy idea!" Several companies have come up with creative ways to remind members not to evaluate, either positively or negatively. For instance, in one company group members take squirt guns to meetings, and whoever criticizes an idea during a brainstorming session gets squirted. In other companies, offending members get nerf balls thrown at them.[8] Lighthearted these responses may be, but they make their point: criticism stifles creativity, and creativity is what brainstorming is all about.

Brainstorming variations.   There are several variations to brainstorming that adhere to the same "no evaluation" theme but are designed to overcome obstacles that sometimes impede creativity. These obstacles can include inhibition of participants, one or two dominant speakers, or fixating on a few ideas.[9] One such variation is **brainwriting.** Brainwriting capitalizes on the fact that group members are sometimes more productive when working alone but in the presence of others. During brainwriting, members are given a specified time limit—10 or 15 minutes—and asked to write down as many ideas as they can generate during that time. They are encouraged to write as fast as they can without stopping and, as with brainstorming, to hitchhike on their own ideas. When the time period has elapsed, members share their ideas, in round-robin fashion, and proceed just as with regular brainstorming.

Another variation, *electronic brainstorming (EBS),* capitalizes on the fact that anonymity can remove inhibitions. Members sit at computer terminals and type in their ideas. No member knows who contributed the ideas, which are displayed on a large screen visible to all. Gallupe et al. found that electronic brainstorming groups generated more ideas, and more high-quality ideas, than oral brainstorming groups, particularly in larger groups.[10] Members were less fearful of being evaluated, and were more satisfied with electronic brainstorming than oral brainstorming.

Finally, there are several brainstorming software programs that have been developed to help individuals define problems and enhance their creativity. Each program has different strengths and weaknesses, and most are easy to use. Computer magazines periodically compare and evaluate them so you can choose the best for your purposes.

Metaphoric and Analogic Thinking

Metaphoric and analogic techniques encourage group members to focus on similarities between dissimilar things, thereby hoping to gain fresh perspective on the problem or issue to be solved. For example, we have heard the story about the man who developed Velcro after noticing, when he returned from a hike in the woods, how burrs stuck to his socks and pants. This illustrates how an idea in one domain may help solve a problem or suggest an innovation in another domain.

An example of a technique that encourages metaphoric thinking is **synectics,** developed by William Gordon.[11] It encourages linking apparently unrelated elements so as to gain an unexpected insight into a problem. It starts by having the individual or group identify the essence of the problem, then identifying a metaphor or analogy that captures that essence. Group members are encouraged to search for metaphors that seem unrelated to the problem and to use a different sensory perception. For example, if the problem is visual, group members are encouraged to develop a hearing or touch metaphor. The point is to make the usual seem unusual, thereby opening mental doors for new insights to occur. The final step of the procedure is to force-fit the analogy to the problem under consideration so the way to a solution may be opened.

Harriman provides an example of how this generation of "distant analogies" works.[12] A food science manager had a problem with organic debris floating in flavored syrup, which detracted from consumer appeal. The only method he knew to remove the debris also wasted large amounts of the syrup. Needing a fresh perspective, he prevailed on a nonexpert colleague for help. Together they created several images (analogies or metaphors) of "debris" in nature: raking piles of leaves, roadside litter, logs floating down a stream, a canoe floating toward a dam, and so forth. The canoe image reminded the manager that tidal currents change the characteristics of water's surface tension, which in turn reminded him that he had once helped clean up a harbor by using this principle. These images and recollections suggested that he could change the surface characteristics of the syrup (i.e., make it less "sticky") to make the debris easier to remove without wasting syrup.

Discussing the following questions, adapted from ones suggested by Miller, can help groups or individuals use analogy and metaphor to arrive at innovative solutions:

1. **Look for a personal analogy.**
   Identify with the object and view the problem from the perspective of the object. For example, if you want to create a safer car, imagine that you are the car and ask, "How could I operate more safely?"

2. **Look for a direct analogy.**
   Look for a direct comparison of events from diverse fields. The earlier Velcro illustration compares something from nature with something human-made.

3. **Look for a symbolic analogy.**
   Imagine different ways of identifying the function or purpose of a solution by filling in the following: "How can we invent [something] that [performs a function] like an [analogy]?" For example, you might ask: "How can we invent [a safer car] that [stays on track] like a [train]?"

4. **Look for a fantasy analogy.**
   Use your imagination to ignore objective reality and discover what new ideas you can find. For instance, imagine that you can shrink yourself to take a trip through your veins and arteries to look for new ways of getting rid of cholesterol deposits.[13]

Metaphoric and analogic techniques may sound odd, but they work by forcing individuals out of their habitual thinking ruts so they can perceive a problem from a different perspective. They may feel uncomfortable to group members because they make what seems like a clear-cut problem ambiguous, uncertain, and strange. But that is precisely the point! If habitual ways of thinking could solve the problem, then innovation would not be needed. Analogy-based creativity techniques provide a potentially rich source of solutions.

CONSIDER THIS

What do you do when you need to come up with a creative solution for a problem? How could you modify your own personal techniques to help a group become more creative?

The **Program Evaluation and Review Technique (PERT)** is helpful during the final stage of problem solving—implementation. Sometimes a solution is highly complicated, involving a variety of materials, people whose work must be coordinated, and steps that must be completed in a specific sequence. Think of what is involved in constructing a large building on campus or making something like the space shuttle. PERT was developed to expedite such detailed operations so they can be done efficiently and so people can keep track of each step of a complex project. The procedure can be simplified to help even a student project group keep track of who will do what by when. Siebold summarized the main points of PERT:

Implementing Ideas with PERT

1. Describe the final step (how the solution should appear when fully operational).
2. Enumerate any events that must occur before the final goal is realized.
3. Order these steps chronologically.
4. If necessary, develop a flow diagram of the process and all the steps in it.
5. Generate a list of all the activities, resources, and materials needed to accomplish each step.
6. Estimate the time needed to accomplish each step, then add all the estimates to get a total time for implementing the plan.
7. Compare the total time estimate with deadlines or expectations and correct as necessary (by assigning more people or less time to a given step).
8. Determine which members will be responsible for each step.[14]

The preceding techniques are for improving group work during specific steps in problem solving. Those that follow use groups to improve the overall performance of organizations in general.

IMPROVING ORGANIZATION PROBLEM SOLVING

Everything we presented in the chapters devoted to problem solving and decision making can be applied to any group in an organization to improve its effectiveness. However, there are a number of specific small group procedures that can be used to tap the personal resources of members for organizational objectives. We have selected the Nominal Group Technique, quality circle, and self-managed team as the procedures you are most likely to use.

The Nominal Group Technique

As we said about brainwriting, often people working individually in the presence of others can generate more ideas for solving problems than the same number of people interacting. Delbecq and Van de Ven developed the **Nominal Group Technique** as an alternative that capitalizes on this while minimizing weaknesses that groups sometimes exhibit. *Nominal* means "in name only"; a nominal group alternates between verbal interaction and individual work in the presence of others.[15] It works better for major problems, like our music department group, and long-range planning than for routine meetings.[16] The Nominal Group Technique helps reduce secondary tension, prevents aggressive conflict, and eliminates the chance for some members to make speeches. In an organization, it allows members to express their concerns without fear of reprisals.[17] This was particularly important for the music department in our opening case, and their dean used this technique to help facilitate discussion. In one recent demonstration of its effectiveness, the Nominal Group Technique was used, in combination with a decision analysis technique, to help a complex organization with many independent divisions select a common integrated computer system.[18] Consensus was achieved and participants were satisfied with the process. On the other hand, the Nominal Group Technique is not by itself a complete problem-solving process, it may reduce cohesiveness, and it can produce less member satisfaction than fully interactive formats.[19]

Essentially, the Nominal Group members (six to nine) individually write their ideas, record them on a chart as a group and clarify them, then evaluate them by a ranking procedure until a decision has been reached. The procedure may vary, but it always involves a cycle of individual work followed by discussion. Following are the steps for the designated leader as outlined by Delbecq:

1. Members are seated at a table facing a chart or board. A large group can be divided into several small working groups, each with a leader.

2. Give the group a clear definition of the problem. At this point, there should be no mention of solutions and no interaction.

3. Allow the group 5 to 15 minutes to brainwrite. Each person is asked to write all ideas for solving the problem that he or she can think of. (The leader also generates a list of ideas.)

4. In a round-robin session that includes the leader, list each new idea on a chart for all members to see.

5. Take the group through the list item by item, for clarification and elaboration, but *not* evaluation. Anyone may ask another person for clarification of an idea on the list. Questions such as "What does number 6 mean?" or "Do you understand item 4?" are now in order for discussion, but no lobbying, criticism, or argument are allowed yet.

6. Give each person the same number of note cards (five or so) on which to write the items he or she most prefers. The person arranges the cards and ranks them according to preference, writing 5 on the top card to 1 on the bottom.

7. All cards are collected. The ratings are added for each item, and divided by the total number of people in the group. Most items will have a fractional rating. Items no one rated are removed from the list.

8. Engage in an evaluative discussion of those items with the highest ranks. This should be a full and free discussion with critical thinking, disagreement, and analysis encouraged.

9. If a decision is reached, fine. If not, vote again on the remaining items and discuss further. This process can be repeated several times as needed until a clear synthesis of a few ideas or support for one idea has emerged. The group then takes appropriate action on the results.

Quality Circles

The name **quality circle** has been given to small groups of employees who meet at regular intervals on company time to discuss work-related matters. We use the term *quality circle* as a generic term referring to any type of committee that meets regularly to improve something. In some companies, such groups are referred to as *work effectiveness teams, continuous improvement teams, cycle time reduction teams,* and other designations. Regardless of what they are called, the ultimate purpose of the quality circle is to increase productivity, improve the quality of what is produced, or enhance employee involvement.[20] Quality circle members share their opinions with management in an attempt to solve all sorts of job-related problems. Quality circle techniques were originally developed jointly by American and Japanese management experts working to help postwar Japan prepare to compete for world markets. The participative nature of quality circles meshed well with Japanese culture, although U.S. managers, who saw quality circles as encroaching on their authority, initially rejected them.

Many American companies have instituted quality circles to help them compete more successfully. Corporations using quality circles or some variation of them include Ford Motor Company, General Motors, Hewlett-Packard, Burlington Industries, Ethyl Corporation, Anchor Hocking, Control Data, Galion, Sheller-Globe, 3M, Dresser Industries, Firestone, W. R. Grace, Sony, Honda, Weyerhauser, Northrup, SmithKline Beecham, American Airlines, Dow Chemical, Procter & Gamble, Xerox, and Kraft Foods.[21] Nonprofit organizations like the Red Cross and Boy Scouts and a number of school systems also have quality circles. Workers participating in these groups perceive improvements in their communication with superiors, subordinates, and peers, as well as positive effects on their power and influence.[22]

Employees in a quality circle meet with a team leader, usually a supervisor, on company time to discuss production problems, or to react to problems presented to them by management. Usually they meet for an hour a week, but time varies from company to company. Quality circles may work on any problem, from how a restaurant can serve customers more quickly to how a country can develop its exports. All ideas agreed upon are submitted to management, which must react to every suggestion by adopting it; modifying, and then adopting it; investigating it further; or rejecting it with an explanation why. Many companies combine the quality circle with employee bonus systems, which reward either individuals or groups for profit-making or money-saving ideas. Often, the quality circles are one part of a *total quality management* or *continuous improvement program* instituted throughout a company. You will note that any of the techniques discussed thus far— standard decision-making and problem-solving methods, the RISK technique, brainstorming, the Nominal Group Technique, etc.—can be used as needed by the quality circle to enhance its effectiveness.

Although quality circles can be quite effective, merely instituting them in a company will not guarantee success. Sometimes unions see them as a ploy to increase production without improving benefits (perhaps a valid criticism in some cases), and occasionally managers implement quality circle programs without having enough foresight into how the programs will work within that company's culture. Potential problems include middle managers who feel threatened and resist the ideas presented, failure to implement ideas, groups becoming discouraged by management's failure to respond, and management's failure to reward groups financially for their contributions.[23] For quality circles to work, management must be strongly committed to the quality circle program, the program must be part of a long-range plan for organizational development, and participants must be adequately trained in small group dynamics and participative problem solving.[24] Employees must know that their ideas for increasing efficiency will not ultimately cost them jobs or earnings. They must know that their ideas will be respected and dealt with and that they will share in the tangible benefits, such as cost savings, their ideas bring. The employees must have a commitment to the company, but must also be assured of the company's commitment to them. If they are used as a trick to squeeze every ounce of work possible out of employees without rewarding them, quality circles won't work.

Self-Managed Work Groups   **Self-managed work groups,** also called *autonomous work groups,* are teams of peers who determine their own work schedules and procedures within prescribed limits. Sometimes the groups have considerable freedom, even up to the point of hiring and firing team members. Self-managed work groups eliminate many traditional supervisory positions and reduce the number of middle managers. The team performs such management functions as deciding which member will perform which job, what supplies to order, and what the work schedule will be. Members are cross-trained so that each member can perform several or all of the jobs needed by the team. For example, the custom-order team for one office furniture manufacturer originally included a salesperson skilled at pricing, a furniture designer, a craftsperson who could create specialized parts, and three skilled assemblers. Members cross-trained each other so now the whole team goes to a prospective client's office to listen and offer suggestions. This team's success has contributed significantly to the company's profits.[25] The fact that members of a self-managed work group are cross-trained provides the team tremendous flexibility to deal with absent workers. Members are less likely to become bored or frustrated, and they are more likely to help each other out than in traditional assembly line organizations. Self-managed work teams are used in such companies as Volvo, Saturn, Sherwin-Williams, and Procter & Gamble. As you may surmise, before a self-managed work program can be installed, workers and managers must undergo extensive training in group attitudes, techniques, and procedures.

A self-managed work group usually elects its own leader, who is *not* a supervisor, but a coordinator with legitimate authority from the group. The company's management establishes the work group's area of freedom and assigns what must be produced, but the work group has considerable latitude to decide everything else. Some self-managed work groups establish their own annual budgets, prepare reports, develop specifications for jobs, and solve technical problems that arise in the course of completing jobs. They may even bid for new company business.

Many of the same concerns about quality circles hold for self-managed work teams. Middle managers and unions often feel threatened by them. However, companies using this technique report a 20 to 40 percent increase in production over traditional work organizations.[26] The self-managed work teams require less supervision time, produce higher-quality products, have less absenteeism, and generally have higher morale and job satisfaction than employees under traditional line supervision.

USING TECHNOLOGY TO HELP A GROUP

In the last decade, technological hardware and software we could recently only dream about are now affordable and available to help groups. These range from simple systems to highly complex ones. For instance, conference calls use existing telephones and phone lines. Electronic mail (e-mail) lets group members use their personal computers to communicate with each other asynchronously, whenever it is convenient for the individual member.[27] Some systems permit members to coordinate their calendars electronically and more easily find convenient times for meetings. Group writing systems permit multiauthored document writing, in which members create, analyze, edit, and revise a single document simultaneously.[28] We will next discuss two key ways technology can help groups: for teleconferences and for group decision support.

Teleconferences are electronically mediated meetings that allow members of a group to meet, even though they may be far apart from each other geographically. This helps companies save travel time and money, because face-to-face meetings can be expensive if members have to travel long distances to attend. Teleconferences can take several forms, including *videoconferences,* which let members see and hear each other; *audioconferences,* which

Teleconferences

let members hear but not see each other; and *computer conferences,* where members send messages to one another that are displayed on computer monitors.

Videoconferences are expensive for most companies, but audioconferences, including telephone conference calls, are routine. Computer conferences are becoming increasingly sophisticated and accessible; we expect the frequency of teleconferencing to increase exponentially in the near future. A number of companies already are developing their own specialized computer software for employees linked to a network to work simultaneously on a variety of tasks. Recent studies have shown that decisions made by computerized conference groups were just as good as ones made by face-to-face groups, but computer groups were less likely to reach agreement.[29] The *type* of computerized technique appears to make a difference. Murrell found that using the window method, which permits each participant to see the responses of all other participants at once, produced higher decision quality than a message system requiring participants to complete a message before they interact.[30] Some studies have found that computer conferences can provide some advantages over face-to-face meetings. Dubrovsky et al. discovered that inequalities due to status and expertise were minimized with electronic mail conferences.[31] Hiltz et al. suggest that computer programs permitting anonymity may help create greater and more equal participation.[32] On the other hand, computer-mediated group decision making leads to more delays, more outspoken advocacy, and more extreme or risky decisions, along with more equal participation, than face-to-face meetings.[33]

From the more than 100 studies of teleconferencing, we can develop practical guidelines for making electronic meetings productive.[34] For audioconferencing, speaker phone equipment is readily available, is relatively inexpensive, and requires no special studios. It can be set up in any office. However, audio conferences lack "social presence."[35] The sense of sharing, belonging, and recognition of each other as individuals can be low. Many key nonverbal cues are absent, and electronic equipment can fail at the most inopportune times. On the other hand, the potential for *greater* equality of opportunity to participate exists in the control equipment used by conference leaders.

For teleconferencing to work best, Johansen, Vallee, and Spangler recommend that the participants hold an extended face-to-face conference beforehand to form a sense of "groupness."[36] A post-teleconference meeting can be useful as well. It seems that for complex tasks, face-to-face meetings are still preferable, with teleconferences well suited to routine meetings.

Several factors can improve routine teleconferences. A trained moderator is essential, all participants should be aware of the rules and guidelines for speaking, and all speakers should abide by specified time limits.[37] Electronic meetings are not qualitatively different from face-to-face ones, but additional coordination efforts are required because less information (e.g., nonverbal cues) is exchanged.

At present, teleconferences are usually recommended for routine meetings and information sharing. For more complex tasks in which the likelihood of disagreements increase, face-to-face meetings are still preferable. As travel costs skyrocket and technological limitations decrease, the need for teleconferences to replace both routine and significant meetings will increase. Several up-and-coming computer-related innovations promise to increase the utility and effectiveness of mediated meetings, even those involving more complex tasks.

Group Decision Support Systems (GDSS) are computer-based hardware and software systems designed to improve the quality and speed of group problem solving, especially group idea generation, information organization, evaluation of options, and decision making.[38] They are sometimes called *groupware, computer-supported cooperative work* (CSCW), *electronic meeting systems* (EMS)[39] or *group support systems* (GSS). The development of such systems has been encouraged by the proliferation of personal computers and interconnected computer systems. Different GDSS systems address different decision-making processes. For example, some focus on the idea generation step of brainstorming. Others attempt to improve the entire decision-making process by providing the structure that groups often need but don't otherwise receive. GDSS are usually used in conjunction with face-to-face meetings and may require specialized training of the meeting leader and the members.

Group Decision Support Systems

GroupSystems and Software Assisted Meeting Management (SAMM) are two of the more commonly known support systems. They include modules to help groups in every area of problem solving, such as helping group management, brainstorming, analysis, policy formation, evaluation and voting, exchanging comments on topics, and so forth. Many find them most helpful during the evaluation of solutions because their procedures are designed to help members react honestly to each other's suggestions and ideas. In 1992 there were over 400 such software programs and they change daily as their developers learn more about their effectiveness.[40]

GDSS systems are fairly new, so you may not have seen one in operation. The following example should help you picture what some sophisticated systems can do. We recently attended a meeting of a local school board that had been having trouble achieving closure on agenda items at its regular meetings. Members found themselves wandering off track, going in a completely different direction from that provided in the agenda. They accepted the offer made by university faculty members to help them by using GDSS technology. The school board members met in a room specially designed to accommodate GDSS meetings. The room had 12 individual computers linked to each other. The computers were configured in a U shape, with a large overhead projection system, visible to all, at the open end of the U. One faculty member served as a group facilitator by organizing the discussion of the two agenda items the school board president most wanted to complete: deciding what communication issues to emphasize and what promotional strategies to use in the upcoming school bond levy. He stood under the projection screen at the open end of the U. The other faculty member served as the chauffeur, running the computer system for the meeting. He, too, was visible behind the operating desk at the top right of the U. Both the facilitator and chauffeur had specialized training in how to use the system.

At their individual computer stations, group members brainstormed about their first item, the issues to be addressed in the campaign. Each member worked alone; then, when all were ready, they sent their suggestions to the central computer with a keystroke. The master list then appeared on the overhead. No one knew who had made which suggestion. The facilitator and chauffeur clarified vague items and combined like items. Group members were then given the chance to make comments, again anonymously, and send them to the screen. With the help of the facilitator, face-to-face discussion occurred concerning several items. Finally, members ranked all the items and sent them to the system, which automatically tallied the rankings and provided an overall ranking and rating of each item. The rankings and ratings were displayed in numerical and bar graph form, which provided visual reinforcement for the members' opinions. Face-to-face discussion followed, with members easily coming to consensus (or realizing that they already had achieved consensus). They addressed the second issue in the same way.

Reaction of the members was highly positive. The school board president noted that the visual display of ratings and rankings emphasized to some of the long-winded members that consensus had already been achieved, so further discussion was not needed. Both the facilitator and chauffeur reminded the school board that the system was designed to *support,* not replace, effective group discussion. GDSS helps groups do what they *should* do, but often don't do, without computer support: analyze carefully, evaluate thoroughly, and give everyone a chance to participate. They also make record-keeping easy because the computer provides an automatic history of all the items that were listed, the comments made about each, and the rankings and ratings of each.

Recent research suggests that GDSS is effective. Olaniran reported that computer-mediated groups produce more ideas than face-to-face groups.[41] However, they take a longer time to come to consensus. Decision quality seemed to be highest when groups used a combination of computer mediated and face-to-face discussion, as did the school board we just described. Poole and his associates, who have studied GDSS extensively, noted several benefits.[42] Using computer support systems seems to focus members' attention on decision-making procedures and improves organization of the decision-making process. It also sparks insight into the decision process, although it does take time for members to learn the system and orient themselves to it. Jessup and Valacich, in their extensive review of GDSS research, concluded that computer-supported decision making is as good or better than traditional decision making, that members of large groups, especially, are more satisfied because participation can be equalized, that time spent in group meetings can actually be reduced with GDSS, and that such systems help members stay on task.[43]

Whether GDSS improves decision making or not depends on a variety of factors. One of the most important of these is the level of GDSS support, which refers to how sophisticated a system is and how much intervention into the group's natural decision-making process GDSS provides. Benbasat and Lim found that more sophisticated level 2 support produced better decisions and higher satisfaction than level 1 support.[44] This is consistent with the findings of Sambamurthy et al., who concluded that simpler is not always better.[45] The particular mediated system used must be well matched to the task, according to Farmer and Hyatt.[46] For example, some complex tasks require information to be processed via many channels, including audio, video, and screen-sharing. However, for other tasks, having an audio channel alone might be sufficient.

Familiarity with the system is another factor influencing GDSS effectiveness. Hollingshead et al. observed that computer group members' poor initial performance seemed to be related to their unfamiliarity with using computer support, but that most of the differences disappear over time.[47] They also noted that face-to-face groups are likely to outperform computer-mediated groups on intellective tasks, where there is a correct answer, and negotiation tasks, where members must reconcile their competing interests. These researchers warn managers planning to institute computer-mediated work groups that there may be initial declines in performance and dissatisfaction until members become comfortable with the technology. GDSS effectiveness is also a function of how tightly it might structure group interaction and some managers themselves may not use these procedures because they do not want their employees to have full access to the information and benefits of computer technology.[48]

The presence of a facilitator also affects GDSS performance. Poole et al. were surprised by their findings that, although groups using GDSS exhibited more organized decision processes, they did not demonstrate improved critical thinking or more thorough evaluation of options.[49] These authors noted that the groups they studied had no facilitator support, and they postulate that this, along with the level of GDSS support as discussed earlier, may have been a key factor hampering GDSS effectiveness. Ideally, a facilitator should have a strong conceptual understanding of the technology and its capabilities, be able to make members comfortable with the technology and help them understand it, select the right technological system for the group, and have it prepared properly.[50] This was a factor in the success of the school board meeting we described earlier.

Scott et al. caution that facilitators need to understand the difference between *faithful* use of GDSS procedures—using them as they were intended—and *ironic* use of GDSS—using GDSS contrary to its purpose or spirit. Scott et al. note that it can be very hard to predict how any GDSS will *actually* be utilized because GDSS implementation is a dynamic adaptation between the user and the GDSS technology.[51] Generally speaking, GDSS is designed to promote anonymity, equalize participation, and balance member influence. But some groups used GDSS in a way that was not faithful to these intentions.

Scott et al. found that GDSS users exhibited a strong need to figure out the sources of messages. Over time, members could figure out the styles of different users. Sometimes users follow the rules of the program at the expense of good decision making. For instance, they change their message style frequently without concern for message effectiveness. Equal influence was also hard to achieve even with GDSS use. Users agree with their own comments, use forms of emphasis, and repeat themselves to assert their opinions. Some users played with the rankings of alternatives in an attempt to manipulate the outcome of votes. Users often felt powerless because they discovered that others did not read their messages. While equal participation is easier to facilitate with GDSS use, as compared to anonymity and equal influence, it may encourage social loafing. Finally, users also indicated little commitment to the group's decision. The GDSS benefits declined over time.

Group Decision Support Systems are much more common now than they were even a couple of years ago. We expect more and more organizations to invest in this technology in the future. Despite widespread research on its use in organizations, few generalizations can be made about the influence of GDSS on group problem solving because these programs are changing daily. GDSS seem to be beneficial for certain kinds of tasks, such as generation and decision making.[52] Face-to-face groups remain better for negotiation and complex, cognitive tasks. As we mentioned above, an important factor in GDSS effectiveness seems to be user familiarity and facilitator knowledge and skill in GDSS use. Groups utilizing GDSS appear to make better decisions, generate more alternatives to problems, and to have more even group member participation. However, these groups can take longer to reach decisions, experience less consensus, and are less satisfied than their face-to-face counterparts.[53]

To summarize, no matter how much these systems grow, we remind you that they are designed to *support,* not *replace,* traditional group decision-making and discussion processes. The most we can say is that they are generally good for groups, although not useful in every circumstance.[54] As long as GDSS procedures are used consistently with their intentions, they can be very effective, but GDSS does not eliminate the need for group members who understand group processes, nor is their use an excuse to slack off on using good communication skills. In fact, GDSS should help focus members' attention on those processes. Knowledgeable individuals who know how to operate the computer support systems as they are intended and who understand groups will always be needed.

CONSIDER THIS

You have been asked to help a group use a new GDSS program for problem solving. Given your understanding of the advantages and disadvantages of GDSS, create a list of guidelines you would use if you were to act as facilitator for this group.

SUMMARY

1. Leaders of committees created by organizations governed by *Robert's Rules of Order* should know and follow Robert's rules for committees, which are simpler and less formal than parliamentary rules.

2. Two techniques are useful to help members identify problems. The problem census uses a polling-posting method to help a group build an agenda for future problem solving, and the RISK technique spots unforeseen negative reactions to a proposed change of policy or procedure.

3. To generate information, focus groups, unstructured group meetings that can be recorded and content-analyzed, provide a wealth of information for numerous applications. Buzz groups allow every member of a large group to participate.

4. Creativity can be enhanced by brainstorming, including its written and electronic variants, which defers judgment, and synectics, which seeks unusual analogies to generate a sudden insight into a problem.

5. PERT can be used to work out how to implement a complex solution by breaking it down into sequential, organized steps.

6. Organizations can be enhanced through the Nominal Group Technique, which helps groups reach solutions with a minimum of secondary tension; quality circles, which meet to improve the quality and quantity of products and the work climate; and self-managed work groups of cross-trained members who manage the details of their own work.

7. Various technologies can help groups. Members who cannot meet face-to-face may use teleconferences. Group Decision Support Systems, which are computer-based hardware and software systems, support traditional group decision making in a number of ways.

EXERCISES

1. Conduct a problem census focusing on the question, "What topics should our class select for discussion that would be intrinsically interesting and involve the whole class?" Use the rank-ordered topics in future exercises.

2. Select a topic from your problem census and use the Nominal Group Technique to discuss the problem. Your instructor will coordinate

and time the exercise, but students should lead each of the groups.

3. Prepare and follow a PERT plan for a major group project. Each member must sign acceptance of the PERT plan.

4. As a whole class or in subgroups of 6 to 12 each, participate in a formal brainstorming session considering questions such as, "What

use might Goodwill Industries make of the thousands of used belts donated in collection boxes?"

5. With the instructor's blessing, form a quality circle of volunteers to meet every two weeks to discuss problems in the class and what might be done to solve them, and other ways the class could be made more interesting. The quality circle should give consensus recommendations to the instructor. The instructor should make some reaction to each suggestion at the next class meeting by either incorporating it or explaining why the suggestion was declined.

BIBLIOGRAPHY

Baird, John E., Jr. *Quality Circles: Leader's Manual.* Prospect Heights, IL: Waveland Press, 1982.

Jessup, Leonard M., and Joseph S. Valacich, eds. *Group Support Systems: New Perspectives.* New York: Macmillan, 1993.

Johnson, Craig E., and Michael Z. Hackman. *Creative Communication: Principles and Applications.* Prospect Heights, IL: Waveland Press, 1995, especially sections 3, 4, and 5.

Krueger, Richard A. *Focus Groups: A Practical Guide for Applied Research.* Newbury Park, CA: Sage Publications, 1988.

McGrath, Joseph E., and Andrea Hollingshead. *Groups Interacting with Technology.* Thousand Oaks, CA: Sage Publications, 1994.

Robert, Henry M. *Robert's Rules of Order, Newly Revised.* Glenview, IL: Scott, Foresman and Company, 1990.

Siebold, David R. "Making Meetings More Successful: Plans, Formats, and Procedures for Group Problem Solving." In *Small Group Communication: A Reader.* 6th ed. Robert S. Cathcart and Larry A. Samovar, eds. Dubuque, IA: Wm. C. Brown Publishers, 1992, 178–91.

NOTES

1. M. H. Butcher, ed., *Fundamentals of Parliamentary Law and Procedure,* 2d ed. (Dubuque, IA: Kendall/Hunt, 1992).

2. Henry M. Robert, *Robert's Rules of Order, Newly Revised* (Glenview, IL: Scott, Foresman, 1990): 471–521.

3. Al Weitzel and Patricia Geist, "Parliamentary Procedure in a Community Group: Communication and Vigilant Decision Making," *Communication Monographs* 65 (September 1998): 244–59.

4. Randy Y. Hirokawa, "Discussion Procedures and Decision-Making Performance: A Test of a Functional Perspective," *Human Communication Research* 12 (1985): 203–24.

5. Norman R. F. Maier, *Problem-Solving Discussions and Conferences: Leadership Methods and Skills* (New York: McGraw-Hill, 1963): 171–77.

6. Alex Osborn, *Applied Imagination,* rev. ed. (New York: Charles Scribner's Sons, 1975).

7. Paul Kirvan, "Brainstorming: It Is More than You Think," *Communication News* 28 (1991): 39–40.

8. Michael Schrage, "Meetings Don't Have to Be Dull," *The Wall Street Journal* (April 29, 1996): A22.

9. Graham Hitchings and Sara Cox, "Generating Ideas Using Randomized Search Methods: A Method of Managed Convergence," *Management Decision* 30 (1992): 58.

10. R. Brent Gallupe, Alan R. Dennis, William H. Cooper, Joseph S. Valacich, Lane M. Bastianutti, and Jay F. Nunamaker, Jr., "Electronic Brainstorming and Group Size," *Academy of Management Journal* 35 (June 1992): 350–70. See also Joseph S. Valacich, Alan R. Dennis, and T. Connolly, "Idea Generation in Computer-Based Groups: A New Ending to an Old Story," *Organizational Behavior and Human Decision Processes* 57 (1994): 448–68.

11. Russell L. Ackoff and Elsa Vergara, "Creativity in Problem Solving and Planning," in *Handbook for Creative and Innovative Managers,* ed. Robert L. Kuhn (New York: McGraw-Hill, 1988): 77–90.

12. Richard A. Harriman, "Techniques for Fostering Innovation," in *Handbook for Creative and Innovative Managers,* 136–37.

13. William C. Miller, "Techniques for Stimulating New Ideas: A Matter of Fluency," in *Handbook for Creative and Innovative Managers,* 124.

14. David R. Siebold, "Making Meetings More Successful: Plans, Formats, and Procedures for Group Problem Solving," in *Small Group Communication: A Reader,* 6th ed., eds. Robert S. Cathcart and Larry A. Samovar (Dubuque, IA: Wm. C. Brown, 1992): 187.

15. Andre L. Delbecq, Andrew H. Van de Ven, and David H. Gustafson, *Group Techniques for Program Planning: A Guide to Nominal Group and Delphi Processes* (Glenview, IL: Scott, Foresman, 1975): 7–16.

16. Ibid., 3–4.

17. Alan Honeycutt and Bill Richards, "Nominal Group Process in Organizational Development Work," *Leadership & Organization Development Journal* 12 (October 1991): 24–28.

18. James B. Thomas, Reuben R. McDaniel, Jr., and Michael J. Dooris, "Strategic Issue Analysis: NGT + Decision Analysis for Resolving Strategic Issues," *Journal of Applied Behavioral Science* 25 (May 1989): 189–201.

19. Andre L. Delbecq, "Techniques for Achieving Innovative Changes in Programming" (Presentation at the Midwest Regional Conference of the Family Service Association of America (Omaha, NE: April 20, 1971).

20. June P. Elvins, "Communication in Quality Circles: Members' Perceptions of Their Participation and Its Effects on Related Organizational Communication Variables," *Group & Organization Studies* 10 (1985): 479–507.

21. William V. Ruch, *Corporate Communications* (Westport, CN: Quorum Books, 1984): 205–19.

22. Elvins, "Communication in Quality Circles," 479–507.

23. E. Lawler and S. Mohrman, "Quality Circles after the Fad," *Harvard Business Review* (1985): 65–71.

24. Gerald M. Goldhaber, *Organizational Communication,* 4th ed. (Dubuque, IA: Wm. C. Brown, 1986): 283.

25. Thomas Owen, "Self-Managing Work Team," *Small Business Reports* (February 1991): 53–65.

26. Henry P. Sims, Jr. and James W. Dean, Jr., "Beyond Quality Circles: Self-Managing Teams," *Personnel Journal* (1985): 25–32.

27. Sue Barnes and Leonore M. Greller, "Computer-Mediated Communication in the Organization," *Communication Education* 43 (April 1994): 129–42.

28. Annette C. Easton, Nancy S. Eickelmann, and Marie E. Flatley, "Effects of an Electronic Meeting System Group Writing Tool on the Quality of Written Documents," *Journal of Business Communication* 31, no. 1 (1994): 27–40.

29. Starr Roxanne Hiltz, Kenneth Johnson, and Murray Turoff, "Experiments in Group Decision Making: Communication Process and Outcome in Face-to-Face versus Computerized Conferences," *Human Communication Research* 13 (1986): 225–52.

30. Sharon L. Murrell, "The Impact of Communicating through Computers" (Unpublished doctoral dissertation, State University of New York at Stony Brook, 1983).

31. Vitaly J. Dubrovsky, Sara Kiesler, and Beheruz N. Sethna, "The Equalization Phenomenon: Status Effects in Computer-Mediated and Face-to-Face Decision-Making Groups," *Human Computer Interaction* 6 (1991): 119–46.

32. Starr Roxanne Hiltz, Murray Turoff, and Kenneth Johnson, "Experiments in Group Decision Making, 3: Disinhibition, Deindividuation, and Group Process in Pen Name and Real Name Computer

Conferences," *Decision Support Systems* 5 (June 1989): 217–32.

33. Sara Keisler and Lee Sproull, "Group Decision Making and Communication Technology," *Organizational Behavior and Human Decision Processes* 52 (June 1992): 96–123.

34. Robert Johansen, J. Vallee, and K. Spangler, *Electronic Meetings: Technical Alternatives and Social Choices* (Reading, MA: Addison-Wesley, 1979): 2.

35. John A. Short, E. Williams, and B. Christie, *The Social Psychology of Telecommunications* (London: John Wiley and Sons, 1976).

36. Johansen, Vallee, and Spangler, *Electronic Meetings,* 113–15.

37. Larry L. Barker, Kathy J. Wahlers, Kittie W. Watson, and Robert J. Kibler, *Groups in Process: An Introduction to Small Group Communication,* 3d ed. (Englewood Cliffs, NJ: Prentice-Hall, 1987): 208.

38. Marshall S. Poole, Michael Holmes, and Gerardine DeSanctis, "Conflict Management in a Computer-Supported Meeting Environment," *Management Science 37* (August 1991): 926–53; Leonard M. Jessup, Terry Connolly, and David A. Tansik, "Toward a Theory of Automated Group Work: The Deindividuation Effects of Anonymity," *Small Group Research* 21 (August 1990): 333–48; Hiltz, Turoff, and Johnson, "Experiments in Group Decision Making."

39. Noshir S. Contractor and David R. Siebold, "Theoretical Frameworks for the Study of Structuring Processes in Group Decision Support Systems: Adaptive Structuration Theory and Self-Organizing Systems Theory," *Human Communication Research* 19 (June 1993): 528–63.

40. Joseph E. McGrath and Andrea B. Hollingshead, *Groups Interacting with Technology* (Thousand Oaks, CA: Sage, 1994).

41. Bolanle A. Olaniran, "Group Performance in Computer-Mediated and Face-to-Face Communication Media," *Management Communication Quarterly* 7 (February 1994): 256–81.

42. Marshal Scott Poole and Michael E. Holmes, "Decision Development in Computer-Assisted Group Decision Making," *Human Communication Research* 22 (September 1995): 90–127; Marshall Scott Poole, Michael Holmes, Richard Watson, and Gerardine DeSanctis, "Group Decision Support Systems and Group Communication: A Comparison of Decision Making in Computer-Supported and Nonsupported Groups," *Communication Research* 20 (April 1993): 176–213.

43. Leonard M. Jessup and Joseph S. Valacich, eds., *Group Support Systems: New Perspectives* (New York: Macmillan, 1993).

44. Izak Benbasat and Lai-Huat Lim, "The Effects of Group, Task, Context, and Technology Variables on the Usefulness of Group Support Systems: A Meta-Analysis of Experimental Studies," *Small Group Research* 24 (November 1993): 430–62.

45. V. Sambamurthy, Marshall Scott Poole, and Janet Kelly, "The Effects of Variations in GDSS Capabilities on Decision-Making Processes in Groups," *Small Group Research* 24 (November 1993): 523–46.

46. Steven M. Farmer and Charles W. Hyatt, "The Effects of Task Language Demands and Task Complexity on Computer-Mediated Work Groups," *Small Group Research* 25 (August 1994): 331–66.

47. Andrea B. Hollingshead, Joseph E. McGrath, and Kathleen M. O'Connor, "Group Task Performance and Communication Technology: A Longitudinal Study of Computer-Mediated versus Face-to-Face Work Groups," *Small Group Research* 24 (August 1993): 307–33.

48. S. Opper and H. Fresko-Weiss, *Technology for Teams: Enhancing Productivity in Networked Organizations* (New York: Van Nostrand Reinhold, 1992).

49. Poole, Holmes, Watson, and DeSanctis, "Group Decision Support Systems and Group Communication."

50. Victoria K. Clawson, Robert P. Bostrom, and Rob Anson, "The Role of the Facilitator in Computer-Supported Meetings," *Small Group Research* 24 (November 1993): 547–65.

51. Craig R. Scott, Laura Quinn, C. Erik Timmerman, and Diana M. G. Barrett, "Ironic Uses of Group Communication Technology: Evidence from Meeting Transcripts and Interviews with Group Decision Support System Users,"

Communication Quarterly 46 (Summer 1998): 353–74.

52. Hollingshead, McGrath, and O'Connor, "Group Task Performance and Communication Technology."

53. Benbasat and Lim, "The Effects of Group, Task, Context, and Technology Variables."

54. Poppy McLeod, "New Communication Technologies for Group Decision Making: Toward an Integrative Framework," in *Communication and Group Decision Making,* 2d ed., eds. Randy Y. Hirokawa and Marshall Scott Poole (Thousand Oaks, CA: Sage, 1996): 426–61.

Observing Group Discussions

15

Central Message

Observers and consultants who understand group communication processes can use a variety of techniques and instruments to help groups evaluate and improve their performance.

Study Objectives

As a result of studying Chapter 15 you should be able to:
1. Explain the benefits of having a consultant observe and work with a group.
2. Prepare an observation guide appropriate for observing a small group.
3. Report observations to groups in ways that are helpful to the group members.
4. Devise and use instruments to assess verbal participation, obtain members' reactions to a meeting, and evaluate both individual members and groups.

Key Terms

Consultant
Content analysis
Critique
Postmeeting
 reaction forms
 (PMRs)

Rating scales
Verbal interaction
 analysis

Sam, the CEO of a small plant that manufactured specialized circuit boards, decided to hire a consultant to help his executive committee overcome several problems. The committee met weekly and consisted of the department managers: Roger, manufacturing; Elgin, quality assurance; Angela, sales and marketing; and Frank, the comptroller. The team had made several costly mistakes in the past several months, which Sam thought were caused by misunderstandings between members, on top of the pressures caused by an expanding business. In one instance, Angela had promised an early delivery to a customer based on what she thought Roger had said, but the circuit boards weren't ready and the company lost the customer. Things didn't seem to be improving, and Sam didn't know whether the problems were due to his leadership style, the competence of the members, ineffective communication at the weekly meetings, or something else. He needed an objective, informed opinion.

Enter Susanna, organizational trainer and consultant who specialized in team performance and teambuilding. First, she gathered all the information she could about the team by interviewing Sam and reading the group's memos and minutes. This didn't take her long because committee minutes were kept sporadically. She observed three meetings, which highlighted to her what some of the problems might be, and took extensive notes so she could provide specific examples to the members. As a last step, she interviewed each of the group members to gain their perspectives on the meetings and their own performance.

Susanna prepared her feedback for the group. She had a long list of things she could mention, but she didn't want to overwhelm or demoralize the team. She selected the few she thought were most problematic, beginning with "housekeeping." The team did not operate with an agenda, nor was anyone regularly assigned to take notes. She noted that the team met in an employee break room that had snacks handy, but because other employees wandered in and out, the room was noisy and distracting. She observed that at each meeting, nearly every member was called away at least once by a secretary or subordinate to answer a question or take a phone call. In her report, Susanna recommended that Sam provide members with an agenda at least a day or two before the meeting, and that if members didn't want to rotate the job of taking minutes, Sam's secretary could attend the meetings specifically for that function. She suggested that members find another place to meet—even if that had to be away from the plant, at a private meetingroom in a restaurant over breakfast, for example. She also recommended that members not allow their secretaries or subordinates to interrupt the meeting, except for a dire emergency.

The next recommendations concerned the process of discussion itself. Susanna praised the group for their obvious dedication to the company and their creativity in solving problems. She noted, however, that because there had been several costly misunderstandings, members exhibited signs of distress and distrust, which she thought they could overcome. Susanna gave the group several examples of how their discussion was disorganized, with members jumping from one topic to another without concluding a topic. At any given moment, there could be three different topics under discussion, and it was easy to mishear or misunderstand information. She affirmed that their problems were solvable and gave them several suggestions for how the group could monitor its own discussion process. She spoke privately with Sam about his somewhat lax leadership style and recommended that he keep firmer control of the meetings.

Finally, Susanna designed a training program for the group, to take place during a weekend retreat. The program succeeded in improving the members' basic communication skills and featured several teambuilding activities that helped the group recover some of the trust their mistakes had recently eroded.

As a member of a group, it's important for you to observe the group communication process while you participate in it. However, you cannot both observe and participate at the same instant. Rather, your attention shifts back and forth between observing and participating, which means that you may miss something. Sometimes you see clearly what your group needs and can supply it (the completer function), but sometimes you can't tell what's missing, what's wrong, or what's needed—or even that there is anything wrong at all! The most skillful among us can become so engrossed in discussing an issue we care about that we lose the observer perspective. That was Sam's situation.

That's when a **consultant,** an observer who does *not* participate in the group's discussion, can be of real assistance in identifying what is going wrong and helping the group correct its problems. Evaluation of group processes has been shown to be beneficial to both small groups and the organizations that created them.[1] Feedback from a consultant can help an entire group, including the discussion leader.

We have two main purposes in this chapter: first, we explain the functions consultants can perform and how they perform them; second, we present examples of several types of instruments that both participant-observers (group members) and consultants can use to gather information and feed it back into the group for improvement of future discussion. Included among these instruments are interaction analysis diagrams, member and observer rating scales, postmeeting reaction questionnaires, and content analysis schemes.

ROLES OF OBSERVERS AND CONSULTANTS

Every student of discussion and group communication needs to spend considerable time observing interaction of discussion groups. As many of our students have remarked, "It looks different when you are sitting outside the circle." We have witnessed the "Ah-ha!" reactions of student observers as they finally *saw* a phenomenon occurring that previously had been only an abstract idea. These observations frequently lead to voluntary change, so we encourage you to observe as much small group interaction as you can.

Preparing to Consult

Before you assume the role of a consultant who gives advice to others, you should spend some time observing different kinds of groups so you can learn as much as possible about the process of group interaction. There are many groups you can observe in their natural settings, for instance, any small group meeting legally declared open to the public, such as most meetings of boards, councils, and committees of governments where a "sunshine" law exists. You can obtain permission to observe many other small groups by describing your purpose as a learner and promising to maintain the confidentiality of details that are the private business of the group. Our students have observed meetings of groups such as church study-discussion classes, project groups in college classes, student activity committees, executive committees of sororities and fraternities, teaching teams, department managers, management staffs, task forces, school boards, boards of regents, quality circles, and self-help groups such as Adult Children of Alcoholics.

We recommend that you conduct your observations as part of a team because that will increase your learning. A team of observers usually produces more insight into a group's processes than an individual observer; team members learn a lot from sharing and discussing insights. An observation team may be able to arrange a fishbowl setup, with observers sitting in a circle outside the discussion group. All observers can focus on the same aspects of group discussion, such as leadership sharing, or each can watch for and report on different phenomena (e.g., leadership, roles, use of information, nonverbal signals, etc.). Observers may be assigned to watch the behavior of specific participants on a one-on-one basis, then later share their observations with the rest of the observation team.

Once you have experience as an observer and as a small group participant, you are ready to consult. Consultants generally provide three functions for the groups they consult for: they *remind* a group of techniques or principles of discussion it has overlooked, they *teach* a group new procedures and techniques to improve the group's performance, and they *critique* a group's performance. Sometimes, consultants do all three of these at once.

Reminding

Often group members need only to be reminded of principles and techniques they already know but have temporarily overlooked in the excitement of a lively argument. When the consultant notices some difficulty with the communication process or problem-solving procedure, he or she may remind the group of the principles or techniques that have temporarily been overlooked. The reminder role is somewhat analogous to that of a coach during pauses in a game. Having a reminder can help a group improve the quality of its decisions. Schultz et al. trained certain group members to serve as reminders, intervening whenever they observed symptoms of defective group decision making.[2] The reminders were instructed not to be aggressive but to remind the group by providing timely questions and suggestions: "Maybe we shouldn't make our final choice until we've looked at all the alternatives." Reminders, particularly those who were regular group members and not the emergent leaders of their groups, significantly affected decision quality.

The fishbowl is an excellent arrangement for training observers.

These researchers suggest appointing a reminder to improve decision making. If the reminder is to be a member of the group rather than a nonparticipating consultant, it might be useful to rotate this reminder role among the members so each has the chance to develop skills without any one person being left out of the discussion for too long. Group members themselves can and should function as reminders when they notice something going astray. Here are a few guidelines to help you *remind* in a sensitive and helpful way:

1. Focus on communication process and procedures, not on issues and content of the discussion.

2. Don't give orders or force the group to change. Keep in mind that the group is responsible for its own changes—your job is to remind and suggest. Phrase most of your remarks in the form of descriptions of what you have observed, questions, and suggestions. Susanna did this for the executive team: "I wonder if the team realizes that in the space of only four minutes, you have discussed _____, _____, and _____?" and "I wonder if Angela and Roger understood each other's proposals?" or "Some members do not appear to have much chance to be heard. Does the group want to do more gatekeeping to ensure that such members' contributions are not missed?" Comments phrased in these ways remind the group of principles of effective discussion without criticizing specific members and possibly arousing defensiveness.

3. Focus on trends and tendencies, as a rule, rather than singling out individual members for comment.

4. Give the group a chance to correct itself before you intervene. Interrupt discussion only when you think the group will not become aware of a problem until it has wasted a lot of time or created harmful quarrels out of what could be productive argument. Allow a little frustration to motivate change, but not enough to lower morale or produce severe secondary tension.

Teaching   Sometimes a consultant can be a helpful teacher by providing basic information about small group processes. Remember, many of the people who participate in groups of all kinds have never studied small group communication and don't know what is normal and what isn't. They need information to know how to resolve relational and procedural difficulties. Just by taking a small group communication course, you are ahead of many group leaders, facilitators, and managers, who may have been thrown into a group with no training.

A teaching consultant can also provide specialized information in the form of procedures and techniques designed to solve specific group difficulties. With the advent of quality circles and self-managed work teams, workers who select coordinator-leaders from their own ranks need both basic and specialized information you may have that is not readily available to most workers.

To serve as a teaching consultant, you will need a thorough grasp of small group communication and a working knowledge of a variety of techniques and procedures, along with a number of observational, feedback, and evaluation instruments. Examples are presented later in this chapter, and there are others available in resources you should know if you plan to serve as a consultant. Here are some guidelines for making your remarks as a consultant more acceptable and effective with the people you advise:

1. First, stress the positive; point out what a leader and group are doing well.

2. Focus on the most important things; don't overwhelm a group with more advice and suggestions than it can handle at one time.

3. Don't argue. Present your observations, opinions, and advice; be sure they are understood as you intend; then leave group members free to decide whether or how your evaluations and advice will be used. You are not an umpire with authority to stop the game or throw players out.

4. Don't interrupt a meeting if you need to give advice to the designated leader. If possible, whisper or write suggestions to the leader.

5. Give advice precisely, clearly, and briefly as possible when you are asked. If the group asks for an explanation or demonstration of some technique or competency, prepare it carefully.

6. Make critical comments in private to a leader (or any member), so the person will not appear to be under attack or lose face with other members.

7. Don't bluff. If a group asks for information or procedures with which you are not familiar, admit you aren't familiar with them and explain that you'll research them for the group. Then feel free to consult print resources or other experts who can help you.

Critiquing   A primary responsibility of many consultants, teachers, and trainers is to provide a **critique,** a descriptive analysis and evaluation of the group's strengths and weaknesses. Communication specialists on corporate training and development staffs are often called on to provide evaluations of both groups and individual members to managers. Fandt demonstrated that such accountability among managerial personnel led to higher levels of performance, higher satisfaction with both process and product, and higher cohesiveness in groups evaluated than in groups not being evaluated to superiors.[3] Greenbaum and associates claim that failure to evaluate adequately the procedures and output of the quality circles is often a major factor in the demise of quality circle programs.[4]

In general, a consultant's critique should cover at least four aspects of a group's discussion processes and culture: (1) inputs to and content of the problem-solving discussion; (2) the group process, including patterns of verbal interaction, member roles (including any ego-centered behavior and ethical lapses), communication process, decision making, and problem solving as a whole; (3) the group product, including how well it has been evaluated by the group, how appropriate it is to the goals or problem described by the group, and how committed members seem to be to making it work; and (4) leadership, especially the role of the designated leader and the sharing of leadership functions.[5] When you critique, make sure you use criteria appropriate to the group—a learning group's discussion shouldn't look or sound the same as a problem-solving group's.

Ethical Principles for Consultants

After observing a discussion, a consultant usually makes a detailed feedback statement to the group, describing selected aspects of the discussion and expressing opinions about strong and weak points. While doing so, it is essential to respect both the individual members and the group as an entity. Consultants should behave so that the group will welcome other observers and consultants in the future. The ethical standards that apply to critic observers are analogous to those that universities use when faculty and students conduct research involving human subjects. The relationship of group members to consultants is similar to that of subjects to researchers. The ethical standards also are similar to those for group members that we presented in Chapter 1. We propose that, as consultant, you adhere to the following standards of personal conduct:

1. Do not harm group members either physically or psychologically by your observation and feedback. Don't knowingly cause embarrassment, emotional upset, physical danger, and so forth. For example, it *would* be unethical for a consultant to make fun of a group member in front of the rest of the group, but it *would not* be unethical to speak with that member privately to describe the effect of the offending behavior on the group.

2. Never lie to people you observe. It would be unethical to tell a group that a critique will not be given to a superior when in fact it *will*. It is also unethical to tell a group that you think its decision-making procedures are vigilant when in fact you think they are sloppy and uncritical.

3. Make your criticism constructive. When you point out a problem, you should also suggest what to do to correct it, as Susanna did when she recommended that the group find a different meeting room, that Sam provide an agenda, and that his secretary take minutes. You are there to help, not to judge. You will be more helpful if you present positive evaluations before talking about what needs to be changed: "I like . . . , but you could improve . . ."

4. Respect the privacy and confidentiality of group members at all times. It is not ethical to share with outsiders what you have observed in a specific group unless: (1) you told the group you were going to do so before observing and the group granted you permission to do so; or (2) you so thoroughly disguise the identity of the group and its members (as in a statistical summary) that no one can possibly identify the group and members in your report. It is not ethical to receive confidential information from one member and share it with another without permission. Unless a group meeting has been legally declared open to the public, you should not report details or the substance of group business to outsiders.

When the purpose for which you are observing includes reporting findings (for instance, reporting your observations to your teacher or class), you will need to get permission to do so from the group members *before* you do your observing. The persons to be observed may be more willing to let you report if you offer to use pseudonyms instead of real names. In general, treat observed persons just as you would want to be treated if your roles were reversed.

Planning to Consult

While consulting for a group you may feel overwhelmed by all that is going on. Planning your observation and consultation in advance will help you focus on variables most important to your purposes and functions as a consultant. You may first want to talk with the group's leader or the person responsible for the group's output for background material about the group, such as what its purpose is, the history of the group, how effective it is perceived to be, and so forth. One way to cope with information overload is to record the group's discussion on audio or videotape (but only after obtaining permission from the group) for more detailed analysis at a later time. That way, you will worry less about missing something important and can make notes about parts of the discussion to review later. Before trying to observe systematically, we suggest you practice observing numerous discussions, including videotaped ones, for which you do not need to make any reports. Practice using the sorts of observational instruments and techniques you intend to use as a consultant. As with any skill, most of us need a lot of practice on a musical instrument before we are ready to perform.

You can use the following questions as a general guide from which to select a more limited list of questions for a specific observation. If you have been asked to observe interaction as a consultant (or even as a participant-observer), this list can help you decide which processes are going well and then focus on characteristics that group members may want to change.

Group Purpose/Goals

What is the group's purpose?

Do members clearly understand and accept the group's purpose?

Has the committee achieved a clear understanding of its charge?

Do members seem to know and accept limits on their area of freedom?

Can members describe what sort of output is needed?

Setting

How adequate are meeting facilities, such as seating arrangement, privacy, and comfort?

How adequate are facilities for recording and displaying group progress (information, ideas, evaluations, decisions, and so on)?

Communication Skills and Network

How competently do members encode verbally and nonverbally?

How carefully are members listening to understand each other?

How equally is participation spread among the members?

Is the network of verbal interaction all-channel or unduly restricted?

Group Culture, Norms, and Communication Climate

To what degree is the group climate characterized by openness, trust, and teamwork?

What attitudes toward each other and the content of information and ideas are members manifesting?

Are cultural, work style, or personality differences interfering with the group's effectiveness?

Are any self-centered hidden agenda items interfering with progress toward the goal?

Are any norms interfering with cohesiveness and progress?

Are arguments being expressed sensitively and being managed to test ideas and achieve consensus, or to win?

Role Structure

Is there a designated leader?

If so, how well is this person performing the role? With what style? Are others encouraged to share in leader functions?

If not, how is leadership distributed? Are any needed services missing?

Are all necessary functional roles being provided?

Are there any ego-centered behavioral roles?

Problem-Solving and Decision-Making Procedures

How vigilant are the group's problem-solving procedures?

Do members seem to be adequately informed or are they planning how to get needed information before reaching decisions?

Are information and ideas being evaluated thoroughly for effectiveness and possible negative consequences, or accepted without question?

Are criteria shared by all group members, or explicitly discussed and agreed upon?

Are there any tendencies toward groupthink?

Has some procedure or agenda for the discussion been accepted by the group? If so, how adequate is it and how well is it being used?

Are information, interpretations, proposals, and decisions being recorded?

Are these provided in some record visible to the entire group?

How creative is the group in finding alternatives?

How frequently are summaries being made and used to focus and move discussion toward the goal?

How are decisions being made?

If needed, is the group making adequate plans to implement its decisions? To evaluate the adequacy of its actual solution(s), and possibly make changes later?

Might procedural changes or special techniques such as brainstorming, committee procedural rules, Nominal Group Technique, or computer charting be beneficial to the group?

Obviously, you cannot consider all these questions at the same time. Concentrate on the one or two factors that seem most important to understanding your particular group or that seem most problematic for the group. With increased experience you will discover that you can pay attention to more factors, or rapidly scan what is happening and then decide where to focus your attention.

INSTRUMENTS FOR OBSERVING AND EVALUATING DISCUSSIONS

Just as athletic teams, music groups, and actors need regular evaluations and advice to perform optimally, so do task forces, standing committees, boards, quality circles, and self-managed work teams. Any group can benefit from periodic evaluation. Regular reviews should be scheduled, whether or not aided by a consultant. For instance, Hill's "Learning Thru Discussion" procedure includes an evaluation of the discussion as part of each meeting of a learning group.[6] If "How are we doing?" sessions are not scheduled, too often no group evaluations occur, or evaluation takes the form of gripe sessions among a few members with little benefit to the group system.

This final section of Chapter 15 is devoted to instruments and techniques for observing and evaluating groups and their members. Many of the forms

Verbal interaction diagram.	**FIGURE 15.1**

Group __G.E. "Tigers"__

Time _____

Begin __1:03_____

End __1:54_____

Place __Conf. Rm. 14_____

Observer __Snow_____

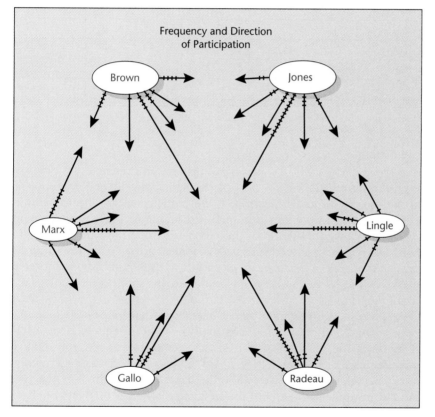

Frequency and Direction
of Participation

were developed for classes in small group communication and leadership. They can be used as presented or adapted to suit particular situations and needs.

A diagram of a **verbal interaction analysis** made by an observer reveals much about relationships among members of a group. The diagram in Figure 15.1 shows relationships among a team called the G.E. Tigers—who talks to whom, how often each member participates orally, and whether the

**Verbal
Interaction
Analysis**

FIGURE 15.2 | **Displaying data from a verbal interaction diagram.**

Group: G.E. "Tigers" Q.C. Place: Conf. Rm. 14
Observer: Snow Date: 10-9-96
Beginning time: 1:03 Ending time: 1:54 pm

TO:

FROM:	Brown	Jones	Lingle	Radeau	Gallo	Marx	Group	Total Percent
Brown	–	5	2	4	2	5	5	23 / 16.1
Jones	3	–	3	4	4	3	13	30 / 21
Lingle	2	2	–	3	2	4	12	25 / 17.5
Radeau	3	3	4	–	0	2	12	24 / 16.8
Gallo	3	3	2	0	–	0	6	14 / 9.8
Marx	8	2	2	3	2	–	10	27 / 18.9
Total number / percent	19 / 13.3	15 / 10.5	13 / 9.1	14 / 9.8	10 / 7	14 / 9.8	58 / 40.6	143 / 100

group has members who do not speak up or who dominate the discussion. Notice the information at the top of the figure that identifies group, time, and persons involved. The names of the participants are located around a circle according to seating during the discussion. Each time a member speaks, an arrow is drawn from the person's position toward the person to whom the remark was addressed, or a longer arrow is drawn toward the center of the circle when a member speaks to the entire group. Subsequent remarks in the same direction are indicated by short cross marks on the shaft of the arrow.

For ease in interpreting a verbal interaction diagram, numbers and percentages can be displayed in charts like the ones in Figures 15.2 and 15.3. Judging from the numbers shown in this example, who do you think was discussion leader of the G.E. Tigers? Are there any other reasoned inferences you can make about this group from the data? You could modify this procedure and instrument to capture the frequency of some nonverbal behaviors such as eye contact and body angles.

Content Analysis

Content analysis procedures examine the actual content of remarks (topics, types of remarks, fantasy theme structure, etc.) made during a discussion. One type of content analysis focuses on who performs what behaviors and how often. From such a descriptive analysis, members' roles can be described. The example in Figure 15.4 classifies members' behaviors according to the functions they carry out during the observed discussion. Specific be-

Another way to display data from a verbal interaction diagram. | **FIGURE 15.3**

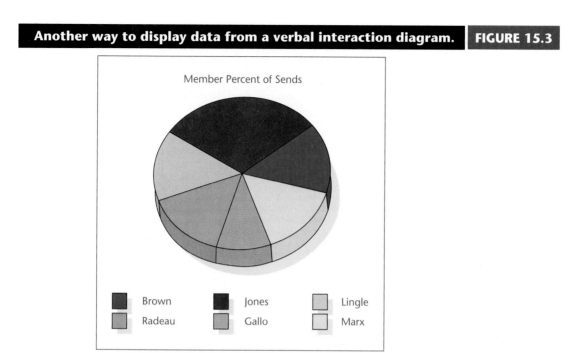

Member Percent of Sends

Brown Jones Lingle
Radeau Gallo Marx

havioral functions are listed along the left side of the chart, and the participants' names in the cells at the head of each column. Each time a member speaks, the observer judges the functional meaning of that statement to the group and places a tally mark in the appropriate cell of the chart. After the discussion the tally marks are converted to numbers and percentages, as shown in Figure 15.5. They can also be converted to pie charts such as the one shown for Jodi in Figure 15.6. From this analysis, can you tell who is probably task leader of this group? Who is the social or maintenance leader? Do any individuals seem to be interfering with the group's progress toward its goal?

A content analysis form could be developed for virtually any set of categories into which observable member behaviors could be classified, such as types of statements, functional stage in problem solving, kinds of questions, ways of expressing inferences, and so on. You might use verbal interaction analysis to trace development of fantasy chains, the progression of an idea from initial introduction through its final form and disposal by the group, types of conflicts, or how information is used by a group. One thing that matters is that the observer is able to classify the remarks consistently, identifying approximately the same behaviors and classifying them about the same way as another independent observer, or with oneself at two different times (using a recording of the discussion).

| FIGURE 15.4 | Content analysis of behavioral functions of members. |

Group _____ Place _____ Observer _____

Date _____ Beginning time _____ Ending time _____

Behavioral Functions	Participants' Names					
1. Initiating and orienting						
2. Information giving						
3. Information seeking						
4. Opinion giving						
5. Opinion seeking						
6. Clarifying and elaborating						
7. Evaluating						
8. Summarizing						
9. Coordinating						
10. Consensus testing						
11. Recording						
12. Suggesting procedure						
13. Gatekeeping						
14. Supporting						
15. Harmonizing						
16. Tension relieving						
17. Dramatizing						
18. Norming						
19. Withdrawing						
20. Blocking						
21. Status and recognition seeking						

Displaying data from analysis of behavioral functions of members.

FIGURE 15.5

Group _EXECUTIVE COMMITTEE_ Place _CU LOBBY_

Observer _ANDY_ Date _8 - 28 - 96_

Beginning time _4:30 P.M._ Ending time _6:30 P.M._

Participants' Names

Behavioral Functions	Mary	John	Edna	Dave	Jodi	Total $\frac{number}{percent}$
1. Initiating and orienting	5	3				$-\frac{8}{5.7}-$
2. Information giving	6	5		2	3	$-\frac{16}{11.4}-$
3. Information seeking			3			$-\frac{3}{2.1}-$
4. Opinion giving	8	8	4	2	1	$-\frac{23}{16.4}-$
5. Opinion seeking			2			$-\frac{2}{1.4}-$
6. Clarifying and elaborating			3			$-\frac{3}{2.1}-$
7. Evaluating	2	4			1	$-\frac{7}{5}--$
8. Summarizing	2					$-\frac{2}{1.4}-$
9. Coordinating	8					$-\frac{8}{5.7}-$
10. Consensus testing				3		$-\frac{3}{2.1}-$
11. Recording			5			$-\frac{5}{3.6}-$
12. Suggesting procedure	3		6			$-\frac{9}{6.4}-$
13. Gatekeeping			1	5		$-\frac{6}{4.3}-$
14. Supporting	2		2	6		$-\frac{10}{7.1}--$
15. Harmonizing				3	2	$-\frac{5}{3.6}-$
16. Tension relieving					6	$-\frac{6}{4.3}-$
17. Dramatizing		5			3	$-\frac{8}{5.7}-$
18. Norming				4		$-\frac{4}{2.9}-$
19. Withdrawing		1				$-\frac{1}{7}-$
20. Blocking	2	5				$-\frac{7}{5}--$
21. Status and recognition seeking		4				$-\frac{4}{2.9}-$
Total $\frac{number}{percent}$	$-\frac{38}{27.1}$	$-\frac{35}{25}$	$-\frac{26}{18.6}$	$-\frac{25}{17.9}$	$-\frac{16}{11.4}$	$\frac{140}{100}--$

FIGURE 15.6	Pie chart displaying Jodi's behavioral functions.

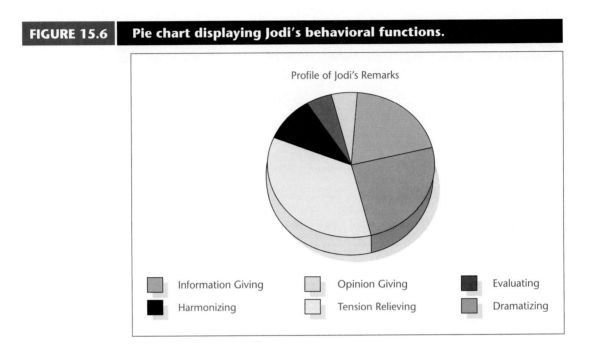

Profile of Jodi's Remarks

- Information Giving
- Opinion Giving
- Evaluating
- Harmonizing
- Tension Relieving
- Dramatizing

Questionnaires and Rating Scales

Many different types of questionnaires and observer forms have been prepared for studying and improving small group interaction. Some of these use open-ended or multiple-response questions; some use rating scales. **Rating scales** contain items that ask a respondent to render a numerical evaluation of some characteristic. You are probably familiar with the 10–0 scale used by judges of some Olympic competitions and the scales by which consumer products are rated in magazines. In Chapter 8 we introduced you to SYMLOG, a rating technique in which behaviors of group members are rated on three major dimensions; these ratings are then entered in a three-dimensional chart to describe group-level characteristics and problems. The scales and other forms that follow are provided for your use and to give you ideas about creating others for specific purposes.

Postmeeting reaction forms (PMRs) are questionnaires given to participants at the end of a meeting to get objective feedback for improving future discussions by the group. Because they are anonymous, participants are likely to be candid and honest in their comments and ratings. A PMR form may be planned by an entire group, a leader, an instructor, a consultant, organizers of a large conference, or by a student of small group communication. The questionnaires are distributed, completed, and collected after a discussion. Responses should be tallied and reported back to the group as soon as possible on a duplicated summary sheet or wall chart. If a group has access to group decision support software, the ratings can be entered

Postmeeting reaction (PMR) form.	FIGURE 15.7

Instructions: Check the point on each scale that best represents your honest judgment. Add any comments you wish to make that are not covered by the questionnaire. Do not sign your name.

1. How clear were the *goals* of the discussion to you?

very clear	somewhat vague	muddled

2. The *atmosphere* was

cooperative and cohesive	apathetic	competitive

3. How well *organized and vigilant* was the discussion?

disorderly	just right	too rigid

4. How effective was the *leadership* supplied by the chairperson?

too autocratic	democratic	weak

5. *Preparation for this meeting* was

thorough	adequate	poor

6. Did you find yourself *wanting to speak* when you didn't get a chance?

almost never	occasionally	often

7. How satisfied are you with the *results* of the discussion?

very satisfied	moderately satisfied	very satisfied

8. How do you feel about *working again* with this same group?

eager	I will	reluctant

Comments:

and tallied simultaneously. The chart provides the basis for an evaluation discussion and planning changes in group procedures.

Questions and scales should be tailored to fit the purposes and needs of the person(s) preparing the questionnaire. Questions can be about any aspect of group discussion: the substance of the discussion, interpersonal relations, procedures, and techniques. Several types of questions may be mixed on a questionnaire, depending on what the preparer of the questionnaire wants to learn. Two examples of PMR forms are shown in Figures 15.7 and 15.8.

Rating scales can be inserted into feedback questionnaires or used by consultants to report judgments about any aspect of the group and its discussion, including group climate, norms, structure, interpersonal relationships,

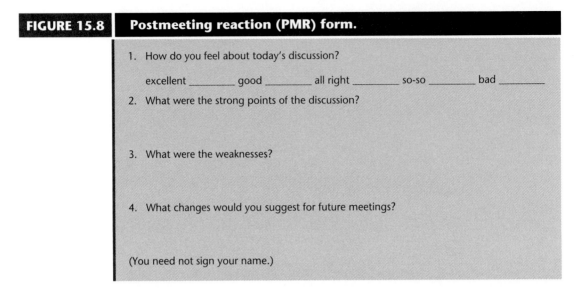

| FIGURE 15.8 | Postmeeting reaction (PMR) form. |

1. How do you feel about today's discussion?

   excellent _____ good _____ all right _____ so-so _____ bad _____

2. What were the strong points of the discussion?

3. What were the weaknesses?

4. What changes would you suggest for future meetings?

(You need not sign your name.)

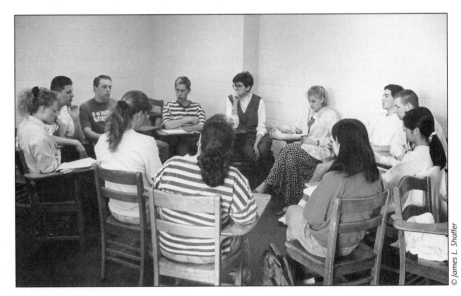

Postmeeting reaction (PMR) sheets can help a group diagnose its own problems.

© James L. Shaffer

speaking, listening, content of remarks, and so on. The set of scales in Figure 15.9 can be used to evaluate any small group discussion. The composite scale in Figure 15.10, based on a similar one developed by Patton and Giffin, may be used to identify deficiencies in problem-solving procedures.[7]

Almost any characteristic of individual behavior can be evaluated with an appropriate scale. Figure 15.11 shows a simple rating form that can be completed by an observer and given to each participant; participants can even complete these scales anonymously about each other, and then distribute

Group Characteristic	5 Excellent	4 Good	3 Average	2 Fair	1 Poor
Date _____			Group _____		
Time _____			Observer _____		
Goal clarity and interest					
Organization of discussion					
Vigilance; evaluation					
Communication: speaking					
Communication: listening					
Cooperation, teamwork					

Instructions: Based on behaviors and interaction you observed, rate the degree to which the group measured up to each criterion.

Poor 1	Fair 2	Average 3	Good 4	Excellent 5

1 2 3 4 5   **1.** Concerns of all members were established regarding the problem.

1 2 3 4 5   **2.** Components of the undesirable situation and obstacles to change were clearly described.

1 2 3 4 5   **3.** The goal was clearly defined and agreed upon by all members.

1 2 3 4 5   **4.** Possible solutions were listed and clarified before extensive evaluation of them.

1 2 3 4 5   **5.** Criteria for evaluation were previously understood and accepted, or discussed and agreed upon by all members.

1 2 3 4 5   **6.** Based on facts and reasoning, predictions were made regarding the probable effectiveness and possible negative consequences of each proposed solution.

1 2 3 4 5   **7.** Consensus was achieved on the most desirable/acceptable solution.

1 2 3 4 5   **8.** A realistic plan was developed for implementing the solution and, if appropriate, for evaluating its effectiveness.

1 2 3 4 5   **9.** Overall, the problem-solving process was thorough, vigilant, and systematic.

FIGURE 15.11	**Participant rating scale.**

Date _____

Observer_____

_____
(Name of participant)

1. Contributions to the *content of the discussion.* (relevant information, issue-centered arguments, adequate reasoning, etc.)

5	4	3	2	1

Outstanding in quality and quantity   Fair share   Few or none

2. Contributions to *efficient group procedures.* (agenda planning, responding to prior comments, summaries)

5	4	3	2	1

Always relevant,   Relevant, no   Sidetracked,
aided organization   aid in order   confused group

3. Degree of *group orientation and cooperation.* (listening to understand, responsible, agreeable, group centered, open-minded)

5	4	3	2	1

Very responsible   Self-centered
and constructive

4. *Speaking competency.* (clear, to group, one point at a time, concise)

5	4	3	2	1

Brief, clear,   Vague, indirect,
to group   wordy

5. *Overall value* to the group.

5	4	3	2	1

Most valuable   Least valuable

Suggestions:

them to the persons rated. Versions of this form (originally devised by a group of students for their own use) have been used extensively by one of the authors. It is easy to understand, can be completed quickly, and focuses on some of the most important variables of a participant's behavior; Figure 15.12 is similar in purpose but more comprehensive. Figure 15.13 is useful for rating the level of assertiveness of participants, while indicating whether nonassertive participation was evaluated as passive or aggressive.

Discussion participant evaluation scale.	**FIGURE 15.12**

Participant's name _____

Instructions: Circle the number that best reflects your evaluation of the discussant's participation on each scale.

Superior Poor

1 2 3 4 5	**1.**	Was prepared and informed.
1 2 3 4 5	**2.**	Contributions were brief and clear.
1 2 3 4 5	**3.**	Comments relevant and well timed.
1 2 3 4 5	**4.**	Spoke distinctly and audibly to all.
1 2 3 4 5	**5.**	Willingness to communicate.
1 2 3 4 5	**6.**	Frequency of participation [if poor, too low ( ) or high ( )].
1 2 3 4 5	**7.**	Nonverbal responses were clear and constant.
1 2 3 4 5	**8.**	Listened to understand and follow discussion.
1 2 3 4 5	**9.**	Openmindedness.
1 2 3 4 5	**10.**	Cooperative, team orientation.
1 2 3 4 5	**11.**	Helped keep discussion organized, following outline.
1 2 3 4 5	**12.**	Contributed to evaluation of information and ideas.
1 2 3 4 5	**13.**	Respectful and tactful with others.
1 2 3 4 5	**14.**	Encouraged others to participate.
1 2 3 4 5	**15.**	Overall rating as participant.

Comments: Evaluator _____

The previous forms can be used as presented or modified to rate designated leaders, but Figures 15.14 and 15.15 were devised specifically to rate leaders. Exceptionally comprehensive, Figure 15.14 has been modified substantially over the years from one originally devised for rating Air Force personnel as discussion leaders. Figure 15.15 is designed to help a leader engage in introspective self-evaluation after a discussion, identifying specific successes and failings, and then providing an overall rating.

FIGURE 15.13	Assertiveness rating scale.

Discussant _____ Date _____
Observer _____ Time _____

The check mark on each scale indicates my best judgment of your degree of assertiveness as a participant in the discussion.

	Nonassertive	Assertive	Agressive
Behavior			
Getting the floor	yielded easily	usually refused to let others take over or dominate	interrupted and cut others off
Expressing opinions	never expressed personal opinion	stated opinions, but open to others' opinions	insisted others should agree
Expressing personal desires (for meeting times, procedures, etc.)	never, or did so in a pleading way	stated openly, but willing to compromise	insisted on having own way
Sharing information	none, or only if asked to do so	whenever information was relevant, concisely	whether relevant or not; long-winded, rambling
Manner			
Voice	weak, unduly soft	strong and clear	loud, strident
Posture and movements	withdrawn, restricted	animated, often leaning forward	unduly forceful, "table pounding"
Eye contact	rare, even when speaking	direct but not staring or glaring	stared others down
Overall manner	nonassertive	assertive	aggressive

FIGURE 15.14

Comprehensive leader rating scale.

Date _____ Leader _____
Time _____ Observer _____

Instructions: Draw a line through any item not applicable to the discussion you have just observed. Use the following scale to evaluate the designated leader's performance as discussion leader.

5—superior   4—above average   3—average   2—below average   1—poor

Personal Style and Communicative Competencies

To what degree did the leader:

_____ Show poise and confidence in speaking?
_____ Show enthusiasm and interest in the problem?
_____ Listen well to understand *all* participants?
_____ Manifest personal warmth and a sense of humor?
_____ Show an open mind toward all new information and ideas?
_____ Create an atmosphere of teamwork?
_____ Share functional leadership with other members?
_____ Behave democratically?
_____ Maintain perspective on problem and group process?

Preparation

To what degree:

_____ Were all needed physical arrangements cared for?
_____ Were members notified and given guidance in preparing to meet?
_____ Was the leader prepared on the problem or subject?
_____ Was a procedural sequence of questions prepared to guide discussion?

Leadership Techniques

To what degree did the leader:

_____ Put members at ease with each other?
_____ Equalize opportunity to speak?
_____ Introduce and explain the charge or problem so it was clear to all?
_____ Control aggressive or dominant members with tact?
_____ Present an agenda and/or procedural and outline for group problem solving?
_____ Encourage members to modify the procedural outline?
_____ State questions clearly to the group?
_____ Guide the group through a thorough analysis of problem before discussing solutions?
_____ Stimulate imaginative and creative thinking about solutions?
_____ Encourage the group to evaluate all ideas and proposals thoroughly before accepting or rejecting them?
_____ See that plans were made to implement and follow up on all decisions?
_____ Keep discussion on one point at a time?
_____ Rebound questions asking for a personal opinion or solution to the group?
_____ Provide summaries needed to clarify, remind, and move group forward to next issue or agenda item?
_____ Test for consensus before moving to a new phase of problem solving?
_____ Keep complete and accurate notes, including visual chart of proposals, evaluations, and decisions?
_____ If needed, suggest compromise or integrative solutions to resolve conflict?
_____ (Other—please specify _____)

FIGURE 15.15	Discussion leader self-rating scale.

Instructions: Rate yourself on each item by putting a check mark in the "Yes" or "No" column. Your score is five times the number of items marked "Yes." Rating: *excellent,* 90 or higher; *good,* 80–85; *fair,* 70–75; *inadequate,* 65 or lower.

	Yes	**No**
1. I prepared all needed facilities.	____	____
2. I started the meeting promptly and ended on time.	____	____
3. I established an atmosphere of supportiveness and informality by being open and responsive to all ideas.	____	____
4. I clearly oriented the group to its goal and area of freedom.	____	____
5. I encouraged all members to participate and maintained equal opportunity for all to speak.	____	____
6. I listened actively, and (if needed) encouraged all members to do so.	____	____
7. My questions were clear and brief.	____	____
8. I saw to it that unclear statements were paraphrased or otherwise clarified.	____	____
9. I used a plan for leading the group in an organized consideration of all major phases of problem solving and all components of vigilant interaction.	____	____
10. I saw to it that the problem was discussed thoroughly before solutions were considered.	____	____
11. I actively encouraged creative thinking.	____	____
12. I encouraged thorough evaluation of all proposed solutions, both for effectiveness and negative consequences.	____	____
13. I integrated related ideas or suggestions and urged the group to arrive at consensus on a solution.	____	____
14. I prompted open discussion of substantive conflicts.	____	____
15. I maintained order and organization, promptly pointing out tangents, making transitions, and keeping track of the passage of time.	____	____
16. I saw to it that the meeting produced definite assignments or plans for action, and that any subsequent meeting was arranged.	____	____
17. All important information, ideas, and decisions were promptly and accurately recorded.	____	____
18. I was able to remain neutral during constructive arguments, and otherwise encourage teamwork.	____	____
19. I suggested or urged establishment of needed ethical standards and procedural norms.	____	____
20. I encouraged members to discuss how they felt about group process and procedures.	____	____

SUMMARY

1. Consultants who observe but do not participate in a group's discussion can help a group by reminding members of principles they have forgotten, by teaching members procedures and techniques, and by critiquing a group's performance. Students should observe many groups first before they attempt to consult for a group.

2. Consultants must plan their observations carefully because it is impossible to keep track of all variables at once. They focus on the most important or most problematic aspects of a group's interaction.

3. Consultants report their findings to groups honestly and constructively, but forthrightly and respecting members' confidentiality.

4. Many different kinds of prepared observation forms and questionnaires can help consultants (and also group members) gather information about a group to assess the group's performance. The forms included in the chapter can serve as models for describing a group's verbal interaction, analyzing the members' behaviors and discussion content, providing postmeeting evaluations to group members, and rating many other aspects of groups.

EXERCISE

Divide your class into project groups of five or six members. Each group should select an existing small group to observe and evaluate. You may want to check your student activities office or similar office for lists of on-campus organizations or groups whose meetings you might observe. Class members may have special access to groups in local business or government organizations.

This project will last for the entire term. Although you may be given some time in class for meetings, expect that you will have to schedule numerous meetings outside class time.

You will need to decide which group to observe, on which aspects of the group to focus (e.g., leadership, roles, decision-making procedures and effectiveness, conflict management, problem-solving procedures, collection and use of information, etc.), and which observation techniques and/or forms to use. Then you will carry out your observations and prepare a report of your findings to the rest of the class, using appropriate visual and other aids. You may also be asked to serve as a consultant to the group you observe and present an oral or written report to the observed group.

BIBLIOGRAPHY

Schwarz, Roger M. *The Skilled Facilitator: Practical Wisdom for Developing Effective Groups.* San Francisco: Jossey-Bass, 1994.

NOTES

1. Patricia M. Fandt, "The Relationship of
    Accountability and Interdependent
    Behavior to Enhancing Team
    Consequences," *Group & Organization
    Studies* 16 (1991): 300–312; Harold H.
    Greenbaum, Ira T. Kaplan, and William
    Metlay, "Evaluation of Problem-Solving
    Groups," *Group & Organization Studies* 13
    (1988): 133–47.
2. Beatrice Schultz, Sandra M. Ketrow, and
    Daphne M. Urban, "Improving Decision
    Quality in the Small Group: The Role of the
    Reminder," *Small Group Research* 26
    (November 1995): 521–41.
3. Frandt, "The Relationship of Accountability,"
    305–7.
4. Greenbaum, Kaplan, and Metlay, "Evaluation
    of Problem-Solving Groups."
5. Ibid., 137–39, 145.
6. W. Fawcett Hill, *Learning Thru Discussion*
    (Beverly Hills, CA: Sage, 1977): 30–31.
7. Bobby R. Patton and Kim Giffin, *Problem-
    Solving Group Interaction* (New York:
    Harper & Row, 1973): 213–14.

APPENDIX A   MAKING PUBLIC PRESENTATIONS OF THE GROUP'S OUTPUT

Often groups must make public presentations of their output, which may take the form of a report, a set of findings or recommendations, and so forth. The group's leader or selected representatives may present a report from the group to the parent organization, a political body, an open meeting of interested community representatives, or another type of public gathering. The members of the audience at such public gatherings may themselves become participants who will discuss the report of the group. The following information presents formats for a variety of public discussion sessions in which group members may find themselves participating.

PANEL DISCUSSIONS

A **panel discussion** is a public presentation in which a small group of people representing varying perspectives informally discusses issues relevant to an important question in front of a listening audience. For example, a panel might discuss abortion laws, solutions to congested parking on campus, what might be done to solve a community's solid waste problem, or the responsibility of society to the victims of crimes. A panel format is sometimes used with a group of aspirants for political office.

Groups may participate in panel discussions in a variety of ways. A group may be asked to plan and conduct an entire panel discussion, in which case the entire group must research and present fairly all relevant points of view about the issue. More typically, a group known to support a particular point of view will be asked to supply a representative to serve as a panelist with other panelists who represent different viewpoints. The **moderator** of a panel coordinates the discussion so it does not ramble and so all viewpoints are represented. Participants need to be both knowledgeable about the question under discussion and articulate in expressing their, or the group's, opinions. Panelists generally have an outline of questions to follow, but their speaking is relatively impromptu. Panelists need not agree on anything except which issues to discuss; the lively argument that often ensues can make for an intellectually stimulating program. The panel format is excellent for presenting an overview of different points of view on an issue of public concern. CNN and C-SPAN often include such discussions in their programming.

Panel and other public discussions call for special physical arrangements and other preparations. First, all discussants should be able to see each other and the audience at all times to facilitate direct interaction. Seat panelists in a semi-circle in front of the audience with the moderator either at one end or in the center; thus, panelists have eye contact with each other and the audience. Second, panelists should be seated behind a table, preferably with some sort of cover on the front. Two small tables in an open V make an excellent arrangement. Third, a large name card should be placed in front of each panelist. Fourth, microphones, if needed, should be plentiful enough and unobtrusive. In a large assembly, if a floor mike is required for questions from the audience, it should be placed strategically and audience members instructed in its use. Finally, visual displays of the topic or question under consideration help keep the discussion organized. A chalkboard or easel can be used for this purpose.

The discussion outline for a panel discussion can follow one of several formats. The one described here is common. The moderator should ask panelists in advance to suggest questions and subquestions for the discussion. After these are compiled into a rough outline the moderator intends to use, panelists should receive a copy in advance so they have a chance to investigate and think of possible responses to each question.

The moderator prepares a special outline and uses it during the panel discussion. The outline has an introduction, sequence of questions to be raised, and a planned conclusion format. The moderator acts as a conversational traffic officer directing the flow of the discussion. Moderators ask questions of the group of panelists, see that each panelist has an equal opportunity to speak, and clarify ambiguous remarks or ask panelists to do so. They do not participate directly in the arguments. They summarize each major topic or have the panelists do so and keep the discussion moving along the major points of the outline. A moderator's outline might look like this:

Introduction

"What should be the law governing abortions in the United States?"

I. Ladies and gentlemen, the question of what the law should be governing abortions in the United States has been a subject of heated argument, physical confrontation, intensive lobbying, court cases, sermons, and pamphlets—and far too little calm, thoughtful discussion.

II. Today we are fortunate to have a panel of thoughtful experts who represent all major points of view on this subject.

    A. Father Jon McClarety has made an intensive study of the Catholic theology and arguments underlying the church's stand against legalized abortions. He is a member of the Department of Philosophy and Theology of Holy Name Academy.

    B. Robert Byron is an attorney for the Legal Aid Society who has served his society in appeals to the Supreme Court that led to the current legal status of abortions.

C. Ms. Martine Giles, founder and director of the Adoption Alternatives Agency, has helped arrange more than 300 private adoptions nationally.

D. Ms. Dorothy Mankewicz, a social worker and volunteer lecturer for Zero Population Growth, has assisted many women who wanted abortions.

E. Professor Maha Kasakrim is historian of ethical and social values at Western State University and author of two books dealing with the abortion law controversy.

III. Our panelists have agreed to discuss four specific issues that are part of the question you see on the poster before you. "What should be the law governing abortions in the United States?"

A. When does a human life begin?

B. Who has the right to decide whether or not a woman should be allowed to have an abortion?

C. What would be the effects of greater restriction on the right of choice to have an abortion?

D. Under what conditions, if any, should abortions be legal?

IV. Each panelist will give a brief statement of his or her position on each issue and the reasoning behind it, then the panelists will question and debate their positions informally. After 50 minutes, the floor will be opened for questions from you, our listening audience. While discussion is proceeding, you may want to jot down questions as they occur to you so you can remember them for the forum period (described later).

Body of the Discussion

I. "When does a human life begin?"

A. Father McClarety: _____

B. Ms. Mankewicz: _____

C. Professor Kasakrim: _____

and so on.

(All four issues are discussed, with the moderator summarizing; seeing that each panelist gets an opportunity to present a position on each issue, and question, support, or argue with the others; and moving the group to the next major question at a prearranged time.)

Conclusion

I. Let's see if we can summarize what we have learned about each other's positions. I'd like each of you to summarize in a minute or less your position and arguments. (Often the moderator does the summing up, with panelists being free to correct or supplement.)

II. I believe all of us in this room are now better prepared to cope with this vital issue. We now understand each other's positions as well as possible, and the values and beliefs supporting them.

III. Now I wonder what questions our listeners have for the panel? Please raise your hand if you want to ask a question, and wait for me to recognize you by pointing. I will give each person a chance to ask one question before allowing anyone to ask a second question. Your questions can be directed to a particular panel member to answer or to the entire group. If you want a particular panel member to answer, state that person's name. Okay, what's our first question? The lady to my right wearing the maroon blazer—please state your question loudly enough for all present to hear.

(Suggestions for conducting a successful forum discussion are provided later in this appendix.)

PUBLIC INTERVIEWS

The leader or selected members of a group may be asked to participate in public interviews about the group's work. A **public interview** may be conducted by one or more interviewers of one or more interviewees at a time. *Meet the Press* and *This Week with Sam Donaldson and Cokie Roberts* are examples of this format, as are press conferences and some political candidate debates. Interviewers and interviewees may agree in advance on a list of major questions or topics to be discussed and on the range of topics for discussion, or the program may be entirely spontaneous. The interviewer's responsibility is to represent the audience by asking questions the audience most wants or needs to have answered, and to help the interviewees clarify their responses. The interviewee's responsibility is to present fairly and clearly the point of view of the group represented.

FORUM DISCUSSIONS

Sometimes when a group presents a report to a large gathering, members of the audience are permitted to ask questions or express opinions about the group's work. **Forum discussion** refers to this period of verbal interaction during which audience members interact in an organized way with the presenters. The term *forum* also refers to a discussion held by a large gathering of people, such as a university faculty meeting or a town meeting. Frequently a forum follows a panel or interview presentation. Audience members should be told in advance that a forum will follow the public presentation so they can think of questions or comments. Microphones often are set up at strategic places for audience members to use. Sometimes, audience members are asked to supply their questions or comments in written form to a moderator, who reads them aloud for the entire gathering, followed by responses from panelists or interviewees.

Strict procedural control is needed for a successful forum. The moderator should control the forum so the discussion is interesting and fair to all participants. The following are guidelines to ensure fairness without letting the discussion bog down on one issue:

1. During the introduction to the panel or other program, announce that there will be a forum or question and answer period. This allows listeners to be thinking of questions and remarks.

2. State whether only questions or both questions and comments will be permitted.

3. Just before the audience participation segment, announce definite rules to assure equal opportunity for all to speak, such as:

   a. Raise your hand and wait to be recognized before speaking.

   b. No one may speak a second time until each person who wants the floor has had it once.

   c. Comments or questions should be addressed either to a specific panelist by name or to the entire panel.

   d. Remarks must be limited to not more than _____ seconds.

   e. Speak loudly enough to be heard by everyone or go to the floor microphone.

4. Tell the audience whether there will be a definite length of time for the forum and stick to the time.

5. If the audience is large, recognize people from various parts of the room in a systematic pattern.

6. Encourage different points of view by asking for them: "Does anyone want to present a *different* point of view from that we have just heard?"

7. If a question cannot be heard by all, restate it.

8. If a question is unclear or long, paraphrase it to the originator's satisfaction.

9. When the allotted time is nearly up, state that there is just enough time for one or two more questions or comments.

10. If no one seeks the floor, wait a few seconds, then thank the panel and audience for their participation and either dismiss the meeting or go on to the next item on the agenda.

APPENDIX B   INFORMATIONAL RESOURCES FOR THE GROUP

A group's output can be only as good as its input and throughput allow. No matter how committed members are to the group and how skilled they are at the process of discussion, critical thinking will be impaired if members don't have accurate, relevant, valid, and complete information with which to work. Groups that attempt to gather as much relevant information as possible *before* they begin their problem-solving or decision-making procedures will produce better outputs—decisions, solutions, reports, recommendations— than groups whose inputs are inadequate.

Appendix B is designed to help group members improve their input resources by assessing the information they have, deciding what additional information they need, and then obtaining it, evaluating it, and organizing it for easy referencing by the group. The four steps, in order, are (1) review and organize your present stock of information and ideas, (2) gather needed additional information, (3) evaluate all the information and ideas you have collected, and (4) organize the information and ideas into a tentative outline. This comprehensive information-gathering procedure is especially useful for important problems and decisions when making a mistake would be costly or worse. In such cases, the search for information should be exhaustive and the evaluation thorough. For problems with little danger of causing a costly mistake, the group can adapt the procedure or focus on just those steps that are most relevant.

REVIEW AND ORGANIZE YOUR PRESENT STOCK OF INFORMATION AND IDEAS

Group members probably already have some information about the subject or they would not be discussing it. Taking a systematic inventory of the information you currently have saves time and makes it easier for you to recall what you have when you need it.

1. **Place the problem or subject in perspective.**
   To what is it related? What will it affect, and what affects it? For example, when the church board mentioned in Chapter 2 decided on a new location for the church, it had to consider the financial condition of the church, long-range plans, the availability of public transportation and parking facilities, types of activities planned for the church, and so forth.

2. **Make an inventory of information you have about the subject.**
   Each member should contribute what he or she knows, similar to the mapping procedure described in Chapter 11. This should be a fairly

unstructured, freewheeling process. All this information should be written down.

3. **Organize the information into a rough draft of a problem-solving outline.**
   Look over the information for main issues, topics, or questions about the problem. You may want to use the guidelines suggested in Chapter 11.

4. **Look for deficiencies.**
   The rough draft will reveal where the group has gaps in its information and suggest specific information to gather and opinions or ideas that need to be supported.

GATHER NEEDED INFORMATION

The group is now ready to plan how it will correct the deficiencies in its knowledge and thinking. *Planning* is important; otherwise, haphazard information gathering produces "garbage in" that results in "garbage out" conclusions.

Groups cannot expect to deal with all this information in a single meeting. Even if members are familiar with the topic in advance, they need time to think about the information and spot gaps. This usually takes two meetings, often more. The following two-step procedure helps ensure that the group overlooks nothing important:

1. **The group should identify and list all the major issues or topics, along with subtopics, that it needs to explore further.**
   These issues were suggested by the rough outline produced during step 1 above. Additional topics or deficiencies should be added as they occur to members. A list should be produced of all additional information needed.

2. **The group should assign research responsibilities to individual members.**
   Items from the list produced in step 1 should be distributed equitably to the members and deadlines should be established for completion of the research. This increases individual responsibility and involvement. Ideally, members are allowed to choose voluntarily the topics of most interest to them. A group secretary or chair should keep track of who has agreed to undertake what research.

As a general rule, all members should do some common background study, with two or more members examining each major source on the topic. This helps offset individual perceptual biases and helps prevent the group from relying on one "specialist" for each topic.

Ways of gathering information are suggested below. Since this information is likely to have been covered in previous communication and composition classes, we review it only briefly.

A note card listing a topic heading, a specific subject, and exact details of the source.

SELF-MONITORING   Why related to leadership emergence

Robert J. Ellis and Steven F. Cronshaw, "Self-Monitoring and Leader Emergence: A Test of Moderator Effects," in *Small Group Research,* Vol. 23, No. 1, February, 1992; 113–129.

> "It is possible that low and high self-monitors are equally effective at identifying the needs of a group, but only high self-monitors are proficient at modifying their behavior to respond to such needs." p. 124

Note Taking

Information and ideas slip from memory or become distorted unless we make accurate and complete notes. Saying that a key piece of information appeared "in a book by some DNA researcher" is useless because fellow members cannot evaluate the credibility of the information or the source. The best system of note taking is to record each bit of information or data on a separate index card or directly into a database via a laptop computer, along with the topic heading and the full bibliographic reference, as shown in Figure B.1.

Note cards and databases provide both accuracy and flexibility. They can be arranged in groups to help synthesize and interpret the evidence collected. They can be sorted in a variety of ways and consulted with ease during a discussion without having to leaf through a disorganized notebook.

Three important sources for gathering information useful to problem-solving discussions are direct observation, reading, and interviews.

Direct Observation

Many times, needed information can come only from firsthand observation by group members, and often only direct observation can breathe life into a table of statistics or survey results. For example, a group of students trying to improve conditions in a self-service coffee shop of a student union spent time observing and recording how many customers did and did not bus their waste materials, the kinds of litter on the floor and tables, and placement and condition of waste containers.

Reading

For many topics and problems, the major source of information will be books, journals, newspapers, government documents, and other printed materials, whether in hard copy or online through the Internet. First, it is important to narrow down the print sources likely to yield relevant information. To do that, you need to compile a **bibliography,** which is a list of published sources on a particular topic or issue. Although ideally you would like to locate and evaluate all recent printed information on your topic before making any final decision, that is not always possible. Internet sources are especially helpful here. Be sure, however, that you do not limit yourself to only one or two sources or to sources that support only one point of view. This will produce a bias in your information with no way to cross-check validity.

To compile your bibliography as efficiently as possible, first prepare a list of key terms—descriptors—on the topic. For instance, a group investigating, "What type of lottery should our state conduct?" might use the following descriptors: *lottery, sweepstakes, gambling, crime, revenue,* and *betting.* Once you start your search, you may encounter additional terms, such as *victimless* or *wagering.* A reference librarian's help is indispensable in using printed sources of all kinds, including *Sociological Abstracts, Psychological Abstracts, ERIC, Facts on File,* and others. The abstract sources are significant time savers because they provide brief summaries of articles or books so you can determine whether you should read the entire publication for details.

Most such sources are now accessible by computer. Computerized databases such as *InfoTrac* and *Sociofile* can be invaluable in locating information about a topic. Although some of these databases may entail a fee, they make it extremely easy for you to locate relevant items quickly, so they are usually worth the money. The list of descriptors your group generates provides a starting point for a computer file search.

A good library manual, available at virtually every college or university library, helps in building a bibliography and locating print materials. Also helpful are bibliographies of bibliographies, such as *A World Bibliography of Bibliographies and Bibliographic Sources* and *Bibliographic Sources.* Bibliographies are also found at the end of most books, doctoral dissertations, and research articles. Do not overlook indexes to periodicals, such as *The Readers Guide to Periodical Literature, The New York Times Index,* and *Education Index.* Federal and state government publications, in special sections of many libraries, also contain vast amounts of information. The *Monthly Catalog of U.S. Government Publications* and the *Monthly Checklist of State Publications* will help you locate relevant information in these publications. Other useful sources include the *Congressional Quarterly Weekly Report* and the *Congressional Digest.*

Even while you start to compile a bibliography, you can begin reading. A good strategy is for all members of the group to read some of the same things to provide a common background, then divide up the rest of the bibliography. When you evaluate a book for usefulness, read the index and table of contents for clues. Skim rapidly until you find something pertinent to your group, then read carefully. Take notes of the most important ideas and facts, and make copies of particularly valuable information for the rest of the group.

For controversial problems or topics, read as many contrasting interpretations and viewpoints as possible. For example, before developing a campus policy regarding use of laboratory animals for research, study the writings of those who favor and oppose using animals. Although it is easier to remember opinions that support your own, making an effort to understand other points of view is essential for effective group discussion and problem solving. Doing that will also help you increase your level of cognitive complexity.

Sometimes you need first-hand information or explanations by a knowledge-able individual; interviews can help you obtain information you cannot get in other ways. Members of the group described earlier that observed the operation of the campus coffee shop also interviewed a number of customers to determine how they felt about its condition and to ask their reasons for not busing their wastepaper and leftovers. They also interviewed the manager to determine why materials that contributed to litter were being used. Most people are flattered to be asked for their information and opinions, but remember that your interviewees are busy and would prefer that you read first, then interview them for clarification.

Interview questions may be open-ended ("Why do you eat in the snack shop?") or closed-ended ("If trash containers were more conveniently located, would you use them? Yes _____ No _____"). In-depth interviews using open-ended questions often yield unexpected information and provide richer data. However, answers to open-ended questions are more difficult and time-consuming to tally. In contrast, closed-ended questions can be asked of many people quickly and are easily tabulated if formulated properly. You may want to use both.

It is invalid to generalize findings from a casual or haphazard sample to a larger population. For example, interviews about location of a new sanitary landfill with 50 people who happen to enter a particular door of City Hall will not provide an accurate picture of the beliefs of residents of that city, or even of people who go to City Hall. A scientifically designed sample (a *representative* sample) must be taken if results of interviews are to be generalized to members of a larger population. Unless some member of your group has been trained as a survey researcher or you can get such a person to help you, *student groups should generally not undertake a sample survey.*

Useful information may crop up anywhere, anytime. You may hear something relevant to your topic or problem while listening to the radio or watching television. Some televised material, such as the program content of C-SPAN, is cataloged and available for purchase or rent. Lectures or public speeches are another source of information. An idea may occur to you when you are not consciously thinking about the group's problem—for example, while riding to school, jogging, or talking with friends. Most of us find it helpful to keep a small notepad or a few notecards with us so we can jot down ideas when they occur, lest we forget or distort them. The important thing is to be alert for unexpected information and record it promptly.

Interviews

Other Information Sources

EVALUATE THE INFORMATION AND IDEAS YOU HAVE COLLECTED

The information and ideas you have gathered must be evaluated for accuracy and credibility. Many of your ideas may collapse in the presence of contradictory information, or some of your information may be spurious, from suspect sources, in direct contradiction to other evidence, or irrelevant. Now is the time for the group to cull the misleading, unsubstantiated, or wrong information so your decision or solution will not be faulty.

In Chapter 12 we discussed ways you can evaluate information and reasoning. In particular, examine the following questions:

1. **Are the sources believable?**
   Is the person a recognized expert? Is there anything—vested interest, known bias—that could have biased his or her opinion? For instance, ideas about medical care in the United States from representative physicians, insurance agents, and pharmaceutical salespeople are likely to be biased in different ways.

2. **Is there a clear distinction made between facts and inferences?**
   Are opinions stated as though they are facts? Can the facts be verified by independent credible sources?

3. **Are statistical data validly gathered, analyzed, and explained?**
   Was the sample representative? Were appropriate statistical procedures used to analyze the data? Are the results appropriately generalized, or overgeneralized?

4. **Are conclusions (inferences) supported by good reasoning?**
   Are there any fallacies that call the conclusions into question? Can you draw different but equally valid conclusions from the same set of evidence?

ORGANIZE YOUR INFORMATION AND IDEAS

The most efficient way to organize the group's information is to write a tentative outline based on a P-MOPS or Single Question sequence for problem solving (see Chapter 11). Ask yourself, "What are the questions that must be answered by our group to arrive at a full understanding of the problem or subject?" Your answers can serve as tentative main points in your outline.

Once you have decided on some tentative major issues or topic areas, you can arrange your notes into piles, one per issue or outline item. Some of the piles can be further divided into subheadings. For example, information concerning the nature of the problem might be arranged under such subheadings as "who is affected," "seriousness of the problem," "contributing causes," "previous attempts to solve the problem," and so forth. Organizing your information like this makes it easier for you to locate pertinent information when a topic arises during group discussion, helps you prepare questions the group needs to consider, and generally helps you and the group conduct an orderly and comprehensive discussion of a complex topic.

When you prepare for a problem-solving discussion, your outline is likely to contain some possible solutions you have found or thought of. You may have evidence or reasoning that shows how similar solutions were tried on a similar problem or even some suggestions about how to implement a plan. However, such thinking and planning should be *tentative*. It is easy to become dogmatic about an issue after you have spent hours preparing to discuss it, but it is absolutely essential that your mind be open. It is inappropriate and harmful to the group for members to come to a discussion prepared to defend their solutions against all comers. Remember that experts at the cutting edge of their fields are usually less dogmatic and sure of themselves than people who know much less.

We emphasize again that the information-gathering strategies we have suggested here can be modified to suit the particular needs of the group. For consequential decisions that will affect many people, something like this full procedure should be used. However, for relatively minor problems with few risks of making a mistake, the group can focus on the parts of this procedure most relevant to the group's problem.

GLOSSARY

Abstract: general, nonspecific, or vague.

Acceptance requirements: the degree to which the solution for a given problem must be accepted by the people it will affect.

Accommodation: the conflict management style, high in cooperativeness and low in assertiveness, where one person appeases or gives in to the other.

Action-oriented listener: a listener who focuses on the task, remembers details and prefers an organized presentation.

Active listening: listening with the intent of understanding a speaker the way the speaker wishes to be understood and paraphrasing your understanding so the speaker can confirm or correct the paraphrase.

Activity group: a group formed primarily for members to participate in an activity such as bridge, bowling, hunting, etc.

Activity orientation: the extent to which a culture emphasizes *doing* or *being,* taking charge or going with the flow.

***Ad hominem* attack:** an attack on a person rather than his or her argument, often involving namecalling; distracts a group from careful examination of an issue or argument.

Administrative duties: one of the major categories of responsibility of a designated leader; includes planning, sending meeting notices, keeping written records, and other administrative functions.

Affective conflict: conflict resulting from personality clashes, likes, dislikes, and competition for power.

Agenda: a list of items to be discussed at a group meeting.

Aggressiveness: behavior designed to win or dominate that fails to respect the rights or beliefs of others.

Ambiguous: a characteristic of any word or statement that can reasonably be understood in more than one way.

Area of freedom: the scope of authority and responsibility of a group, including limits on the group's authority.

Assembly effect: a type of group synergy or nonsummativity whereby the decision of group members collectively is superior to adding together (summing) the wisdom, knowledge, experience, and skills of the members individually.

Assertiveness: behavior that manifests respect both for your own and others' rights as opposed to aggressiveness and nonassertiveness.

Attitude: a network of beliefs and values, not directly measurable, that a person holds toward an object, person, or concept; produces a tendency to react in specific ways toward the object, person, or concept.

Authoritarianism: tendency to accept uncritically the information, ideas, and proposals of authority figures such as a high-status group member or leader; produces preference for strong leaders and subservience as a follower.

Autocratic leader: a leader who tries to dominate and control a group.

Avoidance: the passive conflict management style that ignores a conflict.

Backchannel: nonverbal vocalizations such as *mm-hmm* and *uh-huh* that are uttered while another is speaking; partly determined by one's culture, can indicate interest and active listening.

Behavior: any observable action by a group member.

405

Behavioral function: the effect or function a member's behavior has on the group as a whole.

Bibliography: a list of sources of information about a topic; usually includes books, journal or magazine articles, newspaper stories, interviews, and so forth.

Boundary spanner: a group member who monitors the group's environment to import and export information relevant to the group's success.

Brainstorming: a small group technique for stimulating creative thinking by temporarily suspending evaluation.

Brainwriting: individual brainstorming producing a written list.

Buzz group session: method whereby attendees at a large group meeting can participate actively; the large meeting is divided into groups of about six persons each who discuss a target question for a specified time, then report their answers to the entire large assembly.

Bypassing: a misunderstanding that results from two people not realizing they are referring to different things by the same words, or who have the same referent for different words.

Charge: the assignment or goal given to a group, usually by a parent organization or administrator of the parent organization.

Closed system: a system, such as a small group, with relatively impermeable boundaries, resulting in little interchange between the system and its environment.

Cognitive complexity: the personal trait that refers to the level of development of a group member's construct system for interpreting signals; cognitively complex individuals are able to synthesize more information and think in more abstract and organized terms than are cognitively simple individuals.

Cohesiveness: the degree of attraction members feel for the group; unity.

Collaboration: the assertive, cooperative conflict management style that assumes a solution can be found that fully meets the needs of all parties to a conflict; a problem-solving conflict management style.

Collectivist culture: a culture in which the needs and wishes of the group predominate over the needs of any one individual; the idea of an individual following a path separate from the group is inconceivable.

Committee: a small group of people given an assigned task or responsibility by a larger group (parent organization) or person with authority.

    ***Ad hoc* or special committee:** a group that goes out of existence after its specific task has been completed.

    Standing committee: a group given an area of responsibility that includes many tasks and continues indefinitely.

    Conference committee: a group composed of representatives from two or more groups; members' responsibilities are to represent the interests of their constituents.

Common Ground dialogue: a process of constructively managing divisive conflict where the participants are unlikely ever to agree, by focusing on the goals and values they can share and agree to.

Communication: a process in which signals produced by people are received, interpreted, and responded to by other people.

Communication apprehension (CA): anxiety or fear of speaking in a variety of social situations; reticence; shyness.

Communication network: the interpersonal channels open for interaction; collectively, who talks to whom.

Communicative competencies: the communication-related skills and abilities of members that help groups achieve their goals.

Competition: the uncooperative, aggressive conflict management style where one person attempts to dominate or force the outcome to his or her advantage.

Compromise: the conflict management style that assumes each party must give up something to get something; a shared solution to a conflict situation.

Concrete words: low-level abstractions referring to specific objects, experiences, and relationships.

Conflict: the expressed struggle that occurs when interdependent parties (including group members) perceive incompatible goals or scarce resources and interference in achieving their goals.

Conjunctive task: a type of group task where each member possesses information relevant to the decision, but no one member alone has all the needed information, thus requiring a high level of coordination among members.

Consensus decision: a choice that all group members agree is the best one that they all can accept.

Consultant: a nonparticipant observer who works with a group to determine what it needs, then attempts to help by providing inputs, such as special techniques, procedures, and information.

Content analysis: an analysis of the content (topics, behaviors, specific words or ideas, fantasy themes, etc.) of a group's discussion.

Content-oriented listener: a listener who enjoys analyzing information, dissecting others' arguments; can be seen as overly critical.

Contingency approaches: the study of leadership that assumes the appropriate leadership style in a given situation depends on factors such as members' skills and knowledge, time available, the type of task, and so forth.

Control touches: gentle, positive touching of another person in an effort to get that person's attention or request compliance.

Cooperative requirements: the degree to which members' efforts need to be coordinated for a group to complete its task successfully (see also "conjunctive task").

Criteria: standards for judging among alternatives; may be *absolute* (must) or *relative*.

Critical thinking: the systematic examination of information and ideas on the basis of evidence and logic rather than intuition, hunch, or prejudgment.

Critique: analysis and criticism of something, such as identification of strengths and weaknesses in a small group's process and interaction.

Cultural identity: the identification with and acceptance of a particular group's shared symbols, meanings, norms, and rules for conduct.

Culture: the patterns of values, beliefs, symbols, norms, procedures, and behaviors that have been historically transmitted to and are shared by a given group of persons.

Decision making: choosing from among a set of alternatives.

Defensive listening: thinking of how to defend some aspect of one's self-image while appearing to listen to what another is saying.

Democratic leader: an egalitarian leader who coordinates and facilitates discussion in a small group, encouraging participation of all members.

Designated leader: a person appointed or elected to a position as leader of a small group.

Deviate: a group member who differs in some important way, such as degree of participation, values, or opinions, from the rest of the group members; *opinion* or *innovative* deviates help groups examine alternatives more thoroughly by expressing opinions different from those held by the majority, thus forcing the group to take a closer look.

Devil's advocate: a group member who argues against a proposal to test its validity.

Dialect: a regional variation in the pronunciation, vocabulary, and/or grammar of a language.

Discussion (small group discussion): a small group of people communicating with each other to achieve some interdependent goal, such as increased understanding, coordination of activity, or solution to a shared problem.

Disjunctive task: a type of group task in which members work on parts of the group problem independently, with little or no coordination of effort through discussion needed.

Distributed leadership: the concept that group leadership is the responsibility of the group as a whole, not just the designated leader; assumes all members can and should provide needed leadership services to the group.

Distributive approach: the approach to managing conflict that assumes there are fixed resources to distribute among parties to the conflict; thus, whatever someone wins, someone else loses.

Dogmatism: a tendency to hold rigidly to personal beliefs; closed-mindedness to evidence and reasoning contrary to one's beliefs.

Egalitarianism: belief in the equality of all people, resulting in the preference for participation in problem solving by all group members rather than by just a few high-status members.

Emergent leader: member of an initially leaderless group who, by virtue of information and communication competencies, rises from within the group to enact leadership functions and is viewed as the leader by all or most members.

Emotive words: words that evoke specific emotions, connote more than they denote, and serve as triggers for recalling pleasant or unpleasant experiences.

Environment: the context or setting in which a small group system exists; the larger systems of which a small group is a component.

Ethics: the rules or standards that a person or group uses to determine whether conduct or behavior is right and appropriate.

Ethnocentrism: the belief that one's own culture is inherently superior to all others; tendency to view other cultures through the viewpoint of one's own culture.

Extraversion-introversion dimension: the Myers-Briggs Type Indicator™ dimension concerned with whether one's focus is the external world (extraversion) or one's internal, subjective landscape (introversion).

Fact: a verifiable observed event; a descriptive statement that is true.

Fallacy: a reasoning error.

False dilemma: either-or thinking that assumes, incorrectly, that only two choices or courses of action are possible.

Fantasy: a statement not pertaining to the *here-and-now* of the group that offers a creative and meaningful interpretation of events meeting a group's psychological or rhetorical need.

Fantasy chain: a series of statements by several or all group members in which a story is dramatized to help create a group's view of reality.

Fantasy theme: what the content of the dramatization of a fantasy or fantasy chain is about; the *manifest* theme is the overt, surface content, and the *latent* theme is the hidden, underlying meaning.

Faulty analogy: an incomplete comparison that stretches a similarity too far; assuming that because two things are similar in some respects, they are alike in others.

Feedback: a response to a system's output; it may come in the form of information or tangible resources and helps the system determine whether or not it needs to make adjustments in moving toward its goal.

Focus group: a special group procedure that encourages freewheeling discussion focusing on a specific topic or issue, often used to analyze people's interests and values for market research.

Focused listening: focusing attention on major ideas and issues rather than details of another's message so as to be able to review and recall those issues readily.

Forum discussion: a large audience interacting orally, usually following some public presentation.

Functions approach: the study of functions performed by leaders; the theory that leadership is defined by the functions a group needs and can be supplied by *any* member.

Gatekeeper: any member of a small group controlling who speaks during a discussion; any controller of the flow of messages among members.

Gender: learned and culturally transmitted sex-role behavior of an individual.

Group: three or more people with an interdependent goal who interact and influence each other.

Group culture: the pattern of values, beliefs, and norms shared by group members, developed through interaction and incorporating members' shared experiences in the group, patterns of interaction, and status relationships.

Group Decision Support Systems (GDSS): computer-based software and hardware systems designed to help groups improve a variety of group outcomes, such as creativity, problem solving, and decision making.

Grouphate: the feeling of antipathy and hostility many people have against working in a group, fostered by the many ineffective, time-wasting groups that exist.

Group polarization: the tendency for group members to make decisions that are more extreme (more risky or cautious) than they would make individually.

Groupthink: the tendency of some cohesive groups to fail to subject information, reasoning, and proposals to thorough critical analysis leading to faulty decisions.

Hidden antagonizer: an unintentional trigger word, not intended to offend, that does in fact provoke an emotional reaction.

High-context communication: communication wherein the primary meaning of a message is conveyed by features of the situation or context instead of the verbal, explicit part of the message.

High-level abstraction: a word, phrase, or statement commonly used to refer to a broad category of objects, relationships, or concepts; typically refers to intangibles such as *love, democracy,* etc.

Idiosyncracy credit: additional leeway in adhering to group norms, given to a member for valuable contributions to the group.

Individualistic culture: a culture in which the needs and wishes of the individual predominate over the needs of the group.

Individual-level variables: characteristics of the individual members of a group that affect the group's interaction, such as traits, attitudes, values, beliefs, and skills.

Inequity conflict: conflict about perceived unequal workloads or contributions to the group effort.

Inference: a statement that includes more than a description of some event, thus going beyond fact; an inference involves some degree of uncertainty or probability and cannot be checked for accuracy by direct observation.

Input variables: the energy, information, and raw material used by an open system, which is transformed into output by throughput processes.

Integrative approach: the approach to managing conflict that assumes that solutions can be found to satisfy every party to the conflict.

Interaction: mutual influence by two or more people through the communication process.

Intercultural communication: interaction between and among individuals from different cultures or subcultures.

Interdependence: the property of a system such that all parts are interrelated and affect each other as well as the whole system.

Interdependent goal: an objective shared by members of a small group in such a way that one member cannot achieve the goal without the other members also achieving it.

Intracultural communication: interaction between and among individuals from the same culture or subculture.

Intrinsic interest: extent to which the task itself is attractive and interesting to the participants.

Intuitive problem solvers: people who size up a situation, then arrive at a solution without consciously following any perceptible procedure.

Kinesics: study of communication through movements.

Laissez-faire leader: a do-nothing designated leader who provides minimal services to the group.

Leader: a person who uses communication to influence others to meet group goals and needs; any person identified by members of a group as leader; a person designated as leader by election or appointment.

Leader as completer: a leader who determines which functions or behaviors are most needed for a group to perform optimally, then supplies them or encourages others to do so.

Leader-Member Exchange (LMX) model: the leadership model based on the finding that supervisors develop different kinds of leadership relationships with their subordinates, depending on characteristics of both the leader and members.

Leadership: influence exerted through communication that helps a group achieve goals; performance of a leadership function by any member.

Leadership emergence: the process by which someone emerges as the leader of an initially leaderless group in which all members start out as equals.

Learning group (study group): a group conducting a learning discussion.

Least-sized group: the principle that the ideal group contains as few members as possible so long as all necessary perspectives and skills are represented.

Liaison: communication between or among groups; interfacing; a person who performs the liaison function.

Listening: receiving and interpreting oral and other signals from another person or source.

Low-context communication: communication wherein the primary meaning of a message is carried by the verbal or explicit part of the message.

Maintenance functions: relationship-oriented member behaviors that reduce tensions, increase solidarity, and facilitate teamwork.

Majority decision: decision made by vote, with the winning alternative receiving more than half the members' votes.

Meeting notice: a written message providing the time, place, purpose, and other information relevant to an upcoming meeting.

Message: either a set of signals from one person to others or interpretation/response of a listener to a set of signals.

Minutes: a written record of every relevant item dealt with during a group meeting, including a record of all decisions.

Moderator: a person who controls the flow of communication during a public presentation such as a panel or forum discussion.

Multiple causation: the principle that each change in a system is caused by numerous factors.

Myers-Briggs Type Indicator™: a personality measure based on the work of Carl Jung that categorizes individuals based on how they relate to the world around them.

Noise: interference in the communication process; can occur at any step in the process, from the sender's original encoding of the message to the receiver's decoding of it.

Nominal Group Technique: a special procedure in which group members brainwrite to generate ideas, then interact to pool, clarify, and evaluate these ideas until a solution has been accepted by weighted voting.

Nonsummativity: the property of a system that the whole is not the sum of its parts, but may be greater or lesser than the sum.

Nonverbal signals: messages other than words to which listeners react.

Norm: an unstated informal rule, enforced by peer pressure, that governs the behavior of members of a small group.

Obstacle: something that interferes or stands in the way of solving a problem, such as lack of information or resources, or attitudes of people who must support the solution.

Open system: a system with relatively permeable boundaries, producing a high degree of interchange between the system and its environment.

Output: anything that is produced by the throughput processes of a system, such as a tangible product or a change in components of the system; in a small group, outputs are such things as reports, resolutions, changes in cohesiveness, and attitude changes in members.

Overgeneralizing: assuming that because something is true about one or a few items, it is true of all or most items of the same type.

Panel discussion: a small group whose members interact informally and in impromptu manner for the benefit of a listening audience.

Paralanguage: nonverbal characteristics of voice and utterance, such as pitch, rate, tone of voice, fluency, pauses, and variations in dialect.

Paraphrase: restatement in one's own words of what one understood a speaker to mean.

Participant-observer: an active participant in a small group who is at the same time observing and evaluating its processes and procedures.

Passiveness: nonassertive behavior that allows one's own rights and beliefs to be ignored or dominated, often to avoid conflict, even at the expense of good decision making.

People-oriented listener: a listener who is sensitive to others, nonjudgmental, and concerned about how his/her behavior affects others; can become distracted from task by others' problems.

Perceiving-judging dimension: the Myers-Briggs Type Indicator™ dimension concerning how people organize the world; perceivers are spontaneous and flexible whereas judgers are decisive and sure.

Personal growth group: a group of people who come together to develop personal insights, overcome personality problems, and grow personally through feedback and support of others.

Phase: a stage in the development of a small group or in the process of making a decision.

Formation phase: the stage in the development of a group during which relationship issues predominate as members work out their relationships with each other.

Production phase: the stage in the development of a group during which task concerns predominate after a group has reached some socioemotional maturity.

Phasic progression: the movement of a group through fairly predictable phases or stages, each of which is characterized by specific kinds of statements.

Population familiarity: the degree to which members of a group are familiar with the nature of a problem and experienced in solving similar problems or performing similar tasks.

Postmeeting reaction form (PMR): a form, completed after a discussion, on which group members evaluate the discussion, the group, and/or the leader; PMR responses are usually tabulated and reported back to the group.

Power: the potential to influence behavior of others, derived from such bases as the ability to reward and punish, expertise, legitimate title or position, and personal attraction or charisma.

Power distance: the degree to which a culture emphasizes status and power differences among members of the culture; in low power-distance cultures, status differences are minimized, but in high power-distance cultures, they are highly emphasized.

Preference for procedural order: a trait characterized by need or desire to follow a clear, linear structure during problem solving and decision making.

Prejudice: a preconceived opinion about something based on partial information or limited experience, accompanied by the tendency to reject contradictory information.

Primary group: a group whose main purpose is to meet members' needs for inclusion and affection.

Primary tension: tension and discomfort in members that stems from interpersonal (i.e., primary) sources, including the social unease that occurs when members of a new group first meet or during competition for power among members.

Principled negotiation: a general strategy that enables parties in a conflict to express their needs openly and search for alternatives that will meet the needs of all parties without damaging the relationship among parties.

Problem: the difference between what actually happens and what *should* be happening; components include an existing but undesired state of affairs, a goal, and obstacles to achieving the goal.

Problem census: a technique in which members of a small group are polled for topics and problems that are then posted, ranked by voting, and used to create agendas for future meetings.

Problem question: a question calling the attention of a group to a problem without suggesting any particular type of solution in the question.

Problem solving: a multistage procedure for moving from some unsatisfactory state to a more satisfactory one, or developing a plan for doing so.

Problem-solving group: a group that discusses to devise a course of action to solve a problem.

Procedural conflict: conflict resulting from disagreement about *how* to do something.

Procedural Model of Problem Solving (P-MOPS): a five-step general procedure, based on the scientific method, for structuring problem-solving discussions; P-MOPS is adaptable to any type of problem.

Program Evaluation and Review Technique (PERT): a procedure for planning the details to implement a complex solution that involves many people and resources.

Proxemics: the study of uses of space and territory between and among people.

Pseudolistening: responding overtly as if listening attentively, but thinking about something other than what the speaker is saying.

Public interview: one or more interviewers asking questions of one or more respondents for the benefit of a listening audience.

Quality circle (quality control circle): a group of employees meeting on company time to investigate work-related problems and to make recommendations for solving these problems.

Rating scale: a pencil-and-paper instrument to measure quantitatively some factor involved in a discussion.

Referent: whatever is denoted by a symbol or statement.

Regulator: nonverbal signal used to control who speaks during a discussion.

Rhetorical sensitivity: speaking and phrasing statements in such a way that the feelings and beliefs of the listener are considered; phrasing statements so as not to offend others or trigger emotional overreactions.

RISK technique: a small group procedure for communicating and dealing with all risks, fears, doubts, and worries that members have about a new policy or plan before it is implemented.

Role: a pattern of behavior displayed by and expected of a member of a small group; a composite of a group member's frequently performed behavioral functions.

Rule: a statement prescribing how members of a small group may, should, or must behave, which may be stated formally in writing, or informally as in the case of norms.

Secondary group: a group whose major purpose is to complete a task, such as making a decision, solving a problem, writing a report, or providing recommendations to a parent organization.

Secondary tension: tension and discomfort experienced by group members that stem from task-related (i.e., secondary) sources, including conflicts over values, points of view, or alternative solutions.

Self-centered functions: actions of a small group member, motivated by personal needs, that serve the individual at the expense of the group.

Self-managed work group: a small group of peers who determine within prescribed limits their own work schedules and procedures.

Self-monitoring: the extent to which someone pays attention to and controls his or her self-presentation in social situations; high self-monitors are able to assess how others perceive them and adapt their behavior to elicit a desired response.

Sensing-intuiting dimension: the Myers-Briggs Type Indicator™ dimension concerned with the type of information individuals use; sensers prefer facts and figures whereas intuiters prefer to dream about possibilities.

Sex: biologically determined femaleness or maleness.

Sidetracking: a poor listening habit whereby one group member spins off on a private reverie unrelated to what another group member has said, or whereby one group member moves the conversation in a direction completely different from what was being discussed.

Sign: a signal that has an *inherent* relationship with what it represents, such as a blush or scar.

Signal: any stimulus a person can receive and interpret, including both signs and symbols.

Single Question format: a special procedure for structuring problem-solving discussions that facilitates critical thinking and systematic problem solving, but is more suitable for members low in preference for procedural order than more highly structured linear procedures.

Small group: a group of at least three but few enough members for each to perceive all others as individuals, who meet face-to-face, share some identity or common purpose, and share standards for governing their activities as members.

Small group communication: the scholarly study of communication among members of a small group, among two or more groups, and between groups and larger organizations; the body of communication theory produced by such study.

Social loafer: a person who makes a minimal contribution to the group and assumes the other members will take up the slack.

Solution multiplicity: extent to which there are many different possible alternatives for solving a particular problem.

Solution question: a question directed to a group in which the solution to a problem is suggested or implied.

Status: the position of a member in the hierarchy of power, influence, and prestige within a small group.

Ascribed status: status due to characteristics external to the group, such as wealth, level of education, position, physical attractiveness, and so forth; status given on the basis of a member's input characteristics.

Earned status: status earned by a member's valued contributions to the group, such as working hard for the group, providing needed expertise, being especially communicatively competent, and so forth; status that comes from performance during a group's throughput processes.

Structuration: the concept that a group creates and continuously re-creates itself through members' communicative behaviors; the group's communication both establishes and limits how the group develops.

Structure: organization; arrangement of parts of a system; steps in a procedure.

Styles approach: the leadership approach that studies the interrelationship between leader style and member behaviors.

Subculture: a grouping that sees itself as distinct, but is part of a larger culture.

Substantive conflict: conflict resulting from disagreements over ideas, information, reasoning, or evidence.

Symbol: an arbitrary, human-created signal used to represent something with which it has no inherent relationship; all words are symbols.

Symbolic convergence: the theory that humans create and share meaning through talk and storytelling, producing an overlapping (convergence) of private symbolic worlds of individuals during interaction.

SYMLOG: *SY*stem for the *M*ultiple-*L*evel *O*bservation of *G*roups, both a theory about member characteristics and effects on group interaction, and a methodology that produces a three-dimensional "snapshot" of a group at a given point in time.

Synectics: a special group technique that encourages members to use unusual analogies and metaphors to create innovative solutions to problems.

System: an entity made up of components patterned in interdependent relationship to each other, requiring constant adaptation among its parts to maintain organic wholeness and balance.

Systematic problem solvers: organized problem solvers who follow a definite series of steps or sequence, such as those provided by P-MOPS.

System-level variables: features or characteristics of the group as a whole, such as cohesiveness, interaction patterns, norms, roles, and so forth, that affect the group's interaction.

Task difficulty: degree of problem complexity and effort required.

Task functions: task-oriented member behaviors that contribute primarily to accomplishing the goals of a group.

Teambuilding: a set of planned activities designed to increase teamwork, cohesiveness, or other aspects of group performance.

Technical requirements: the degree to which the solution for a given problem is technically feasible or must meet standards of technical excellence.

Teleconference: a meeting of participants who communicate via mediated channels such as television, telephone, or computer rather than face-to-face.

Thinking-feeling dimension: the Myers-Briggs Type Indicator™ dimension concerned with how individuals prefer to make decisions; thinkers are objective and fact-based whereas feelers are subjective and emotion-based.

Throughput: the actual *functioning* of a system, or how the system transforms inputs into outputs.

Time-oriented listener: a listener sensitive to time; may be impatient or try to move group prematurely to closure.

Trait: a relatively enduring, consistent pattern of behavior or other observable characteristic.

Traits approach: the approach to leadership that assumes leaders have certain traits that distinguish them from followers or members of a group.

Uncertainty avoidance: the degree to which members of a culture avoid or embrace uncertainty and ambiguity; cultures high in uncertainty avoidance prefer clear rules for interaction, whereas cultures low in uncertainty avoidance are comfortable without guidelines.

Variable: an observable characteristic that can change in magnitude or quality from time to time.

Verbal interaction analysis: an analysis of who talks to whom and how often during a discussion.

Vigilant Interaction Theory: the theory that suggests that group members not only must have expertise about a problem, but must also be knowledgeable about the *process* of problem solving, especially to ensure that all aspects of the problem have been examined and that the pros and cons of all the alternatives have been thoroughly assessed.

Worldview: one's beliefs about the nature of life, the purpose of life, and one's relation to the cosmos.

Author Index

Subject Index